THE ART OF PRAYING LITURGY

THE ART OF PRAYING LITURGY

by

Gregory Manly, C.P.
and
Anneliese Reinhard, M.S.C.

SPECTRUM PUBLICATIONS
MELBOURNE
1984

First published by
Spectrum Publications Pty Ltd
PO Box 75, Richmond, Victoria 3121

Copyright Gregory Manly C.P. & Anneliese Reinhard M.S.C.

Printed in Australia by
Brown Prior Anderson Pty Ltd.,
5 Evans Street, Burwood Vic. 3125

Photography: David Galloway
Design & Illustration: Anneliese Reinhard
Typeset by Spectrum Publications Pty Ltd

ISBN 0 86786 066 9

ACKNOWLEDGEMENTS

To you
Sister Brendan, Sister Francis and Sister Gabriel
Father Jerome and Father Denis
our superiors during the time of this book's development
and composition
our most sincere appreciation
for your trust and understanding of us and our work
over the years.

To you
laity, sisters, brothers, priests
of our own church and other Christian churches
who, in our courses
helped us to clarify our thinking and refine our methods
and encouraged us to persevere;

with special mention of you, sisters and staff,
of Assumption Institute
our grateful acknowledgement
of your contribution to this book.

To you
our publisher, Henry,
always enthusiastically encouraging
our thanks for your initiative and support.

To you
so many in number
who have contributed your time, your energy, your skills
to the production of this book,
our thanks for your generous service

To you
our parents, families and friends
our deepest gratitude
for the gift of Life and Prayer.

ACKNOWLEDGEMENT OF QUOTATIONS

The publisher and authors gratefully acknowledge permission to include copyright material from the following: Collins, New York for quotations from *The Common Bible, Ecumenical Edition*; Collins, London, *Prayers of the Eucharist: Early and Reformed*, R.C.D. Jasper and G.J. Cuming, 1975. International Committee on English in the Liturgy, Inc., *General Instruction of the Roman Missal, The Roman Missal, Directory for Masses with Children*. Geoffrey Chapman, *The Documents of Vatican II*, Walter M. Abbot, S.J.; *Christian Celebration: The Prayer of the Church*, J.D. Crichton, 1976. National Conference of Bishops, U.S.A., *Music in Catholic Worship; Environment and Art in Catholic Worship; Newsletter*. Ave Maria Press, Notre Dame, *Merton's Palace of Nowhere*, James Finley. International Consultation on English Texts, *Song of Zechariah*, ABC, 'By the Way', Talk by Rev. Brian Phillips, December 1975. Sheed and Ward, N.Y., *Thomas Merton, Monk: A Monastic Tribute*, ed. Patrick Hart, O.C.S.O., 'Man of Prayer' by David Stendl-Rast; *Man's Search for Himself*, Leo Scheffczyk. Dove Communications, Melbourne, *Stages of Faith*, James W. Fowler; *The Mystics*, Veronica Brady. Penguin Books, William Blake, 'Auguries of Innocence'; *The Way of Zen*, Alan Watts; *The Cloud of Unknowing*. Doubleday & Co. Inc., *The Story of My Life*, Helen Keller; *Reaching Out*, Henri J.M. Nouwen; Image Book, *Conjectures of a Guilty Bystander*, Thomas Merton. Faber and Faber, London, *Collected Poems*, W.H. Auden, 'In memory of W.B. Yeates'. Harper and Row, Inc., *Stride Towards Freedom*, Martin Luther King; *Motivation and Personality*, Abraham Maslow. Routledge & Kegan Paul, Ltd., London and Henley, *Zen in the Art of Archery*, Eugen Herrigel. Paulist Press, New York/Ramsey, *The Book of Sacramental Basics*, Tad Guzie. The Herald, Melbourne. Liturgical Press, Collegeville, *The Mass*, J.A. Jungmann; *Mean What You Say*, Clifford Howell, S.J.; *Worship*, 1975, 'Prayer and Emotion: Shaping and Expressing Christian Life' Don E. Saliers. Clarendon Press, Oxford, *The Spiritual Nature of Man*, Sir Alister Hardy, FRS. E.J. Dwyer, *General Instruction on the Liturgy of the Hours*, translated by Peter Coughlan and Peter Purdue. Macmillan, *Introduction to Religious Philosophy*, Geddes McGregor, 1964. S.P.C.K., *Myth and Symbol*, ed. F.W. Dillistone, Paul Tillich, 'The Religious Symbol'; *Liturgy Reshaped*, ed. Kenneth Stevenson, David Tripp, 'Shape and Liturgy'. Gujarat Sahitya Prakash, Anand, India, *The Song of the Bird*, Anthony de Mello, S.J., 'The Word Made Flesh,'. Princeton University Press, *Collected Works*, C.W. Jung, Vol. XVIII. Darton, Longman and Todd, *The Early Liturgy, J.A. Jungmann. Benziger Brothers*. Benziger Brothers, *The Mass of the Roman Rite*, J.A. Jungmann. National Association of Pastoral Musicians, Washington D.C., *To Give Thanks and Praise*, Ralph Keifer. Publications Office, United States Catholic Conference, Washington, D.C., *Letter to the Presidents of the National Conferences of Bishops Concerning Eucharistic Prayers*. Irish University Press, Shannon Ireland, *The Church at Prayer: The Eucharist*, ed. A.G. Martimort. University of Notre Dame Press, *Eucharist*, Louis Bouyer. Catholic Book Publishing Company, N.Y., *The Liturgy of the Hours*. Dacre Press, *The Shape of the Liturgy*, Dom Gregory Dix. Studia Anselmiana, Rome, 1977, David Power, 'How can we speak of the Eucharistas Sacrifice'. Diocesan Liturgical Centre, Melbourne, *The Summit; The Directory For Masses with Children*. The Liturgical Conference, Washington D.C., *There Are Different Ministries*, Robert J. Hovda; *The Ministry of Music*, William A. Bauman. *Journal of Ecumenical Studies*. A.C.T.S. Publications, Melbourne, *Instruction on the Worship of the Eucharistic Mystery; Instruction on Music in the Liturgy*. World Library of Sacred Music, Ohio, *Spirit and Song of the New Liturgy*, L. Deiss. Alcuin Club/SPCK, *Daily Prayer in the Early Church*, Paul F. Bradshaw. *New Spectator*, Melbourne, 'A Dismissal to Ecumenical Witness and Service' Harold Leatherland.

If through inability to trace present copyright owners, any copyright material has been included for which the required permission has not been sought, apologies are tendered in advance to those concerned.

CONTENTS

Section Six: EVALUATING-PLANNING A EUCHARIST

Section Seven: PRAYING THE LITURGY OF THE HOURS

INTRODUCTION

Our aim in this book is to help people to experience their celebrations of the Eucharist, and all liturgy, with more meaning, more prayer, more life and more joy. We believe that liturgy can be 'the activity in their lives surpassing all others', as the Constitution on the Liturgy describes it.

It is our view that the promulgation of the New Order of Mass in 1969, and its later appearance in different languages, gave to the Church not just a translation of the Latin Roman Missal of St Pius V which had been in use since 1570; we were given a new rite of a completely different type. It required of priests, ministers and people activities not hitherto associated with the Mass — at least, not for many centuries. New needs were born in regard to the celebration of liturgy: needs which opened up new parameters and dimensions in the study of liturgy. It is a situation not unlike that of the time of the Carolingian renaissance in the ninth century when Latin was no longer understood even by Romanic peoples and changes had been introduced into the ritual of the liturgy. To meet the people's needs, they began for the first time to 'teach liturgy' — something unnecessary before that situation — especially in the form of written *Expositiones Missae* ('Explanations of the Mass').

As, at that time, the disappearance in liturgy of a language that could be understood and new rites gave rise to what became a new ecclesiastical subject, namely liturgiology or liturgics, so the recent disappearance of Latin and the introduction of a new rite seem to call for a new way of 'teaching' liturgy. After a decade of working with Catholics and Christians of other churches, laity young and old, religious, seminarians and clergy, we are firmly convinced that the type of course customarily given in liturgy, either in seminary or parish, no longer meets the need of Catholics celebrating the

Eucharist of the 1969 Order. There is need of a new subject with new content, form and method, even of new goal and aim. What we consider these to be the reader will discover as the book unfolds.

Our conviction, born out of, and nurtured by, our experience of people seriously trying to improve their participation, has led to the evolving of our approach to liturgical education, or as we see it, liturgical *formation*. Our emphasis is reflected in practically every section of this book: more importance given to the experience than to information, more emphasis on the *people* celebrating the rite than its structure; first concern placed on participation seen as a prayer from the heart, rather than 'doing' things.

It is our experience with groups that the best way to introduce them to our approach is to explain to them how we ourselves have come to our present position. In other words, to tell the story behind it: the way we journeyed separately and together, to arrive at the experience and knowledge we present in this book.

To introduce the book, we would like to introduce ourselves.

MY STORY — GREGORY MANLY

My present ideas on liturgy, as presented in this book, are the fruit of work and experience during a period of more than twenty years. To say how I arrived at these ideas is to describe more than a radical change and progress in my thinking; it is to tell of a change in myself: what truly was a conversion.

I completed my seminary studies in Dublin, and was ordained there, in 1950. To prepare me as a seminary lecturer I was sent to study theology and scripture in Rome and Jerusalem. By the time I had completed my degrees in those subjects in 1955, and begun my life of lecturing, I had become a confirmed academic, completely won over by scholastic philosophy and theology and the scripture study methods of that time. I loved my life lecturing seminarians — little realizing then that I was going to spend thirty years at it. My inclination being towards the academic, during the later years

I spent in Dublin and Rome I entered more and more deeply into that world.

The first little change in me came in 1961, when I left Europe and came to Australia to lecture in our Passionist seminary, then in Adelaide. At that time I started to lecture in systematic theology, a new subject for me after ten years devoted to scripture. My struggles with it brought me in touch, for the first time in my life, with catechists: a group of people who influenced me greatly and to whom I am very grateful. Then, too, especially with the help of Father Marcellus Claeys, C.P., also lecturing in our seminary — a man to whom I am deeply indebted — I became acquainted with the abundance of new theological thought available at that time in European publications, including existentialist and personalist thinking. That was the time when, through a special attraction sacramental theology had for me, my interest in liturgy was born.

The transfer of our seminary to Melbourne (because of the increasing number of vocations in 1965!) gave me new opportunities of learning from the large number of lecturers from the various religious congregations and different Christian churches, as well as the Melbourne catechists, who used to meet for theological and scriptural discussions. I joined the ecumenical liturgical group 'Studia Liturgica', later to become the Ecumenical Liturgical Centre, which gave me an opening for a liturgical apostolate, as well as enriching my liturgical knowledge, as by this time I was a very keen student of the subject. However, it was the religious sisters in Melbourne, and their particular need at that time, who were responsible for drawing me into an increasingly engaging liturgical apostolate. This puzzled me at the time, since I could claim to be a professional theologian, but a liturgist only by interest and enthusiasm. The requests continued to multiply, and eventually, in response to what I heard as a call in the Church, I left other areas of work to occupy myself exclusively with liturgical education.

The method I used was inadequate, I see now; but it was the only way I knew to give help in liturgy: that is to give a better understanding through talks, discussions and the like. It was what everyone else was doing, and I knew of no other way. I began to be aware of its defects. In response to requests for help with a community's celebration of the Eucharist or Office, I would go to them on a Sunday afternoon and give a talk; maybe follow it with a discussion period. Then I left them. I found myself asking the question, How were those sisters when, on the morning after I spoke to them, they assembled at 6.30 for the Office and Mass? I had to respond, No different from how they were any previous morning: my talk would not have brought about any change in them that made any difference to their praying next time they went to prayer. If I had asked them to write a paper on the content of my talk, I am sure they would have written very well. However, to cater for their needs in chapel, something else was needed. Something then beyond my knowledge. The problem became more acute for me when, in 1968, I was asked to lecture in the new Assumption Institute in liturgy: part of a year's renewal for religious sisters. This much I did realize: my goal was to help the sisters to *pray* better at liturgy, rather than to know more about it as was my concern in the seminary. I saw, too, that the most effective means of giving the help they needed was good experiences of celebrating liturgy prayerfully. Yet nagging at me was the thought that there must be something else.

The first break-through came during a sabbatical year which I spent as guest lecturer at the East Asian Pastoral Institute, Manila. One of the questions I hoped to have answered was, what goes into a liturgy course? By this time I was dissatisfied by the type of course given to seminarians and laity, and really searching. I made a point of hearing a few of the other lecturers at the E.A.P.I., and one thing struck me forcibly: that was the way they drew on the experience of the students, most of whom were experienced missionaries. For me that was a new way of teaching. I saw its value at once, and quickly realized that this was the missing element I had been seeking. The people I had been teaching in Australia had had years of experience in prayer, and in faith. Why add more information? Why not tap their experience and develop that?

That was 1971. Later in the year I continued my search in Europe and the U.S.A., and became even more convinced that a liturgical education had to contain the experiential and be a behavioural type of course. I returned to Australia, still without an answer to my question about a liturgy course. Certainly I knew that it had to be experiential. That, however, raised a new problem due to my complete lack of competence in that area. Having nothing but a passing acquaintance with the behavioural sciences, I had no idea how to implement my new discovery.

The following year saw the decisive event for me: I met Sister Anneliese, a Missionary Sister of the Sacred Heart, at that time mistress of novices. She had joined a course in the Formation of Liturgical Directresses which I was giving to representatives of sisters' congregations in Melbourne. I can still remember well the evening she told me about her method in helping her novices with their prayer: no talks or discussions; but walks in the garden, and stopping and reflecting. I realized excitedly that this was what I was looking for: Anneliese was using every day that missing element I had been searching for, and was quite at home with it, as well as utterly convinced of its value. Soon afterwards we started to give courses together, and have continued since then to work together.

At first, Anneliese catered for the experiential element and I would add my informational contribution. In the years that followed our gifts 'overlapped'; she was a natural theologian, and she learned a lot of new theology and scripture. I, for my part, came to see the limitations of my academic approach, although it is still part of me and my work in liturgical education. It just did not cater for all the needs of people in liturgy. With Anneliese inspiring and guiding me, I had opened to me a whole new world: I learned about the human person, human feelings, human development, and human realtionships. I acquired the skill of reflecting and responding; I grew adept, not only in coming to inner quiet myself, but in leading others to come to it. I discovered the connection between liturgy and life, and new horizons in regard to presiding at the Eucharist. In those years, and not without a lot of dying and some suffering, I lost my fear of entering into the personal, the psychological world — although I did not recognise it as fear; I saw it as defending truth! I was changed; it was truly a conversion. It happened to me in my middle and late fifties; I am saying so much about it to give encouragement to any who, through reading this book or any other reason, would like to change but consider that it would be impossible for them.

That is my story of my coming to life as the person and liturgist who writes in this book. It is now time you heard Anneliese.

MY STORY – ANNELIESE REINHARD

No matter how many times I stand before a group to begin yet another course, I am always very apprehensive and anxious. This moment proves to be no exception; on the contrary, these feelings seem to be intensified, since I am not a writer and since even my speaking needs the support of a lot of body-language, so, I wonder just how I will ever be able to communicate, in book-form, something which has not only been my ministry in the Church over the last twelve years, but is at the very heart of what motivates me and gives my life meaning and direction.

Whenever I begin to share a little of my story as a means of introducing our course, my anxiety level drops considerably because, as I am speaking, the group communicates to me, although non-verbally, something like: 'This is our story, too,' 'Yes, I agree' or 'Oh boy, don't I know it!' or just 'Yes, I know what that feels like.' And so I go on, our experience being re-awakened in the hearts of everyone listening. May it happen to you, as you read on.

What gives me the audacity, the qualification, above all, the courage to speak or write as a liturgist, is not a degree in scripture or theology or liturgy, but rather an experience of living and praying which began way back, when I was very young and growing up in my homeland, Bavaria, in south Germany.

I remember vividly the Sunday mornings, when all of us, with Mum and Dad, set off in our Sunday-best, to our parish church for High Mass, accompanied by the sound of the church bells and the sound of the customary Bavarian greeting 'Gruss Gott' sounding all around us as we greeted all the people we met on the way. Soon we would kneel alongside Mum and Dad to pray. Little did I realise then that what absorbed my attention, what made me stand on tip-toes to see more, what made my elbow secretly nudge my brother, had a lot to do with praying: the light of the sun filling the saints in the stained-glass windows and dancing off the shiny vessels on the altar, the billowing clouds of incense, the long procession of priests in heavy gold-looking vestments, altar-boys galore, and the commanding sound of the brass-band — all of it building up to a moment I will always remember, when I would sneak a look at Mum and Dad to see what they were doing. All sounds in the church had stopped. It seemed as if this was the moment when one would even stop breathing, lest *that* would interfere with the stillness. It was the moment of consecration, as I was to learn later.

At the end of High Mass, probably to give Mum a chance to get the Sunday dinner ready, Dad would take us for a walk: down the valley, up and over the meadowed slopes of *Kalvarienberg*, along the edge of the forest or through the forest. We would run and jump, or linger behind and stop to look at things Dad had noticed and we had missed. We would stand to watch a bee buzzing inside a flower, or a butterfly resting on a flower, raising and lowering its wings in rhythm as we watched.

Depending on the season of the year, we would stand and watch little stars dance off blankets and blankets of freshly fallen snow no one had trodden on. We would lie in the snow and, using our arms, 'make angels' in the snow. We would stand back to look at our creations, hearing Dad say: '*You* did that!' What a thrill it was to fall into, and disappear in a trough of snow along the edge of the forest, or even roll in it! Then there was spring and the little patches of green grass and moss emerging again as the snow-crust lifted and gently melted away again. Dad had us convinced that the snowdrop looked like it does, with a strong green petal at the back of the white cup, in order to help the snow-crust to lift more easily. And did Mum ever like our bunches of 'little suns' (dandelions), our coloured leaves and dry grasses and buttercups which ended up filling every vase or bottle we could find!

I remember the first time we reached the top of the mountain. We wanted to shout and give voice to our sense of triumph. But Dad gently let us know that speaking did not fit in with that moment; and so, special moments like that, we did not speak much; they felt more like *the* moment in the church that morning, when all sounds had stopped and even our breathing was too loud. I know now that these were moments of 'touching Holy Ground'; not because Dad spoke about God or faith; but he led us to feel it, to see it and to hear it. *He awakened HIM in us!*

Then there was the horizon! I used to say to Dad: 'Dad, can we go to where the sky touches the meadow?' Of course, we could. So we would run and run and stop to look at the horizon, no closer, so it seemed, and at Dad, only to be urged on again: 'Go on, run!' I never knew then, what I know now, namely the transforming power of a symbol!

During my growing-up years, these Sunday morning walks became a bit of a nuisance. I preferred to go with my friends to other places than meadows and forests and mountains. I felt too grown-up for that 'kid stuff'. And it seemed as if that which had been brought to life went into a dormant state.

It was not awakened, I am afraid, when I joined the Missionary Sisters of the Sacred Heart in Hiltrup, Westphalia, in north Germany. I felt no 'holy ground' feeling as I sat, with a huge meditation-book at five o'clock in the morning in the convent chapel, nor as I knelt quiet and straight, copying the professed sisters, who looked as if they had arrived at sheer ecstacy. Prayer now didn't feel like it felt on those Sunday mornings at High Mass, or on the mountain, or when Mum put us to bed with the last prayer of the day. My reaction was, Well, never mind, if it didn't *feel* like it; I just *must* do what a sister *does*. 'Two years will be over quickly,' I thought, and then, well, one never knows, I might be sent to the foreign missions!

And so it came: 1958 saw me on a cargo boat, bound for Australia! I mention this trip of five weeks duration, because of the effect it had on me: what seemed to have dried up of feelings and emotions re-awakened in me. The endless up-and-down movement of the water in its various moods; the sky, the cry of the albatross, the long hours of watching the ship cut through the water, taking me further and further away from home — which, I believed I would never see again — were powerful stimulants to bring 'me' back again and all that I was experiencing.

When I arrived in Australia, the experience of home-sickness was intensified by my inability to communicate in English. Oh, yes, I had learned a little of the language at secondary school, but when I heard the sounds of the English language in the harbour of Melbourne, I knew that I did not know how to speak 'Australian', and so I determined to listen and watch — quite fascinated, I might add, since the sounds seemed to come out of what looked like mouths that did not open.

In a short time I had sufficient English to be a primary teacher. I loved teaching: all of me seemed alive in the classroom — alive until the moment, when on my return to the convent, it was time to go to chapel to pray. How was it I felt so happy, involved and really living when with the children and parents, and so devoid of all spark when it came time to pray? Again, all I would do was sit still with my meditation book, appearing still, trying not to go to sleep, appearing recollected, kneeling straight and looking prayerful. I must have felt something — I don't remember much; all I remember is saying to myself: 'Oh, well most of the hours of the day are really good, and I feel happy; never mind about this awful time in chapel which I can't manage; perhaps one day I will!' Never once would I have suspected anyone else of having similar problems.

Around the time of my final vows, I became a bit desperate. After all, the thing that a religious ought to be able to do is to pray, and it hadn't happened to me. How could I go on, making it look as though it had! Well, I did go on, temporarily calmed in my anxiety by the suggestion made to me: 'These temptations come to all of us around this time.'

My appointment to be in charge of the Art Department at the Teachers' College in Oakleigh, then Christ College, pushed me to the limits of my personal needs at the time.

Yes, I had my degree, but how would I go as a *religious?* I will *look* like one, but more was needed and I didn't feel that I had it. Under the pretext of needing to learn to help young people to live Christian lives, I became very interested in Review of Life activities engaged in by the Y.C.W. movement here in Melbourne. The simplicity and genuineness of these young working boys and girls really moved me, as they looked at their daily lives, reflected together and seemed to move with such Christian enthusiasm into their daily activities. 'This is all right, actually quite possible for me,' I thought, 'all I have to do is stop, look at my life, think about it a little more, to the point where Christ makes all the difference to it.' A thrill of hope fired me to try it. Then followed the thrill of discovering that I no longer needed to leave my work, the children I taught, the parents, my friends, their concerns, my worries and love for them, *outside* the chapel. I could take them *with* me, and even think about them and know that my response was an experience of prayer, given by Christ in my heart. Living, and living the life of the Spirit, began to be one reality for me. What a relief!

Living by faith became a possibility for me, and very much symbolised, by my work in art, and my appreciation of the artist as a person with a heart-vision, who draws close to whatever stirs her heart, but always sees more than the surface appearance of things.

As a preparation for a new appointment, I studied theology and took courses in counselling. The studies in theology, and especially the tract on Faith and Revelation, confirmed my experience, and put words to what I had begun to trust and to work from in my heart.

The 'Holy Ground' experience of years ago returned as I found myself in counselling and spiritual direction situations, and as I sensed that all I had to do is believe in the life of the Spirit in the other person and his power in me to awaken the 'MORE' that wanted to live.

For me, that process of awakening, which began many years ago, continues to go on, facilitated by many experiences, such as a year in Chicago at the Institute of Spiritual Leadership, where I was able to hear and to work with those hidden realities inside me, which some fearful experiences in my earlier life had sent into hiding.

And now you might well ask, if you haven't done so already, what has all *that* got to do with liturgy? Why tell us all that in a book on liturgy? The answer, which will unfold as you read on, is that —

what I bring to liturgy,
whether celebrations of liturgy
or courses in formation in liturgy
is MYSELF.

Our Method and Scope

Have you ever attended a lecture on liturgy, say on the Eucharist, and been so impressed with the ideas, insights and suggestions that you resolved to incorporate them into your celebrations and your own prayer; and. . .

A week later they are still ideas, memories in your head, notes on paper. . .

Six months later. . .gone, evaporated, lost — mostly because you did nothing with them.

This unfortunate happening is something we set out to avoid in this book. Our method includes a process which can help to integrate ideas and insights into your praying.

From what we have said about ourselves, it will be obvious that we do not see liturgy as another subject, like scripture, theology or history, to be 'learned about.' You will also see that our concern is not to help you to gather more information about matters liturgical. Our aim has something in common with authors of books on such subjects as Making Salads or Yoga: they intend their readers to prepare and enjoy salads, or to practice and benefit by Yoga. They would be very disappointed if their readers stopped short at *reading about* it.

Take another illustration: the difference between a 'music-ologist' and a 'musician'. A 'music-ologist' is a scholar who is concerned with systematized knowledge about the musical art (similar to a psychologist or biologist). A 'musician', in contrast, is an artist who performs on a musical instrument (a pianist, violinist, etc.).

In this book we are not writing for the liturgiologist-scholar, but for the praying participator in liturgy. Although some history is included, the book does not contain a system-atized history of liturgical rites; there is some theological reflection, but not for its own sake. The aim is not scholarship, but prayer. Hence if it appears that some explanations are over-simplified, lacking in depth, and neglecting finer points and nuances, this is not an oversight but done deliberately. Nor are we setting out to give ideas on how variety can be introduced into celebrations, nor to expound on what 'you have to do', or what can, or cannot, be done in liturgy. For the same reason, we are not offering reading lists, nor even encouraging extra reading; the books most helpful, and indeed necessary, while using this book are the Missal/Sacramentary, Lectionary and Breviary.

It is to YOU as part of the worshipping congregation that the book is first directed. Only when you have been helped in your own praying at liturgy (Sections One to Four) can you be helped as a Minister (as in Sections Five and Six). The temptation may present itself to you to ask, 'How could I use this. . . in class. . .for the children?' or 'How would I go about presenting this to the people of the parish?' It is a very real, and ever-recurring, temptation: that we know from past experience, especially in the case of teachers or those who are in a situation where they can influence others. Very real, and very urgent — but nevertheless, a temptation, and we suggest that it is not something to be banished, nor forgotten, but just delayed until the appropriate time comes in the book.

In regard to method, the basis will be your *experience*, and for the most part, your experience of liturgical celebrations. We will try to help you to expand and deepen your experience, by clarifying your ideas and giving you a terminology in which to express it, thus leading to a more conscious awareness of what you have been experiencing.

As we always explain to our groups, the course is not so much a programme as a process: each section flows out of the previous one. Or better, you are prepared in each section for the next one. Hence, if people join us after the course has got under way, they will not be able to appreciate all that is going on. The same applies to this book: if you were to dip in here and there to look in a particular chapter for some topic or point, without having worked through what has gone before, you would run the risk of being misled. It is designed as a progression to facilitate the process in YOU.

This process can only happen through *reflection*, and so you will be asked, from time to time, to stop reading and to spend some time in reflection. We will offer you activities and reflection-aids to help you to assimilate and integrate the material into your life and prayer. You will be alerted to the change to reflection by the insertion of a 'reflection-sign' at this point in the text, with the activity or reflection aids which follow enclosed in a 'frame'. There will, therefore, be three types of material:

1. EXPLANATIONS
2. ACTIVITIES
3. REFLECTIONS AND PRAYER-AIDS.

A word in regard to the style of the book. We are not so much writers as speakers/facilitators. The material was originally prepared for, and used in sessions with groups. Obviously, what we present now in written form could not be just a transcript of what went on in the sessions. We have had to adapt it for writing; it is almost inevitable that its original 'spoken' character will reveal itself, however. In a sense it is a 'Self-help', a 'How to. . .' book. More precisely, it is a book for reflection: to help you to reflect on your own faith and prayer-experience, so that you may come in a new way to join a congregation to participate in liturgy, or to minister to them.

Section One

PARTICIPATION

1

LITURGY IS. . .

The meaning of 'liturgy' is our starting point. We will begin by investigating what this book is all about.

Liturgy is a generic name given to the celebration of the Eucharist and the other sacraments, and the Liturgy of the Hours. The question which concerns us is, what does it tell us when we say that something is 'liturgy'?

What do you think?

If little or nothing is coming to you, take some time at this point — and, if it helps, pen and paper — to become more aware of your ideas on what liturgy is.

What does liturgy conjure up in your mind:
any picture, or image, or words?
Ask yourself this question: "If I want to describe what the Mass is, what words or phrases first come to my mind?"

Note: Ignore what you may have read, or heard someone say. Don't quote; it is YOUR ideas that matter now.

You could have thought of:

- — a meeting with God;
- — the sacrifice of Calvary renewed;
- — a celebration of life;
- — official worship;
- — the renewal of the New Covenant;
- — prayers and rites according to Church law;
- — the action of Christ and the Church;
- — the sacrifice of Christ made present: etc.

These are the kind of responses we have got from groups of people to whom we have put that question. Others have used phrases like:

- — people assembled to worship;
- — the Christian community praising God;
- — coming together to listen and pray;
- — the congregation offering the sacrifice of Christ;
- — a group of believing people;
- — a manifestation of faith by the parish;
- — etc. etc.

Both of these lists represent how different people were actually experiencing their celebrations of the Eucharist at that time. The phrase each one used would have come from recent thoughts or insights from prayer, or from something he or she read or heard; as well as from earlier upbringing and later growth in Christian faith. To be noted about the two lists is that the first consists of concepts that are abstract; the second of more concrete expressions: it is possible to form a picture of 'people assembled', a community, people coming together. Two different types of phrases, expressing two different ways of focussing on the Mass. If you wanted to differentiate between the two categories, the first summary of phrases looks on the Eucharist from the theological point of view, the second from the liturgical point of view. They are samples of the difference between the interest and approach of the theologian and the liturgist. The first list contains theological statements explaining what the Mass is, and gives answers to the questions which theology asks; the second list reflects the kind of questions the student of liturgy asks about the Mass; for while they both ask questions about the same matter, they ask different questions. Theology asks, what is the essence of the Mass? What is the meaning of the Mass? The liturgist then makes use of the theologians' answers to ask a further question — the liturgical question: HOW DO YOU DO IT?

Theologian and liturgist: different approaches

To illustrate the difference between the concern of the theologian and the liturgists we often use the example of a sister of our acquaintance who is a member of a missionary congregation. She spent four years in an Institute of Technology studying food technology, her objective being to work in the area of nutrition as a preparation for an apostolate in New Guinea. During the years of study she went deeply into the question of food and nutrition and made use of most sophisticated equipment; but she never cooked anything, so different from others who studied food, and did courses in which they learned and practised skills and techniques, and cooked food which was eaten and enjoyed. This difference is somewhat akin to that between theology and liturgy as a study. Theology is a science and gives the theory. The liturgy of a sacrament, making use of what theology offers, is concerned with how it is celebrated in the ceremony of the sacrament.

Take the example of the sacrament of baptism. If you read a theology of baptism it will speak of baptism as initiation into the People of God, living the life of the Holy Spirit; becoming one with Christ as a witnessing and saving people, and such facts: all providing the meaning of the sacrament. Liturgy, however, will tell of the best way to celebrate this meaning in a ceremony: to bring out this meaning, where should it be celebrated? Who should be present? What actions and words of the parents, the godparents and the congregation would best bring out the meaning of their role? Briefly, in the ceremony what should be said and done, and by whom?

In the case of the Eucharist, one series of questions would be: what does it mean? what is the role of the priest? what is the bread and wine about? Why have scripture readings? How is Christ present? These are theological questions. A different question — the liturgical question — is: What is the congregation supposed to be doing: what prayer are they supposed to be praying? etc.

This distinction is relevant to our aim in this book. To understand more deeply the meaning of the Mass can be very helpful towards participation, but it does not answer all our needs and difficulties. Theological understanding helps only when the *need* is in the nature of explanation or motivation. People can also have difficulties that are not theological, but liturgical: 'I know what to do, but I cannot manage to do it,' sort of difficulty. To give such people a theological explanation as a means of helping them is quite insufficient, and maybe even harmful. It would be like this human situation: picture a five year old girl taking leave of her mother to go to school. To her mother's surprise, tears begin to flow as the child clings to her and protests that she does not want to go to school; she feels so needful of her mother that she cannot bring herself to part from her. Imagine, then, if the mother were to deal with the situation by saying to the little girl: "Just sit down for a few minutes and I will tell you of the advantages of a good education in Australia today." About the last thing she needs is an explanation! Yet, this is more or less the treatment given to help people who experience dissatisfaction with their celebration of Mass. The general practice of giving theological solutions to liturgical questions might well be one factor accounting for the notable loss of interest in the celebration of the Eucharist among Catholics of all ages and types in recent times.

Liturgy: Participation

The distincition is also relevant to the question we are considering, 'What does liturgy first bring to your mind?' The items in the list representing the interests of the liturgist all refer to people doing something or other. Hence, in the way the liturgist looks on the Mass, the first thing that we need is PEOPLE. Hence —

LITURGY IS PEOPLE, and
PEOPLE DOING SOMETHING

The Constitution on the Liturgy presents it as AN ACTION of the People of God: "No other action of the Church can match its claim. . .", it states in paragraph 7.

What is this action? Put simply and basically, it is PRAYING. Therefore,

LITURGY IS PEOPLE PRAYING. . .

From this it follows that:
> the choir singing is not liturgy;
> what is printed in the Missal/Sacramentary is not liturgy;
> the reader proclaiming the readings is not liturgy.

They are only means to bring about liturgy. Liturgy happens when the congregation prays. Not *every* prayer is liturgy. Anticipating what we will treat in detail later in the book, we could say:

LITURGY IS PEOPLE PRAYING
> — *a special prayer*
> — *IN A SPECIAL WAY*

The special, or specific, prayer which liturgy is, and the special, or specific, way in which it is prayed, will be treated at length in Section Two.

What has been stated is only expressing in other words what is said about 'participation' in the Constitution on the Liturgy. Active participation has been called the 'refrain' of the Constitution. It has been the principal concern of the liturgical movement in the Roman Catholic Church. It was a new idea when Pope Pius X wrote about active participation in 1903. Before that, personal involvement in celebrations of liturgy was a matter of little or no interest. Liturgy was viewed as a rite, and the aim was the exact performance of a fixed text and rubrics. Since the rite was performed by the clergy, liturgy was considered to be an exclusively clerical preserve.

The model was a soirée at court, with all its pomp and grandeur. Hence the most that was offered to the people was to admit them as onlookers: to stand afar off and admire the ceremonial. It was taken for granted that they would have no active part, and that they would not understand what was going on. At one time it was even said that they *should not* understand. The high point of the Eucharist for the people was to look at the host at the elevation. No help was given to them to pray: their prayer was not associated with the idea of liturgy.

Through the work of the liturgical movement the situation changed slightly. Hand-missals with a vernacular translation gave the people the opportunity of understanding what the celebrant was saying, and of praying with him. But they had to do so silently. They were released from the silence, although still confined to Latin, by the coming of the 'dialogue Mass' which became popular in the 1950s. This allowed of different degrees of participation in the congregations responses to, and recitation with the celebrant. The dialogue Mass was introduced only into the more liturgically advanced parishes, and remained unknown to most Catholics — as did any experience of active participation. So it was really only after the Constitution on the Liturgy had recommended the use of the vernacular in the Mass, that Catholics in general got their first acquaintance with active participation.

Its importance receives the strongest emphasis, as in paragraph 14:

"Full and active participation
by all the people
is the aim to be considered before all
else."

The participation which is recommended is sometimes misunderstood. It is not just keeping the congregation busy, nor occupying their interest; it does not mean singing, saying, using gestures or movements. It is something that involves the *whole of a person* in action — including external actions, but only as expressing the more important action of mind and heart. Paragraph 11 states the necessity "that their thoughts match their words."

In the course of this book, we will always use participation as meaning 'prayer participation': people praying liturgy.

The aim of work and efforts

From this understanding of liturgy there are some very significant consequences. The first is that whatever work is put into any aspect of liturgy, whether that be during the celebration or outside of it, it has one purpose: *to help the people to pray better.* Whether you are proclaiming a reading, leading the singing, or taking up the collection; whether you are planning a celebration, buying new music, attending a liturgy committee meeting, or reading this book — all of these activities have one aim, and one aim alone: that is, to help a congregation to pray as 'fully' as they are capable of praying.

Good liturgy is people praying well; poor liturgy is when people pray poorly. There is no place for anything, or any person, in a celebration that does not contribute to help the people to pray. The criterion for all that is said, sung or done is, what help does it offer to the people to pray this special prayer, in this special way which is liturgy?

Growth in prayer-participation

A further consequence: when we speak of helping people with their participation, what we are speaking of is helping them with their prayer. This is the kind of help that is indicated, for example, in the Directory for Masses with Children: what is described there as 'a liturgical and eucharistic formation.' The Rite for Christian Initiation of Adults contains a similar reference: the catechumen is to be provided with 'a pastoral formation and training . . . to learn to pray to God more easily.' This is the kind of help and formation we too have in mind.

Not only because of the very personal nature of each person's prayer, but also, and even more so, because prayer is always a gift, a grace of the Holy Spriit, any help that we, or anyone else, offers in relation to prayer, is in reality a removing of whatever is preventing the work of the Holy Spirit. "Prayer happens when the heart is open."

Of the many forms in which help can be given, and the varied types of activities that are possible to facilitate the work of the Holy Spirit, the essential activity that is needed for growth in prayer is actual *praying.* Reading, listening, thinking will avail nothing, if time is not devoted to serious praying. As already mentioned, the success of this book in leading to improved prayer at liturgy presupposes that there are regular times of prayer. Indeed, it is this — your prayer — which will be the most effective agent of growth during the time of using this book.

It would be useful for you to stop at this point in order to gather together and become more aware of the implications for you of what you have read; and to prepare for moving on to the next step in regard to praying liturgy.
A reflective reading of the following may help you, especially in regard to motivation and trust.

Interest in liturgy
is an interest in improving praying
liturgy:
my own praying, and others', too.
To this I am called by God
all the time.
It is a part of my growth into Christ:
   growing to deeper faith
   to firmer trust
   to a love more concerned and
     committed
   and growing in prayer.
As a Christian, I acknowledge that there
is nothing in me that cannot grow.
Growth must be there, because of God's
   presence.

I live through the Holy Spirit,
   who is transforming me,
   and I grow in every way.
"Speaking the truth in love,
we are to grow up in every way
into him who is the head, into Christ. . ."
I can never say, My praying liturgy is
all right; I don't need to look to its
improvement.
Do you find in your heart a need
or desire to grow in prayer?
What motivation have you now?

"It is God,
for his own loving purpose,
who puts both the will
and the action
into you."

Speak to God of your hope and trust
in regard to your prayer:

     "Who by the power at work within
     us is able
     to do far more abundantly
     than all we ask or think."

(Eph. 3:20)

2

THE FOUR AREAS

It is common experience that a person's praying liturgy is not always on a constant level of prayerfulness. There are celebrations of liturgy from which she or he may come away with a feeling of having prayed well; and others from which it may have been with a sense of dissatisfaction, and even frustration. This difference happens because of the varying factors which affect our praying liturgy, and indeed, all prayer: our prayer can be helped, or it can be hindered, by a variety of factors.

Our next step is to reflect on our experience of past celebrations of liturgy, in order to become more conscious of what these helps and hindrances are. This will lead to an awareness of our needs and what can be done to improve praying liturgy.

The following activity will help you to come to this awareness:

Make two lists, under the headings:

1. What I have found is a HELP to me in praying liturgy	2. What I have found is a HINDRANCE to me praying liturgy

Note:
You may include in your reflection any liturgies you have experienced:
Masses, the Office, baptisms, marriages etc.

You can now make use of these lists to see that there is not just one area of possibility, but *four areas* in which things can be done to improve the liturgy. The areas will be referred to as A,B,C, and D.

AREA 'A' IS THE *PLACE:*
AREA 'B' IS THE *TEXT AND RITE:*
AREA 'C' IS THE *MINISTERS:*
AREA 'D' IS THE *CONGREGATION.*

Most likely each of these areas will be represented in your, or any, lists.

Table: THE FOUR AREAS

THE PLACE	THE TEXT AND RITE	THE MINISTERS	THE CONGREGATION
Belonging to this area are: *The church or chapel, its arrangement, furnishing and decoration; the altar the lectern/ambo, the chair — their design, and visibility; the seating for the congregation — its suitability for praying, for seeing and hearing; the acoustics; the lighting; the heating/cooling; and all that is in the space in which the liturgy is celebrated*	This area includes: all that will be said and done in the celebration; *the ceremony as it was planned; the prayers, readings hymns and other music whatever is composed* (e.g. the homily); *options which have been selected* (e.g. procession with the gifts, greeting of peace, etc.) *commentaries; time for silent reflection* etc. It is the particular *format or design of a* celebration; all the elements that are put together to produce this rite or order of ceremony.	In this area are the people who have some particular role or function in the celebration, that is, apart from their participation which they share with all the congregation. They include: *the priest who presides; servers; commentator; instrumentalists; leader of the singing special ministers of Communion;* etc.	This area consists of *of the people who assemble to pray liturgy.* It is ME/US, whose participation and growth in prayer participation, is our concern.
A	B	C	D

Take time to become familiar with the FOUR
AREAS as described in the accompanying table.

In order to gain a more concrete picture of the
Four Areas, on the lists you have made place the
appropriate letter — 'A', 'B', 'C', or 'D' alongside
each item you have included.

Our concern is with what can be done to improve our
praying liturgy. Whatever is done for this purpose will belong
to one of the first three areas: 'A' — the Place, 'B' — The
Text and Rite, or 'C' — The Ministers. The influence that
they have on participation will have been learned from the
above reflective activity. Everything in these areas is supposed to be helpful to the congregation's participation.

However, what they contribute towards good participation —
the degree to which they affect the people present at the
celebration — depends ultimately on the *people themselves.*
A well-led prayer will get no response from a person who is
distracted about something else. A well-proclaimed reading
will do nothing for a person who is not listening. The words
of institution pronounced over the bread and wine will have
no meaning for a person who has not got the Christian faith.
Hence, the effectiveness of each of these areas presupposes
something in the *people* in the congregation. While there is
no denying that they do help, along with them something is
required *in* the people, before the Place, the Text and Rite,
and the Ministers can be of help to them in their prayer
participation.

This is the reason for the fourth area: *Area D — The
Congregation.* Change and improvement is to be sought first

and foremost, not in the wood, metal or cloth; not in what is on the printed page; nor even in the ministers, but in the People. It is really the neglected area: the area most needing attention and getting least. In the course of the centuries, little or no interest has been shown in doing anything other than in what comprises Areas A, B, and C. A look at what has happened in these four areas since the liturgical movement began will make this clear.

Area 'A' — The Place

A church is a place for worshipping people, not a monument or a museum. Therefore, all is to be evaluated not just as good art, good taste, but from the help they offer to the people to pray liturgy in a celebration. This is the focus of the Constitution on the Liturgy, which in Chapter VII, *Sacred Art and Sacred Furnishings*, continues the early interest in liturgical art and architecture; the architecture of the place of worship; its decoration; the design and placing of the liturgical furniture; the vessels and vestments. It was a very alive area for liturgists. Efforts of renewal of *ars sacra* — sacred art as distinct, and very different, from 'profane art' at the end of the 19th century, gained momentum through renewal societies and publications, especially in the U.S.A. and Europe. Through liturgical art periodicals many became familiar with the new post-war style, for example, the church designed by Le Corbusier in L'Arbresle, and St John's Abbey, Collegeville. Many will remember the change in vestments and vessels from the forties on. The liturgically-minded priest — described popularly as a 'litnik' — could be recognised by his chasuble, which was in the full, neo-Gothic style rather than the very ornate, fiddle-shaped style of the past. Chalices — as likely as not brought from Germany — tended to be less of the Gothic style, tall with conical cup, richly ornamented with filigree, and to be more of a lower shape with prominent cup.

How important a factor this Area A is still considered to be, can be seen in Chapters V and VI of the *General Instruction of the Roman Missal* (Arrangement and Decoration of Churches; Requisites for Celebrating Mass); and in the publication of the National Conference of Catholic Bishops in the U.S.A. in 1978, *Environment and Art in Catholic Worship*, which speaks of its 'vital role' in the people's participation.

Area 'B' — The Text and Rite

At the same time as the interest in liturgical art and architecture, there was a vital interest in church music. From the time of Dom Gueranger and the Benedictines of Solemnes, and the efforts of Pope Pius X to promote a renewal in church music, singing at Mass has probably received more attention than any other element in liturgy. The Gregorian renewal was followed by a wider vision which brought liturgists to encourage the use of music other than Gregorian. The *Instruction* of 1958, permitting what it called 'popular religious hymns' to be sung during a 'read Mass,' led to the introduction in English-speaking countries of what had been in use in Germany for quite a while: the *Betsingmesse*. This has stayed with us in Australia in the popular form of what has been termed the 'four-hymn sandwich' (singing at the Entrance, Procession with the Gifts, Communion and Recession.)

In the document of the bishops of the U.S.A. mentioned in the last section, on Environment and Art, it is said: "Historically, music has enjoyed a preeminence among the arts of public worship, and there is no clear evidence to justify denying it the same place today." The attention given to singing at Mass, at the parish level and in religious communities, and the proliferation of religious songs in folk style in the past few decades, leaves no doubt about the great hopes that have been placed, and are still being placed, in music as a powerful means of improving the praying participation of the congregation.

The highlighting by the Constitution on the Liturgy of the important place of the elements in Area 'A' and of music (Area 'B') in participation was clearly not due to any new questioning or recent research; it had been traditionally valued, and accepted and included as such. By omitting any reference to the relation between the architecture, art or music to different types of congregations or celebrations, the

Constitution continued the attitude of the past, requiring good quality, but saying little on the matter of 'relativity'. The concept is introduced, however, in connection with the recommendations of adaptation of the text and rite to the culture and traditions of people in 'General Principles', The Reform of the Sacred Liturgy, section D. Underlying it is the principle that what is good and helpful in art, architecture and music *is relative to the particular congregation (in regard to size, age, background etc.) on this particular occasion (whether it is a special occasion or a daily celebration, solemn in character or simple).* This principle applies to each and every item in the three Areas, A,B, and C. The most obvious example of relativity is the change to the use of the vernacular in liturgy. Because of the obstacles to participation in Latin liturgy, as early as 1884, translations of the Roman Missal in the vernacular appeared in the form of hand-missals. While these hand-missals gave the people the opportunity of understanding what the celebrant was saying, and of praying with him, their use was restricted to a minority of Catholics. Participation really became possible for all when, in 1964, not only the readings, but also the chants and parts of the Ordinary were allowed in the vernacular. The situation was vastly improved when the Eucharistic Prayer in the vernacular was introduced a few years later.

Relativity in Text and Rite: Planning

The content of Area 'B' is the official Text and Rite as given in the Missal/Sacramentary and the General Instruction which deals with the 'Structure, Elements and Parts of the Mass,' (Chapter II), 'Different Forms of Celebration' (Chapter IV), and 'Masses and Prayers for Various Occasions' (Chapter VIII), and planned and prepared according to Chapter VII, 'Choice of Mass Texts.' That is, availing of the options offered, and the possibility of the 'introductions' outlined in paragraph 11 of the Instruction. In any celebration, what pertains to Area 'B' is what we end up with on paper when we sit down, by ourselves or with others, to plan a particular liturgy.

Before the 1969 Order of Mass, planning of this kind was unknown and uncalled for. In practice, anything of its kind was confined to the organist or choirmaster. The 'priest' could just open the book and go straight through. The only preparation expected of the priest was his homily, and his personal preparation immediately preceding the celebration. These are still expected of him; and much more, in addition. To keep a distinction between the two activities, we have found it helpful to use 'planning' to refer to the thinking and paperwork activity; and to reserve 'preparation' for the personal activity of the celebrant, or other ministers, in making himself or herself ready to act in this role. The rite of the Eucharist today is so designed that previous planning is unavoidable. The celebrant, before the celebration, must have made a choice of which greeting he will use; he will choose the penitential rite, and possibly compose it; the Opening Prayer has to be selected on weekdays in Ordinary time; the homily is to be composed, and also the General Intercessions, including the introduction and concluding prayer; the Preface, Eucharistic Prayer, Acclamation have to be selected; and so on. There are about fifty places in the Eucharist in which selection and composition is indicated. The other rites of the sacraments also require previous planning. For the purpose of catering for different circumstances and situations they offer a multiplicity of prayers and readings to choose from. The principle directing planning is stated in the General Instruction, paragraph 313:

> "The pastoral effectiveness of a celebration depends in great measure on choosing readings, prayers and songs which correspond to the needs, spiritual preparation and attitude of the participants. This will be achieved by the intelligent use of the options described below.
> In planning the celebration, the priest should consider the spiritual good of the assembly rather than his own desires. . ."

The significance of this principle of relativity is highlighted in the Constitution on the Liturgy. Having established that in the promotion of liturgy the primary aim is 'full and active participation by all the people,' it puts forward, as the means to attain this participation, the need of a 'general restoration of the liturgy itself. . . in which texts and rites. . . not only may but ought to be changed.' (paragraph 21). Hence, one of the General Norms for reform is: 'the liturgical books are to be revised as soon as possible.' (Paragraph 25). If we are looking for the area in which most hopes were placed for an improved participation, we certainly find it here in Area 'B', the Text and Rite. This is true of all levels, the official, Roman level, and the local, parish level. On the official level, the body set up in 1964 to execute the recommendations of the Constitution, the *Consilium ad exsequendam Constitutionem de sacra liturgia*, commonly called the 'Consilium', provided a series of changes in the rite of the Mass in 1965, 1967 and 1968, and then the new form of the rite in which we now celebrate the Eucharist: the Order of Mass in the Sacramentary/Missal, with the General Instructions of the Roman Missal; and then the new Lectionary. New texts of the other sacraments and the Office were composed and published; and other new texts, including new Eucharistic Prayers. On the local level, most of the efforts of priests, catechists and all who were making efforts to improve participation directed their attention to this same Area 'B'. A new type of music has been introduced and new instruments; there is a continued search for more suitable hymns; the procession with the gifts, and the greeting of peace in the congregation are very popular; less acceptable are the alterations made to the text and rite in the form of re-writing it, omitting or interchanging elements in a quest for improved meaning: the Our Father as part of the General Intercessions, the Fraction Rite as part of the Narrative of Institution, for example; and the fascination by variety and innovation.

All of this is evidence of the conviction that the Area most productive of better participation is undoubtedly Area 'B'. So much is this the case that, in the minds of many, 'liturgy' has tended to be identified with, and restricted to, the text and rite. A typical exchange is: "We had a marvellous liturgy today."
"What did you *do?*"

This is hardly surprising, since the tendency can be seen in no less a document than the 1963 Constitution on the Liturgy. Although in its first section it presents liturgy as an action of the people, when in the General Norms for the Reform of the Liturgy, it uses such phrases as 'the regulation, (or the revision) of sacred liturgy,' it is obviously not referring to people but to texts and rites as printed in the liturgical books.

This attitude towards the text and rite is open to the danger of thinking that a better ritual automatically means better participation by the people. There is a gap — and it is necessary to be aware of it always — between what is on paper in the printed text, and what is going on in the people in the congregation. There is no doubt that a better environment, better music, and better translations of improved texts and rites *should* result in better participation. That they do not always succeed in doing so is a universal experience. This gap has been recognised in the *Directory for Masses with Children* (1973), which devotes one of the three chapters of its content to 'The Introduction of Children to the Eucharistic Celebration'. The situation was very well summed up in a Commemorative Statement in anticipation of the fifteenth anniversary of the Constitution on the Liturgy by the U.S. Bishops' Committee on the Liturgy, in November 1978. Grateful for what had been accomplished in that period of time, in looking to the future they recognized areas of true concern and new challenges. One of these was: "We have the revised books. . . In a sense the books must be 'unpacked'."

The ones who do the unpacking are in —

Area 'C' — The Ministers

The new rite of Mass has introduced a difference in regard to Ministers: it includes not only ministers who are active in the altar area, as the celebrant, servers, readers, but also those who perform their ministry outside the altar area, such as the commentator, the leaders of the responsorial psalm and the petitions of the General Intercessions, the instrumentalists, and singing group, ushers and collectors. Ministers, it should be noted, are not included in a celebration in order to help them, the ministers, to feel involved. If people's participation presents a problem, the solution is not to give them something to occupy them as ministers, the opportunity to 'do' something! That would be an abuse.

Ministers in liturgy, according to their different functions and gifts serve to bridge the 'gap' between text and rite and the people, as mentioned above. They are not to be considered useful; nor only as important; they are indispensable. In a celebration of liturgy everything is 'ministered' to the people. The congregation, for example, are not handed a printed text, when they enter the church, which they will read and pray themselves. Between the text and rite and the people is always a *person*: a person who 'serves up' the text and rite. Never is there a 'self-serve' situation. To give another example, at Communion, the body and blood of Christ is always personally ministered by someone acting as a minister.

There is good ministering and bad ministering. Ministering plays a critical part in the success or failure of text and rite to evoke prayer participation; it can bring it to life, or can kill it. So much so, that of the two areas, 'B' – Text and Rite, and 'C' – the Ministers, the latter group exercise the greater influence. Whereas a good text, such as a reading, can be rendered ineffective by bad ministering, an indifferent text can be used to good effect by good ministering. Father G. Broccolo writes of the critical role of ministers in these words: "When a man with the gift of spiritual leadership prays in the midst of his people he stimulates them to prayer by his manner of praying. The forms or structures he uses are secondary in importance."

In order that ministers can be most effective it is now common practice to provide them with a preparation and training: for seminarians as a preparation for ordination, and also for readers, commentators and special ministers of communion.

As is the case with the other areas – the Place, and Text and Rite – relativity applies to this area, too. Ministers of different types will be more effective in different circumstances; for example, according to the size of the congregation, the age of the participants, and their background. Like the Planning of Area 'B', this is a new area, brought into existence by the new Rite of Mass. It has not been given anything like the attention Area 'B' has received; it was slow to be recognized as important – or at all. There are factors and influences which result in holding it back, mostly connected with an understanding of the difference between the pre-1969 rite and the present one: the past attitude towards the congregation as present at, but not participating in the rite, so different from the need seen today of communication between ministers and the people so that the congregation may be able to participate. Nevertheless, the area and its importance have been established by the Constitution, in paragraph 11: 'pastors of souls must realize that, when liturgy is celebrated, more is required than the mere observance of the laws governing valid and licit celebration'.

More important than the Place, or the Text and Rite, are the Ministers. What has the greater influence on the people's prayer participation is not the songs selected, nor the words delivered, nor even the official Text and Rite, but the persons who minister them. Yet none of these is the most important area: the most telling factor in prayer participation is —

Area 'D' — Me/Us: the People praying liturgy

In seeking for some authoritative backing for this area, we have found only one statement, a statement in the Constitution on the Liturgy, paragraph 17; referring to seminarians, it says: "they will need proper direction so that they will be able to understand the sacred rites and *take part in them wholeheartedly.*" (The italics are ours.) This is how we see Area 'D': the people participating and the help they need in order that they may be able to 'take part wholeheartedly.'

Of the four areas, it is the most critical, and the one in which attention will reap most fruitful results. If it is neglected, it is because too much in it is taken for granted. Children are given a preparation for first communion, first confession, and confirmation; too seldom are they given a preparation for the celebration of the Eucharist. It seems to be taken for granted that if they are brought to Church, they will respond and pray as easily as they respond to their favourite TV shows — and that applies to adults as well. Yet the celebration of the Eucharist is the most complex activity that most people will ever engage in; and the most demanding action that could be asked of any human being. (This point will be taken up later in connection with the Rite of the Eucharist.)

It is our conviction, and it has been our practice in liturgical formation, that the area with which to begin is this Area 'D': with ourselves. We will, therefore, be concentrating on ME/US praying liturgy for quite a long time in this book, before dealing with the other areas.

1. Select a liturgy (Mass, Office etc) which you celebrated recently.
2. Reflect on it in order to discover, and list,
   (a) what were the significant things that were there *outside* of you, that is in Areas 'A', 'B' and 'C';
   (b) what was significant *inside* you: Area 'D'.
3. Were there any 'gaps' between (a) and (b)?
4. Did you notice times when your words, gestures and movements did not correspond to what was in your mind and heart?
5. Read and reflect on *Isaiah 29:13-14.*
   What is it saying to you?
   What is it asking of you?

3

ME/US PRAYING LITURGY

Following through our concern with people praying liturgy, and the improvement of that praying, the three areas of factors which influence the quality of prayer participation and which are *'outside'* a person, have been investigated in chapter 2. This chapter will take up the factors *'inside'* a person — the personal factors — which operate to affect prayer participation.

The activity at the end of the previous chapter will have supplied you with some examples of what these factors are in you. You will be able to appreciate the relevance and extent of them if you have a fuller list of examples. This you can do by some further reflection, as in the following activity.

List: what you feel you need in order to improve your praying liturgy.

Note: The needs under consideration are *personal* needs; not the needs that belong to the three 'outside' areas.

A typical list, and one we have often received in our workshops, would be:
— to want to pray
— to understand what is going on
— to be forgiving
— to feel at one with the other people
— to be calm and relaxed
— to be in touch with myself
— some previous preparation
— to have an interest in the celebration
— knowledge of scripture
— the practice of personal prayer
— faith: conviction in the value of the Eucharist etc. etc.

An examination of these items brings out different types or classes of needs:

a need of understanding; more information; explanation of the elements of the ceremony; human needs, like being able to be in touch with what I am experiencing; feeling at one with other people; tolerance of others; able to be committed;

a need of Christian faith, in regard to a Christian life, scripture, the Eucharist

the need to be able to practise, or bring into action, internal states, such as being tolerant towards *this* priest; calm and relaxed *right* now; to want to pray at *this* time.

There are other types of needs, but before mentioning them, we will have a closer look at each type of need, as revealed in the list.

1.   **Understanding**: Praying liturgy presupposes a certain knowledge of the Christian faith. To find meaning in the rite and respond to it a person needs to have some familiarity with the history of salvation; to be acquainted with the mystery of Christ and the Church; as well as knowing the meaning of the particular sacrament they are celebrating.

This need is well catered for by the many publications, courses, seminars, talks, tapes that are available for any who wish to make use of them.

2. **Personal development**: More than how well informed they are, people are going to be affected by their *own selves* in

praying liturgy. For example, how they relate to other people; what their self-image is; the freedom with which they can accept themselves, make choices and make a commitment; their sense of responsibility towards society; and their ability to deal with their emotions, like anger or anxiety. The reason for this is that people are the very same people in a celebration of liturgy as they are outside of it. They do not undergo any transformation as they pass through the doors of the church; nor do they leave any part of themselves outside the church. At liturgy they are — just *themselves, as they are.* Consequently, the people they are affects their prayer participation; participation draws on certain psychological qualities. For example, people whose state of development is such that their motivation for going along to the church on Sundays is fear of punishment or a sense of duty or to perform one of life's rituals — while their presence may be an expression of submission and obedience to God, and they may well pray — yet they will not be able to participate 'fully', for this requires that they act out of free choice, and not out of a 'should/must'. Again, those whose feelings are not yet sufficiently awakened will be able to do no more than hear ideas, and make only a 'head' response of assent to them. For if they are not able to make a 'personal' response, a response of the whole person, there is no experience for them, and that means a prayer participation which is partial only. Similarly, participation will be restricted to the extent that their growth allows people to experience a sense of feeling at one with their family or friendship group only; neither parish community nor 'the Church' will be a felt reality for them.

This can be summed up by saying that if, as was discovered in the last chapter, ME/US is the finally determining factor in prayer participation, then *our state of development as a person is necessarily a critical factor.* If this seems to be a new notion, it is because personal participation is new to us, for it is only about twenty years ago since we in the Roman Catholic church were able to attempt it.

3. **Faith:** Participation, that is prayer, is based on a faith in Jesus Christ, the Son of God, which includes commitment to him in his Church in trust and love; faith in our baptismal

life of the Holy Spirit; a conviction of the value of the *celebration that matters.* Regrettably these skills are not part acceptance of Christian values; a regular prayer-life and some facility in prayer.

These, what we call 'faith needs', are too easily taken for granted: difficulties and problems that many have in regard to celebrating the Eucharist in their parish on Sundays can be, not a problem with liturgy at all, but weakness, and possibly a lack, of faith. This can often be the case with people in their adolescent stage. They are really a part of what was dealt with in the above section, 'Personal Development': a particular aspect or dimension of a person's human development. They are needs people have in regard to their prayer participation; factors operating to help or hinder that prayer from 'inside' a person.

4. Skills: As well as being affected by their personal development, 'who they are', people are also influenced by 'how they are', that is at the time of celebrating liturgy. There are permanent qualities a person has; with them habitually, and not appearing and disappearing, such as: having a forgiving attitude towards people; being a reflective, prayerful type; trusting in God; or having the habit of regular prayer. A person can also be influenced by experiences of a temporary nature, for example, if she or he, as Mass is about to begin, experiences anger and feels like doing anything but praying. Is the only option to leave the church, or to drop out of prayer participation, that is to go through the external motions only, and leave it at that: "I am so annoyed right now, I could not possibly pray!"? That would be unthinkable. There *is* something else he or she can do: has a *need to be able to do.* This is one of the needs that come under the heading of SKILLS.

Some of the typical skill needs are: to be able to come to quiet; to deal with distractions and with strong emotions; to concentrate for the length of the celebration; to listen; and to respond in prayer. They play a decisive part in anyone's prayer, for *it is how a person is at the time of the liturgical celebration that matters.* Regrettably these skills are not part of our culture; our culture is noisy, busy and unreflective, interested more in 'usefulness' than meaning. People cannot stay attentive for very long; their span of attention, it has been said, is the length of time between television commercials. It is sad to find so many excellent people who want to pray more deeply, and cannot, because they have not got the ability to stop: people who feel threatened by a notable period of silence.

Who I am, and *how* I am, on the psychological and faith levels, are what ultimately determine how I pray liturgy, that is, how I respond to whatever is present in the other three areas of Place, Text and Rite, and Ministers.

There is a very important discovery that we have made in working for over ten years with thousands of people: never have we met anyone with a problem in praying that was specifically a liturgical problem. What appeared to be a problem with liturgy turned out, when looked at more closely, to be a symptom of a problem in life. There are few, if any, strictly speaking liturgical problems; only human ones.

Another observation in this same context. So often one hears the question: What connection is there between liturgy and life? This is the connection: ME/US. The same ME and US in everyday life and in the church; acting in the same way in both; acting in the way I act because of who I am, because of my stage of development, psychological and faith; and because of the skills I have developed and can bring into operation as they are needed.

You have an illustration of this in the list of items you drew up in the last activity (page 38). You can see it by doing the following activity:

Take the list of personal needs (Area 'D'), and consider each item carefully, *as a factor*, not now in your prayer, but as *affecting your life in general.*

Liturgy and life are not two unconnected and independent activities. Praying liturgy is one activity in life, one of the many activities along with others such as working, going to school, being with friends, bringing up a family, living as husband and wife or as a member of a religious community. They are all *part* of a person's total life; and so is liturgy. To celebrate liturgy a person does not step out of life, but moves from one of life's situations to another, as a mother or father returning from work to their family, or a child returning home after school. To any and every situation in life each one brings himself or herself, with his or her qualities as a person and communicating skills and learning skills, and so on; she or he uses these skills; *is* himself or herself. Participating in liturgy is just one of these situations.

Liturgy is so much a part of life, and so indistinguishable are the needs of liturgy and day to day living that the best help that can be given to people with their liturgical praying, is help with their *personal needs*; what they need for liturgy is what they need for life. The presence or absence of personal qualities and skills becomes evident in both; though possibly they show up with greater clarity in liturgy, since it is such a concentrated span of activity and time. "There is nothing in life that is not in liturgy." There is no human activity in which anyone engages in life that is not drawn on in liturgy. It is all there: being called to a situation, and being sent to people; listening and responding; hearing people's needs and helping them in loving concern; being silent and speaking; and many more instances, which will all be elucidated in the course of this book. Here, though, it may help anyone who is feeling sceptical about what has been said so far, to know that it has been summed up in one phrase in the Constitution on the Liturgy in describing liturgy as 'the summit' of a Christian's activity.

We hope that it will not now come as a surprise when we present the help we offer as a *Formation in Life and Liturgy*. As we see it, you cannot help a person with their liturgy, at least in any depth, without helping them with their living; and, any help given with living is a help with liturgy.

**There IS nothing in life
that is not in liturgy.**

This following activity is placed here with a view to giving you a broader basis for what will be considered in this chapter:

Becoming conscious of one's behaviour in liturgy

Select a specific Eucharist which you celebrated, in order to reflect on it, on yourself and your behaviour in it.

Ask yourself:

* What did I like about it?
* What did I not like about it?
* What was my attitude towards the other people: the people in general, and individuals in particular?
* How did I respond to the ministers?
* How was the music/singing, if there was any? if not, how did I feel about that?
* How was I during the homily?
* What did I take away from the celebration?
* How was I present: was I involved, alive and vital or dead and just looking on?
* Was my Christian faith active, or not?
* Where was 'I' evident in it —the *real person I am?*

Ways of being "at Mass"

There are different states in which you could find yourself during the celebration of the Eucharist.

You could be there PHYSICALLY only:
> Your body is there in the church;
> but no more than your body.
> Your mind and interest are anywhere but
> in the church or on this celebration.

Whatever other value there may be in this, there is no participation or prayer in it.

You could be there OBSERVING:
> You are the same as when you watch a religious service
> on TV: you give your attention to what you see and
> hear, such as the place and its decoration; the ministers'
> dress and performance. You register your likes and
> dislikes;
> you evaluate and pass judgement,
> maybe you suggest alternatives, improvements.
> You could pass such remarks as,
> "The people do not know this Entrance Hymn; they
> should have chosen another one." "I like that reader;
> it's easy to see that he put a lot into preparing it."
> "That homily will not do any good; he is altogether too
> patronising in it."

This is not prayer participation, either. Being there in this
way would give you material to give an evaluation, or write
up a report on the celebration afterwards.

You could be there LEARNING:
> You would then be there
> the same as you are when at a lecture;
> you listen to the facts, and the teachings
> of the readings and responsorial psalm;
> you note the thoughts and ideas expressed
> in the prayers.

Neither is this prayer participation, but simply a learning
situation about scripture, theology and the Christian life.
You would be there to collect ideas that would be useful
later on in catechetics class or prayer services.

You could be there
AS A PRAYING CHRISTIAN:
> The only way of being there praying:
> the only way in which to participate.
> Mere physical presence is not participation. A person
> may not be able to avoid it at times, but to be satisfied
> with it would be harmful. The time for an evaluation of
> liturgy is not during the celebration; it is impossible to
> participate and evaluate at the same time, so it has to be
> done after the celebration. Liturgy makes use of prayers
> and scripture readings, not to *instruct*, but to bring us to
> PRAYER.

> There is only ONE way
> to be present:
> *as a participating person,*
> *a Christian praying.*

Your own growth in participation makes it necessary for
you to be in touch with how you are when you are 'at Mass'.
This activity will exercise your awareness:

Discovering the ways I am at liturgy

Describe yourself when you are (a) only physically
present at Mass; or (b) only observing; or (c) just
learning. What goes on inside you: your feelings,
thoughts, attitudes?

From the awareness of ME/US in liturgy, this reflection could lead on to a deeper responsiveness to the real ME/US in God's sight.

Reflection

"God knows your hearts" (Luke 16:15)
"You know me, Lord you see me,
you probe my heart." (Jer. 12:3)
God sees me, and nothing is hidden from
his sight:
he sees all I do
he hears all I say —
    what I am really saying
    (no matter what the words are);
    what I am really doing
    (no matter what the actions are).
His 'eyes' see through me, into *me*:
what is of importance to him
is what he sees going on
inside me.
"Oh, you Pharisees! You clean the outside of the
cup and plate, while inside yourselves you are
filled with extortion and wickedness.
Fools! Did not he who made the outside make
the inside too?" (Luke 11.39-41)
    Is God not at all interested in the outside?
    Does he not see my external acts?
    He is interested in *me*: me the human
        person.
    The real me is the 'inside', and that
        is who he wishes to listen to.
    He does not hear the sound of my voice
    as if it were a tape-recorder;
    he does not hear the sound of my words

but the sound of my heart,
the sound of my feelings, intentions. . .
He does not see what I make or accomplish
as though I were a machine, a computer.
God wants to see more in me;
he can see more than the outside;
what I mean,
what I am expressing
    about myself, my relationship with him,
    and people,
my values, attitudes, hopes. . .
In his sight
the outside becomes a sacrament:
and he hears it speak —
me.
"There is no sound tree that produces rotten
fruit, nor again a rotten tree that produces sound
fruit. For every tree can be told by its own fruit. .
A man's words flow out of what fills his heart."
(Luke 6)
    What more could he see inside?
    Many things,
    like peace, joy, and happiness,
    a caring and compassionate heart,
    gentleness,
    sensitivity and responsiveness,
    and much more. . .
At any moment, in any situation
I can ask the question: What does God want to
see inside me now?
What does God wish to find inside me
when I am. . . (select a typical situation in your
life, e.g. at work, driving, at home etc.)?
What does he expect to hear inside me
when I participate in liturgy?

Pray Psalm 138 (139).

4

ELEMENTS IN A FORMATION
IN LIFE AND LITURGY

We have discovered what is needed in order to improve prayer participation, and so we are in a position to come to an understanding about what help will be most beneficial to a person who sets out to improve in liturgical praying: or, to put it in another way, what elements constitute a course that has this aim. This chapter, then, will round off the enquiry begun in chapter 1, and specify what will begin in the next section, Praying Liturgy.

Each of the elements will be developed in some detail. We hope that it will not deter readers from entering into the process of working with their prayer. However, because the book does not follow a well-known path — our courses are frequently described as 'different' — it could happen that a question is raised, Why do they do it like this? or What has this got to do with liturgy? To forestall any distracting questions or possible confusion, this chapter presents a rationale for the content of the book, and the method we pursue. At the same time it presents our ideas concerning liturgy courses in general.

Method

The principal needs that surfaced as prayer needs are personal needs. Hence the kind of help required to improve prayer will be in the nature of a 'formation'. A formation rather than an education, since it is concerned with the whole person: the mind, of course, but, more importantly, what is referred to in biblical imagery as the 'heart'. To think about improving prayer participation is to think about personal growth and human development.

A formation in life and liturgy, as we consider it in this book, aims at catering for people's *personal prayer needs*. Their personal needs are what determine the content, context and method of the formation. Typical needs have been discovered and analysed in the previous chapters: they are what constitute Area 'D', and they were grouped into (1) understanding, (2) personal development, (3) faith and (4) skills.

Giving help to a person in his or her need is often referred to as 'supplying what a person needs'. The nature of prayer participation in liturgy calls for a different image from that of giving what is lacking, or filling holes, as it were. We consider it more suitable to think in terms of 'awakening', 'drawing out', 'eliciting', 'educing' or 'identifying'; that is, bringing to life what is already there. In other words, we use a *method that is experiential*. What is first done is to tap people's experience — their experiences of faith, long or short; their experience of praying, satisfactory or not; and their experience of living. We move on from there, expanding and deepening the experiences. This process is used in regard to each of the following elements in formation.

(1) Understanding

Content: The understanding, knowledge and facts which are necessary and useful include some rather basic familiarity with details, and even some memory work, such as knowing the prayers and responses which the congregation uses in the celebration of the Eucharist, or being able to find one's way through a breviary. The important requirements, however, which come under this heading are:

— an adequate understanding of the Christian faith:

adequate, that is, to find meaning in the text of the celebration;
- an understanding of liturgical worship: its nature and its demands;
- a knowledge of the rites which are regularly celebrated: the Eucharist, the Rites of Reconciliation; and, for those who use it, the Liturgy of the Hours.

The information is easily available on these subjects in books, on tapes, in courses and workshops of varying length and depth.

Context: Of greatest consequence is the context in which the information is imparted. The context is 'we/us praying liturgy'; the concern is with *ourselves participating* in liturgy. The question to be answered is the liturgical one, 'How do I do it?' In courses we have given, we have noticed in groups an attraction for the impersonal, 'out there' question, What are you allowed to do? Do you have to. . .?

The focus in the questions is on the text and rite, the interest is centred on the prayers, hymns, ways of doing things, etc. — almost going back to an interest in a rubrical stance. There seems to be a natural gravitation to this aspect and this question. There is a place for imparting information about possibilities in the rite; for example, when dealing with planning liturgies or ministering. However, in the situation of a *formation in participation* the context needs always to be praying, answering the question 'How will *this* help me to pray?' rather than 'What can be done?' — as could be asked, for example, about the Introductory Rites.

In other words, the context is not what liturgy looks like, but *what liturgy feels like.*

Method: The information and explanations, as well as being offered in this special context, also need to be integrated into the faith, and prayer, and lives of the listeners. This can be achieved only through *reflection*; a sufficient period of time after a lecture spent in 'hearing' what the facts awakened in them: holding up their past experience in the light of what has been told them; registering any change they are conscious of in their attitudes, values, feelings; accepting the difference between what they experience in their parish liturgy and what has been proposed to them. In short allowing the information to seep through their heads into themselves. They can be helped in this by offering them suggested points for reflection, or questions to put to themselves. It will be a further help if they are given the opportunity to share in small groups, and, if suitable, to allow the total group to hear feedback from the small groups.

No matter how it is done, if anything is to be gained from a lecture, tape or article in regard to participation, TIME must be provided for reflection in a SPACE/ENVIRONMENT suitably quiet. There is no alternative.

Understanding, when thus integrated into experience will meet some needs that people have, and give a help with some of their difficulties with prayer participation. Emphasis is on the *some*. It is not to be assumed that people will pray better if they know more; least of all to expect that prayer automatically improves through reading or attending lectures.

To put this in another way, people have many other needs in liturgy besides intellectual ones, and to offer them nothing but what contributes to their knowledge would produce very meagre results. Yet so many liturgy courses and seminars give just that and no more: lectures, talks, reading lists, discussions.

In our estimation, the intellectual dimension of understanding liturgy is on the lowest rung of the ladder of needs and requirements and the means to use to help people to improve their praying liturgy.

> *Since a mere reading of this book will be of very little use to anyone's prayer, and because the reflective exercises are so important, to encourage you, at given points, to stop reading and begin to reflect, we place all reflective and prayer passages in a frame like this.*
>
> You are invited to stop and reflect now, to ask yourself:
> * in my experience, what help to my praying liturgy has information or understanding given me?
> * what needs still remain unanswered even with a greater understanding?

(2) Skills

The abilities, facility, skills that are used in liturgy, and which contribute to a person's prayer participation are:
— the ability to come to inner quiet; to be in touch with how one is (e.g. in regard to preoccupations, feelings, emotions, body sensations, etc.); to be attentive to what is going on in the celebration;
— to be totally present; to maintain concentration;
— to listen: to listen, that is, not to the sounds or the words, but to the person and what he or she is 'saying' to us.
— to reflect: associating memories and ideas; seeing at a deeper level; becoming aware of implications;
— to respond: for example, to the readings, with a response that is from the *total person*; a response from mind and heart, as distinct from thoughts and ideas (a head response only) or even a mere reaction.

These skills are called for in everyday life as much as in liturgy, and they make for successful and peaceful living as much as for good participation in liturgy. There is yet one more skill needed, and it is necessary because liturgy is prayer; it is:

– to allow one's Christian faith to be activated; to think,
reflect and respond as a person of faith.

All these separate skills are included and contained in *the
one basic liturgical skill: responding to a symbol*. It arises
from the nature of liturgy as symbol. All liturgical rites are
symbols; furthermore, all prayer participation is a response
to the symbols; and prayer, when externalized in any way, is
also a symbol. To pray liturgy is to be drawn into the world
of symbols, and a person needs to be at home in symbolic
action. Hence the skill: *to respond to a symbol in a symbol*.

This one skill, which includes several skills, is the subject
of Chapter 10 – which is probably the most important in
the book – and it will receive a lot of emphasis. Most of the
time and attention given to these skills will be in the form
of exercises; skills are learnt and developed only by repeated
exercises. In them people come to experience the freedom
that is possible in the midst of distraction, and even in
emotional disturbance; they will come to see that their
prayer needs not be impaired or destroyed because of what
is going on inside them – *how* they are.

To engage in these exercises also calls for TIME and a
PLACE/ENVIRONMENT suited to these special activities.

(3) Praying

The place and role of prayer in relation to formation in
liturgical praying has already been touched on in Chapter 1,
when treating of Growth in Prayer Participation. In the workshops which we conduct, we are always most insistent that
the times when the group prays together are not only part of
the workshop but the most important part: an intrinsic
element and not just accompanying the other elements.
Because of this essential, and maybe unique, role, whatever
else that may be omitted through change of programme or
shortness of time, the prayer sessions are never left out.

The prayer we envisage is not always liturgical prayer,
that is Eucharist or Liturgy of the Hours. We compose
Prayer Services that arise from and externalize the experience
of the people in the group – the result of work we have

recently completed with the group, whether of an 'under-standing' or 'skill' nature, suited to the occasion and the development of the group. It can be quite short, meaning by short, about ten minutes. Since emphasis is on the quality of the prayer rather than on the quantity, it is often a help to the quality to reduce the length, especially in the beginning stages of a workshop. The prayer can be held in the chapel, prayer room, or in the same room in which the work sessions are being held. What is important is that it is taken seriously, and given the thought and attention, both in preparation and execution, that is due to its status. In this way, they get a more definite taste and experience of their prayer from the heart; they become more sure of what they can expect in their prayer participation in liturgy. Continued over a period, these experiences of prayer can bring them to a feel of prayer at a depth they had not known before. This point will be taken up again in the next chapter.

(4) Human development: deepening faith

We made the assertion in the last chapter that the state of anyone's development, on the psychological and faith levels, is the ultimate determining factor in praying liturgy. An improvement in this prayer, therefore, cannot take place without growth and development. How is growth to be fostered? In the very same process, we believe, as has been described above in regard to Understanding, Skills and Praying. The essential activity in promoting human develop-ment is reflection: reflection on oneself in life; on one's seeing and being in the world and with people; on one's behaviour and values; on experiences and events, feelings and attitudes. Whatever else may be needed in order to grow, it is impossible to grow without reflection. This requires that a person —

1. stops doing things, becomes disengaged;
2. becomes consciously aware of himself or herself
   (how am I right now?)
3. spends time reflecting and listening.

Some can do this on their own, in time chosen by them-selves; some need the help of a friend, or a spiritual director. The elements in this life-liturgy formation process offer the

aid of a structure: at various times it summons us to reflection, and gives direction as to how to do it. You have already
been introduced to some exercises of this type in the previous
chapters. Exercises like this will continue to the end of the
book, and will be the most effective sections right through;
the rest of the content will be a lead into, or the outcome of,
the reflection and prayer which is indicated.

(5) Evaluation

A part of the process of formation in liturgical praying is
keeping in touch with one's prayer: it is necessary to 'evaluate'
current prayer participation in terms of needs and relevant
factors. It is a work of discovery and discernment; it is one
aspect of the reflection that is necessary for growth and
development. If it is to be done properly and effectively, a
person needs to know how to go about it: what questions
to ask, what to look for. Hence, to offer the person something in the nature of a method would be very useful. Initiating people into the practice is an integral part of formation in liturgical praying, and for that reason, evaluation
is included here as one of the elements of formation in
liturgical praying.

Summary of Section One: Participation

We have arrived at this framework for a course in liturgy
through starting with a specific concern and point of view:
the concern of the liturgist, as distinct from that of the
theologian: that is, the people's prayer participation.

Through reflection on past experiences of praying liturgy,
there emerged four different areas; constituted of factors
which significantly affect people's praying, through being a
help or a hindrance to them in their participation. Three
of these areas affect a person from 'outside' him or her (A
— the Place; B — Text and Rite; C — the Ministers) and are
already receiving attention from liturgists through committees,
centres, courses and the like. The fourth area (D — the
Congregation) is made up of *personal needs*; it is the area
receiving least attention, and is the one to which we will
first direct our interest.

An analysis of personal prayer needs revealed several classes or types of needs, which, however, are no different from what people need in the other situations and activities in their lives. Liturgy has thus got this in common with life: it is the same person in both. *Who* I am, and *how* I am are the most significant factors affecting anyone's prayer participation.

The different types of needs indicate the method, context and content of any undertaking aimed at meeting these needs; and the elements which would be included in a formation: a Formation in Living and Liturgy. These have been considered and developed in this chapter. Every effort to improve liturgical praying belongs to one, or several, of the elements; and this will be the case in other sections of this book.

To allow you to enter now into your formation process, we have chosen one element which will give you a useful sample of a reflection. The following gives you the opportunity of learning about, and experiencing, an Evaluation of your praying liturgy.

Evaluating my participation

(This Evaluation will be of recent celebration(s) of the Eucharist. The Evaluation may profitably be repeated in this form, until we come to the fuller treatment of Chapter 22)

Ask yourself:

How, in general, did I pray?

Did I have any striking difficulties in praying?

How was my conscious awareness of the others who were present with me?

How was my attention
- to the ministers (the priest, the readers, etc)?
- to the text (the prayers, readings, Eucharistic Prayers)?

How responsive was I?

What took my attention from the ministers or the text?

Was I willing to allow my thoughts and attitudes to be led?

How was my sincerity and sense of involvement?

What would I single out as *my* most significant NEED?

How would I care for that need in the next celebration of the Eucharist?

In order that the sacred liturgy
may produce
its full effect,
it is necessary
that the faithful
come to it with proper dispositions

Mother Church earnestly desires
that all the faithful be led
to that full, conscious, and active
participation
in liturgical celebrations
which is demanded by the very nature of
the liturgy. . .
This full and active participation by
all the people
is the aim to be considered before all
else.

Because it is
an action of Christ the priest
and of His Body the Church,
every liturgical celebration
is a sacred action
surpassing others.
No other action of the Church
can match its claim to efficacy,
nor equal the degree of it.

Constitution on the Liturgy. nn. 7, 11, 14

Section Two

PRAYING LITURGY

5

PRAYING LITURGY I:
BEGINNING TO PRAY

In view of all that has been said in Section One about liturgy — liturgy as praying: the factors which influence it, outside the person and inside; the help that can be given in the nature of a formation which caters for better understanding, greater skill, times of prayer and evaluation of prayer — the question could well be asked, Why make so much of it? Why make it look so complex? The answer is, because of the nature of liturgical prayer, above all, because, as prayer, liturgy is 'the most.' In this Section Two we are going to look at what it is that gives liturgical prayer such a unique status; and in doing this it will become clear what constitutes a prayer as liturgical prayer: when is a prayer liturgy and when is it not? That is to say, our concern in this section is with 'the nature of liturgy.'

Liturgy: a prayer surpassing all others

The claim to pre-eminence is to be understood in light of the consideration of liturgy as people praying: the unique character of liturgy as the unique prayer of the people. The

Constitution on the Liturgy, pointing out the connection between the effect of liturgy on the participants and their dispositions in the celebration, says: "In order that the liturgy may be able to produce its full effect, it is necessary that the faithful come to it with proper dispositions." (paragraph 11) These dispositions are a component of liturgy's unique character: in praying liturgy the people have specific dispositions which are proper to liturgy. Paragraph 14 contains the oft-quoted phrase describing liturgy as a prayer which is *full, conscious and active participation,* internal, of course, as well as external. Is there a variety of dispositions which people may have in prayer; are there degrees of fulness, consciousness, and activity in prayer participation? There are.

In people's prayer-lives there is a wide variation in the degree of intensity and depth in their prayer at different times, on different occasions, and in different situations. To give some instances: a brief visit paid to the Blessed Sacrament is different from a time of formal meditation when we settle down for a substantial length of time. Or, compare the general, implicit advertance to God's presence during work with a very striking insight about him. There is prayer which keeps us going from day to day, as distinct from the prayer that gives us new direction, or the prayer that is a conversion experience. Compare normal daily prayer with prayer on a special occasion such as a retreat or a feast. There are, in effect, different degrees of attention and concentration, of settling down and thoroughness, or listening and response; different depths and different effects. Without in any way intending to take away from their importance as part of anyone's prayer life, some of these can be called 'lesser' times of prayer, and in comparison with them there are times that are 'more', and a prayer that is 'most'. *The 'lesser' times need, depend on, and are supported by the 'most' serious time. Without it they will die.*

It is the same in life situations. Take, for example, a relationship between two friends, or husband and wife. Brief greetings, casual statements, exchange of jokes and superficial conversations will not be sufficient to keep the relationship alive. They serve a purpose, but there must be some time of really deep sharing of ideas, of values, of feelings and hopes, etc. Without this 'most' time, the 'lesser' avail little by themselves in what concerns a relationship. Similarly, coffee breaks, flopping into a comfortable chair, or occasional cat-naps will not provide sufficient rest; there is also need of a sufficiently long period of continuous sleep. The need for nourishment will not be met by a diet of 'grab and gulp' or 'a bun on the run.' Rest and food and relationships between people, and many other aspects of life, have need of a 'most' time; and prayer is one of them. The time of prayer which is 'most' prayer is undoubtedly liturgy. Described as an 'action of Christ and his body,' it is presented in paragraph 7 of the Constitution as 'a sacred action *surpassing all others. . . no other action in the Church can equal its efficacy by the same title and to the same degree.' The action of praying liturgy surpasses all other prayers; prayer which is prayer participation in liturgy is, can be, and is intended to be, the most growth-giving prayer in the Christian's life.*

An image

Liturgical praying and the growth it promotes is well illustrated by the image of the tide coming in on a beach. The water line moves inward from where it was when it was low tide, to the high tide point. It does so, not in a steady progression, but in a series of waves and wavelets. Little wavelets, lapping in with a gentle whispering sound, do not advance the water line at all, no matter how many of them there are. Then comes a bigger wave, accompanying its arrival with a notifying *whoosh*, and it moves in further than any of the previous ones. When it recedes, its point of arrival can be clearly seen: it leaves its mark in a thin necklace of sand and shell. Many smaller waves succeed it, none of them advancing beyond its line — until the next big wave which moves the water line yet further up the beach.

Such is the effect of one's liturgical prayer: there are many smaller waves, lesser times of prayer; and there is the bigger wave, the 'prayer surpassing all others' which leaves its mark on one's person. This is one of the strongest convictions in the liturgical movement, and the great endeavour has been to make it a reality in the lives of the parish congregation: to have them experience their Sunday Mass as 'the fount of power' for them. This may be considered to be a vision of what the Eucharist can be in people's lives; but it is no idle dream. In giving us the Eucharist to celebrate, Jesus Christ intended it to be precisely this unique experience in his People's lives. It may also be considered to be an ideal; and if so, it is just one of the many ideals of our faith. As there is an ideal love in 'love one another as I have loved you'; an ideal faith in 'If you have faith as a grain of mustard seed you could say to this tree, "Be rooted up, and be planted in the sea, and it would obey you.' (Luke 17:5); so there is an ideal prayer, that is, the liturgy, and above all the Eucharist.

'An impossible dream?'

When people are presented with this ideal and hear what is required of them in order that their Sunday Mass will become their 'prayer surpassing', their response very often is, 'But that's very hard!' What they are really thinking is that it is impossible; and it is a good observation, no different from the disciples', 'In that case who can. . .?' to Jesus after the encounter with the rich young man. Jesus' answer to them is applicable to this ideal of liturgy: 'With men it is impossible, but not with God; for all things are possible with God.' (Mark 10:27) Liturgy is the opportunity to aim at the ideal and to attempt the impossible which Christianity is. It being the will of Christ that we assemble for the celebration of the Eucharist, our faith and trust is that the Holy Spirit will place in us the prayer that is participation, moving us closer to the attainment of the ideal — one more of the bigger waves leaving its mark on us. The impossible ideal concerns me/us: growing and maturing in faith; at the time of the celebration attentive, concentrating, responsive; with faith activated consciously in Father, Jesus Christ and Holy Spirit.

Another response we have often heard is: 'That is all very nice. But you should be at our parish Mass. No one could pray there the way you describe.' This is not an uncommon problem. The first step in dealing with it is to acknowledge that there *is* a tension there; without making a judgment as to what should be, or should not be, to look at *what the situation is*. We ask, then, that for the time being, the tension/problem is allowed to be present, to be faced later. To insist on solving it at this point would close a person to what is to be presented in these pages. It is a real difficulty, and as with every genuine difficulty in regard to praying liturgy, it must be faced and not swept under the carpet. We will most certainly address it, and, when the necessary basis has been laid, offer help.

Beginning to pray

The time we are most likely to become aware that this celebration of liturgy is not going to be a 'prayer surpassing', that there is something lacking, and that there are needs in us calling out for attention, is at the very beginning of our praying liturgy. In those final minutes — or, sometimes, final seconds — before the celebration begins, we discover that we cannot engage in, are not ready for, 'full, conscious and active' participation.

To help in this difficulty in the situation of liturgy, we are now going to transfer our attention to *life;* not just the time of praying liturgy, but day to day, moment to moment, life. Why? This little episode in our, your authors', lives will tell you why. It is a moment that has become very important for us.

A story

For several years Anneliese and Greg had been working together in Liturgical Education, quite caught up with enthusiasm for their work and its potential, always reviewing and looking for ways of improving it. It was very demanding and taxing. One day, during the time when Anneliese was Directress of Novices, and Superior of the congregation's Australian mother-house, as well as being involved in liturgical work in Melbourne and interstate, during a conversation about their work, Anneliese burst out, in exasperation: 'Greg, there is more to life than liturgy!'

At this point, Greg retired, but with a niggling feeling that there was something worthwhile he could say — more to her statement than to her, be it confessed — but he was not sure what it was. It came to him later, and at their next meeting, judging the atmosphere to be right for it, he brought up the matter.

"Remember, the last day I was here, you said, 'There is more to life than liturgy.' Well, I have been thinking about it, and I thought of something: *There may be more to life than liturgy, but there is nothing in life that is not in liturgy."*

This has been verified more and more for us over the years, and has become one of the fundamental principles on which our attitude to prayer participation is based, as well as the method we have adopted to give help to improve it.

Another way of stating it is: *The 'ME' in liturgy is the 'ME' in life.* You will have the opportunity of testing this for yourself. At this point, let us look at what is involved in being 'fully, consciously and actively' in *life.*

A good way of coming to this is by reflecting on our actions in daily life.

Reflection on my daily actions

1. Make a list — as full as possible — of things you did in the past twenty four hours.

2. When you have completed it, alongside each item place a number, 1, 2, or 3.

First, place a 1 at those things which you did
    MECHANICALLY, AUTOMATICALLY.

Now place a 2 at those things you did as a
    'SHOULD', a 'MUST', a 'HAVE TO'.

And place a 3 at the things you did
FREELY: as a result of your own free CHOICE.

3. Reflect on this to discover:
    (a)   what does it tell you about how
       a PERSON ACTS?
    (b)   what does it tell you about
       YOURSELF WHEN YOU PRAY?

The activity will have shown that we do many things in a
day which are not of our free choice, but mechanically
performed, or done from a 'should/must'. Note that what we
are concerned with is not the matter of *obligation*, whether
physical or moral (like being held up in traffic, or going to
work in the morning, doing home work, keeping under .05,
etc.) but, of *motivation; why*, in the final analysis, did you
do it?

Applying this to prayer, neither of these ways of acting
would rate as 'full conscious and active' participation. Still
looking at life, let us take our appreciation of what is meant
by 'full, conscious and active' participation further, by means
of the help of this activity.

Being 'wholly present'

Think back to an occasion, or a situation,
of which you can say that you were
really 'wholly present.'

What did you experience in that situation,
which enables you to say:
'I was really wholly present in it.?'

Note these indications in a list.

Reflection on the activity would have shown you that if you are wholly *in* something, wholly present, you will be able to say something like:
I knew that the *whole person* was involved because —
  — there was communication,
  — there was involvement,
  — I was affected — physically, emotionally,
  — I *felt* things,
  — I was present,
  — time seemed to just go,
  — I was different after it,
  — I will never forget it,
  — something had been done to me,
  — I said things I had never said before.

This gives an insight into the way we perform in life. Now, what has been listed above in regard to the way that person performs in life also applies to them praying, especially when there is praying that is full conscious and active. At prayer there will be involvement and communication; we will feel things, be affected; we will be different after it; above all, we will be present.

The point has been made that prayer is a gift from God. I do not move myself to prayer; I receive prayer that is given to me. The prayer I 'make' is placed in my heart by the Holy Spirit. What is more, I receive the prayer as I am at the particular time; that is, to the extent of my receptivity. In other words, to the extent of my *presence*.

The 'presence' under consideration is *my presence to God*. God's *presence to me* is something else; he is always present to us, to his creation, and it cannot be otherwise. My presence to God, however, being a human activity on my part, is subject to change. The 'prayer surpassing' which is participation that is full, conscious and active requires that I am wholly present. It is not an added extra, nor an optional accessory, but of the very nature of liturgy. *It is only when we are present that we can receive the prayer that is given to us by the Holy Spirit.*

Both scripture and the prayers of liturgy repeatedly refer to this presence and action of the Holy Spirit in us, making use of *heart* to include the whole person:

> "Come back to me with all your HEART."
> (Joel 2:12)
> ". . . for our inner selves to grow strong, so that Christ may live in our HEARTS through faith."
> (Eph 3:17)
> "Send your Holy Spirit to live in our HEARTS"
> (*Tuesday, 7th week of Easter*)
> "Hear our prayers, so that we may leave our former selves behind and serve you with holy and renewed HEARTS." (*Saturday, 7th week of Easter*).

The two activities given above show that, more often than not, we are not wholly present in life; and, we can conclude, not wholly present when we want to pray. Therefore, we are not in a position to receive prayer. "Prayer happens when the heart is open", and we often are not open. Probably what is basically lacking is that we are not present to ourselves. I cannot be present to God, without being first present to myself. There can be no full, conscious and active participation without my first becoming *present to myself*; how I am; how I am experiencing myself.

The question, then, is, What can I do to come with an open heart? What can I do to prepare myself to receive this gift? While acknowledging that we cannot give a prayer to ourselves, nor produce a prayer, we can prepare ourselves to be receptive. The way we will approach the answer to the question is to look at what goes on in a person who has decided to pray. First, the theory; and then the experience.

From 'outside' to 'inside'

What happens in a person when she or he sits down for a chosen length of time, in order to receive the gift of a prayer?

Praying, as we saw earlier, is one activity in our living. Keeping in mind the parallel between living and praying: the person who comes to pray is the person who lived and was active in a variety of activities in the hours previous to the time of prayer. At that moment of settling down to pray, each of these activities is still present in the person. At the time of engaging in them they affected the person, and on three levels — *body, feelings and mind.* How they affected the person can be discovered by tapping into these three levels. We will see that it is necessary to do so by getting in touch with our body, our feelings, and our mind, before we can receive prayer. These levels embody our experiences; they absorb them, and retain them. For example, the hours of teaching affect my legs, and perhaps my throat and head. Although we *say* 'I' am tired, really it is just the body that is tired. In our feelings, too, we have been affected: I can still feel pleasure because the students responded well; or discouraged and upset, because the students resented me, or mistrusted me. We *say*, I've had it; that class makes me mad. More correctly we should say, Part of me is really mad. Or I may experience a mixture of feelings: I hate them, and yet I love them. My mind, too, is probably racing. All the things I have to do, demands that are being made of me, are still preoccupying my mind.

We see from this that we are pretty busy within ourselves: very active, unquiet, often in turmoil; and certainly not in touch with *self*, that deeper-down part of us, our centre. That is where 'I' am. This is the 'heart' to which Christ calls us; the heart in which the Spirit dwells, and where he places his prayer for me. This is where I receive it — provided, of course that 'I' am there. 'I' am *not* there as long as I am held on to and restrained by those parts of me, or one of them. For example, a body sensation may hold my attention, a feeling may dominate me, or my mind may be preoccupying me. The experience of being under control of part of me is often expressed by the phrase, I was not myself then. Indeed, that is true. It was not my 'self' acting; part of me was.

The first movement in beginning to pray — that is, becoming capable of receiving the prayer — is to *my centre:* to come from 'Outside' to 'Inside'. The movement can begin only when I acknowledge *where* I am now; that is, by getting in touch with *how* I am now; focussing on what is going on in me. To do so, I consult separately and in turn my body, my feelings and my mind. Usually, as soon as I become aware of what is going on on these levels, I will become free of their hold on me. All I have to do is look, and know what is there.

We seem to be conditioned to place feelings into the categories of 'good' and 'bad', that is, 'acceptable' and 'unacceptable'. Going with this is the opinion that while 'bad' feelings are certainly a hindrance to prayer, the person with 'good' feelings is already centered. This latter is a mistake, and a trap. *All* feelings 'hook' us: keep us 'out there' from being centered. No matter what the feeling, we need to be freed from it, so that we do not act out of it, out of this *part* of us.

> "The journey into prayer
> is a journey directed towards
> a fundamental return to the heart,
> finding one's deepest centre,
> awakening the profound depths of our being
> in the presence of God,
> who is the source of our being and our life."

> (Thomas Merton, quoted by James Finley,
> *Merton's Palace of Nowhere*)

It may well happen that something — a body sensation, a feeling, an idea, an image — will not let go, but holds on tenaciously, 'hooking' me. In this case, I choose to dwell with it. What I have is a 'distraction'. We used to be advised to 'get rid of' distractions. 'Put them away, or aside,' was another way of stating it. What we advise is different: deliberately dwell with it, gently hold it; let it speak to me; speak to it, and ask it to speak to me, and to tell me more about itself, until it retires, or 'lies down" It is very like what happens when a child tugs at its mother's skirt to get her attention. If the mother rejects the child, speaks harshly or impatiently, the child will withdraw, but only for the time being. The little one will return, and now tug again, but with more insistence, this time. If, however, the mother is gentle and understanding, and listens to the reason why the child wants her attention, the child will retire in peace, quiet and satisfied. Being 'hooked' is like an experience that can happen when cutting roses, and getting caught by the thorns. Tugging energetically is no way to get free; that only causes damage. The only way is to identify where the thorns are holding, and then gently unhook each thorn, leaving one free to move.

The 'hooks' stay there, but they no longer overpower us.

The 'hook', whether it comes from body, feelings or mind, does not want to overpower us or control our activity; it just wants to be heard. It is not tugging and holding on for nothing; it just wants to be given an opportunity to say something, and to get our attention for the necessary length of time. If we realize that, and welcome what there is in us by listening to what it will say to us — hear its need — then we will be free. Then we will be in the centre; then we are our 'selves'.

I will know when I am at my centre by the quiet, the calm,. the gentle acceptance of myself here and now: when there is a silence in me, so that I can hear and listen.

This is not yet prayer, by any means. In fact, something else may happen before I am ready for prayer. This is the time, and the opportunity, when 'the more' within me that wants to make itself known, can speak. From inside me memories, fantasies, day dreams, images, dreams and symbols are awoken. They are very important: they are data of previous experiences, which I had not heard because I was not quiet enough for long enough to hear them. So I gratefully receive them, and reverently deal with them in the same manner in which I deal with the 'hooks' which I experienced.

Sometimes, from my deeper self, a 'life-form' persists in staying with me. It could well be that the Lord is offering me his prayer through it now. And so, I look at it, dwell with it, listen to it, to receive the prayer that may be offered to me through it. If, however, I am getting ready for participation in liturgy, (in which case, as will be seen in Chapter 7, the prayer will be offered through the text and rite) a different approach is called for. In this situation, I respectfully ask this strong feeling or thought or whatever it is, to allow me to be free now, promising to return to it later — a promise, experience tells, I must keep at my peril! Then, gently placing it on one side, I find myself free to receive the prayer of the liturgy.

What we have described is the process of centering. Summing it up: *I begin with myself and how I am: how I am experiencing myself. I focus on what I am experiencing, and then gently let it go, to the point of readiness to be given and to receive the prayer the Holy Spirit wants to awaken in my heart. To receive the given prayer in my centre is Christ's call to me, his gift for me.*

> "Blessed be the Lord, the God of Israel;
> he has come to his people and set them free. . .
> free to worship him. . ."
> (The Song of Zechariah)

If you now find yourself asking 'Are they still talking about liturgy; or have they been talking about other prayer times, like meditation time? then you are in good company. Many have raised this query — very often, as a protest! Yes, we are talking about liturgy: about prayer participation that is 'full, conscious and active'; about praying liturgy as the 'prayer surpassing all others'. It was not ever imagined that such a prayer could come in a moment: an 'instant prayer.' Liturgy always provides an Introductory Rite, even in the Liturgy of the Hours, taking it for granted that people are not in a prepared state to begin to participate. What the rite provides to get us ready may be sufficient; on the other hand, it may not. It will be sufficient if it is successful in leading through the process of centering, such as we have been describing; and we have had experiences of the short Introductory Rites being enough on their own. These were occasions when the group was engaged in reflective activities prior to the liturgy. However, to place side by side the two pictures of ourselves in our daily lives, and ourselves praying a prayer from the heart, a prayer that surpasses all other prayers, the 'most' prayer of all, with participation that is 'full, conscious and active', will give enough evidence of the 'bridge' that is necessary, and the time to make it. *An allocation of sufficient TIME for preparation is an indispensable pre-requisite for participation — if it is to be what Christ intends in our lives, and produce its full effect.*

The Reverend Brian Phillips of Adelaide has spoken these words on prayer in the ABC programme, By the Way:

"Anthony Bloom (an Orthodox Archbishop) suggests that we begin looking, not for the prayer that fires outward towards God, but the prayer that penetrates inward through the outer shell to the still point at the centre of our being. The God who is near neither speaks nor hears until we recognize that prayer is from the centre of our being. . . Unless the words we say are those capable of penetrating to the centre then they are not prayers. They do not come from our whole being. Our words are not prayer until they arise from the centre of our being. . .

Prayer is the response which comes from the still centre of our being. It is there that the Holy Spirit shapes us, and it is there that the Holy Spirit prays our prayer for us before God the Father."

For most people, unfortunately, their Sunday Mass has not got a high rating as a time of heart-stirring prayer. If it was the experience of prayer alone that brought people to Mass, there would be even fewer present on Sundays. There has been much condemnation of our present Rite of Mass, of our churches and priests; a lot of lamentations that 'it does not work', 'it has no appeal'; and an amount of experimentation – which did not 'work' either. If the truth be told, the Rite never had a chance. How could it have succeeded in giving the people an experience of a prayer from the heart? It never did, never could, with an unprepared congregation. As a little boat tied to a jetty may be carried a little distance from it by the tide and wind, only to be jerked back again by the rope, so can we be tied down from praying. Once the rope is untied, and only when it is, the boat will move freely and without resistance wherever the wind and current take it. And so will we be moved by the Spirit in prayer when we are freed – and only when we are freed.

The thoroughness or depth of a centering will depend on the past experience of a person in centering, and on the time devoted to it each time. Normally, a greater depth would be expected of, and attempted with, a prayer group than at a Sunday parish Eucharist.

In the course of our work we have had experience of a centering done by the priest, as part of the Introductory Rite (see Chapter 14); by a leader before the celebration began; and sometimes left to the congregation themselves, that is, of course, when they were skilled in it. There is no short-circuiting it; there is no quick or 'instant' way to it. If it needs time to become centered, then it is going to take time. It is like sitting in a car by the footpath, waiting to pull out into the flow of traffic. Until there is a break in the flow, allowing you to move with safety, there is nothing to do but wait; no matter in how much of a hurry you are, or how impatient you feel. Our prayer is not going to come any sooner because 'there are things I have to do', or because I do not like centering. Indeed, we have a built-in warning signal in us: *as long as I feel anxious or impatient to begin praying, it is sure that I am not yet ready, for I am not yet centered.*

A price has to be paid for the experience of prayer participation, and it is *preparation*. The only way anyone could be convinced of this is by experiencing what a centering preparation can do, and what a differerence it makes.

Thomas Merton has said: "If we really want prayer, we'll have to give it time. . . We have what we seek, we don't have to rush after it. It is there all the time, and if we give it time, it will make itself known to us."
(David Stendl-Rast, 'Man of Prayer' in *Thomas Merton, Monk: A Monastic Tribute,* Patrick Hart, O.C.S.O., (Ed.))

You might like to test this for yourself, in one of these centering activities:

A.

Find a comfortable position
Become aware of the room
the chair you are sitting in
any pressure points
the carpet under you
your feet in your shoes
the height of your body
the shoulders — both
Notice the structure of your body —
vertical. . . from your toes to the tip of head
horizontal. . . trace a mental line from your right
  shoulder across your back to your left shoulder.

Now, become conscious of your breathing. . .
really focus on every breath you take. . .
notice how your body moves

Focus on your face. . . how tense or relaxed it is
focus on the most unrelaxed part of your face. . .
mentally give a gentle massage to that part. . .
gently care for that part. . .
let that go. . .

Now focus on what is going on in your feelings. . .
don't give your feelings a name — but a colour. . .
What sort of texture has it. . .
if you wanted to describe your feelings,
  how would you do it: what would you say?
Perhaps there is more than one feeling. . .
just focus on them, and let go. . .

Now focus on your mind. . . and thoughts. . .
note the most present one
stay a little longer with that one. . .
is there anything you can do to make that
  thought less powerful over you?
let go. . .

B.

A Centering — with a candle

Become conscious of where we are. . .
the room we're in. . .
the chair you're sitting on. . .
feel the pressure as your back leans against it. . .
feel the carpet under your feet. . .
your feet in your shoes. . .

Now become conscious of your breathing. . .
follow each breath. . .
Now, take a deep breath. . .

How does your face feel. . . relaxed, tense?

Take note of any particular feeling you are
  conscious of. . .
allow yourself to feel it all. . .

Now, focus on your mind. . .
any particular thoughts that may be occupying
  you. . .
welcome any thoughts that may want to come. . .

Think of a particular person in this room. . .
and another one. . .

breathe *with them*. . .
Now, light the candle.
Take notice of yourself and what you are
  experiencing. . .

Let's focus on the candle. . .
It's flickering. . .
something is making it flicker. . .

Something in *me* is flickering. . . is alive. . .
is feeling
Because someone is making it live!
My Father — Our Father. . .

6

PRAYING LITURGY II:
PRAYING A COMMUNAL PRAYER

> *Let us draw near with a true*
> *heart in full assurance of*
> *faith. . .*
> *let us hold fast to the*
> *confession of our hope without*
> *wavering. . .*
> *and let us consider how to stir*
> *up one another to love and*
> *good works, not neglecting to*
> *meet together. . .*
> *but encouraging one another.*
>   *(Heb. 10:22-25, passim)*

Liturgy is: PEOPLE PRAYING — A SPECIAL PRAYER —
IN A SPECIAL WAY (Chapter 1). The 'special way' arises
from the fact that liturgy is always Communal Prayer. In this
chapter we will look at what is involved in making a prayer a
Communal Prayer.

A group of people gathered together in the same place, at the same time, praying the words of the same prayer would seem to be doing all that is necessary for communal prayer. However, that group could be just a gathering of people *simultaneously praying their own private prayers.* Communal prayer requires more than that: the 'extra' quality necessary is in their ATTITUDE and BEHAVIOUR. To be present with others praying, really *with* them and present *to* them requires something special inside the person: a special attitude; this attitude affects the person's behaviour in the prayer. It is necessary to know what this attitude and behaviour is. We will take it in stages: first, we will be looking at the meaning, value and characteristics of communal prayer by presenting the theological basis for it. Secondly, we will consider the necessary attitude and behaviour. This will lead to some observations on the difference between liturgical prayer and devotional prayer.

Theological Basis

There are two important considerations which throw light on the meaning and value of communal prayer. The first is:

EVERY GOOD THING WE DO, WE DO IN CHRIST

Take as an example someone we love and care for. We love that person only because we have a share in the love which Christ has for her or him. Or take our attitude of reverence and obedience towards God. This, too, is nothing but a sharing in the worship of Christ of his Father. We cannot do anything — good, that is — independent of Christ; there is no good in us apart from him, no real life in us except his. As St Paul saw it: "You must consider yourselves. . . alive to God IN Christ Jesus." (Rom. 6:11)

When we pray, the only means of access to God for us is IN Christ. Imagine for a moment the prayer that Jesus Christ is praying, arising from his attitude to the Father and passing between him and the Father. If we want to pray, we must get into that 'current' of prayer; there is no access to God in prayer independent of it. To use what may seem to be a crude comparison: what arrives at the Father is not a whole lot of separate individual *prayers*, but ONE prayer comprised of the prayer of Jesus Christ and that of all praying people caught up in it. St Augustine wrote, "Each one of us cries as part of the whole Body. Thus, there is one Man continuing on to the end of time, and those who cry out are always his members."

The consequence is that all prayers — my prayer, your prayer, and everyone else's prayer — all get taken up into the ONE prayer of Jesus Christ. This point was made a lot during the early days of ecumenism in Australia. When a group from different Christian churches would come together to pray for the first time, so often it was remarked that although this was the first time they had actually gathered to pray together, in reality they had always been praying together, because their prayers were joined in the one prayer of Jesus Christ. A great ecumenical figure, the Abbe Couturier, put it in these words: "Since all the baptised have the life of Christ in them, they must be described — both corporately and individually — in the light of the wonderful relationship which St Paul describes in 1 Corinthians 12. Into my poor prayer, then, runs like lifeblood the prayer of others."

"And so we join the angels
and the whole company of heaven
who, through Christ, offer their prayer of adoration,"
as we enter into the great Eucharistic Prayer.

The second consideration, which is a basic principle in liturgy, is:

A HUMAN REALITY IS NOT AS REAL AS IT CAN BE UNTIL IT IS EXTERNALIZED

This is the way we are; God has made us like this. If there is a thought in a person's mind, that thought — a human reality — becomes more real when the thought is expressed in some way, like writing it or speaking it. If we love someone, that love is a human reality within us; and when we do loving things for the person we love, our love for them becomes more real. The externalizing of our love has the effect of making our love more real. This is one reason God has given us our bodies: to use them to externalize the reality of our relationship with God in Christ.

When anyone prays, the reality is that he or she is praying *with* other people *in* Christ. This will become more real if it is externalized, and the way to externalize it is to come together, and to be with other people while praying. It is this externalization which gives communal prayer its special value and meaning. It is more than just the psychological value of mutual support arising from doing the same thing with others. Communal prayer has a theological, a 'sacramental' value, which means that as a form of prayer, because of what externalization adds, communal prayer is a superior form. This is not taking away from the necessity and importance of private prayer.

"The inward performance is only complete, or at any rate only deeply and genuinely complete, when it is objectivized outward." (Fr John Cowburn, S.J., quoting K. Rahner, in *Love and the Person*)

All liturgical forms of prayer are communal prayer – although, obviously not all communal prayer is liturgy – and although it may not always be possible, are intended to be prayed with others. When prayed privately, as happens often in the case of the Liturgy of the Hours, this is not the full form of the prayer, because of the absence of externalization.

What we need to know is what we have to do, besides being with the group and reciting the same prayer, in order that prayer will also be a communal prayer.

Attitude and Behaviour

In communal prayer we are WITH others, praying WITH them. Since all that concerns ourselves and others comes within the scope of Christ's commandment to love one another, communal prayer can be understood as an activity in which *in our praying along with others, we fulfill Christ's command to love one another, by acting in a loving way towards them.* If we look at communal prayer as one way of fulfilling Christ's command of love, we will discover what we need to know if we want to pray communally. We will begin, therefore, by looking at the reality of love, *agape*, in life generally, in order to discover and see how it applies to liturgy. Let us look at some basic features of this love: at what is asked of us in order to be loving; then, at what would be unacceptable behaviour in a Christian, to reinforce our discoveries.

(a) In the light of Christ's command, we see that the most important thing on earth for a Christian is *PEOPLE*. Of the many beings which elicit our concern in the world, PEOPLE occupy first place. Everything else which God has made is *for* PEOPLE. We are concerned about them and committed to help them to the best of our ability at any time. Hence what is important about these people is their *NEEDS*.

(b) We are to love people, not just by having a loving feeling towards them, but by doing practical loving deeds. We cannot know what to do for them unless we know their NEEDS. In other words, the concrete form our love will take is indicated by their NEEDS, the very many different needs that people have. Loving a person does not begin with us, but with them and their needs. We are placing this emphasis on NEEDS in connection with loving — the significance of *their* needs in our loving them — because of the possibility of making others, albeit unknowingly, 'victims of kindness.' This occurs when someone acts in response, not to the needs of another but to his or her own likes or whims (or needs!). "I would like to do this for you; " "You cannot go without. . ."; "Come on, have another drink." These are frequently heard forms of what may be mistaken for loving. It is not, because it starts with the person themselves, whereas love starts with the other: her or his needy state, and PARTICULAR NEED. Loving is helping, as best we can, in that NEED.

(c) At different times, in different situations, people have different needs. At one time their need may be for companionship or support; at another time, advice or money; yet another time, to be listened to, or to be left alone. Loving is responding to what a person *NEEDS HERE AND NOW* so that part of loving is 'hearing' what a person needs at *that* moment.

(d) Attitude and behaviour enter into loving: an attitude of loving concern and willingness to help; and behaving as a listener to discover needs and then doing or giving what one can. The thrust in loving is *GIVING: BEING FOR* others. Christ has been described as 'the man for others', and the Christian as 'being FOR the brother.'

A brief look at what is unacceptable in a Christian because of the commandment of love, will complete the picture. Continuing the same line of thought, that is, the importance of people, the worst of all would be to IGNORE PEOPLE as people: to live and act as if there were no other people on earth besides myself; making myself the centre of the universe, the only one who mattered. This tendency is in all of us, though thankfully not in this extreme form: we are, because of our sinfulness, to some degree selfish and self-centered. While it would be impossible to ignore the fact of people in the world with me, it is possible to ignore them as PEOPLE, and treat them as 'things', of no different significance than my phone or T.V. set, my car or my dog; they are there just for my benefit, to use, turn on or not as I please; it is possible to respond to people in other ways than as persons.

It is also possible to fail to respond to people in their need: TO IGNORE THEIR NEEDS, to refuse to act lovingly towards them. Yet another instance of failing to love is the insensitivity which fails to hear and respond to their NEEDS HERE-AND-NOW.

The attitude and behaviour associated with lack of love is to GET: others are there FOR ME.

The thrust in the behaviour:

Loving Behaviour	Unacceptable Behaviour
I ———→ OTHERS	ME ←—— OTHERS
for	for
GIVE	GET

Now let us look at how what is involved in loving others, that is obeying Christ's command, applies in the context of praying a communal prayer with people.

(a) In communal prayer it would be unacceptable behaviour to ignore the people who are present.

That is, to be there as though others were not present; to

fail to respond to their presence. There are, of course, times when this is precisely the type of behaviour which is called for, for example, at times of meditation people do not pay any attention to anyone else near them; when reflecting, we pass others by without adverting to who they are. This is the first point of difference between private prayer and communal prayer: in communal prayer there must be a response to the others present; that is a consciousness that they are 'with' one another in prayer. The people may not know one another; they may never have been together before, yet they are called to respond to one another.

From this we see that the first attitude in communal prayer is *an attitude towards the group of people who are praying.* To this praying group of people, I come; to be praying with them, in the way Christ said I should be with a group – responding to them all in love. Hence –

(b)   **In communal prayer each responds to the NEEDS of the others present.**

To come to others lovingly is to come in an attitude of 'being for' them, committed to help them in their needs; an attitude of willingness to do the best one can for them in the circumstances. In biblical terms, it is to come as 'servant', like Jesus, 'not to be served but to serve.'

Communal prayer is, therefore, as well as being prayer, an act of service to the members of the group. They may be complete strangers to one another, yet they have concern for one another. The bond is special, and one that is possible through Christian faith only. The fellowship has as its basis the experience of sharing a common faith and trust and love. It is not their past acquaintance with one another, but what they *now believe* about one another because of their Christian faith; how they place *trust* in one another, and how they feel *loving concern* for one another in virtue of their faith in Christ. Faith gives meaning to coming together to pray: a meaning and value that no other motivation or consideration can give. There are a variety of reasons for which a group will gather; a variety of motivations, too. A special motivation is necessary if he or she is to pray communally.

It is to be hoped that what has been stated in (a) and (b)

will not be taken as confirming an opinion sometimes expressed that we can pray communally only with, or better
with, people whom we have known or with whom we have
common interests or shared experiences. This is not so; it is a
dangerous fallacy. It is certainly not necessary that we be
acquainted with people before we can pray a communal
prayer with them; it is not necessarily advantageous, and
could even be a disadvantage. The reason for this is that the
source of the bond, the particular oneness and special communication of communal prayer has its base in *Christian faith
and trust*. The experience of oneness with others, the interest
in being with them, the concern for them and commitment
to help them, now — that human experience which feels no
different from any other feeling or interest, concern and
commitment — has not got its basis in their previous acquaintance with one another, nor in what they have learned and
know about one another, least of all because they like one
another and enjoy one another's company. It is not the
experience of a support group in community prayer, but of a
faith community; hence *the basis is in what we believe about
the risen Christ and these people and ourselves, and the trust
and love that it brings to life in us.*

We mention the past closeness of the group as a possible
disadvantage, because this is what it so often is. Take the
situation of our joining a group of friends for prayer, a group
with whom we feel very comfortable, and who provide us
with an experience of being accepted and of being free to be
ourselves; a group whose interest we have at heart, including
their growth in prayer. So, it's all there, we think: the people
present are important to us, and we are a group that cares
about the needs of each. Isn't this all we need to make our
prayer communal? It is in this that the danger lies: that we
will be satisfied with our feeling of oneness, rest in it, and not
move to *faith experience of one another*. On the other hand,
picture joining a group we do not know, and of whom our
first impressions are not at all favourable. Right away we are
aware that something is lacking, and we easily come to see
that only by looking on them through our faith could we
ever pray with them. The very lack of feeling at one with
them is the stepping off point that causes our faith, trust and

love to be activated: being with them then becomes an experience-in-faith. It is not that the first group, the group we know, could not have done the very same for us, and given us a faith experience. The point we are making is that we can pray communally both with the support group and the stranger group, but whether we can or not depends ultimately on our *faith*. For the same reason activities sometimes used for the purpose of facilitating communal prayer, such as getting to know one another, saying something to the person beside you, may well turn out to be counterproductive. These activities will fail if they stop short of awakening the people's faith consciousness.

(c) **In communal prayer, the here-and-now needs to be responded to are the people's prayer needs.**

The deepest needs of the people present may not be known, nor need they be known. Loving concern will respond to their *here and now needs*, and these *are* known; for if the people have come to this group they have come to pray, and their needs are: to be quiet inside and attentive, to have their faith activated, to listen and to be responsive — and all the kinds of personal needs that are in Area 'D'. These are the needs to be responded to now: all that the others need in order to pray as well as they can now.

The loving attitude is summed-up in a commitment to help these people in their prayer needs, and so, we come to communal prayer with a double responsibility: to pray well myself and to help others to pray well. No one will deny that we have a responsibility towards others in our daily living, and we do not leave that responsibility outside the church or prayer room. Indeed, if ever we have a responsibility towards others, surely it is when they are trying to pray and we are with them.

(d) **In communal prayer we help one another by our behaviour.**

From the attitude that is required to make prayer communal, there follows a special behaviour: the behaviour that gives an answer to the question, How do you pray a communal prayer?

Briefly, the behaviour is such that it helps the others in their prayer.

1. Remembering the kinds of needs they have — to be attentive, to concentrate, to be serious about their praying, to be aware of the presence of Christ in the group — the least I can do is not to make it more difficult for them by placing hindrances, by anything that would cause disturbance or interruption. This is only negative, but worthy of consideration; it is sufficiently important to give thought to it from time to time to discover if there is anything in our behaviour in church or chapel that adds to the difficulties of the others. It would be of great advantage to the members of religious communities to meet to speak about one another's behaviour at liturgy.

Praying communally includes a consideration of, and sensitivity to, the others present that keeps us from adding to their needs.

2. Is there anything more that can be done: any other way — a positive way — to help? There is. The possibility is there because through our shared life, and activity, of the Holy Spirit, our attitudes and enthusiasms are infectious: we communicate them, share them with others, mainly through 'body language'. This type of communication is very apparent in situations other than communal prayer. One such situation is a meeting, like a parish committee or a religious community. Take the instance in which one person strongly disapproves of discussing a certain matter, thinking that the meeting should never have been called as this matter should not be discussed by this group, and feeling very angry about it. Without saying one word, non-verbal communication can be so strong that he or she is 'shouting' thoughts and feelings. Waves are going out from that person, chilly, paralysing waves, which little by little have the effect of dampening the enthusiasm and deadening the interest of the others, so that the meeting accomplishes but little. The opposite can happen too, for example, when into a rather dead party comes a very alive person, whose very presence makes others feel more alive themselves, more interested and more ready to enjoy themselves.

This is the kind of influence that can be exercised in communal prayer through non-verbal communication: our presence giving an uplift to the others' prayer — our *praying presence*, that is. So, the first thing we can do in order to exercise a helping influence, is to be praying myself.

In communal prayer, our praying influences the praying of the others, and we help them in their praying by the sincerity and depth of our praying.

3. Is there anything else we can do? Yes! Communal prayer externalises: the people make sounds; and, in liturgy especially, use gestures and movements. Let us first look at these gestures and movements.

From the moment I enter the church, my movements can be a help — or the opposite. I reverence the altar, or genuflect towards the tabernacle; I enter the seat and take up some position. These few, seemingly unimportant movements all 'speak': maybe, that my mind is miles away, and I am not at all aware of the presence of Christ; or that we believe in his presence, are responding to him with reverence, and are very committed to our praying. This does not mean that we are to 'put on an act.' It means that we act responsively and responsibly. There is always an appropriate way to act. In the situation of communal prayer, we let our faith be transparent; 'We believe in the presence of Christ; we want to help you in your faith in him; as we hope that you will help us,' is what we are saying in our movements throughout the time of prayer. Because there is never a moment when we are not communicating, 'speaking' a helping word of faith and prayer, there is a liturgical way of standing-praying and sitting-listening that looks not quite the same as ordinary standing and sitting.

There is also the sound; this, too, can be helpful or not. Sometimes the singing sound is such that it is sheer agony: a penance to be endured until the blessed moment of release when the hymn ends. Other times, the singing of the congregation is such that it is a real joy the way it carries us along with them. Communal prayer should have a sound that is a 'supportive sound.' A sound that takes us up and carries us along in our praying. A sound of this quality is needed not just in singing, but also in what is said: think of what an 'Amen' sounding strong with faith, conviction and commitment could do for the congregation; or an 'Our Father'

D

that conveys the atmosphere of needy children before their generous Father. With the quality of vocalized sound that is usual in our Australian parishes, one wonders if it would not be a good idea to call a moratorium on singing for a year, and instead explore the possibilities of cultivating a 'said'-sound!

In communal prayer we respond to the presence and needs of the others by our prayer externalized in our movements, and by contributing to a supportive sound.

People praying in this special way is called communal prayer. What is in the person's mind and heart — what is 'inside' — makes a prayer a communal prayer. The fundamental difference between it and private prayer is an attitude towards the group: the group specifies the value of the prayer and the motivation. Private prayer, including devotional prayers, spiritual reading, spiritual exercises and the like, is chosen and evaluated according to how useful and helpful it is found to be. In communal prayer it is otherwise: it is the *others*. We go to help one another. Of course, we in our turn are helped by the others in our prayer; we get from them just as we contribute to them. However, that is not our motivation, to GET; as in all Christian love, we grow and gain by our loving, but we do not love in order to get. Hence, the often heard objection to Mass and Office: 'That does nothing for me; I get nothing out of it,' shows a lack of appreciation of the nature of communal prayer and what motivates a person to pray communally, and hence it is irrelevant as an objection. In communal prayer we are not in that kind of activity: to get something out of it, to be turned on by it.

The difference between communal and private prayer can be illustrated by the difference in the way we are when we are going to visit someone who is sick, and when we are going out for a pleasant evening with friends. In the latter, we have certain expectations, a pleasurable anticipation about the evening. At the end of it, it would be expected that we say, 'I enjoyed that,' or 'That evening did not turn me on.' However, when we are on a visit to the sick person, we do not know how we will find him or her, but our attitude is that we will do the best we can to respond to them and their needs as we find them. Most certainly, we would not say after such a visit that we had not enjoyed it, or that we had got nothing out of it; we are not supposed to; we do not go for that purpose — although it may turn out to do a lot for us. It is the same in communal prayer.

Why do we go to communal prayer? For the others: they would appreciate, and be helped by, our presence; we can help them by our efforts at praying. Christ has commanded us to love, and has given us the gift of loving, and we feel called to use it in this way for these people.

Sometimes we may feel that the people we pray with are beyond any help that we could give them: that nothing we could do would have the slightest effect on their prayer. That, however, must not change our intention and efforts to help them. First, we never know for certain how we are affecting other people. Further, if we do not have the attitude of wanting to be *with* them, to *help* them, out of a sense of responsibility; and if we do not behave and pray in a manner that is helpful to them, then our prayer will be a private prayer, with the consequence that it will NOT be communal prayer — nor liturgy; for liturgy is always a communal prayer.

In communal prayer, our motivation for being present is to help the others.

Liturgical Prayer and Devotional Prayer

A lot of difficulty and a lot of pain have been felt by many people in recent years through not appreciating the difference between their liturgical prayer and their devotional prayer. This is especially true of Catholics, for whom virtually all their prayer for centuries has been what is termed 'devotional', and that even at celebrations of liturgy. The situation was that, apart from those who were imbued with the spirit of the liturgy and made use of hand-missals in vernacular translation, the congregation was forced by the Latin liturgy, with its absence of active participation, into a choice of either just looking on as a spectator, or praying their own devotional prayers, such as the Rosary or prayers from a devotional prayer-book.

By 'devotional' is understood here those prayers which are characterized by a limited interest, are selective in attitude and mostly come from a particular spirituality. Examples are: prayers to the Sacred Heart of Jesus, devotions in honour of the Passion, the Precious Blood, or the Five Wounds; different devotions to the Blessed Virgin Mary under various titles, such as Our Lady of Lourdes, Our Lady of Fatima, Our Lady of Mount Carmel, the Mother of Sorrows; prayers to the saints; all in different forms such as prayers, litanies, novenas, the nine first Fridays, the thirty days prayer, etc. These prayers are not, and are not intended to be, as strictly and fully theological as liturgy. They are composed to have a greater appeal to the emotions, as can be seen from the thought-content and language they use. They afford a means of praying that is less learned and sophisticated; they are 'popular devotions.' They are intended to build up the faith, hope and love of the people, and therefore, if they are authentic, must have a theological basis. This they have in common with liturgy. They are different, however. Let us take as an example the treatment of the Passion and Death of Jesus Christ. The classical place for this in liturgy is the Good Friday liturgy, and what it presents, to lead to a prayer response, is the *meaning and value* of Christ's death. On the other hand, 'devotions' to the passion of Christ, and a devotional approach as used in popular preaching, in order to elicit a response of prayer, portray the *physical and psychological sufferings* of Jesus in a very graphic and vivid manner.

Devotional prayer, as well as the devotional approach, is not only useful but even necessary in the Church; and in different amounts for different people, or different communities with different spiritualities. In order to 'satisfy their devotion', people are free to choose what they will, and use them as suits them best. They are intended to cater for different needs. The Constitution on the Liturgy 'warmly commends' popular devotions. It is up to each person or community to select what devotions, and what form of them, they find helpful to satisfy their devotional needs.

What has been said above about the difference between private prayer and communal prayer applies to devotions.

Failure to recognise the difference between the two and the necessary place devotional prayer has in the Church along with liturgy, has had two bad results. When, in the 1960s, there arose a new interest in celebrating liturgy, the enthusiasm for liturgy as the 'summit' came across as if liturgy were now the only prayer. It was offered in the place of devotions, and they were allowed to deteriorate and die; for example, with the coming of evening Mass on Sundays it was felt that this now should take the place of Sunday devotions, and that Benediction was a thing of the past. There was even a tendency to view devotions as though they were just for the old, the simple and spiritual invalids.

The other bad effect has been on people with a very alive devotional life. They expected liturgy to do the same for them as their devotions had done in the past. There was a widespread effort to handle liturgy, and to modify it, so as to give it the same characteristics as devotions, and to make it play the same role; for example, celebrating the Eucharist in a manner that gave it the same atmosphere as a charismatic prayer meeting. This has done a lot of damage to liturgy: so mishandled, re-arranged and disfigured that it can hardly be said to be the original rite at all. It could be compared to what you see when a father and his children play with a ball on the beach — and call it cricket or football.

Meeting different needs, as they do, both forms of prayer should be available in a parish or religious community, in the manner and proportion which is found most helpful to them. Liturgy has now been given attention in the Church and parish, but devotions have remained mostly unaffected by renewal. Unfortunately, they are often treated as an offshoot of liturgy by liturgy committees and commissions, but because they are so different, the personnel of liturgy commissions are not the people most suited to care for devotional life. The devotional life of our people deserves and needs attention, first, so that their devotional life may not be starved but their devotional needs met; secondly, so that liturgy may not be abused, but allowed to be the 'summit' prayer, and the communal prayer, it is supposed to be. To mix the two diminishes the value and effectiveness of both.

Our experience of human behaviour, in ourselves and in

others, has a lot to say to us about the attitude and behaviour
we bring to communal prayer. This reflection will raise your
consciousness of your attitude and behaviour in one situation
as compared to the other.

A Reflection

People assemble
    in the railroad station and the airport
    in a sports stadium and the theatre
    in a line at the take-away food counter.

They come together, in this place, at this same
time because
in this place, at this time
    the train or plane departs
    the game, the show begins
    or they want to eat now.

A multitude of individuals (and twos and threes)
with one aim: the plane, the game, the food
finding themselves
at the station, the stadium, in the line and,
therefore,
not through choice, but of necessity
together.

It is not their desire to be *with* the others
"I hope it's not crowded"
"I hate standing in line"

    What do these people feel, or not feel, about
    one another?
Do people ever come together
just to *be together*, to be WITH one another
PRESENT to each other?

A family gathering at Christmas
a class re-union
a celebration of a birthday, an ordination,
a team's victory.

How do I feel about the others
when I am at a gathering like that?

A time of tragedy, crisis, common need:
the death of someone close to us
a flood,
our team being defeated
an urgent appeal for blood.

When did I experience one of these situations?
When we got together, how did I feel
about the others?
What was I able to do there and then?

At communal prayer
people are there WITH one another
feeling RESPONSIBLE for one another
HELPING one another.

What could the others do for me
to help me in my praying?
What could I do for the others to
help them in their praying?

Reflection on our behaviour in these situations to raise consciousness is helpful; more so, perhaps, is an opportunity which helps me to experience myself with a group, and, on observation, *lets me see how I performed* as a member in this communal activity. We offer the following to lead individuals to an experience of inter-action in a group, similar to that of praying communal prayer.

(1)   Write down TEN words which are
      important to you right now:

(2)   Out of these words, select THREE which
      mean *most* to you right now,
      Share with each other, saying *why*.

(3)   From what is now a 'group-treasury',
      compose a 'Community-poem'; a
      'Community-prayer'; a 'Community-
      anything'.

(4)   After the project is completed, there
      is an interval for some *private
      reflection* on the following points,
      before the group activity is resumed:

- Look at the ten words: where did they come from? Ask yourself: what level did they concern themselves with: outside me, or inside me?
- Continue to ask: When I shared, how much *feeling* was in me?
- Did I experience the group listening to me?
How did I know they were listening; what indications did I have?
- What was their response to me?
- What was my manner of sharing: clever ideas, or felt experiences?
- In the process, was there any experience of dying, in the form of yielding, submitting, giving of myself?
- Did I withdraw from the group: at what point?
    How did I feel?
- What value, if any, can I see in this experience?
- at the end was I happy
    that we accomplished the task?
    accomplished the task?
    — because it is very much *us*?
- Is my behaviour in this group reflected in my praying communally?

(5) In the group, share on what the experience meant to you.

(Note: *If there are several groups, a communal sharing would be appropriate at the conclusion.*)

7

PRAYING LITURGY III:
PRAYING THE PRAYER OF THE CHURCH

> *"Each of you*
> *should form a choir*
> *so that, in harmony of sound*
> *through harmony of hearts,*
> *and in unity*
> *taking the note from God,*
> *you may sing with one voice*
> *through Jesus Christ*
> *to the Father."*
>
> *(Ignatius of Antioch)*

'The Prayer of the Church' is often used nowdays in Australia as another name for Morning and Evening Prayer of the Office. It certainly includes this prayer, but it is wider: it is one and the same as 'Liturgy'. This chapter will complement the two previous ones, and continue with the understanding of the liturgy as PEOPLE PRAYING – A SPECIAL PRAYER – IN A SPECIAL WAY. The last chapter dealt with liturgy as Communal Prayer (the special way); this will deal with the 'special prayer': liturgy as the Prayer of the ᴄh.

Not every prayer is liturgy, not even communal prayer. What is it that makes one prayer liturgy, and another not? As a prayer, liturgy has some specific qualities of its own. These are in regard to:

— the attitude and behaviour of those who are praying; and
— the content of the prayer text.

What these qualities are will emerge as we look at liturgy from the point of view of Prayer of the Church.

Prayer and experience of God

There are many forms of prayer: silent and vocal, long and short; the prayer of a child, of an adult, of a mystic. There are also different attitudes expressed in prayer: mainly petition, repentance, thanksgiving, and praise. Whatever the form of prayer, and whatever the attitude is expressed, prayer always has as its basis *an experience of a relationship with God*. It has meaning for the person praying because of that experience, and without it the prayer would have no meaning at all. What is in a person's heart at prayer speaks from that experience.

It is the same as in our relationship with people. We speak to other people, and treat them, according to what we experience between us. Because a relationship grows and deepens, our behaviour towards people changes: for example, the first time we ever entered a friend's home there was a certain reserve on our part, a little unsureness; years later, things are different, because we and they are different. If we were to behave today as we did on that first visit, they would get the impression that something was wrong — that we felt offended, or upset with them. On the other hand, if we had behaved at that first visit the way we behave today, we probably would not have been asked back! There is a seemliness in the way we act towards, and speak to, others which is indicated by the relationship we experience between us; certain boundaries are set, and offence is taken when anyone steps outside of them.

The way we feel in God's presence is because of the relationship we experience with him. Christians experience God as their merciful Father and, because of it, we pray to him in a certain way. If we experienced him as a powerful being, just watching and waiting for us to step out of line so that he could punish us, we would never say the things we pray in our Christian prayers such as the 'Our Father.' *Our prayer is an articulation of the relationship we experience with God in our present situation.* When we have a very real sense of our sinfulness, or feel needy and helpless, we address God as we experience him in intercession. At another time we may feel different, and so when we are conscious of many good things in our life, we say *different things to God: we thank him and praise him, but always from the same experience we have of him.*

Looked at in this way, *the prayer of the Church is an articulation of an experience of a relationship with God on the part of the Church.* This statement will be clearer if for 'Church' we substitute the equivalent phrase, 'Christian people.' The prayer of Christian people: an articulation of the experience which this People has of their relationship with God. Who are to be included in this 'People', this prayer? Certainly, all Christians living today: *their* prayer, based on the Christians' shared experience of God through Jesus Christ. However, to limit this experience and this People to Christians now living would not represent the real situation; for their experience of God was received from other people, possibly now dead; who, in their turn received it from others. The experience of this relationship is one that can be traced back in a continuous stream to the very first people who experienced God through Jesus Christ, that is, the people who were the first Christian community. An experience, living, handed on; and if living, also growing.

Indeed, it can be traced back further. The first people to experience our God were not the Christians. Yahweh was known by people several thousand years before the final revelation by Jesus Christ. The prayer of our People is, therefore, the prayer that has been prayed from the beginning of salvation history until now: the prayer coming from the experience, living and growing, which the bible presents as sweeping from Abraham until this present time.

It is *their* prayer; *their* articulation of *their* experience of Yahweh, in Old Testament times, and of God, the Father of our Lord Jesus Christ, in Christian times. It is how *they* experienced the covenant relationship – old and new – with God.

This is the first quality which makes the Prayer of the Church different from any other prayer: it is the articulation of the experience of a whole People.

The Prayer of the Church

We began our thoughts on the Prayer of the Church by considering prayer in relation to our own personal experience of a relationship with God; we have now arrived at the consideration of a whole People's experience. Clearly, there is a difference between an individual's experience, or even the experience of a group, and that of an entire people. In that living experience of the whole people there is a completeness and totality that cannot be found anywhere else: it is *all* there. Furthermore, it has an authenticity which no other prayer can claim; it is the source of all prayers, in that they all draw on it; all prayer is in some way a share in it.

The age-old living prayer of our People was handed on from generation to generation. Each of us has an experience of a 'handing on' in our own learning to pray, from our parents or others in our lives. It has always been done by word of mouth; sometimes also by the written word. The prayer of our People is now to be found printed, in Missal/ Sacramentary, Lectionary, the Rites of the sacraments, and the Breviary. Possibly it exists in other texts, but if so, we do not know, for only the accepted and approved books carry with them the assurance of our People, the Church, that this is authentically their prayer. The Prayer of our People – collectively called 'liturgy' from the Greek *leitourgia*, derived from *laos* ('people') and *ergon* ('work' or 'service') – is the prayer they pray in the celebration of the Eucharist, the other sacraments and the Liturgy of the Hours. We do not know who composed them – unless we say it was composed by the well-known 'Anon', who composed ballads and the old folk-music – for no one person composed this prayer; a People contributed to its composition. The Psalms and other prayer passages of scripture are a concrete illustration: their origin rooted in history, their development the result of their being sung by generations of our praying people, and their final form, their refinements resulting from the people praying together. Unfortunately, the 'freezing' of liturgy for the past few hundred years has prevented the people of those years from making their contribution to the growth of their prayer. It is to be hoped that this will no longer be the case. The 'prayed over' characteristic of liturgy gives it a unique quality: a perennial, lasting worth as a prayer; very different from the worth — and it is a real worth — of the 'throw-away' prayers composed in our own day, even by ourselves, which although good, have no lasting quality about them. Just like the popular music of recent times: all but a fragment of it is forgotten and dies. If any of it lasts long enough, it may eventually lay claim to be a part of the heritage of 'a people'. The method of procedure that was followed in the composition of the new rites of the sacraments followed from this 'handed-on' (or *traditional*) quality. Those to whom the task was given did not see themselves called to 'create' new texts, beginning with a clean canvas which they would fill with their own ideas; nor even the ideas of their contemporaries. The Lectionary of 1969 was composed with consultation of lectionaries that were used in the Church in the celebration of the Eucharist. The question that the commission had to ask, What will we put into the Lectionary? had to include in it the further question, What passages of scripture have our People been using in the past? Hence, the readings for Lent, Easter time, etc., are what our People have experienced as the most suited to give Christians the spirit of Lent, of Easter. The selection was influenced by insights from today's new understanding of scripture, the result of contemporary biblical scholarship; but always as part of our People's experience.

Liturgy is a prayer handed-on, given to us, received by us.

In this view of the Prayer of the Church, the similarity between it and our faith will be evident. Faith, in God's plan, is transmitted, handed on by means of 'tradition.' It is received from members of the believing community. So is our prayer. The normal way we Christians — and others, too — learn to pray, is by being with people who are praying, hearing them pray, and joining in with them, starting with our parents, teachers or some prayerful person or group. We then continue to grow in prayer through the same process of 'handing on.'

This similarity is not to be wondered at, because of the affinity between prayer and faith. Prayer includes, of necessity, an articulation of faith. One of the most effective ways in which the faith is preserved and handed on is in the Prayer of the Church. Liturgy contains a much more complete statement of faith than, say definitions of General Councils, which, at best, are partial and selective, since they aim at a particular aspect of the Church's faith under threat at that time.

To come to 'know' God better — using the word in the semitic sense of 'experience' — we come to people who experience a special relationship with God, in the very act of expressing their experience of him: we join them in their prayer. To come to the faith of the Church, it is necessary to come to the People's knowledge-experience of him, that is, their liturgy.

If I want to test my faith, I hold it up against the faith of the Church. Authentic faith is the experience of our People, the Church. If I should discover that the God I experience is very different from the God of our People, then I have diverged from the 'true faith' of the Church, and produced my own little god. The same applies to prayer: the prayer of our People is the standard and model of all prayer.

This reflection will help you to deepen your appreciation of receiving from our People. You will need ONE HOUR for it, and so you need to provide for that time before you commence.

A Reflection

Get comfortable; you want to be yourself.
Now, try to become conscious of your faith in
God's presence in your life right now. 'I am with
you.' 'I am your Father and I love you.'

    Conscious of God's presence, go over your
    past life, looking for only one thing — the
    PEOPLE who share your life with you.

Go back as far as you can remember.
Recall your parents, your family, your neighbour-
hood friends. Picture them; in your mind write
down their names. Let yourself live your life
again.

    Come forward through the years.
    See the people who have been God's gift
    to you.

Go slowly.
Your life has not just happened;
you have lived it. And others have shared it.
Think of them.
Talk with God about them. Thank him for them.
Present their needs to him.

    Notice, you have never been alone.
    There have always been people in your life.
    There are NOW.

At this point, renew your faith in God's presence
right here and now. 'I am with you.'
'I am your friend and I love you.'

    Go back as far as your memory will take you.
    See the people who were a blessing to you.
    Maybe it was just on one occasion.
    But they were a healing *gift* to you.
    Picture them. Mentally write down their
    names.

Think of a concrete way you could use to thank
them for their 'gift-ness' to you.

    These people did not just happen,
    any more than you did. Through them,
    God blessed you.

'You were sick and I healed you. . . through
him/her.'
'You were discouraged, and I cheered you up. . .
through him/her.'
'You were confused, and I listened until you
became peaceful. . . through him/her.'
'You were lonely, and I sent him/her to you.'

WHO?   WHERE?   WHEN?

DON'T YOU SEE – 'I HAVE LOVED YOU –
THROUGH THEM – WITH AN EVERLASTING
LOVE.'

Attitude and Behaviour

A whole People's prayer based on their corporate experience of their shared relationship with God, is so different
from the prayer and experience of one single person or group,
that any one of us who joins in the prayer of our People will
experience being *extended* in his or her prayer: stretched
beyond oneself to a prayer that was not anticipated, and
indeed, quite beyond a person's own capabilities. In our
People's prayer we come to a prayer, and a growth and
experience of God, that is new to us.

In liturgical praying we are in what could be called a
learning situation: learning to pray in the school of prayer
which liturgical praying is. A good illustration of 'learning'
to pray is given by Morning Prayer in the Liturgy of the
Hours. Consider our mornings, with the process of waking up,
and getting out of bed, with the movement to conscious
awareness. If we were to pray by ourselves then, would the
prayer not be a rather restrained acknowledgement of our
condition – a bit lifeless and none too bright, although not
without hope of improving as the morning advanced. The
externals accompanying such a prayer would portray our
weakness in bowed head, muted voice, and fewness of words.
In contrast, look at the prayer we are led to pray if, in that

morning state, we join our People in Morning Prayer, Listen to them; and look at them: "Come, ring out your joy to the Lord; hail the God who saves us! Alleluia." No muted voice here; we may even sing it. No bowed head nor restrained tones pray "with songs let us hail the Lord." This marvellous prayer with which our People provide us! Is it not like someone shaking us in bed, 'Come on, wake up.' Our People say, 'Come on, join us in responding to the day as a Christian.' It can well be called 'A Prayer for sleepy people', for it is not intended that we become wide awake before praying Morning Prayer; it is intended to do that for us — maybe with a bit of a jolt, too. Who of us, left to ourselves, would launch into a prayer of praise and thanks to the Father, think seriously of our coming day, enter into it blessing God for his continued promises to us to free us and to 'guide us on the way of peace'? Yet, this is the effect of choosing to pray liturgy as Morning Prayer, if I allow it to do this in me.

The liturgical year, as presented to us in Sunday and weekday Eucharists and Morning and Evening Prayer in the liturgical seasons and yearly cycle, takes us through a practical course in spirituality, in which we are exercised in all the key responses of the Christian life.

Consider a parallel in everyday life. To keep ourselves healthy we are advised to take regular exercise. We can choose our own exercises, and doing them day by day exercise our 'favourite' muscles. We can, on the other hand, go to a professional in a health and fitness centre and take on exercises designed by him which affect, not just those favourite ones, but every muscle in our bodies — with quite painful consequences for us. Similarly, if we choose our own prayer, we will exercise our own favourite 'prayer muscles' only. If, however, we allow ourselves to be guided and led, we will exercise them all in liturgy — all our praying capacity, also, possibly, with some painful consequences.

This comparison brings to our attention how a prayer that is 'structured' is different from one that is 'spontaneous'. Not a little difficulty is experienced by people in liturgical praying through not realizing the difference: difficulties expressed in phrases like: 'Liturgy does not say what I want to pray right now.'

A spontaneous prayer is the prayer we pray during a short visit to the Blessed Sacrament, or at meditation time: when we stop whatever activity we have been engaged in, become quiet inside, and aware of God in our lives, receive the prayer which wells up in our hearts. It is a prayer which has its beginning *inside* us. From what is in us — our feelings, interests, pressures, and so on — we move to prayer.

A structured prayer is when we make use of a prayer formula composed by someone else. Instead of using our own spontaneous prayer, we decide to avail of a prayer formula, such as the 'Our Father', something from a prayer leaflet, or an act of contrition which we know by memory. When we choose to pray this prayer formula, we adjust our thoughts and attitude to it. If we just repeat the words, it is not prayer. What our prayer will be depends on, and is determined by, the words of the prayer formula and our adapting to them. In which case, the prayer can be said to begin *outside* us.

This explains the difference *in behaviour* in private prayer and the Prayer of the Church, which is always, in this sense, a structured prayer. *In liturgy, to be brought to a fuller share in our People's experience of God, we allow ourselves to be brought to their prayer*, coming to it without any choice or presuppositions as to what we will pray. It could be likened to going to hear a lecturer: any expectations about what he will, or should, say closes our minds to what we could hear. The more open we are, to be more prepared to accept what is different, or even unacceptable to us, the more we will learn. We submit; and that is what we do in praying the Prayer of the Church: submit to the prayer offered.

There is a special value in this aspect of liturgy, that is, in submitting to a prayer which has been chosen and composed by someone else, which is not there when the choice of the prayer is made by us. It leads to a response in which there is less of us and more of the Holy Spirit. In all aspects of life, true living is responding to a situation with all its circumstances; we cannot live by trying to arrange, or manipulate, situations into what would be of our liking and choosing. To attempt it would be frustrating and fruitless; there would be no growth in it, and little happiness. Truly happy people are not those who have all they want — actually impossible — but those who freely accept what the Lord offers in their situations. How a person is, and what is going on inside them, in regard to someone or something, whether chosen or not, constitutes their happiness and success in living. Prayer is no exception to this rule: we exercise more deeply human qualities in accepting the prayers of the liturgical text.

Furthermore, it is a great expression of trust: trust in the People who have given us this prayer. Our forebears who prayed it were no more saintly than we are: just ordinary People. Yet we trust that this prayer which they give us as a heritage is the *best* prayer for us today, the living People. Our People prayed their prayer; and the prayer that was in their hearts they expressed in a rite, a ceremony — words, songs, symbols, movements, etc., and handed it on to us. *To receive the prayer we accept the People and the Rite.*

It is something like ourselves when we are visiting a place for the first time. To see the place, two possibilities are open: to try to find our way around ourselves by trial and error; or to take directions from someone who knows the place. A necessary condition, however, in the latter would be to put ourselves trustingly in the guide's hands; the more we question their guidance, the less the guide can do for us. The more we esteem the guide's knowledge and experience the more we benefit. Praying the Prayer of the Church means trusting the People *and* the rite they give us: viewing the rite as containing and communicating their prayer to us, esteeming it as such, and valuing it with its numerous components — for liturgy is always a rich and complex rite. This respect for the rite, and desire to be faithful to it, may look like 'observing the rubrics', but it is very different from it; It is the behaviour which follows from the attitude that constitutes praying the Prayer of the Church.

Summary

To pray liturgy, the Prayer of the Church,
the prayer of our People
I must come to it
open and willing to be led to this prayer
allowing myself to be extended in my prayer
submitting to this prayer now offered to me
by the Church, my People;
trusting that this is their prayer
trusting them, and their experience of God
and their response to this experience.
Trusting in God
that through this People
and their prayer
he will give me a true prayer in my heart
give me growth in my prayer
and form us all into his praying People.

*The concept 'our People' can remain for us just a concept,
and no more. To pray the Prayer of the Church, our People
need to be people we have experienced in some way. The
following activity could help to deepen that experience for
you:*

A — Read reflectively Psalm 114 (113A).
   Deepen your awareness of its content by
   asking yourself the following questions:
   — what does it say of our People's past?
   — what does it say of our People's attitude
      to Yahweh?

B — List for yourself
    (a) what you have received from your People:

    (b) what you will receive from them:

NOTE: In this activity there should emerge a consciousness of who 'our People' are.
    It would enrich your awareness if you could share your lists in B with others.

Psalm 114 (113A)

When Israel went forth from Egypt,
    the house of Jacob from a people
    of strange language.
Judah became his sanctuary,
    Israel his dominion.

The sea looked and fled,
    Jordan turned back.
The mountains skipped like rams,
    the hills like lambs.

What ails you, O sea, that you flee?
    O Jordan, that you turn back?
O mountains, that you skip like rams?
    O hills, like lambs?

Tremble, O earth, at the presence of
the LORD,
    at the presence of the God of Jacob,
who turns the rock into a pool of water,
    the flint into a spring of water.

The Content

Liturgy is the prayer surpassing all others: because of the attitude and behaviour we bring to it as prayer of the whole person; with the special attitude and behaviour towards those present with us, which makes it a communal prayer; and the special behaviour towards the text and rite. Further, there is the content. Because of the totality and completeness of the Prayer of our People, we can expect, in praying it, that it will exercise us:

— *in all the principal prayer attitudes:* that is, petition, repentance, thanksgiving and praise; and

— *in a prayer which is a response to our relationships with God the Father; with his Son, Jesus Christ; and with the Holy Spirit; as well as to our relationship with one another as members of the Church.*

What we have in mind is the response which is 'conscious and full'. First, a conscious response: we can, and we do, respond to God without being consciously aware of him or his presence to us. This occurs in the helpful deeds we do, the caring words, the good intentions in our hearts, and any change of heart we experience. In short, insofar as we are doing God's will we are responding to him. However, we are not *consciously* aware of him. To respond in conscious awareness of him, liturgy leads us to 'name' him: to have him explicitly in mind; to address ourselves to *him*: God, the Father of our Lord Jesus Christ, who has brought us into the special relationship of the New Covenant relationship of our baptism.

Liturgy further leads us to respond to the *fullness of this relationship.* As has been said above, we respond according to the relationship as we experience it; whether with God or with anyone else. To help with our appreciation of what happens in liturgical prayer and the quality of fullness it offers, consider the relevance of relationships when, for example, a girl states of another, 'She is like a sister to me', to express how close they are to one another; or when, of a young man who marries an older woman, it is remarked, 'It is a mother he is looking for.' Again, take the situation of two people, a young man and young woman, working together, and developing a good 'working relationship'; who, in time, come to be friends — a different relationship, now; later, they marry one another — and another kind of relationship begins between them. The relationship has to change: from one of co-operation to the deeper trust and sharing of friendship; and from that to the unique intimacy of husband and wife. With the change of relationship is a change in their response to one another; a change of attitude and behaviour as well. It would be a sign that things were very wrong between them as husband and wife, if they saw one another, and felt towards one another, just as two friends, or worse, if they just did a job of work together. Let us apply this to responding to God, and the difference in the responses to God the Father, to Jesus Christ, and to the Holy Spirit.

Liturgical prayer leads us to experience *God our Father* as 'source of life and goodness', and to respond to him in a dependence that is absolute and with an obedience that is unconditioned. To him, as the 'God of power and might', and at the same time 'rich in mercy' — all-loving, for he is love — we respond with unwavering and unquestioning trust. He has no activity in our regard but to give to us out of his love and faithfulness towards us. We have no activity in his regard but to receive from him; accept unmerited graces, unearned favours. Our response is the loving trust of well-loved children towards their Father who cares and provides for them, to the limit of all he has to give: for having given us a share in his divine nature, what more is there for him to give?

The high point of the Father's giving to us is the sending of his Son, *Jesus Christ* as our Redeemer. All the gifting of the Father is done THROUGH Jesus Christ. A new dependence: we receive FROM the Father, THROUGH Jesus Christ, who sharing our human state, is 'a man like us in all things but sin', living to the full human dependence, human obedience, human receiving, and human loving trust towards his Father.

Into this man and Son of God, we are *incorporated in baptism*, setting up a relationship WITH him: we share with him, his dying-rising, his risen glorified life. With him we depend on the Father; with him we receive all from the Father, including the status of having God as our Father, too. To accept Christ is to receive a transformation: to become

children of God (John 1:12); a change into a true image of
Christ the Son of God (Rom 8:29); made into the one
single new man (Eph 2:15) to the extent of sharing his life:
'It is no longer I who live, but Christ who lives in me.' (Gal
2:20); 'united to him in a death like his. . . united with him
in a resurrection like his' (Rom 6:5), the Christian becomes
another Christ, ONE PERSON WITH HIM — an experience so
beautifully expressed in the Office of Readings for Holy
Saturday, in the words of Christ to Adam and Eve after his
resurrection: 'Rise up, work of my hands, you who were
created in my image. Rise. . . for you are in me, and I am in
you; together we form only ONE PERSON and we cannot be
separated.'

All of this happened to us because *the Holy Spirit* has been
sent to us: 'the Holy Spirit was sent on the day of Pentecost
in order that. . . all believers would have access to the Father
through Christ in the one Spirit.' (Constitution of the Church,
n. 4) The Holy Spirit is, as it were, our 'contact Person': the
Person under whose direct influence we live. We live by the
Spirit; we walk by the Spirit; we act by the Spirit (Gal 2:25);
we are led by the Spirit (Rom 8:14); the Spirit prays in us
(Rom 8:26). Living in us he transforms us: 'filled with the
Holy Spirit we become one body, one spirit in Christ.'

Basil the Great, in his treatise on the Holy Spirit extends this
transformation to the utmost: 'Through the Spirit we acquire
a likeness to God; indeed, we attain what is beyond our most
sublime aspirations — we become God.'

*The threefold experience which, although shared with all
our People, is also unique in each of us, is something like the
following. Allow yourself to be re-awakened to your experiences of the Father, Jesus Christ, and the Holy Spirit.
You might then like to put your own experience in writing.*

BY THE WORKING OF THE HOLY SPIRIT

prayer is given to me.
Feeling assured, I await it
and confidently listen.
I find it in my heart,
placed there by the Spirit
who dwells within me:
gently donated to me;
heart-felt favour,
gift received, not made.
No work, no doing but
allowing him to enable me
I am wafted into prayer

T
H
R
O
U
G
H

C
H
R
I
S
T
.

W
I
T
H

H
I
M
.
I
N

H
I
M

WE — ME and THEM and HIM — the total Christ,
inter-loving, co-praying; in shared experience of
grace and favour; abiding in him; living in him; and
he in us — our identity; as one person; one body, one
soul shared by us all; shared prayer; his prayer; our
prayer: a living sacrifice of praise

before the Father
as his children in
submissive obedience,
trusting dependence,
unwavering hope,
thankfully receiving
joyfully praising
him who has blessed us with
every spiritual blessing

TO WHOM SALVATION AND GLORY AND POWER
BELONG

8

PRAYING LITURGY
AND HUMAN GROWTH

Liturgy throws a searchlight on a person and on communities. It lights up their state of human development; it exposes how they are living; and what may be underneath their external behaviour. This becomes especially noticeable when difficulties are experienced in liturgy: things are done, or not done, which are unacceptable; a sense of uncomfortableness is felt; it seems not 'real'; detached from real life; has nothing in common with life in the world. That liturgy throws a searchlight on these human experiences and exposes them more concretely, was graphically illustrated for us on the occasion of a request to help a community with their liturgical prayer. The community was split in two in its ideas on liturgy; so divided, that they decided that the members would meet to pray only in their 'faction' groups. It was the hope of the superior that our work with them on their praying would re-unite them. It did anything but that! At the end of a full week's work with us on the liturgy they were even more hardened in their positions, but the underlying malaise was surfacing: the lack of community spirit and, in individuals, insufficient development for community life.

The difficulties they experienced individually and as a community, arose out of their stage of growth: the stage revealed by difficulties experienced with regard to the content and practice of the previous three chapters on Praying Liturgy. They experienced difficulty in centering; they were not convinced of its necessity; they were not willing to sacrifice time for it. Because of their stage of growth, their experience of living had to focus on their own individual needs, rather than on 'being for others'; hence the ideal of communal prayer had no meaning for them. Again for the same reason, when presented with the Prayer of Our People their experience found them reacting to it as an imposition, an obligation to follow a set form, which took away their freedom; their stage of development did not enable them to appreciate it and receive it as the powerful means it is to help their growth in prayer. Once again the connection between living and liturgy became obvious.

This chapter will deal with the stages of human development and their relevance to liturgical praying. Lest the context be lost, it is well to repeat here what has been said about praying as 'gift'; our praying is Christ praying in us. However, while it is all God's work, it does not leave us out, nor does it happen without us. More specifically, without our receptivity, our allowing it, the prayer cannot be given to us; cannot happen in us.

In this chapter we will address one specific obstacle to a 'full, conscious and active participation.' The obstacle we will consider arises from the fact that we are all people in a process of growth — hence lacking in personal and faith-maturity. If this factor in us is not to be an obstacle, we need first to recognise and acknowledge it in ourselves, and secondly have the skill to use what we find in ourselves to be growth-promoting for both praying and living. (See chapter 3)

Stages in Human Growth

We would like to preface this section and those following, by pointing out that they contain no more than our reflections on what we have experienced in our work in Formation and Living and Liturgy. They are not by any means intended as a scientific presentation on a deep level of psychological and faith-development.

We live in a process of growth; a development in which there are identifiable stages. Corresponding to our psychological stage of development is our experience of God and also our prayer. We can find ourselves in any one of these stages at different times, although we would have the experience of a 'home-land' where we belong. My prayer, at any time, corresponds to where I am; I speak to God from the relationship I feel (or, maybe, do not feel). That is, I pray always from a level of my inner psyche.

We will now look at these stages and the corresponding prayer-experience of the person. Our 'home-land' is where we are when we are centered. When we are not centered, – when we do not give the time to become centered, – we pray from a superficial level: from only a part of us; the part which, at this particular time of sitting down to pray, most affects us; it thus is holding us away from our true centre and home.

a. Just alive

Each stage has a sort of centre, which need not be my real self. When we are born and in our very early days and weeks, we are alive, but not *conscious* of being alive. We cry, we laugh, we eat, but we cannot say 'I eat', 'I' am hungry' – hence there is no identity.

b. Part alive

Not too much later, between the ages of two and four, I can say 'I' and experience myself as such: so much so, that I am completely identified with the experience of the moment: I feel hungry and that is all; I feel tired and I cry and cry. It becomes: I am hunger; I am tiredness. My vocabulary is 'I want', 'I don't want', 'give me'. The sound of my language is definite, determined and emphatic. My behaviour too is expressive of this stage: unless I get my way I go into a corner and sulk: or I throw things, or lash out. The word that best describes me at this time is EGO-CENTRIC: not yet a person in the strictly defined sense. (I) am an enclosed 'I', the centre of my universe: (I).

What we have described so far is the experience and behaviour of a human being at that stage of development; it is appropriate at that stage and quite acceptable. The same cannot be said when it is seen in a person later in life, whose experience and behaviour is that of a three-year old! What this person and the small child have in common at this time is *that both completely identify with a part of them: that* part, which at that time is most alive. The experience is often expressed in such statements (often explosive!) as 'I am tired;' 'I can't pray;' 'I am fed up with her;' 'I won't have any more to do with her ever again!' 'I can't stand him; the way he says Mass turns me off completely!'

These examples show how a person in later life may find himself or herself in that stage: maybe just temporarily — quite a common experience — maybe fixated.

Whether temporarily or permanently in this stage their behaviour is characterised:
— by an inability to make a response; so they react; what motivates them is gratification, satisfaction.
— there is no inner freedom, no ability to make a free choice; nor is commitment possible. The direction for their lives comes from outside of them; they look to authority, e.g. Church, peer-group.
— because of the fragility of their 'I' they have not the security to ask questions, to reflect, to see connections between the present and the past and the future. Life lives them rather than they living life. They are surface-people, drifters; they go with the crowd — not able to have a personal stance; their competence is in being practical, pragmatic, efficient, but always from a role.
— feelings become the impetus for action; a lot of protest and 'anti-behaviour.'
— because of their lack of self-identity there is no awareness of other people as *'Persons'* (that is, I-Thou). They do kind things but their actions come from a role, not a relationship.

c. **Alive with**

We grow out of this stage through people approaching us. When we allow them into our lives the result is the weakening of the enclosure around my 'I' and the beginning of an

experience of feeling related to; a sense of belonging to.
This experience of relationship strengthens my 'self' sufficiently to make a choice. From the experience of I-with I
can choose to be 'for others'. Of course I will still experience
all those 'ego-centric' drives as spoken about above, however
I can choose OTHER than — MORE than — them. In fact, I
have already chosen as I let down the enclosure around myself,
allowing others in; I have learnt to move beyond myself. I
can choose to be *for others*'; whether I will do it or not is
another matter — at least if I do not, I know that I do not. I
am no longer drifting.

Further characteristics of a person at this stage of development, along with the ability to choose, to relate to others,
are:

— the ability to reflect: to make connections between the
present and the past and the future; to experience myself as
more than what at any moment I am feeling ('I am hungry —
but I can wait for food!' 'I am tired, but others need me at
this moment.') — I am *more* than my feelings. This ability to
see *myself* as more, enables me to see more in everyone, in
everything. It moves me to ask questions; to search out
meaning.
— I dare to risk, to make mistakes, to face the unknown.
— I can make a commitment.
— I can experience more deeply.
— Instead of letting my feelings drive me to action, they
'speak to me' and I hear them, but *I* claim my freedom to do
what I choose.

d. Wholly alive

As the process of growth continues in us we become more
authentic persons. Integration is deepening on all levels: I
am open to all experience, inside of me and outside of me; I
have the ability to accept *me* on my feeling-level; none are
rejected as being incompatible with becoming whole.
— My acting matches my core, my centre; I choose options
which correspond with who I am, and I am ready to accept
the consequences of my choice.
— I am a transparent person: who I am shines forth, and can
shine forth because no hiding is needed.

— I grow in experience of being with others, of being for others.

This activity is meant to help you to be more aware of yourself, and 'where' you are living — in your home-land or in a part of you.

Our aim in liturgy is that our participation will be FULL, CONSCIOUS AND ACTIVE.

Think back over your day. Note the times you were that way 'in life' — and were not.

Stages in Faith-growth

Corresponding to these stages of human growth are stages of spiritually only if I am consciously aware of what is happening in more detail these stages, it might be helpful to know, what value this knowledge can be to us. Briefly, it is a help towards the removal of the obstacle we have referred to above; why I am interested to look at myself as a person in a process of living and praying is because I can grow humanly and spritiaully only if I am consciously aware of what is happening in me. I need to know where I am in order to cooperate to be open to be moved to more.

Since I relate to God from the level of which I live or am living at any particular moment, the experience of God, and my prayer, will have characteristics corresponding to the different stages of human growth. In the one day, even in the one prayer time, I can possibly move through different 'stages'.

An illustration from life

A novice in a religious congregation was on retreat prior to her first commitment. All preparations and arrangements had been completed, one of the most exciting being a long-awaited visit of her mother and father from interstate. On one of the last days of the retreat, she received a telephone call telling her the disturbing news that her father had had a heart attack. Immediately thrown into panic, experiencing alarm, turmoil and fear, as soon as she left the phone she went straight to the chapel. There she prayed. Out of her panic and desperation her prayer was: 'God, don't let anything happen to dad now!'

Later in the day she prayed again. In the meantime she had spoken to her mother, had talked to her community, and as a result her whole emotional wave had subsided. She felt her body more relaxed and her mind less occupied with all the thoughts that had crowded in. This time in chapel, she did not experience the need to pray a panic-prayer, nor pour out pleas. Now she was calm enough, centered enough to listen: to hear what the Lord was saying to her in this event; and to receive the prayer the Holy Spirit was placing in her heart.

Different prayers, from different levels of the same person. Both authentic: both coming from the 'authentic self' each time. Depending on what level I am living on, my experience can be of being:

Part alive

This is the ego-centric level. Movement begins from me; this 'me' is all important. I don't see anything else. 'Me', in and from my need, prays.

If *I* am in the centre, God is an 'outside' God. I call on him when, and only when, I need him; he becomes a use-ful God, a magic God; a supplier of my needs.

I experience myself with a need and I wholly identify with that need. Having identified wholly with that need, I *am* that need and the only reason God exists for me is to supply now what I need, e.g. to pass an exam, for someone sick to get better, to find a parking spot, a fine day for our fete. When things happen that please me, my 'faith' response is: 'Isn't

E

God good'. If the opposite happens, I say 'He's let me down; God has forgotten me.' As I go up and down, God goes up and down. I give up going to Mass, because, 'I get nothing out of it;' then I experience psychological guilt and I go to Mass again. (I am full of shoulds and oughts.) As we call this section being 'part alive', so is the prayer *part of me praying*.

Further, because my prayer begins from 'me', God becomes what 'I' make him. At one time he is all loving and generous, at another I have to bargain with him, appease him.

> We give God a name. We then equate God with the name we have given him, and in doing so we make ourselves, in effect, God's God. Instead of acknowledging God as the source of our identity and existence, we make ourselves the self-proclaimed source of God's identity. God then becomes the one made in our image and likeness.
> (James Finley, *Merton's Palace of Nowhere*)

I do not distinguish between 'God' and 'Jesus.' These titles are general symbols for transcendence for me. I also have others, e.g. faith, grace, sacrament.

Alive with

As happens in human growth, so now in faith-growth I am prepared to enter this stage by experiences of dissatisfaction, meaninglessness, a sense of incompleteness: 'There must be more to prayer,' and I feel a longing, a desire, an urge to search.

In this stage, God is still not central to me. I call him by name, but *my* experience is still the important thing, the focus. So I pray, speaking about my experience but addressing it to 'God' or 'Lord'.

'Lord, I had a terrible day today — almost too much — I had to struggle all the time — and I got help from no one — . . . . .'

While I name him, *he* makes no difference to my experience. It is only a mental recognition without any change happening to me. I might as well be talking to myself or to my friend for all the experience of God that there is.

Since the characteristic of this stage of human development is an awakening to relationship, God is often friend, lover, father, mother. The experience of Jesus — not yet of living 'in Christ', 'another Christ', of Jesus as risen Lord — is mainly expressed in secondary responses: admiration of his qualities as a hero; closeness and support as of a friend; learning from his example, his wisdom, as from a guru; inspiration from his political/revolutionary stance. Rather than a clear concept of his specific role in salvation, a subjective and strongly emotional response flavours my faith.

Prayers are characterised by a lot of words, by reflecting, analysing, summing up. It is a time of discursive prayer rather than contemplation; of petition more than praise and thanks. There are the beginnings of 'we' prayer as the sense of 'we' develops in a person, along with the growing ability to trust, to submit, to surrender. Prayer becomes something a person chooses to enter into, not out of whim, but from a deeper motivation.

The direction emerging is more God-centered and less me-centred.

Wholly alive

Corresponding to this stage in human growth is a deepening of faith and prayer-experience which is 'a growing in all ways into Christ.'

God is the God of the New Covenant relationship. Movement begins from him; he initiates, he calls and I but *receive and respond*. I can wait; I can surrender; I can be receptive; 'My heart is ready, Lord; my heart is ready.'

To hear his call, his invitation, I LISTEN in the core of my being.

> Instead of *my* reading, analysing and extracting the meaning of a biblical text, in contemplative prayer I began to learn how to let the text read me and to let it bring my needs and the Spirit's movements within me to consciousness.
>
> (James W. Fowler, *Stages of Faith*)

Since it is at the core of my being that I can have an experiential awareness of my relatedness to others, in my prayer I am conscious of responding with others. Through them I reach Christ and through them he reaches me. We are the Body of Christ where we experience our shared, adoptive sonship. Our experience in the fulness of our relationship with God the Father of Our Lord Jesus Christ, and revealed by Jesus Christ, the Word made flesh.

Our life is the Holy Spirit: the life of the People of God.

In this growing faith and prayer, we feel drawn to, and at home with, the prayer of Our People, Liturgy; and the high-point of our response, thanksgiving and praise.

The faith and prayer-experience of a person in this stage is beautifully articulated in Eucharistic Prayer III, in which we pray:

> Father, you are holy indeed,
> and all creation rightly gives you praise.
> All life, all holiness, comes from you
> through your Son, Jesus Christ, Our Lord,
> by the working of the Holy Spirit.
> From age to age you gather a people to yourself,
> so that from east to west
> a perfect offering may be made
> to the glory of your name.

In this activity you will become more conscious of the importance to your prayer of what stage you are in, or what level you respond from.

"What determines the quality of my praying in liturgy — and whether prayer can happen at all — is ME: how I am at that time."

Spend some time reflecting on this statement. How does it match your experience?

Praying Liturgy: Conclusion and some questions

'There is nothing in life that is not in liturgy.' The person who comes to liturgy is ME/US. As we are in daily living so we are when we celebrate liturgy.

Our daily living consists of responses we make; for we do nothing but respond — in life and in liturgy. Living is being present to. . . making choices. . . being free from whatever, outside us or inside us, could 'hook' us. . . free to be our real selves — and so is liturgy.

Living and celebrating liturgy is being with others, being for others, receiving from others, acting in cooperation with others.

Living, and liturgy too, require that I care for myself out of respect for who I am; they lead me to want to act according to my full human potential — and also my divine potential.

Liturgy needs time and interest and commitment, as life does. Liturgy, as much as daily living, reflects the stage of our human development, and our stage of faith-maturity.

This is a suitable place to bring up the questions and difficulties that are regularly raised by groups in our courses in connection with this section of Praying Liturgy — and to answer them.

1. *Looking at prayer in this way — the requirements of centering, communal prayer, prayer of the church, the prayer of a person 'wholly alive', — doesn't it make prayer very complicated?*

If the person who raises this question is using 'complicated' in an emotive way, and is really expressing his or her frustration at this presentation, they would be indicating that this is only a 'presenting problem', and that the real problem is more of a personal nature.

If by complicated is meant complex, composite, consisting of a combination of elements, the answer is Yes. In this sense any human act is complicated, and here we are dealing with 'a sacred action surpassing all others.' To know and acknowledge that it presents difficulties is good; for to know where I am in my living and praying can make me more compassionate towards myself and others; and my acceptance of my limitations can make me more free from shoulds/musts etc. and hence open to receive the prayer given by God.

2. Why is it necessary to bother about what 'stage' I am in?

This question came up in a different form during a lecture given by a psychologist on 'Stages of Faith'. One of the audience, a teacher of religious education, denied flatly the whole idea of stages, and put the cap on his outburst with; 'Next you will be telling me that I am in some stage or other!'

The growth in prayer — faith — life is helped by the acceptance of the fact of growth in myself. As stated above, the consciousness of my growth process and of what is happening in me facilitates my growth. This has always been recognised; it is the reason for the many writings on prayer by the classical masters of the spiritual life and for seeking help in prayer and life from a spiritual director.

3. If I have to have grown into fulness of relationship — to have arrived at the last stage — in order to pray liturgy, does that mean that I cannot pray it, since I am not yet at that stage?

Just as adult behaviour or an adult response can be given by a (psychological) adult only, so full, conscious and active participation in liturgy is possible for a person of a certain stage of human and faith development only. However, a person not yet an adult is capable of participation in liturgy — as in life — to a degree. Furthermore, one of the necessary means of growing and developing in prayer is being exposed to the faith-experience of our people; just as a person grows humanly by being exposed to life-experiences. In neither prayer nor life will there be development without modelling by others (more mature people) and other learning activities. By no means is a child thrown into life — nor liturgy. On the other hand she or he is not completely withdrawn and 'protected' from it. It could be expected that an adult will find most of his or her prayer activity in liturgy. A child will certainly not, but will need preparation of the type suggested in the Directory for Masses with Children.

4. What about the person who has not the skill to center? or has little interest in the others present, least of all in the total church?

These factors point to where such a person is in life, as well as in prayer. They should be encouraged, first, to know and accept where they are — and be allowed by others to be there. If they feel bored with liturgy, no attempt should be made to relieve their boredom by giving variety or some form of 'entertainment'. Rather is their feeling the starting point of their growth. Hence, secondly, we invite them to come to the celebration, *with* their bored feeling: it is one of the places in which they can grow and develop.

Through our sinfulness we can all find ourselves in any of these stages. When we experience ourselves, perhaps dis-appointedly, as very ego-centric, it is something to be accepted not kicked against. We *are* growing, and our experience of limitation does not hinder the Holy Spirit; only our refusal to accept it does that. He is equally present to us whether we are struggling to give bare attention, or are rapt enthusiastically into praise of God. And where the Spirit is there can be prayer.

How typical and widespread these limitations are came to light a few years ago as the result of an investigation made by the Liturgical Education Committee, one of the committees of the Diocesan Liturgical Commission. The Committee considered it necessary to know more about the liturgical needs of the parishes in Melbourne in order to be able to give more effective help. A priest-sociologist designed a programme with a two-fold aim: (a) to discover, informally and formally, what are the *real* liturgical needs of a parish; and (b) by studying three parishes to determine whether a general method of investigating real liturgical needs is possible. The programme involved three groups of seminary students; each group worked in close cooperation with the parish priest, and had experience of different parish activities over a period of four weeks. These activities included Sunday Masses; week-day, school and home Masses; other liturgical functions (funerals, weddings etc.), meetings and gatherings in the parish, and visiting families. The three parishes selected were of a very different character. The seminarians were given guidelines on how to proceed. After a period of private reflection on each activity they attended, each group met with its supervisor, (a sociologist) to read a report; to evaluate, critisize and synthesize the previous phase, and plan the next one, (having been warned not to discuss initial feelings with one another or the parish priest, to avoid 'contamination'). At the end of the four weeks all reports were handed in to the priest who organised the whole programme. After a meeting with all the seminarians involved, he gave the Liturgical Education Committee the final report.

We have included all this detail in order to show how thorough the investigation was, and therefore, how reliable was the conclusion arrived at. *It was that the needs of the people in these three praishes were not of a liturgical nature; their needs were concerned with themselves and their faith.*

So, what then? Were we to suggest that all liturgy be suspended for a time in the parishes, while they took on a renewal programme? By no means. What was indicated was the need of celebrations of liturgy, so planned and ministered, that they took into account and catered for these limitations which had been discovered.

Section Three

RESPONDING TO A SYMBOL

9

RESPONDING TO THE WORD OF GOD
IN THE READINGS

Participation, or in other words, praying liturgy, the subject matter of the two previous sections, is always a *response to a symbol.*

People's praying in liturgy is their response to what is presented to them, what they see and hear, in the *Areas A,B, and C:* that is, a response to the Ministers *(C)* who minister the Text and Rite *(B),* in the Place *(A)* (Section One); as well as a response to themselves, the people with them in the congregation *(D),* and the whole Church (Section Two).

We begin this section on Responding to a Symbol with a typical symbol: the proclamation of the Word in the readings of the Liturgy of the Word. A reading of scripture — sometimes short, sometimes long — is an essential element in every liturgical rite. When the Rite for Reconciliation of Individual Penitents appeared in 1973, with the then novel idea of the possibility of reading a text of scripture as part of the Rite, the question was widely raised, 'Is it practical to have a reading in confession?' It would have been a better question to ask, 'Is it practical *not* to have a reading?' This chapter will explain why a reading from scripture is part of every liturgical rite: every sacrament, and each of the Liturgical Hours. First, we will give a presentation of the theology of the Word of

God in liturgy; it will be simple and short, and just sufficient
to give a basis for what is to follow, namely, an explanation
of the people's response to the readings. This latter, we see as
a special skill — one instance of the basic liturgical skill of
responding to a symbol (see chapter 4, page   ); our treatment
answers the 'liturgical question' how do you do it?

The Word of God in Liturgy

The importance of the readings, and the character of the
people's response to them, arises from the nature of the Word
of God.

The expression 'Word of God' was used by the Israelite
people centuries before the coming of Jesus Christ: the idea
of 'God speaking' is in a creation account in Genesis, 'And
God said, "Let there be light"; and there was light.' (1:3)
The way of thinking that gives it its very profound meaning
and importance for us goes back even before the time of
Israel as a nation. Hence, if we are to appreciate all that is
implied when a reading is called the Word of God, we need to
go to the people of the ancient near East and learn what they
were thinking and what they were saying, when they used
this expression Word of God; and, indeed, what they had in
mind in regard to the 'word' of a human being, especially of a
person in authority like a king.

First, we have to appreciate that their use of their word
'word' was very different from our use of it today. We find
no difficulty in accepting the difference between people's
'words' and their 'actions'; We can accept that there can be a
gap between what they 'say' and what they 'do'. This difference and gap did not exist in the kind of thinking we are
looking at in the people who gave us the expression Word of
God. Word implies action; word both 'says' and 'does'. A
word is a WORD — ACT, an EVENT. This use of the word
'word' will be familiar to any who have heard the older
English translation of Luke's Gospel, in the passage 'and his
mother kept all these *words* in her heart'. It was not only
what she heard *said* that Mary kept in her heart, but 'all
that happened'; 'all these *things*' is the generally accepted
translation today (*Luke* 2:51).

The story of Isaac giving his dying blessing (*Genesis*, chapter 27) is a good illustration of the power of a spoken word. Isaac wished to bestow his blessing on his first-born son Esau, and grant him the right of inheritance. While Esau was out hunting game for a meal for this special occasion of the blessing, the younger brother, Jacob, through a deception suggested by his mother, tricked the blind Isaac into thinking that he was the older brother, Esau, and into giving him the blessing. When Esau returned from his hunting, he and Isaac quickly realised the deception that had been played. Isaac 'trembled violently' and Esau 'cried out with an exceeding great and bitter cry, and said to his father, "Bless me, even me also, O my father." ' In our way of thinking we would have expected Isaac to rectify the situation immediately and do what he had intended to do: to pronounce the blessing over Esau. Yet, what we hear him express is his powerlessness to do that. "Your brother came with guile, and he has taken away your blessing," he said. In other words, he tells Esau that he has accomplished something in blessing Jacob which he cannot reverse. The blessing pronounced over Jacob not only expressed the wishes and prayer that were in his heart, in regard to Esau; the blessing effected something in *Jacob*, and there was nothing anyone could do about it now. The word was said, and through it something 'event-uated'; *WORD-EVENT*.

For the people who gave us the expression 'Word of God', the words spoken were as important, and as productive and effective, as acts performed. The WORD of GOD was a WORD-ACT.

This is the kind of action implied when the phrase 'God said' is used, and the consequences of God speaking his Word. The power of the word was considered to be in proportion to the power of the one who spoke it. So 'God said' indicates the infinite power of God.

> For as the rain and snow came down from heaven,
> and return not thither but water the earth,
> making it bring forth and sprout, giving seed to
> the sower and bread to the eater
> so shall my word be that goes forth from my mouth;

it shall not return to me empty,
but it shall accomplish that which I purpose,
and prosper in the thing for which I sent it.

(Isaiah 55:10-11)

On the other hand, a word of God which does not accomplish what it says is inconceivable *(Deut.* 18: 18-22).

This is the manner in which we see God exercising his power in his creation: he speaks his Word. Being a *saving* God, his Word is a *saving* Word: it effects those changes in people, in situations, in nature, which is his salvation.

He sends forth his command to the earth;
  his word runs swiftly.
He gives snow like wool;
  He scatters hoarfrost like ashes. . .
He sends forth his word and melts them;
  He makes his wind blow and the waters flow.
He declares his word to Jacob,
  His statutes and ordinances to Israel.

(Psalm 147:15-16, 18-19)

The Word of God plays a very important part in the ministry of the prophets. So often we hear them say, 'it is Yahweh who speaks, ' 'Thus says the Lord.' In these utterances the prophet is not just passing on to the people some admonition or new truth. The communicated Word is a dynamic word, with power to direct history and alter behaviour. This is what is implied in the call and sending of Jeremiah, 'Behold, I have put my words into your mouth' (1:9), and of Isaiah, Ezekial, Hosea, Joel and others. Their role was to lead the people to 'hear the word of the Lord' and respond in faithfulness.

The Word of God: Jesus Christ

'In many and various ways God spoke of old to our fathers by the prophets; but in these last days he has spoken to us by a Son.' *(Hebr.* 1:1-2)

When Jesus Christ came on earth he *was* the Word of God. In his public ministry Jesus spoke the Word of God. The nature of the Word of God, its power and the effects of it are presented in the Gospels. By a word he controlled nature, calming the storm, blighting the fig tree, arranging a catch of fish and changing the water to wine. By a word, too, he healed the crippled, gave sight to the blind, restored the sick to health, even raised the dead to life. This , because it was the Word of God he spoke, with all its divine power.

In connection with this, there is that sad comment of Matthew about Jesus' ministry in his home town Nazareth; 'And he did not do many mighty works there because of their unbelief' (13:58). One's immediate reaction is to query, Why not? Did he find it in some way distasteful or un-becoming? Did he consider the people unworthy of his miracles? The fact is that the lack of faith in the people restricted him in using the power of the Word to save them. They left him powerless, at least in regard to themselves. He, who could speak the Word of God all-powerful, found himself incapable. Amazing though this may seem, it was nothing new in God's relationship with his people. This is the experience we are told of in Hebrews, speaking about the Israelites: 'For the good news came to us just as to them; but the message which they heard did not benefit them, because it did not meet with faith in the hearers' (*Hebr.* 4:2)

How can it happen that the Word of God is rendered powerless and does not have an effect on people? The reason is very obvious when we consider the relationship that God established between people and himself. God never does violence to anybody; never pushes us around or drags us by the hair of the head. He never influences us in any way that would infringe on our freedom; for having made us *free*, he will have us act in no other way but freely. God fashioned us to freely choose what we do. As a consequence of giving us this gift of freedom, he will not act in us without our free consent; and so he approaches us with an offer, *an invitation* – for our consent, our acceptance. He leaves us perfectly free to say, No: to refuse his offered gift. (Of this we have all plenty of experience!) Writing on the Verbal-Diological Existence of man, Father Leo Scheffczyk says very beauti-fully:

> In the Old Testament, conscious and formal
> expression of the response to God is reserved to
> man alone. Originating from a particularly solemn
> and exalted word of God ("let us make mankind in

our image and likeness"), man alone is capable of
giving and *being* the fully valid answer of creation
to God. Relatedness to God, which is essential to
man, thus becomes a living dialogue in which man
has the role of the answering partner. His whole
existence is fulfilled in the fact that he answers as
the one addressed by God. As viewed in the Old
Testament, man is a being essentially related to the
verbal movement of God; man's is a "response-
giving" existence. (*Man's Search For Himself*).

This dialogic situation made possible the situation in
Nazareth on which Matthew comments. Their lack of acceptance of Jesus, their refusal of him and what he offered to
them put up a barrier which he could not penetrate. For all
the good he did them, Jesus may as well not have come to
them. In contrast to this, those who did receive and acknowledge him did benefit by his coming as seen in his miracles
and forgiving of sin. St John points to the *change of status*
in those who accepted Jesus: 'to all who *received* him, who
believed in his name, he gave power to become children of
God' (*John* 1:12). Jesus made it the primary aim of his
mission to have the people accept him, not for his own
affirmation or support, but for the sake of the people: there
was no other way to the Father than through faith in him as
'the one sent'. It is in him that God now speaks his Word.

The Word of God in the Church

The Word of God is still spoken by Jesus Christ: in the
Church, his People; with the same effects, under the same
conditions. The Church was built up by the preaching of the
Word by the apostles: 'not merely a message coming from the
Lord, but in the word in which Christ himself imparts himself
to men' (Scheffczyk). St Paul writes: 'the Good News: it is
the power of God saving all who have faith' (*Rom.* 1:16).
Note, first, *the power* in the proclamation of the Good News
of Jesus Christ dying and rising; it is *the* event, *the* word of
God which saves the world. Then note the *condition*: faith in
Jesus Christ; the RESPONSE of faith-trust-commitment to
this man who is the Son of God.

It is in each person's heart that God speaks his Word to him or her. What can be called the *normative source* of the Word of God is the proclamation of the Good News from scripture. That is to say, although we believe that God speaks to us in innumerable ways and diverse forms; that although he is actively present in every person and every event of our lives, there is a quality and power in the proclamation of Scripture by a reader-minister that gives it a precedence; it is an event in which the Word comes to its fullest reality. Hence the Constitution on the Liturgy can state in paragraph 7: 'Christ is present in his word, since it is he himself who speaks when the holy scriptures are read in the Church.' This is the reason why liturgy always includes a reading of scripture: because it is 'a sacred action surpassing all others', of its nature it must include what has the strongest 'claim to efficacy.' Nothing can surpass the power of the Word-Event to effect a prayer in a person's heart. St Thomas says, that 'it produces an interior instinct compelling and moving us to believe.' This is the reason why we would never substitute the scripture readings in liturgy with another reading not from scripture.

To give a practical illustration of the power of the Word: suppose, in a liturgy of the Word, the reader proclaims this passage of St John's gospel (13:34-35):

> 'A new commandment I give to you, that you love
> one another; even as I have loved you, that you
> also love one another. By this all men will know
> that you are my disciples, if you have love for one
> another.'

That Word, proclaimed in this reading, has the power to *transform* the person who hears it into being as loving as Jesus Christ was in his life on earth, and as he is now in his glorified life. It would bring about that marvel, if it were fully accepted; or, to put it more fully, if Jesus Christ were fully accepted and his word responded to with complete submission and obedience. Our experience is that we do not accept fully: we would be scared to be as loving as Jesus; see where it got him! So much in us gets in the way: fear, independence, prejudice, willfulness, and in short, all the aspects of our sinfulness, our lack of growth. A person cannot respond beyond her or his stage of human development and maturity of faith; but corresponding to the response given, there is a transformation — not something cataclysmic, but nonetheless a growth; perhaps very faint, and still weak, yet quite real.

It is this faith in the power of the Word we profess in each celebration of the Eucharist, when in preparation for Holy Communion we pray:

'Lord, I am not worthy to receive you
but only say the word
and I shall be healed.'

Emphasis is on the 'shall': not might be healed, nor possibly, nor could be, nor anything else than *will be healed* by the word which Christ is even now speaking to us.

The response

The response comes from listening-in-faith. There is first of all *a listening*: the hearing of what is being 'said' to us by another; a listening of a type that hears another's words, and also their feelings; their needs and pleas; their offers and invitations. In the case of the proclamation of the Word in liturgy, the congregation is to hear an invitation to conversion, an offer of growth, deepening and intensifying of the Christ-life in them in its various manifestations. The offer may come in the form of an episode in the history of the Israelites, or in a piece of advice on good living; an expounding of faith, or an exhortation of trust; a parable told by Jesus, or an account of a miracle he worked. What has to be 'heard' by each is what is being proposed to him or her, what is being held out for acceptance in these different forms of offer and invitation. This listening is no different to the listening taking place when two people are wholly present to one another.

To this listening there is added *faith and trust in Jesus Christ present to each person;* for it is the Word of God: so different from the word of a man or woman. The latter can try to be helpful, for example by offering good advice whether it be on being successful in business, bringing up children, or how to take care of your skin. They instruct on what is to be done, clearly and completely; but give no further help. They say 'do,' 'you should,' 'if you follow...' — and it

is a case of 'over to you, now you are on your own!' A diet
plan promises loss of kilos and centimeters — many start it,
but few can witness to the truth of its claims, because few
persevere with it. More is needed than instruction or a device.
The Word of God is different. It does not just suggest or
instruct: it *does it* in us; it is the 'power of God' effecting
that which it promises. *The invitation carries an in-built*
power to accept. When God addresses us in his Word, we do
not have to do anything at all: just get out of the way and
cause no obstruction to it!

This response will be seen, in view of all that we have said,
as of the utmost importance. All that happens to us through
the Word is certainly by the power of Jesus Christ; yet it
does *not* happen without our acceptance, our response. The
only point in having a reading is to evoke a response in the
congregation. Hence, the congregation's response is of the
greatest consequence. What has been outlined here, namely
God offering his Word, and we invited to respond, is typical
of what goes on between us and God. God's only act in our
regard is to *give*; all we ever do, all we can do, is *receive*. We
do nothing in life but respond; everything we do is a response.

The ceremonial surrounding the proclamation of the
Word is intended to stir a better response: a special minister
for proclaiming; the proclamation performed in a special
place, at a striking piece of furnishing, the lectern; the book
of superior quality binding, the lectionary; surrounding the
proclamation with music, lights, incense. *More important*
than the proclamation of the reading is the congregation's
response. As far as the people are concerned, the Word is an
EVENT — is productive and effective — on the condition of
their response. The Word proclaimed is not a Word for them
unless they give a response. This must be what St Ignatius of
Antioch meant when he wrote to the Romans, begging them
to allow him to be martyred, and for this reason to keep
silent. He wrote: 'If you keep silent about me, I become a
Word of God; but if you love me in the flesh, I become a
meaningless cry.'

The skill of responding to the Word

Following on the explanation just given of the meaning of the Word of God and its proclamation, and the value of a person's response to the Word as a result of their listening in faith and trust, we come to the very practical question. How does a person go about making a response? What does a response sound like? What goes on inside a person who is responding?

To speak of responding to the Word as a skill may give the impression that something very unusual is expected of a person in order that they may respond. This is not so. It is very simple; but it is necessary to know what to 'do'. A specific activity is required; a distinctive procedure. Just as, for example, when we sit in conversation with a friend, a certain way of acting is expected of us, and we gladly engage in this activity in order to respond to him or her. By way of contrast, think of how different we are when sitting watching the news on T.V. We may be sitting in the same room, even in the same chair, and in the same relaxed way — but how different we are. It does not need much imagination to appreciate what our friend would feel about us if we gave her or him the same treatment as we give a TV show.

To come to the liturgical situation, and to the response to the Word, consider what happens at the Eucharist: At the beginning of the Liturgy of the Word a person, the reader, appears at the lectern; he or she reads aloud to the congregation. The congregation listens and hears, receiving the proclamation in faith and trust in this Word of God. What then? Is the listening and hearing the response? No, something more is required; a further activity.

For the sake of clarity let us leave for a moment the matter of responding to the Word, in order to consider another activity in which the people engage in liturgy: that is, being led in a prayer. When the priest reads the Opening Prayer, a certain activity is expected of the congregation: they pray this prayer in their hearts as they hear him pray it. They allow their praying to be the same prayer: they receive the same prayer. If he prays, 'Help us to know your will, Lord; and to do it with courage and faith', that is what the people pray in their hearts.

To return to responding to the Word and to the point under consideration: responding to the Word is not the same activity as responding to a leader in prayer. Supposing, for example the passage read were:

'After John's arrest, Jesus appeared in Galilee proclaiming the good news of God: "This is the time of fulfillment. The reign of God is at hand. Reform your lives and believe in the good news." ' (Mark 1:14-15)

If a response were to be made to this reading after the manner described above in regard to people responding to a prayer, it would be something in the nature of: 'Yes, indeed, Jesus did proclaim this good news; he did call us to repentance.' That would hardly have much of faith and salvation in it. What goes on in responding to the Word, is better illustrated by this situation: somebody says to me, 'Listen! the phone is ringing.' The response expected of me is not, 'Yes, how true. The phone is definitely ringing.' Rather is it expected that I will say, 'I'll answer it'; or even 'Go and answer it yourself' — or some *response* or other. I am expected to respond to, not repeat, what I hear said to me.

To express this difference in a diagram: when I am led in prayer, the leader prays 'A', and I pray 'A'.

A – A

In the activity of responding to a proclamation of the Word in a reading, the reader says 'A' — and I make my response, 'X', whatever my response is. Thus:

A – X

The Word is addressed to me now; God speaks to me as I am at this moment. I listen to hear what he is offering me. Having heard, I then proceed with the specific activity of making my response to him: my acceptance. *It is not sufficient just to hear what is said, to register the content of the message or the offer. I respond only when that Word activates me in a response to the One who is present, inviting me.*

To give a sample of what a typical response might be, we will take a reading, and look at what kind of a response we, or someone else might make to it, in the following activity.

An Example of a Response

Suppose that the reading is from chapter 4 of Acts: Peter's speech before the Sanhedrin, when he and John were arrested after curing the cripple.

'Peter, filled with the Holy Spirit, said to them, "Rulers of the people and elders, if we are being examined today, concerning a good deed done to a cripple, by what means this man has been healed, be it known to you all, and to all the people of Israel, that by the name of Jesus Christ of Nazareth, whom you crucified, whom God raised from the dead, by him this man is standing before you well. . . And there is salvation in no one else, for there is no other name under heaven given among men by which we must be saved."' (*Acts* 4:8-10,12)

The MESSAGE is the saving power of Jesus Christ. The obvious OFFER is of a deeper faith and trust in Jesus Christ.

Ask yourself:
— what specific message do I hear addressed to me?
— what do I hear God offering to me now in my actual situation at this moment?
— in view of that, what will I RESPOND?

Typical responses would be:

- 'I place my trust in Jesus Christ.'
- 'Praise and thanks to God for sending us his Son, Jesus.'
- 'Forgive me, Lord, for not trusting you in the past.'
- 'I certainly need his power in me.'

The response is basically one of faith and trust, hence it is in the form of a prayer; a short, simple and heart-felt act of repentance, petition, thanks, praise, commitment etc. There is no one response to any reading. Each person responds as the Word touches *him* or *her*, at *that* time. Every person's response is her or his own, and therefore may not be the same as someone else's. Further, a person may make one response today, and at some other time, to the same reading, an entirely different response — because he or she is different.

This is the reason why the same reading can be heard profitably again and again. If the purpose of the reading were to give us information to refresh our memories only, a familiar reading would have as much effect on us as a joke we have heard too often. Our response would be 'I know that', 'Yes, I have noted that before.' Responding to the Word is a different activity from studying scripture, which is directed to the meaning of a passage in its context and all that goes with that activity of discovery. It is also different from the activity of a scripture discussion group. Different, too from spiritual reading in the sense of 'lectio divina.' In responding we allow the reading, or something in it — maybe its total message, maybe a sentence, or even just a phrase — to evoke a response; to strike us; to stir us; to spark off something in us. The reason for different readings on different days, as also for a choice of Eucharistic Prayers in the Mass, is not to avoid boredom by offering variety, but to extend to as full as possible for us the proclamation of the measureless bounty of God's graciousness. Responding happens when, and only when, a person is touched, affected and moved by what God says. What he says in his Word is addressed to, and the response comes from, the heart — and not the head.

Let us see this in another example:

> **Another Example of a Response**
>
> This reading is from a gospel.
>
> 'Passing along the Sea of Galilee, Jesus saw Simon
> and Andrew the brother of Simon casting a net in
> the sea; for they were fishermen. And Jesus said to
> them, "Follow me and I will make you become
> fishers of men." And immediately they left their
> nets and followed him.' (*Mark* 1:16-18)
>
> -- Once again, discover the MESSAGE: using your
> mind to find ideas, insights, etc. This is 'head'-work.
>
> — Now STOP THINKING. Focus on your feelings,
> and what is in your heart in regard to Jesus Christ
> speaking to YOU in this reading.

Typical responses that could be evoked, all of them
including a feeling — resulting from being moved, stirred by
Jesus' call and offer to follow him — would be:

-- 'I am ready to follow you, Lord.' (feeling secure in Christ.)
— 'Whatever you want for me, I welcome' (feeling strong and
  trusting).
— 'I choose you, Lord; and freely leave all else' (feeling
  confident that I can).

The response comes from me, here and now. It need not
be put into words. However, to use some words, image or
other expression is a good discipline to ensure response and
prevent us being fanciful, or false, or quite mechanical. It

is a check on the incompleteness betrayed by a response such as 'Faith in Jesus Christ' (which is just an *idea*) or 'People could or should' (which is not *me* responding). It also prevents the substitution of a *resolution* in the place of a response. If, for example, I were to respond to the reading on the commandment of love with 'The next time I am with John I will be much kinder to him,' that is not a response here and now, but a resolution bearing on a future moment. If, at that future moment, God wants me to behave more kindly towards John, he will speak his Word to me *then*, for that response.

We are, of course, speaking of a response from the heart, from my centre, as developed in Chapter 5. If I find myself *reacting* to the reading, I can be sure to have moved from my centre; I am reacting from a *part of me*.

The greatest trap we can fall into is to respond with a thought, a consideration, an insight, a resolution for the future. Such are not a personal response: they are reflections, applications, some kind of association of ideas. We have coined a word to refer to such 'head responses': we call them *MIAOI* — a Merely Intellectual Association Of Ideas.

There was a familiar TV commercial for disposable razors. It presented a man in the course of shaving, being observed by a girl: very alive and very interested. Both were French, adding a certain appeal to the dialogue, which went:
She: 'You always use this razor now.'
He: 'Yes, it's very good.'
Having, with amazing rapidity completed the shave, he puts the razor down. She takes it up, and we come to the punch line — for us, that is:
She: 'It's very light.'
He: 'Yes, it's all in the head.'
All In The Head — *AITH*.
When the heart is touched and a feeling stirred, that *Feeling* experienced transforms an AITH to Faith. There is no personal faith response without some feeling. The power of the Word to enable a response therefore includes the power to feel.

In order to respond we need *time*. The Good News proclaimed can produce a heart response only if people are allowed a sufficient time of silence after the reading. Ideas come to us instantaneously; feelings do not: it takes time for them to make themselves known. It is impossible for a human being to make the type of response we have been considering in this chapter 'on the run'; it is something that 'wells up' in a person's heart. A period of silence after a reading is not a luxury; it is not an option; it is a necessity. It is worth repeating what was said earlier, namely that it is questionable if there is any value of having the reading of the Word if *time is not allowed* for a response.

The communal response

Very rich samples of personal responses to the Word of God are to be found in the Psalms. No wonder, then, that with very few exceptions, the communal response to a reading is taken from the psalms.

After our own private response, the liturgy often leads us to a communal response. For this a psalm is selected which expresses a response suitable to the reading. It may turn out to be the same response as a particular person has made; and it may well be different. The activity of the congregation is to allow their hearts to be moved to the prayer of the psalm, sharing the response with the others in the congregation, with the whole people of God, and with our Head, Jesus Christ.

This activity has as its aim to give a practical appreciation of the fact that we do nothing in life but respond.

"We do nothing in life but respond."

List some things you remember doing/saying today.	*To what was that activity of doing/saying a response (outside you or inside you)?*
1.	1.
2.	2.
3.	3.
4.	4.

The following exercise is intended to be used by a group:

Responding to a Reading: Communal Activity

This exercise may be used with any passage of scripture such as those in the Lectionary or Liturgy of the Hours.

(1) The group takes time to quieten down, to center.

(2) All read the selected passage silently, sufficient time being given to find the MESSAGE: what is it OFFERING me.

(3) A brief SHARING on what has been discovered in (2).

(4) One of the group READS ALOUD the passage; the others listen without reading it.

(5) A period of silence to seek and receive a RESPONSE.

(6) If the group wishes, they can now share this personal response.

Note: sharing of this kind depends on how close the members of the group are to one another, and how far they are prepared to wait for the Holy Spirit to give them the response. On this see Chapter 10.

10

'SEE MORE' TO RESPOND

In this chapter we come to the very core of liturgical praying; to the basic activity in liturgical participation. What that activity is, emerges from all that has been considered up to this point: the nature of liturgy as people praying, ourselves at prayer and in life, communal prayer, the prayer of the Church, and the Word of God.

There is a principle which bears on each of these, which could be stated thus:

A person's prayer depends on the person's ability to 'SEE MORE'.

Consider the matter of the last chapter; prayer in response to the Word of God proclaimed. If what I hear in the reading is nothing more to me than an incident in history, or a theological explanation of the christian faith, or an incident in the ministry of Jesus, then the reading will not move me to prayer. Only if I *see more* than that, only if I hear God speaking to me, will I respond in prayer.

If I only see bodies around me in the congregation, I will not pray a communal prayer. That prayer will happen only if I *see more*; if I see people, in whom the Holy Spirit dwells and who have assembled to pray now, with me, and I with them in Jesus Christ.

If I see the celebration — Eucharist, baptism, marriage, ordination, or the Office — as something connected with this group only, I will not pray the Prayer of the Church. To do that I must *see more* in the occasion.

If I see the act of participation as just rubrics, movements and singing, and saying prayers, I will not pray. It is necessary that I *see more* in the ceremony and rite. Similarly, I will not succeed in praying unless I *see more* in myself: see myself in the light of faith.

These are just some examples of what is at the foundation of liturgy: the ability to *see more*.

First we will give a presentation of the concept 'See More'. This will be followed by an explanation of a technique that will help to put it into practice, and then apply it to prayer as a response — a response to a symbol.

In more ways than one, the presentation of 'See More' is very special to us. We look upon it as the key to the essential, liturgical activity of responding to a symbol; it has become in our courses and work, (indeed, in our lives) without exception, *the* element, most light-giving and life-giving.

For this reason, so as to awaken the heart more than the understanding, we present it in a special way, and spoken by one person, Anneliese.

It is quiet in the room
I have asked the participants
to surrender note-paper and pens
because what I intend to do now
is simply to re-awaken what lives
in them: the ability to —

SEE MORE in order to
RESPOND more deeply

At this point I use three powerful stimulants:
— I turn on the light of the overhead projector;
— I place an ordinary bit of dry grass on the
  lit-up frame, resulting in quite a transformation
  in both: grass and onlooker;
— I read two lines from the book of Ecclesiasticus:

"HE PUT HIS OWN LIGHT IN THEIR HEARTS
TO SHOW THEM THE MAGNIFICENCE OF HIS
WORKS."

(17:18-19)

The silence in the room
becomes deeper still.
What happened when I
placed that first bit of
grass with the light?

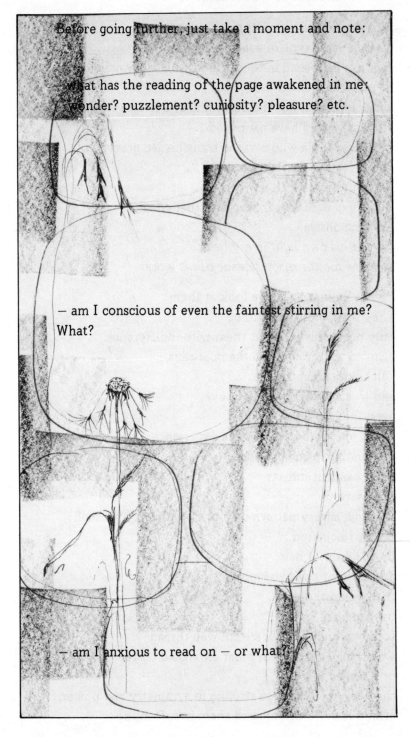

Before going further, just take a moment and note:

— what has the reading of the page awakened in me: wonder? puzzlement? curiosity? pleasure? etc.

— am I conscious of even the faintest stirring in me? What?

— am I anxious to read on — or what?

Whatever it was that happened in you
was the same type of awakening
that has happened in those who saw the dry grass on the
lit-up frame.
That, I believe, was the beginning of a heart responding.
Nothing would have happened
in those people who saw the transformed grass
had I not put the light on.
Without light
the dry grasses would have 'left them dead' —
non-responsive.
He put his own light in my heart
to show me the magnificence of his works.

Things look at us, as we look at them.
They seem indifferent to us
only because we look at them with indifference.
"But to a clear eye," so the poet says,
"all things are mirrors,
and to a sincere and serious eye,
everything is depth."
All of us would have had the experience
of standing in the presence
of a beautiful sunset;
or observed
the lazy, silvery pattern on a brick wall left by a snail;
or felt fascinated
by the drop of dew,
at the tip of a wisp of moss,
that wouldn't fall;
or wondered
for how long the delicate cobweb-thread
would play with the dry leaf entangled there;
or watched
the heavy contours, so striking in symmetry and power,
after a heavy truck created them in soft mud;

or noticed
the fragile design painted on a tarred road
by the branches of trees casting their shadows;
or stood trembling
by the awakening life in a new-born child;
or the deliberate taking of breath by someone afraid to die;
or felt accused
by the hollow eyes of a starving child;
or shocked
by the bloody mess of an accident victim;
or wanted to cry
in the presence of so much loneliness in another person.

We saw,
we noted,
but because we moved on
and did not see more
the light in our hearts could not show us more
and so, we did not respond deeply.
We saw the surface appearance
and 'responded' or better 'reacted'
from the surface.
'Seeing More' results in responding deeply.
I respond to the depth of my seeing.

I was preparing for a session at Assumption Institute. It was my intention to give each student an object which they would hold and look at. So, here I was, with my plastic bag in our beautiful garden, in search of objects. One of our older sisters saw me there, and surprised to see me with a plastic bag (only our primary school-children would be seen there with a plastic bag and for one purpose — to collect tadpoles from our lake, and *that* the sister couldn't imagine *me* doing!) She stopped me, enquiring what I was doing. "Oh," I said, "I just want to collect some objects to give to my students so that they can watch them change!" Her face showed obvious puzzlement: "What objects change as you

F

watch them?'' was her question. When I replied, "Oh, it doesn't really matter,'' her puzzlement intensified quite obviously and she just walked away. William Blake was saying what I wanted to say:

> To see a World in a grain of sand,
> And a Heaven in a wildflower,
> Hold Infinity in the palm of your hand,
> And Eternity in an hour.
>
> (*Auguries of Innocence*)

Of course, the grain of sand remains sand, the dry grass on the overhead projector remains dry grass, the stone in my hand remains a stone, but because *I* hold it. *I* look at it, *I* dwell with it, the light in my heart will show me more and awaken me to a response to much more than the surface appearance of the thing I hold or look at.

> My spirit saw directly
> through all things
> and I knew God in and
> by all creatures even
> in herbs and grass.

(Jacob Boehme, quoted by Veronica Brady, *The Mystics*)

Have you ever heard
someone (myself?) say: 'That
does nothing for me'!
That remark is
a comment, not on 'that'
but on ME.
When I find myself saying,
'This does nothing for me'
(be this a picture, or a song, or a flower, or a weed,
or a word, a symbol, a ritual, a person, etc.)
I am really saying:
my inner light
is clouded over,
my seeing is
dimmed,
dull,
grey.

The heart no longer sees, feels understands or responds.
Outside realities become only shells,
dry bones devoid of flesh and blood;
and the pulse-beat of
the inner spirit living there
cannot find echo in the world around me;
I cast the shadow of my darkness
rather than the light of
my heart.

Confirmation

Several incidents confirmed me in this outlook. They occurred during my years of teaching art in a Teacher Training College, then Christ College and now the Institute of Catholic Education, Oakleigh. I was never more assured in the particular approach I took in the teaching of art, than when the following incident occurred. At the beginning of each new year, it was the custom for the second-year students to show the new first-year students around the college. This day I was working in the preparation room which was situated between two art lecture rooms, when I overheard an older student, who was showing a new student around, saying:
'See this?' — "this" was a lovely piece of bark of a tree I kept on my lecture desk — 'See this? You might think it is just any old. . . But wait. At the end of the year *you'll see more!'* I believe that it was then that the phrase 'See More' was born for me. So thrilled was I, I could barely keep from rushing out to express my delight to the student. She would never produce a painting that would be hung, or a folio earning her the title of a good art student. Yet she had the essential quality of a true artist: the ability to respond from within — giving her a vision for 'more'. An artist never *just sees* a blade of grass, a tree, a city scene, a face or hand. Whoever she would be in life, teacher, or wife and mother; whatever she would do, she would bring to it something that would give added depth and meaning to it, for she would be capable in everything, of 'seeing more'. As a result she would never just exist; she would *live*.

Another incident occurred when I was asked to open an art exhibition. I had never even been to an opening of an art exhibition before, so I was at a loss as to what to do. I thought of enquiring about what usually happened, but thought better of it. For if I could not do it, then I would even be more stuck. So I thought I would just do it my own way. I went to view the exhibits, but as they represented the widest range — from 'chocolate box flowers' which you could almost pick off the canvas, to the 'most' in abstract — they gave me very little to help me with this fifteen minute talk I was to give at the beginning of the opening ceremony.

What could I say that would help the viewers appreciate and respond to the exhibits with greater spontaneity and feeling? Already I had formed a (not very helpful) picture in my mind of the people who would be present. I had been told that the exhibition was in a very upper-class suburb; that it was an annual affair, held for the purpose of fund raising! The picture I had, then, was of sophisticated, fur-clad matrons, walking around in a detached sort of way while sipping sherry and nibbling cheese, who, lacking the spontaneity of a child who could wander and marvel and exclaim, 'isn't it BEAUTIFUL!', would give voice to no more than perhaps an echo of whatever another felt or said: 'Isn't that nice?' 'Yes, I think so, too.' What I wanted to address myself to, was therefore, How should I be as I move around the exhibits? To raise this consciousness I told them a story. I repeat the story here because of what happened afterwards in the course of the evening, which has considerable significance.

The story is of a Chinese artist who painted a pig asleep in a sty. When the painting was finished he showed it to his friend. The friend looked at it and remarked: 'Oh, a dead pig in a sty.' Artists are used to comments like this, and so, this artist said nothing. He went back to his little pig, pulled up a stool to sit with the little pig and to try again. For hours he sat with his sketch-book, looking closely at the pig and making sketch after sketch. Having filled his sketch book, he put it away, but stayed there just looking at his little pig. He became fascinated by the little beady eyes, just half open; by the curly tail; he wondered what the hairs on the pig's skin felt like; did it 'say' something with the twitch in its nose or the gentle grunt? He found himself breathing in time with the pig's breathing. As he quietly sat and watched and wondered and imagined, having put away the sketch-book, he began to really see the pig, so much so, that it became important for him to paint again what he saw: a sleeping pig in a sty. When he showed the picture to his friend this time, the friend looked at it and exclaimed: 'Oh, a sleeping pig in a sty.'

What brought about the difference between the first canvas, showing a *dead* pig, looking like a cut-out, an outline, an empty shell, not alive; and the second showing a sleeping pig? It was the time the artist had taken to stop, to sit with his pig, to listen, to wait and to listen again, to wonder and question, to admire and to listen again. . . until all his sensibilities became more and more alive; he was more awakened, came to life more, and in turn, came to live more. Finally, it became urgent for him to let the life that had been awakened in him flow over and out on to the canvas; his life, his breath, took on form that *breathed* a *sleeping* pig.

I don't know what happened in the people who listened to that story, except for one man, who much later that evening, approached me as I was walking around the exhibition joining the others in sipping sherry and nibbling cheese. He introduced himself as an Anglican priest, and said, 'Sister, that little story you told us earlier in the evening, have you ever thought about it in relation to prayer?' (I really had not. I had used the story to stimulate art classes, but that was all.) 'We pray a lot of psalms in our church; and it came to me, that the words of a psalm, like that dead pig, can be just like so many empty shells sitting on the line: black print on a white page. I need to do what the artist did: I need to sit with them, look at them, listen to them, wonder about them, so that my seeing more with the light in my heart will bring me to live more, and my living more and breathing more will flow over and out, filling the word with breath of His Breath, life of His Life, changing the word into the Word of God, giving me an experience of God alive with me/us.'

I wish very much that I could speak to that Anglican priest and tell him of all that has happened since he spoke to me that night! His words gave even deeper meaning to a saying of Picasso, of which I had become very fond: 'If you want to know whether a painting is good, bring it to a mirror: that

mirror ought to become covered with steam.' Or when he
said: 'I paint just as I breathe.' His subjects are his loves; he
never painted an object with which he did not have an
affectionate relationship.

I know that by this time in the presentation of this material
I am running the risk of being labelled 'unrealistic,' 'a bit
airy-fairy', 'feet not on the ground'. In the past when speaking
to groups like this, I got the distinct, non-verbal, but definite
feed-back: 'Is she real?' Up to five years ago, although quite
convinced of the reality of my experience, I had no reply to
those remarks, or the courage to expose, through reflection,
what may have been underneath the comments. Now I
question what they would mean by 'real', 'real life'. If by
'real' they refer to what they experience of life on a level of
outward appearances, the shape, the form, or the face of
things, then 'reality' is the phenomena, the facts of a situation.
'You and your sitting and looking! You should be in my
situation — that's the *real* world: school all day, with pupils,
teachers and parents to deal with, insufficient funds, lack of
understanding of those in charge, impossible expectations,
meetings at night. *That's* what is real. But preparations. . .
quiet time. . . prayer. . . well?!' Reality comes to mean, then,
the limited, empirical situation, what can be measured,
controlled, and proved statistically. Artists, poets and prophets
are, therefore, considered unreal: living in an unreal world,
not at all practical, because what they do is not useful; (and
isn't utility the only value?!), doesn't bring anything in (and
isn't this what counts: what I can get out of things?!), like
the economist, the geologist, the statistician. Reality then
excludes spiritual realities: meaning, value, beauty, love,
response — these become, then, the things that are *not*
'real'!

'only with the heart. . .'

> How high the corn is this summer! What joy there
> is in seeing the tall crests nod ten and twelve feet
> above the ground, and the astounding size of the
> silk-bearded ears!. . . there through the door in the
> enclosure wall, over the little bridge, and down
> into this paradise of tall stalks and leaves and
> silence. There is a sacredness about the beauty of

tall maize and I understand how the Mayas must
have felt about them. . . How can we not love such
things?. . . The completely irreligious mind is, it
seems to me, the unreal mind, the tense, void,
abstracted mind, that does not even see the things
that grow out of the earth or feel glad about them:
it knows the world only through prices and figures
and statistics.

(T. Merton, *Conjecture of a Guilty Bystander*)

*'It is only with the heart that one can see rightly; what is
essential is invisible to the eye.'*

(Antoine de Saint-Exupery, *The Little Prince*)

Padovano once wrote in one of his reflection books
that the tragedy of life today lies not so much in the suffering, war, killing, violence, etc. but in the fact that there is
'so little poetry.' He certainly is not speaking about people
writing verse, but about a way of living that sees more than
the obvious; more than the so-called reality that ties us down,
hems us in, limits us, frustrates us, binds us to the earth. *That*
reality is the 'tomb-situation': the tomb which 'contained'
('limited') Jesus from Good Friday to Easter Sunday — a
temporary experience. But Jesus burst the confines of the
tomb and became free, at the same time breaking the bonds
that retain and restrain us. That liberation is the reality of
Jesus Christ. The reality of the Holy Spirit is his coming to
set us free from the earthly — to spirit-ualize us. Father Kevin
O'Shea, C.Ss.R. once wrote than when humanness is stretched
to the limits, the transcendent happens. Of course we will
experience the limitations of our various existential situations,
but that is only the start to the possibility of seeing more
and the response from our hearts — freed — and tasting that
freedom in the experience of a child of God, loved by his
Father and full of praise. Faith in that possibility living in
the heart of men and women is movingly captured in this
poem:

In the nightmare of the dark
all the dogs of Europe bark,
and the living nations wait,
each sequestered in its hate;
intellectual disgrace

stares from every human face,
and the seas of pity lie
locked and frozen in each eye.
Follow, poet, follow right
To the bottom of the night,
with your unconstraining voice
still persuade us to rejoice. . .
. . . in the deserts of the heart
Let the healing fountain start
in the prison of his days
Teach the free man how to praise.

(W.H. Auden, *In memory of W.B. Yeats*)

An image with deep meaning for me is the horizon line. I remember my father taking us for walks on a Sunday morning through forests, fields and meadows. The horizon captivated me, prompting me to say: 'Dad, can we go where the sky comes down to the meadow?' He would reply: 'Of course we can; go on, run!' Off we would go, and when we looked back at him, weary, yet no further to the goal, he would keep on saying: 'Go on, run, catch the horizon!' I know now how real was the vision he gave us. It is only when we follow into the beyond of our existence, to see the more of life, that our full life emerges as real.

A truth that Jesus taught is that our eyes and ears can be handicaps to seeing and hearing: just because we have them we *think* we are seeing and hearing.

You will listen and listen again
but not understand;
see and see again,
but not perceive,

he said, quoting Isaiah (*Matthew* 13:14).

Only a person who was not handicapped by ears and eyes can show us what it is like to see more since it is a seeing from the heart; a response from one's deepest self. The person I am referring to is Helen Keller. In *The Story of My Life* she tells of her first experience of 'seeing.'

No 'Seeing' is quite the same again

Helen Keller, who was
born blind, deaf and dumb,
writes about this incident with her teacher:

She brought me my hat,
and I knew that I was going out
into the warm sunshine.
This thought,
if a wordless sensation
may be called a thought,
made me hop and skip with pleasure.

We walked down the path
to the well-house,
attracted by the fragrance of the
honeysuckle with which it was covered.
Someone was drawing water
and my teacher placed my hand
under the spout.

As the cool stream
gushed over my hand
she spelled into the other the word w-a-t-e-r
first slowly, then rapidly,
I stood still, my whole attention fixed
upon the motion of her fingers.

Suddenly I felt a misty consciousness
as of something forgotten —
a thrill of returning thought;
and somehow the mystery of language
was revealed to me.
I knew then that w-a-t-e-r meant
the wonderful cool something that
was flowing over my hand.

That living word awakened my soul,
gave it light, hope, joy,
set it free!
There were barriers still, it is true,
but barriers
that in time could be swept away.

I left the well-house eager to learn.
Everything had a name,
and each name gave birth
to a new thought.

As we returned to the house
every object which I touched

seemed to quiver with life
that was because
*I SAW EVERYTHING WITH THE STRANGE NEW SIGHT
THAT HAD COME TO ME.*

   (Helen Keller, *The Story of My Life*)

   And only one like Helen Keller can pass this comment on
those of us who fail to see:

BLIND

I have walked with people
whose eyes are full of light
but who see nothing in sea or sky,
nothing in city streets,
nothing in books.

It were far better to sail for ever
in a night of blindness. . .
than to be content
with the mere act of seeing.

The only lightless dark
is the night of darkness
in ignorance and insensibility.

   (Helen Keller)

   When making this presentation of 'See More', I invariably
stop speaking at this point, and invite the group to either sit
or walk outside for some time in order to 'hear' and 'see'. . .
MORE.

   *We make use of the opening verses of the First Letter of
St John to deepen our appreciation of the MORE in our
lives. . .in us.*

'That which was from the beginning,
which we have heard,
which we have seen with our eyes,
which we have looked upon
and touched with our hands,
concerning the word of life —
the life was made manifest,
and we saw it, and testify to it,
and proclaimed to you
the eternal life
which was with the Father and was made manifest
to us. . .'

•   •   •   •   •

During your reading about 'See More', your heart
may have been stirred at some point or other, in
some way or other. Return to that point and listen
to the 'More' awaiting you there: to be seen, and
heard, touched and received.

Framing

To 'see more' is a skill; hence it would be useful to have some help to develop it. We now introduce a technique that may help a person to 'see more.'

A — 'Stay in the Frame'

Sit in front of a framed picture.

Look at the picture, and keep looking at it for three to five minutes, careful to stay within the frame.

• • • •

At the end of that time, make a list of the things you found you had to do *in order to stay within the frame.*

1.   6.

2.   7.

3.   8.

4.   9.

5.   10.

People with whom we have done this activity have given us the following feed-back. You may like to check out your list with this one:

I had to concentrate
I needed to keep attentive
I looked at the detail of the picture
I wondered about what happened. . . what feelings. . .
I made up a story
I dwelled on how like me it is
I allowed it to move me to feelings of sadness/joy
I thought of a time something happened to me
I felt like doing something
I remembered things associated with it

B — 'Come back into the Frame'

Did you move out of the frame?
Did you allow yourself to be distracted by wandering
away from it?

If so, what did you do to bring yourself back to the
picture in the frame?

There is only one way you would have come back to the
frame:

Become conscious that you had left it.
and choose to return to it.

Note, that to dwell on thoughts, or feelings it awakened in
you is not leaving the frame. Rather is it 'going in' deeper
into it; allowing yourself to be taken *into* the picture, and
further than the picture, to allow yourself to 'see more'.

You may have looked cursorily at that picture many times;
glanced at it in passing, and even passed some remark, like,
'Isn't her face very sad?' 'Aren't the colours very alive!' You

had much more to think about, and feel about it – and remarked about it if you had chosen to – when you stayed looking at the picture. These depths were awakened in you only because you were asked to stay with the picture for some minutes. Because you did stay with the picture, it drew you *in,* and took you to deeper levels of *yourself.*

The technique we make use of here is to 'frame' the picture. It is only a technique, but in the experience of many people, a very helpful one: we put a *frame* (mental or actual) around what we wish to see more about. The frame will *hold* us in, lock us on to, fix our focus. The result will be that we move from one level of ourselves to a *deeper level.*

– First we just register the existence of something;
merely note the fact; this is only a *superficial 'response'.*
Strictly speaking it is not even a response but only a *reaction.*

– Through staying, we become *more present* to it; more consciously aware of it. We are present, and we respond, perhaps just with a thought at first.

– Continuing in presence will result in *feelings* being stirred; so that our body becomes involved as we externalize them in face or movement or sound.

At this point it would be of great help to engage in some 'framing activities'. Here are some suggestions:

A.

Select some ordinary object in daily use.

Mentally place it in a frame.

Fasten your gaze on it; see details:

> compare
> remember
> associate
> etc.

Let it flow as it wants to.

A FLOWER	AN ORNAMENT

A SECTION OF CARPET	YOUR HAND

B.

Frame something that has 'memories', something of 'sentimental value' for you:

In addition to what you did in the last activity, be watchful for any slight movement of feeling or emotion, e.g. a little elation, surprise, amusement, nostalgia; or the more basic feelings of joy, sadness.

AN EVENT	A PERSON

A PHOTOGRAPH	A GIFT

A Slice of Life

We will now take an event in a person's life and frame it in order to see what happens when a person stays with it, sees more, and is led through it to a deeper level of self — a level where he or she can respond deeply. The person is Martin Luther King. The event is:

But now I am afraid

One night, towards the end of January
I settled into bed late, after a strenuous day.
Correta had already fallen asleep and just as I was about
to doze off, the telephone rang.

A An angry voice said:
"Listen Nigger, we've taken all we want from you;
before next week you'll be sorry you ever came to
Montgomery."

B I hung up, but I couldn't sleep.
It seemed that all of my fears had come down on me at
once.
I had reached the saturation point.

I got out of bed and began to walk the floor,
Finally I went to the kitchen,
C and heated a pot of coffee.
I was ready to give up.
With my cup of coffee sitting untouched before me
I tried to think of a way to move out of the picture
D without appearing a coward.

In this state of exhaustion,
E when my courage had all but gone,
I decided to take my problem to God.
With my head in my hands, I bowed
over the kitchen table and prayed aloud.

F The words I spoke to God that midnight
are still very vivid in my memory:

"I am here taking a stand
for what I believe is right.

But now I am afraid.
The people are looking to me for leadership,
and if I stand before them
G   without strength and courage
they too will falter.
I am at the end of my powers.
I have nothing left. I've come to the point
where I can't face it alone."

At that moment I experienced the presence
H   of the Divine
as I had never experienced Him before.
          (Martin Luther King, *Stride Towards Freedom*)

● ● ● ●

We FRAME an event
in order to SEE and SEE MORE
so as to RESPOND –
    to identify the response
    made in the heart:
GIVEN in the heart as Martin Luther King dies to himself
and NEW LIFE is born in him.

The event in the life of Martin Luther King paints a
picture of a heart opening: opening so that prayer-response
can happen.

    'Prayer happens when the heart is open.'

Let us look more closely at the account he gives of his
experience, to appreciate what happened in him.

A   Martin Luther King as he is in this situation:
the facts, circumstances, what happened.

B   He reacts.
He is affected in his body; he cannot sleep.
His emotional life is awakened: 'all of my fears'.

C   He begins to 'see more' — 'saturation point'.
     He loses control: leaves bed, begins to walk.
       (he leaves more than bed; he wants to walk away
         from the situation)
     heats coffee — does not want it
     An urge to DO.
     HE THINKS — at this level: solve the PROBLEM.

D   What he wishes is 'to move out of the picture' —
     to move out of the frame.

E   He becomes aware of HOW HE IS:
     exhausted in body; fear taking over; courage waning.
     Humanness stretched to the limits.

F   He remembers the 'MORE'
     He surrenders; abandoning, helpless, lost, needy, poor,
     dying to self.
     He bowed.
     The confident, broad, firm, straight back and shoulders
     now curve, bend, soften, give way:
     a gesture of weakness, all firmness gone, yielding,
     pliable.
     He owns, and names, 'how he is'.
     Prior to this he was feeling it all right;
     now he admits it, confesses it
     to another — to God

G   What he prays — coming from 'where he is'
     is a summary of how he feels at that moment.
     Not so much a prayer, as a recital of his psychological
     state which he addresses to God.
     He needs to say to himself how things are.

H   He surrenders his central position,
     Moves out of the centre of the situation,
     creates space
     emptiness
     'the tomb'
     and he can LISTEN and RECEIVE
     THE RESPONSE FROM THE HOLY SPIRIT.

He is CHANGED: a tangible experience
of God-with-him, and with it all God offers.

He feels peace
 strength
 confidence
No problem is solved for him;
now it is no longer a problem!
The result of his 'seeing more' is that he now sees
'with his heart'

The form in which the transformed Martin Luther King
will appear before others has not yet appeared. It will —
as we know from his life after this night.

*   *   *

This event, represented in a diagram, shows the process in
which Martin Luther King, from the phone call to his RE-
SPONSE, passed from a reaction, through 'seeing more',
to a RESPONSE-RECEIVED.

The phone call can be considered as the 'seed event'. The
RESPONSE comes through 'SEEING MORE' in it.

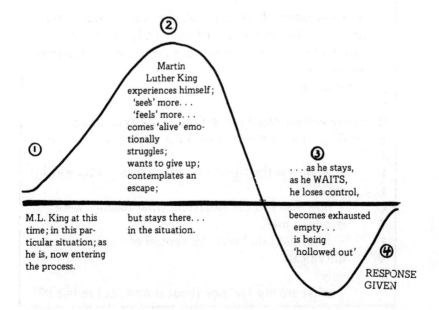

The following activities will give you some practice in framing-responding. The first is suitable for a person working alone; the second for a group.

A   **For use alone**

As you read through Martin Luther King sharing an experience from his life, you may have remembered an experience of your own which had some impact on your life too.

You can go through the same process as he did — and *respond anew* — by going through the following activity:

• Center yourself: relax physically; ask yourself, how am I now? Become aware of your body-sensations, your feelings, your desires, your mental preoccupations, images etc.
Let these go.

R • Deliberately recall the details of the experience.
E Dwell on it with the help of some of these questions:
F
L   — what was the situation? where was I? who was I
E   with?
C   — how was I in the situation; what feelings were
T   strong in me?
I   — what did I do? was this typical of me or
V   untypical?
E   why?
       — what are my feelings about it now, as I re-live it?

• Let your thoughts, memories, associations etc. run for 10-15 minutes.

Note the PROCESS you have just gone through. It might help you to write it down.

In it all you have been the INITIATOR: *you* were doing it.

The process changes; to enter into it —

• CENTER again

• LISTEN — JUST LISTEN — to hear what is presented to you from deep within you.
give it time: 10-15 minutes.

Be a RECEIVING LISTENER.

R
E *Again, note the PROCESS.*
C Write down what happened in this receptive
E stage.
P
T *To complete this activity and to deepen the experience*
I *now go on to reflect on the whole experience;*
V
E What did you experience as you progressed from centering. . . to reflection. . . letting go. . . receiving.

What comments have you to make? what questions to ask?
Keep a record of this for the next activity.

B   **For use in a group**

In a group of four to six, prepare to go through a process — the same as Martin Luther King in the experience he shared — of framing to 'see more' to respond. The 'seed object' is a SHOE a real, or imagined, one.

R • Individually, center: that is do what you normally
E   do to bring yourself to quiet.
F • Ask questions about the shoe: when? where? why?
L   who? what? Recall memories, associations etc.
E
C   Let your thoughts go on for 10-15 minutes.
T   Remember, at this stage you are the INITIATOR.
I
V   *Note the process* (individually).
E Talk to the others about the process you went
        through.
        Exchange your experience with them.
        Prepare for the next stage:

R • Center again.
E • LISTEN - to hear what is surfacing in you from
C   within you.
E   Give it time: 10-15 minutes.
P   This time you are a RECEIVING LISTENER.
T
I   *To complete this activity and to deepen the experience*
V   *now go on to relfect on the whole experience.*
E
        Note the process that went on in you
        (individually).
        Reflect on the experience especially as you pro-
        gressed from centering. . . to reflection. . . to
        letting go. . . to waiting. . . to receiving.

        Exchange your experience with the others.

        For the purpose of the next activity record your
        reflections in writing.

The Process of Responding

At the conclusion of the activity on framing-responding at the end of the last section, whether done alone (p. 172), or in a group (p. 174), it was indicated that it was necessary to note in writing what you experienced. This section will be a comment on the progression through the various stages of the Process of Responding.

We would like to make two points to preface this treatment of the process involved in responding. First, we are speaking about a response, *not a reaction*. That, as explained in Chapter 5, is what happens when I am not in my centre, and hence acting out of a part of me — a bodily sensation, a strong emotion, or a thought. Neither are we concerned with the intellectual — and ideas-response through association — mentioned in the last chapter.

Secondly, it is necessary to analyze the process in order to understand it. In actual responding it is not necessary to be conscious of all that is happening. There are some distinct consecutive steps or stages, however, and when I am aware of them I am in a position to facilitate movement, make choices, and whatever else is called for (as in the activities at the end of the previous section.)

We will use as our starting-point either of these two activities, and ask you to continue it (or them). What you will do in the activities which follow will enable you to see more clearly, and in greater detail, what would have taken place when you were doing them.

What follows here is based on the experience of our past groups. The process as explained here grew out of their comments, their questioning, their difficulties and their successes as they struggled — to learn to respond.

Now take up your record of your reflections on the activity A or B.

What did the activity say to you about the 'skill' of responding?

In particular, what qualities (characteristics, elements, ingredients) were part of your coming to a response?

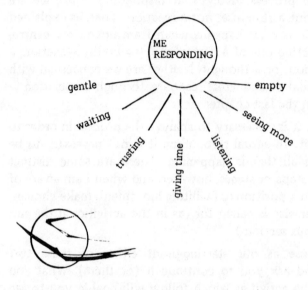

Look carefully at the diagram and write down what comments you have to make in view of your own experience in RESPONDING.

Look at your own list. Were there some active words in it, that is, indicating that you took the initiative? These are not really RESPONDING words —

Not responding

take time
effort
remember
associate
DO it!
perseverance
TRY HARD

but rather

listening
quiet
patience
openness
trust
let it speak
accepting
receiving

While you are saying such things as —

> . . . then I thought. . .
> . . . then I became aware. . .
> . . . then I realized. . .
> . . . then I found. . .
> . . . then I looked at. . .
> . . . then I made myself. . .

YOU ARE NOT REALLY RESPONDING!!!

RESPONDING IS WAITING TO BE GIVEN

Ask yourself now, What am I like in a *waiting state?*

This activity could bring you closer to an awareness of yourself as a waiting empty person.

'E M P T Y'

RESPONDING
happens when you *listen*
and *wait* to
receive the RESPONSE.

> To *receive*
> I have first to be empty;
> To *receive*
> I have to be open.

The Master Nan-In had a visitor who came to
enquire about Zen.
But instead of listening, the visitor kept talking
about his own ideas. After a while, Nan-In served
tea. He poured tea into his visitor's cup until it was
full, then kept pouring.
Finally the visitor could stand it no longer.
'Don't you see it's full;' he said,
'You can't get any more in!'
'Just so,' replied Nan-In, stopping at last,
'And like this cup, you are filled with your own
ideas.
How can you expect me to give you Zen,
unless you offer me an empty cup?'

> — What do I feel like on those occasions when
> I am like the young man, wanting to TALK?
> — What do I have to let go of in order to be as
> Nan-In wanted him to be?
> — How do I feel when I am empty — waiting
> to hear?

REFLECT on images of 'EMPTY':
for example
— an *open* sea shell;

— a cup from which I have drunk tea or coffee. Is
it really empty when I finish drinking?
— my hands: how do I hold them to *receive*? What
is in them then?
> (How do I hold them to give?)

What is an image of yourself
— talking and not listening?
— waiting and listening?

Observable stages in responding

STAGE 1

I enter into the process — as I am, at this time;
with what is going on around me and in me:
my feelings, whatever they are,
body sensations,
preoccupations,
desires, or lack of them,
motivation, or lack of it.
I deliberately focus on what I am experiencing to
raise my consciousness and to
be able to direct my focus.
Thus:

ME entering the process

STAGE 2

As I stay with myself and focus on the particular person, object, event, or whatever is calling
for a response at that time, I begin to accumulate
to gather a 'treasury':
facts, insights, associations, comparisons,
memories, details, awarenesses;
new feelings, thoughts, desires, body sensations.

I am pretty 'busy' reflecting.
I let it all come. . . even stay with it for a while;
listen to it.
When it feels right, I let go. . .
a feeling of acceptance of myself here and now
makes me feel calmer, quieter inside, thus:

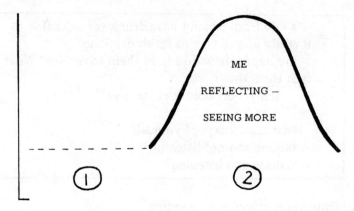

ME

REFLECTING –

SEEING MORE

STAGE 3

At a certain moment, it feels right to discontinue reflecting.
I make a deliberate choice to do this.
I STOP all thinking activity,
so that I will be able to hear from a deeper level of myself.
I GIVE TIME to 'aimless waiting,'
thus:

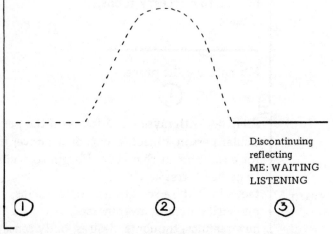

Discontinuing
reflecting
ME: WAITING
LISTENING

A quiet surrounds me – it is in me – I seem to have surrendered the central position; my body feels relaxed and my feelings are no longer tugging at me for attention.
I sense 'more' about me, giving me a feeling of new

STAGE 4   life, renewed confidence and trust; that which
seemed to 'tie me to the earth' has given way to
the free movement of the Spirit in me, enabling me
to see anew — hear anew — respond anew: from
my heart,
thus:

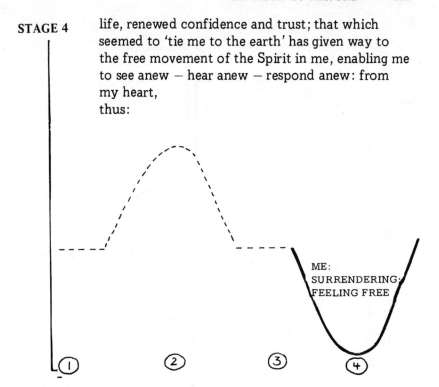

ME:
SURRENDERING:
FEELING FREE

Illustrations:

In the Liturgy of the Word, we RESPOND to the minister
proclaiming the reading. If we were to look at it closely we
could identify several stages:

    STAGE 1. I take ME (present) to the Word.
    STAGE 2. I FRAME what I hear: SEE MORE in it.
    STAGE 3. I WAIT — LISTEN — BECOME EMPTY.
    STAGE 4. A RESPONSE STIRS IN MY HEART.

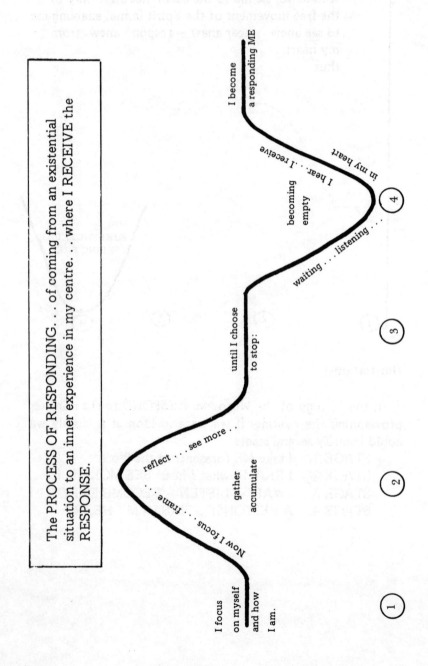

The PROCESS OF RESPONDING. . . of coming from an existential situation to an inner experience in my centre. . . where I RECEIVE the RESPONSE.

I focus on myself and how I am.

Now I focus . . . frame . . .

reflect . . . see more . . .

gather accumulate

until I choose to stop:

waiting . . . listening . . .

becoming empty

I hear. . . I receive

in my heart

I become a responding ME

1   2   3   4

STAGE 1. Being 'wholly present' is the content of Chapter 5, and all that is said there is relevant to, and required in, the Process of Responding.

STAGE 2: The Reflecting Stage — Framing, Seeing More — is like the rocket that puts a space module into orbit: as soon as the module is in orbit, the rocket is jettisoned. So, we do not need to go on too long with the reflection.

The stage, however, cannot be omitted: we cannot go immediately to waiting and listening. We just could not manage that. We have a need to be in control; we feel an urgency to 'DO' first. We are 'ego-centered' and that state requires that 'we' work at it first. We would not have the security to 'let go' otherwise.

STAGES 3 and 4. This is a stage we may cross and re-cross several times. Impatient in our waiting to get results, we go back to our 'doing'.

While here we are in *tension*: between *doing* and *stopping*, between being *active* and *letting go*.

Since this tension-experience is a very common experience, we will share here the experience of a person in tension, and how he, *through* tension is led to a response. This experience of tension is the experience of Eugen Herrigal, a German philosopher who went to Japan and took up the practice of archery toward an acquiring of Zen mysticism; for he was told that it was hopeless for a European to attempt to penetrate into this realm of the spiritual life unless he began by learning one of the Japanese arts associated with Zen. His wife chose flower arrangement and painting, while the art of archery seemed more suitable for him — on the completely erroneous assumption that his experiences of rifle and pistol shooting would be to his advantage. By archery the Japanese does not understand a sport, but a religious ritual. Consequently by the 'art' of archery is understood an ability whose origins is to be sought in spiritual exercises: it is a contest of the archer with himself.

Before he ever shot an arrow, he spent a year learning just to draw and release the bow 'spiritually" At the end of four years, he had not yet acquired the art of 'loosing' an arrow 'spiritually.' That absence of success was in spite of diligent and conscientious practice. He tells of some of the conversations and exchanges between the Master and himself. Some of these are very enlightening – and consoling – in our efforts to 'let go.'

'The right shot does not come because you do not let go of yourself. You do not wait for fulfilment, but brace yourself for failure.'

'What stands in your way is that you have a much too wilful will. You think that what you do not do yourself does not happen.'

'What must I do, then?'

'You must learn to wait properly.'

The following is a beautiful illustration from nature of how to be 'in tension.'

'Stop thinking about the shot.' the Master called out, 'that way it is bound to fail.'

'I can't help it,' I answered, 'the tension gets too painful.'

'You only feel it because you haven't really let go of yourself. It is all so simple. You can learn from an ordinary bamboo leaf what ought to happen. It bends lower and lower under the weight of snow. Suddenly the snow slips to the ground without the leaf having stirred. Stay like that at the point of highest tension until the shot falls from you. So, indeed it is: When the tension is fulfilled, the shot *must* fall, it must fall from the archer like snow from a bamboo leaf, before he even thinks of it.'

Then, not accepting the true situation, but blaming some-one else for failure, and thinking up a manageable way – 'I can do it,' 'I know better' – he came to the conclusion that the fault could not be in lack of purposelessness and egoless-ness, but in the very *physical fact that the fingers of the right hand gripped the thumb too tightly*. He devised and practised a technique which had 'beguiling affinity with the technique of rifle shooting,' but which had the unexpected result that the Master, discovering that he tried to cheat, discontinued the lessons. Eventually, through the intercession of an inter-mediary, the Master agreed to resume the lessons – on condition that he begin again – after four years – at the very beginning.

Weeks went by without his advancing a step. Only once did the Master refer to his deceit, when he said quietly, 'You see what comes of not being able to wait without purpose in the state of highest tension. You cannot even learn to do this without continually asking yourself, "Shall I be able to manage it?" Wait patiently, and see what comes – and how it comes.' (This puts the finger on some of the causes of the tension we experience ourselves in Stage 3.)

The pupil learned of the 'movement by a power beyond' in this exchange, when he felt it was impossible to get out of the rut. One day he asked the Master, 'How can the shot be loosed if "I" do not do it?'

' "It" shoots', he replied.

'I have heard you say that several times before, so let me put it in another way: How can I wait self-oblivious for the shot if "I" am no longer there?'

' "It" waits at the highest tension.'

'And who or what is this "It"?'

'Once you have understood that you will have no further need of me. And if I tried to give you a clue at the cost of your own experience, I should be the worst of teachers and should deserve to be sacked! So, let's stop talking about it and go on practising.'

Then came the conversion point. He discovered that failure did not disturb him in the least. 'Whether I learned the art or not, whether I experienced what the Master meant by 'It' or not, whether I found the way to Zen or not – all of this seemed to have become so remote, so indifferent, that it no longer troubled me. . .'

Then – success! One day, after a shot, the Master made a deep bow and broke off the lesson. 'Just then "It" shot!' he cried. 'I stared at him bewildered. And when at last I understood what he meant I couldn't suppress a sudden whoop of delight.'

'What I have said,' the Master told him severely, 'was not praise, only a statement that ought not to touch you. Nor

G

was my bow meant for you, for you are entirely innocent of the shot. You remained this time absolutely self-oblivious and without purpose in the highest tension, so that the shot fell from you like a ripe fruit. Now go on practising as if nothing had happened.'

One final word of encouragement for us all in this explanation of why we have to fumble and fall before we learn: the words of a Japanese friend of Eugen Herrigal —

You had to suffer shipwreck through your own efforts before you were ready to seize the lifebelt he threw you.

That comment made to the German philospher during his baffling task of learning to 'let go of himself,' is well worth keeping in mind in these exercises in responding, and responding activities of any type in which you may engage.

We have completed our presentation of 'see more' — framing-responding. You can now test its validity by holding it up to your own experience. We suggest the following activity

Your Experience of Responding

Go back to a recent prayer-time in which you experienced yourself receiving a prayer-response. Look at yourself and ask:

— What was I like as I started? What was going on inside me?

— What was I doing before it? Anything special about me at that time?

How was my body, feelings, desires, mind?

— What did I do with myself to bring myself to quiet?

Any particular difficulties? What was my quietness like?

— What did I focus on? What held my attention?

As I stayed with my experience what happened?

What was I doing as a reflective/doing person?

— What prompted me to discontinue reflecting?

— What was I like as a waiting/listening person?

Did I experience tension in the waiting?

How did I handle myself then?

— What was it like receiving the response?

An Experience in Responding

We include here a 'see more to respond' activity made by a religious sister, who is skilled in this practice, during a period away from her own community. As will be clear, the 'seed event' was Mass at the beginning of Church Unity Octave.

One morning, at the beginning of the Eucharist the celebrant began with the words:
'Got a letter from the Arch — says something about Christian Unity — I didn't read it at all — went into my waste-paper basket — like most letters coming from there. . . So, Christian Unity Week!
What does it mean? A few ecumenical meetings a year? Possibly an ecumenical service once a year? Why bother? Well, I don't bother. . . should I bother? I don't think so!'

By this time, everything inside me was reacting: How could he talk so glibly! So lightheartedly! After all, it's THE issue! I remembered all the people in Melbourne who slave their hearts out working for Christian Unity! There is Kevin and Cath and Robert. . . If there is anything we are sure of it's this call for Unity!. . . How can he say 'Should I bother?' That's what Christ's call is all about! That's why he became man — died, rose. . .

Mass went on: 'I confess. . .' but I didn't; I lost him; I lost connection with the people with me; I felt angry and more than ever upset with him: something in him just gets to me. . . he seems so sure; so absolute; so full of himself. . .

The Liturgy of the Word tried to call me back. . . I heard the Alleluia sung, but I didn't hear the call. I couldn't come. . I had 'walked out' — not actually, I wouldn't have been game enough, but in my heart I had said: NO!
'No' to him; to what he was doing, saying; to all that was beyond, underneath all that he was saying and doing;
'No' to the people there;
'No' to the responsibility I had for them to help them in their praying;
'No', to all, except to me. . .
and that precisely stopped me from saying 'Yes'.
'Yes' to the MORE that was hidden even in this situation.

Mass had ended. . . I left — physically — as I came; nothing had happened — could happen — because I was closed. And yet, on another level, a lot had happened. Although Christ's offer to join him in his response to the Father was there — his call to re-commitment in praise and thanks to all of my life was given — nothing could happen to *me*. . . I — my angry self — was in the way.

At personal prayer-time the next day: Here I am, still mad with him and what he is not; unable still to confess to what was not in me, or rather to what *was* in me!

Why does he get to me like this — so sure; so full of himself — so absolute? Am I casting my shadow on him? Is that how *I* am? 'THE ISSUE!' I said. That's an absolute. What was I defending? What was it *in* me that felt attacked — was weak and needed to be protected?

Exposed to my own weakness and fragility,
I sat and listened —
an avalanche of inner turmoil surfaced —
I felt bombarded
I wanted to run
restless and tense —
but I stayed. . .
Gradually, very gradually, I could look all these 'things' in the face and I encouraged them to confront me.

More quiet came over me as I owned this reality in me very gradually, as I managed to disidentify a quiet came over me, an image surfaced on my mind: a square; the square that framed all our communities in Australia (in a recent letter I had received). I had looked at this square on the transfer list the day before; didn't like them all to be in a *square*.

Wouldn't a circle be better?
Wholeness — unity — etc., etc. . .
I listened and waited —
No, not a circle around *all*
until, each *one* can have a circle for herself.

Yes, that's right: We are *all*, everyone of us:
potential wholeness!

A new call came to me: this unity week:
to see with new eyes: eyes purified in my own confession of
my lack of unity within me,
each one of my sisters.
Daily for the rest of the week,
during prayer-time, I listened:
to each of their lives
as I experienced them
as I hoped for them
as I believed in the 'More' about each of them.
Yes, there was potential wholeness in each of them.
I drew the circle
and waited to be given the image of their 'wholeness'.
A wonderful experience of:
light and darkness
colour and shade
line and shape
as a symbol emerged for each one of them — my own, too,
with them, born from my relationship with each one of
them.

I felt a closeness, a unity with each one of them,
especially in our incompleteness;
I felt a new call to each of them
not without a sense of regret for what I had
prevented from coming to more wholeness,
because I did not 'SEE MORE.'

And how was I? I felt 'sobered',
brought low through the experience,
more ready to pray at the Eucharist: 'I confess. . .'
more ready to be raised again
by that inner power, that hidden strength, that Self,
that now had 'room' to move; to 'be at work.'
I felt the reality of Unity Week in my own heart,
a connectedness in me, a presence to me and to *all* of it —
to my sisters in the various communities, to Pat next door;
to Father X,
to OUR Father, who is desiring this unity
for me and all his people
and *will* bring it about through Christ, his Son, living in me.

11

THE EXPERIENCE
OF RESPONDING

What we *feel* in liturgy, in contrast to what we *see* in liturgy, is a distinction we have already used in order to point to our emphasis and approach to liturgy in this book. It was stated in this form in order to draw attention to our primary concern: not with 'what we see in liturgy', that is the ceremony, which is the Text and Rite as ministered to the congregation; but with the PEOPLE and what goes on in them — their *experience*: 'what we *feel* in liturgy.'

Everyone at Mass on Sunday, or any celebration of liturgy, is having an experience — of some kind or other. They may be aware of it or completely unconscious of it; it may be quite deep and strong or hardly detectable. The experience may be one of spiritual feelings, uplifting and supportive; or it may be of guilt or anger, or frustration, irritation or impatience. By the fact that they are alive and human, people are affected — unless they suffer from some mental illness — by stimulus events (what goes on outside them) and their own sensations and internal events (what goes on inside them). In a word, they have an experience — which, however, may or may not be the experience which is intended. The Text and Rite of liturgy is designed, planned and ministered in order to give a very definite and specific experience. In point of fact, it is this specific experience which is not just the aim of the rite, but is the *source and origin* of it: the experience of our People gave rise to, and is 'contained' in, this rite (see Chapter 7, 'The Prayer of the Church'). Hence the connection between the experience (what we feel) and the rite (what we see).

The purpose of 'seeing more', of using the technique of framing, and of going through the process of responding is to make this connection. The response is the experience: the authentic experience which is a share in the prayer-experience of our People — a share in the experience of Jesus Christ. This experience is, to borrow the words of William James in his *Varieties of Religious Experience:* 'the most important biological function of mankind'; or as it has been considered in Chapter 5, 'the sacred action surpassing all others.' It is experienced when we respond to the rite: not any response, but to the rite as the *symbol* it is.

The experience has specific characteristics and several elements to it. In this chapter we will first deal with these characteristics and elements; then we will consider the function of the rite-symbol in the experience. But before going any further, let us give this specific, authentic, response-experience a name: we will call it the *liturgical experience*.

Before considering the 'liturgical experience', it would be helpful to have as good an appreciation as possible of 'experience.' The word is used a lot: 'What an experience that was!' we say; or, 'I didn't experience a thing'; 'Meeting God in my experience' is an often-used expression; the advice is given to us to ' "stay with" your experience'; and prayer is spoken of as a 'prayer-experience.' What is the word 'experience' meant to express in these phrases? The following activities will give an understanding of 'experience' *through* experience.

EXPERIENCE I

Select, and perform, ONE of the following
activities:

* Sit quietly and listen to your breathing for five
  minutes.
* Fill an empty page with question marks.
* Sit in a chair facing an *empty* chair.
* Walk in the garden — or round your room — and
  touch *everything* you see.
* Sit in front of an unlit candle.
* Very deliberately, and with full attention, peel
  and eat an orange.

In the above activity there were two necessary 'ingredients':
— there was the 'outside' stimulus (that is, whatever activity
you chose to do);
— this stimulus 'did' things *in you*:
it stirred something in you; awakened parts of you: and that
on three levels — body, feelings and mind, as explained in
Chapter 5. To get in touch with the experience you have to
tap into your body, feelings, mind.

You might find it helpful to do this now:

EXPERIENCE II

'I know that I have experienced something —
because I was *affected*'

Ask yourself:
  How was I affected? Did I have an immediate,
lively response in the activity? Or what?
  How was my body during the activity? What
particular sensations were felt by me?
  What was I feeling: before I began? As the
activity went on? After it was completed?
  What was going on in my mind in the course
of the activity: what did I think about what I was
doing? Any memories? Any associations?
  Was there anything else for me in the experience? Anything still stirring inside me?

Being affected on those three levels is being involved. We do
not have an experience, we cannot even talk about an experience, if we are not involved. For example, I notice a
car-accident; I am aware of it, and I drive on. . . It is not an
experience for me. But if I stopped and stayed, and took in
all the details and consequences. . . a whole lot of things
would begin to happen inside me. . . I would be affected by
it. . . involved in it. *An experience involves me as consciously
aware* of, and present to, what is happening.

  Further, I could go back on the experience at a later time.
I am not there, some of the details may be forgotten by me. .
l + the effect of it is still with me. An experience happens

deeper down than on the level of the external stimulus. Someone hurt me in the past, for example, a person no longer in my life; yet I am still affected by that hurt, to the extent that it is still part of me; sometimes it feels that it is more than part of me; it is so big that it can almost take over and control me. *An experience involves us, affects us, changes us and all this happens on a deeper level.*

In *The Book of Sacramental Basics*, Tad Guzie, writing on festivity and story, in 'The rhythm that makes life human', notes the difference between what he calls a 'raw' experience and a 'lived' experience. The difference is between the insignificant event and the significant one, a difference consisting in 'an awareness that the experience does touch the quality of my life'. We think it would be saying the same thing to say that the 'lived' experience evokes a real response in me: brings me alive in response. Any alive response or reaction in the course of a liturgical celebration, be it of amusement or annoyance, is an experience. It may not, however, be a liturgical experience.

The Liturgical Experience

Depth of feeling

A celebration of liturgy will, if it is a liturgical experience, be of some significance and of sufficient depth to stir feelings noticeably — just as in the case of the experiences dealt with above.

The ceremony is the stimulus; the experience is the person's *response*. The response will be an experience only if it has those qualities discussed in Chapter 5, where, in connection with Beginning to Pray, it was seen how the status of liturgical prayer as 'most', the 'prayer surpassing all others', required the conscious awarenss of a person who is wholly present, so that I can receive the prayer in my heart: not a part of me acting (or reacting), but ME responding from my centre.

It is necessary to insist on this *depth* of response required; for there are different levels of 'response' — or what passes for response but in reality hardly qualifies, and is no more than a reaction. The difference is how a person is *affected*. It is not necessary that he or she is aware of being affected, or how; just that it sparks a significant response. Let us consider, by way of illustration what goes on between people in conversation. Many conversations — probably most — take place without the people being aware of what is going on inside them: their responses/reactions here and now to what they hear, which now cause them to bring up different topics, pieces of information, jokes. On the surface they are just passing the time having a chat, but the topics are (unconsciously) chosen, and the content of the conversation, are all connected with a feeling. What they say to one another, their reason for wanting to tell of one thing more than another, is their feeling about it. When somebody says, 'I *must* tell you about such-and-such,' for that person the way she or he *feels* about such-and-such is more significant than the facts about it. The prices on the Stock Exchange, times of plane flights, the weight of a piece of meat, and such like may be announced without any feeling accompanying the information. The information may be heard and received without any feelings being aroused. This is a rarity; only automatic, mechanical actions and reactions are devoid of feeling. Feeling may not be noticed, but it is seldom absent.

Different levels of response come from different levels of living. We ask you to read these two examples of conversation, in order to deepen appreciation of different *levels of response and feeling:*

'The Echo'

Many are the strange and marvellous methods used by animal species to greet their fellow creatures.

But none quite so bizzare as that of the species homo sapiens.

Rife with tradition and curious custom, the means we humans use of hailing our friends and associates is a tribal rite rivalling anything from the jungle villages.

To start with there is the Echo.

This is performed by two humans passing each other, both of whom use unanswered questions, thus. . .

Fred: How are ya?

Joe: How are ya?

Fred and Joe then walk on happily, neither knowing how the other actually is or waiting to find out.

The alternative to The Echo is the traditional chant 'Not bad.'

Fred: How are ya?

Joe: Not bad.

Depending on time available, this can be lengthened to a variation on The Echo, thus. . .

Fred: How are ya?

Joe: Not bad — yourself?

Fred: Not bad.

When Fred asks: 'How are ya?' he isn't really asking how you are. He is seeking the traditional response, 'Not bad.'

If a human dares break this honoured rite he is treated either with (a) mirth or (b) shocked confusion, thus:

Fred: How are ya?

Joe: The doctor's given me six months to live.

Fred: Haw, haw, ha, ha, Good one mate. See ya.

Alternatively. . .

Fred: How are ya?

Joe: I'm having my leg amputated tomorrow.

Fred: Ah, oh, gee, um, er, well, see ya Joe.

The strange part of the tradition is that the stock reply 'not bad' is given regardless of how the respondent is feeling at the time.

Such is the ingrained nature of the rite that even if Joe is half-dead, has eyes red and swollen, throat raw and back aching, he will still come out with the appropriate response.

If Fred goes to visit him in the intensive care ward, entering with a cheery 'How are ya?' Joe will drag himself up from the pillow, the drip-feed tubes rattling in his arm, and croak through an oxygen mask. . .

'Aw (cough) not bad mate.'

The above extract, taken from a newspaper, the Melbourne *Herald* was illustrated with a cartoon of two tombstones carrying the names 'Joe Blow,' and 'Fred Nurk.' From Joe's grave comes the question "How are ya, Fred?' From the other grave comes the answer, 'Not bad!'

* * *

Here is another (and different) level of response:

Holy Ground

I vividly remember the day on which a man who had been a student in one of my courses came back to the school and entered my room with the disarming remark: 'I have no problem this time, no questions to ask you. I do not need counsel or advice, but I simply want to celebrate some time with you.' We sat on the ground facing each other and talked a little about what life had been for us in the last year, about our work, our common friends, and about the restlessness of our hearts. Then slowly as the minutes passed by we became silent. Not an embarrassing silence but a silence that would bring us closer together than the many small and big events of the last year. We would hear a few cars pass and the noise of someone who was emptying a trash can somewhere. But that did not hurt. The silence that grew between us was warm, gentle, and vibrant. Once in a while we looked at each other with the beginning of a smile pushing away the last remnants of fear and suspicion. It seemed that while the silence grew deeper around us we became more aware of a presence embracing both of us. Then he said, 'It is good to be here,' and I said, 'Yes, it is good to be together again,' and after that we were silent again for a long period. And as a deep peace filled the empty space between us, he said hesitantly, 'When I look at you it is as if I am in the presence of Christ.' I did not feel startled, surprised or in need of protesting, but I could only say, 'It is the Christ in you, who recognises the Christ in me.' 'Yes,' he said, 'He indeed is in our midst.' And then he spoke the words which entered into my soul as the most healing words I had heard in many years, 'From now on, wherever you go, or wherever I go, all the ground between us will be holy ground.' (Henri J.M. Nouwen, *Reaching Out*).

* * *

In these examples different levels of responding can be readily sensed; and that level which is necessary for a liturgical experience: a response from the centre, of which we have been saying so much in this book.

Eugene Gendlin in his book *Focusing,* introduces a term he has coined himself: it is 'felt sense', which he describes as 'a taste. . . or a great musical chord that makes you feel a powerful impact, a big round feeling.' It has emotional components in it, along with factual components. He presents it as 'the inner aura' that comes into existence when you let your attention dwell on someone: a rich, complex experience of recognition, one felt sense. It seems to express very well a component of liturgical experience: a *felt sense* of God and Jesus Christ.

Before going on to consider a further aspect of the religious experience, this activity could be a help to appreciate more fully the 'feeling-experience' we have been considering:

Experiencing a Person

Dwell on someone you know, a person about whom you have feelings.

How would you describe yourself experiencing that person?

Religious experience

Liturgical experience is not just *any* deep experience. It is a religious experience; and, therefore, also an aesthetic experience. It is possible to mistake other experiences for a religious experience — as Rudolf Otto warns us in his classical work, *The Idea of the Holy* — by 'interpreting "aesthetics"' in terms of sensuous pleasure, and "religion" as a function of the gregarious instinct and social standard.' That is to say, if what we experience at liturgy is the same as what we experience at any gathering — say in family, club, or pub — it is definitely *not* a liturgical experience. Religious experience is a unique, original feeling-response to some reality — that is to a Person — beyond oneself.

There is a distinctive atmosphere about it, as this poem suggests:

Like the empty sky it has no
boundaries,
yet it is right in this place,
ever profound and clear.
When you seek to know it,
you cannot see it.
You cannot take hold of it,
but you cannot lose it.
In not being able to get it,
you get it.
When you are silent, it speaks;
when you speak, it is silent.
The great gate is wide open
to bestow alms,
and no crowd is blocking the way.
                    (Ancient Chinese Poem, quoted by
                    Alan Watts in *The Way of Zen*)

The response-experience in liturgy is this special experience. It has got both cognitive and affective aspects: it is a feeling-response with content. It is an experience to which we give expression, not with 'How interesting' nor 'Now I understand', but with 'HOLY, HOLY, HOLY!'

We will now look at these two aspects, and their integration which makes up the liturgical experience.

The cognitive aspect

People have different ways of expressing their feelings. One very typical way is by telling a story, especially a story about what happened to themselves. This is what those people engaged in conversation with one another, as mentioned

above, were doing. They were giving facts about some situation in which they, or someone else, was involved; but uppermost in them were their feelings about it. They pass on an
item of news, but it is not its 'newsworthiness' that prompts
them to speak about it, but how it has affected them. When
they mention that they met somebody, it is because of how
they felt about the meeting that induces them to speak of
it. Different stories — events, situations, news, thoughts,
meeting people — they are all charged with feelings and the
expression of feelings. It may come as new to us to know
how often we give expression to our significant lived experiences in story form. Tad Guzie says: 'Storytelling is our
most spontaneous and basic way of *naming* an experience.
Lived experience and story are so closely linked that they
finally become hard to distinguish.'

There is a perfect example of this in the bible, and in the
scripture used in liturgy. The story told in Jewish-Christian
worship is about the dealings of God with his People: what
happened through God's intervention and man's sinfulness;
what God did for the People, and with them, in the course
of their history — salvation history. The story in our liturgy
is the Good News of salvation for us: saving events that
happened, and *the* event, Jesus Christ. Our story tells of his
coming, and his death and resurrection; what happened in his
People, the Church, after his ascension; what is happening to
people because of Jesus sending the Holy Spirit: their new
status in baptism. It is the story containing the experience
which is our faith. The response to this story is the Prayer of
our People (Chapter 7): our PRAYER-EXPERIENCE.

We Christians all know this story; we re-hear it in every
celebration of liturgy. Why, then, is the religious experience
which is the liturgical experience so often missing? What
happens that makes it go wrong? The mistake is in hearing
and treating the story as a vehicle of facts and ideas only: to
understand the *thought* content and no more. What happens
then is what happens, for the most part, in the study of
theology: 'truths' of our faith are heard, expressed and
explained without any feeling being aroused in anyone.
*So when people at liturgy make a response which is devoid
of affect, they are really theologizing, repeating theological*

formulas; but they are not praying. This point is made by Don E. Saliers in his paper 'Prayer and Emotion: Shaping and Expressing Christian Life'. He wrote that ' "expressing" certain beliefs and ways of regarding the world in the language of prayer requires the having of an emotion. The language of prayer provides us with cases in which emotions are given articulation and expression in language which asserts what is believed about God and the believers in relation to God.' *(Worship, 1975).*

One of the most powerful forces responsible for lack of attention to feeling as part of the liturgical experience is the place given to the intellectual. It is understandable that the situation is as it is when so many efforts are channelled into *knowing*: the faith, *knowing* your prayers, *knowing* the commandments, your duties, and the answers in the cate- chism. That this almost exclusive emphasis has been there is evidenced by the religious education programmes of the past, and also in seminary programmes. The results are being experienced by that large number of Christians who are struggling to integrate that vague, mysterious activity called prayer into their lives.

These profound thoughts of the author of *The Cloud of Unknowing* are most applicable:

> For whoever hears or reads about all this, and thinks that it is fundamentally an activity of the mind, and proceeds then to work it all on these lines, is on quite the wrong track. He manufactures an experience that is neither spiritual nor physical. He is dangerously misled and in real peril. So much so, that unless God in his great goodness intervenes with a miracle of mercy and makes him stop and submit to the advice of those who really know, he will go mad, or suffer some other dreadful form of spiritual mischief and devilish deceit. . . So for the love of God be careful, and do not attempt to achieve this experience intellectually. I tell you it cannot come this way. (4)

The affective element

To write about the affective element in the liturgical

experience is difficult. Our People, in order to convey it to us, gave us the collection of stories and thoughts which make up the bible. That was their way of putting their experience into words. When people like us try to treat of the experience, the best we can do is write 'around' it, rather than write about it; and so it must remain inadequate. For this reason, rather than describe what the experience is, this chapter will be content to say what *kind* of experience the liturgical experience is.

We will draw on two main sources: Rudolf Otto, already mentioned, and Sir Alister Hardy, FRS, in the study he produced in 1979, *The Spiritual Nature of Man*. In Christian worship, Otto says, although we meet with feelings familiar enough in a weaker form in other departments of experience, such as feelings of gratitude, trust, love, reliance, humble submission and dedication, that does not exhaust the content of religious worship: not in any of these have we got the special feature of the quite unique and incomparable experience of solemn worship.

Hardy describes the experience as 'specific, deeply felt, transcendental, quite different from any other type.' While it induces in the person concerned a conviction that the every-day world is not the whole of reality — that there is another dimension to life — it is still part of everyday living: it affects the way a man looks at the world, it alters behaviour and changes attitudes.'

In case there might be any misunderstanding, we would like to make it clear that the experience we are speaking of in liturgy is not something rare and unusual, like a conversion in 'a moment of truth,' or the receiving of a new call from God. Nor are we envisaging something of the intensity of a 'mystic experience.' It is not necessarily — though it is to be hoped that at times it will be — the 'peak experience' de-scribed by Abraham Maslow (*Motivation and Personality*), '. . . feelings of limitless horizons opening up to the vision, the feeling of being simultaneously more powerful and more helpless than one ever was before, the feeling of great ecstasy and wonder and awe. . .' The liturgical experience is of a lesser degree of intensity — possibly a mild experience, but nonetheless a real experience.

There is an awareness in the liturgical experience which is a *sense of presence*, 'a deep awareness of a benevolent power which is beyond and greater than, the individual self.' The experience of God in relation to myself; the sense that 'somebody is there,' *somebody* being near, and of thus having a certain attitude towards me. . . in me. . . who knows me and all about me. . . to whom I belong. The effect on me — or affect in me — is composite: a feeling of *awe*, a sense of wonder and humility and of nothingness; a 'creature feeling,' a creature consciousness' and a sense of helpless dependence; a feeling of extreme *reverence* and a feeling of *warmth*, of being loved, cared for by a benevolent Providence; a sense of receiving, being favoured with unasked-for gifts; a feeling of *appreciation and gratitude*.

— a sense of *peace* and equinimity;

— a sense of *security*, strength, support protection;

— a sense of *joy*, happiness and well-being;

— a sense of *victory*: being taken into a triumphant, all-conquering plan;

— a deeper certainty in commitment, clearing away fears and reluctance; a more *free choosing*;

— feeling *strong* to endure trials calmly; or overcome them with inner power;

— *buoyed-up* by a sustaining power which is given to me, to persevere;

— a feeling of being encouraged; of *hope* and optimism;

— the feeling of *surrender* of the words 'Thy will, not mine, be done';

— a sense of harmony with others, raised above differences which were divisive;

— a developed feeling of affection for another person, or for people in general;

— a sense of shame and sorrow for my attitude and behaviour towards God; of sadness for failure to help someone in need;

— a willingness to be 'nailed to the Cross';

— a sense of the 'giftness' of prayer;

— a new zest for life and apostolate.

We have included this rather long list partly to allow it to be seen how rich and complex the liturgical experience can be, and partly to offer the opportunity to recognise what can happen to us, and has happened to us, in liturgy. They constitute the affective content of liturgy: what we are drawn into in the celebration. 'The language of religious faith is the language of emotion. . . the language of the heart.' All the prayers of the liturgy include feeling. This, of course, is to be expected, since the prayers are our People's experienced-response to God's presence. A marvellous example, indeed the very best, is to be found in the Psalms. They can hardly be surpassed in richness and variety of feelings.

The General Instruction on the Liturgy of the Hours says of the Psalms:

> Whilst certainly offering a text to our mind, the psalm is more concerned with moving the spirits of those singing and listening. . .
>
> Whoever sings the psalms properly, meditating as he passes from verse to verse, is always prepared to respond in his heart to the movement of that Spirit who inspired the psalmists. . .
>
> Whoever sings a psalm opens his heart to those emotions which inspired the psalm.
>
> (The Psalms and their Close Relationship with
> Christian Prayer)

In order to come to a deeper appreciation of this affective aspect of the liturgical experience, it would be helpful to pause here and spend some time in this activity:

Experiences in the Psalms

1. Read slowly and reflectively the following excerpts from the psalms: allow yourself become aware of what feelings are being expressed in them:

Blessed be the Lord
who has shown me
the wonders of his love
in a fortified city. *Ps. 31 (30)*

My heart is stricken within me,
death's terror is on me,
trembling and fear fall upon me
and horror overwhelms me. *Ps. 55 (54)*

Come and hear, all who fear God.
I will tell what he did for my soul. *Ps. 66 (65)*

Save me, O God,
for the waters have risen to my neck. *Ps. 69 (68)*

Be a rock where I can take refuge,
a mighty stronghold to save me;
for you are my rock, my stronghold.
Free me from the hand of the wicked,
from the grip of the unjust, of the oppressor.
Ps. 71 (70)

What else have I in heaven but you?
Apart from you I want nothing on earth.
Ps. 73 (72)

Why, O Lord, do you hold back your hand?
Why do you keep your right hand hidden?
Ps. 74 (73)

• Select one of the excerpts from above — the one
which is close to a feeling you often have — to
bring you to a deeper feeling and prayer.

First, take time to become centered.

Then, Pray the whole psalm, allowing it to
deepen these feelings in yourself.

12

THE LITURGICAL EXPERIENCE AND SYMBOLS

A person will experience liturgy through responding to the rite *as a symbol*, and *only* through responding to it as a SYMBOL. If the response to the rite is not a response-to-a-symbol, it will not be a liturgical experience, although it may be an experience of a different type.

This may seem to be a rather sweeping and, for some, a devastating statement. However, it should not come as unexpected: it has been implied in previous things we have said. When writing about the skills required for participation in liturgy in Chapter 4, we said that the most important and over-all skill needed was the ability to respond to a symbol. 'Responding to the Word of God in the Readings' (Chapter 9) gave one instance of responding to a symbol. In the last chapter, the liturgical experience was linked with responding to the rite as the symbol it is. There, too, mention was made of one way of failing to do this: that is, by hearing the 'story' of the Good News as facts and ideas only.

Every liturgical rite is designed and presented for this

*'symbol-treatment' and for no other response, and the litur-
gical experience depends on it.*

What other responses could be given by people: responses
that would deprive them of the liturgical experience? The
most common failure — and we have very wide experience of
this — is to mistake the symbols for 'signs': to give the rite
the 'sign-treatment.'

Writing on this reminds us of a very earnest priest we once
had on a course. One day we found him sitting in front of a
setting, consisting of an arrangement of cloth, flowers and a
candle, such as we customarily use as a prayer aid. He was
looking so intently at it, that it was not seemly to interrupt
him. When he became aware of our presence, he looked at us,
with real pain on his face, and said: 'What *does* it mean?' He
was trying to understand it; to get some kind of an idea from
it. Of course, it was never intended to convey the slightest
idea — just an atmosphere. It was well-nigh impossible to
wean him away from the association of the setting with
'meaning/understanding'; the greatest difficulty for him
seemed to be that to allow it stir some feeling in him was too
simple to be of any value.

Another time a catechist came to us for help with a
project she was preparing for a meeting of teachers. She had
been asked to help them to bring symbols to life. Her method
was to prepare information for them on the origin and
meaning of a large number of Christian symbols. We found
ourselves in the position of having to tell her that explanations
do not lead people to respond to symbols; and if her explanations helped the teachers, it was towards something
other than an experience. In effect she was giving the symbols the treatment that signs need.

Similarities and differences

A symbol is a type of sign; what they have in common is
that they all point to something other than themselves.

There are also very distinctive differences. The following
is a brief outline of those relevant to our concern, that is
participation which is a liturgical experience:

(a) A sign gives information: a symbol awakens an experience.

It is this quality of a symbol, namely to awaken an experience, that distinguishes it from other kinds of signs. Signs tell us 'this is the road to Melbourne' (a road sign); 'there is a fire over there' (smoke); 'you can get take-away food here.'

Symbols do not just tell us something; they stir *feelings* in us. For example, a gift stirs those feelings associated with security, belonging; a photograph, those associated with commitment.

(b) A sign needs to be understood, and it needs an explanation so that it may be understood; a symbol needs a 'see more response' and a **previous experience**.

Signs are always very clear and obvious, as long as a person knows what they mean. Yellow lines on the street may be meaningless to a visitor to Melbourne: they need an EXPLANATION. An object cannot operate as a sign unless there is UNDERSTANDING of it. But this presents no difficulty; the meaning can be STATED IN WORDS. Once this has been done for a person, the sign 'says' all that the words say.

A symbol is not just a concept-bearer as a sign is; it is an *experience-bearer*. Hence, it has not got the clarity of a sign; there is always something of mystery attached to it. Dom Odo Casel has said: 'There is a mystery when we consider things that are other than those we see.' That is, 'mystery' in the sense in which sacraments are called 'mysteries' in Greek. There is always something still hidden about a symbol; more to be seen. Hence the response to be given is of very necessity a SEE MORE-RESPONSE (Chapter 10).

Obviously, therefore, words can never be a substitute for a symbol, as they can for a sign. A famous ballerina, when asked the 'meaning' of some of the more complicated items in her repetoire, replied: 'If I could tell you in words, I should not go to the so great trouble of dancing it.' The reality that a symbol strives to convey is very much beyond conceptual grasp; the reality is not understood, but felt.

In order to respond to a sign a clue or 'key' is necessary. In the case of a symbol the 'key' is a PREVIOUS EXPERIENCE.

> There is no conceivable way in which a symbol
> could be of any use to anyone who does not already

have some kind of experience of what it symbolizes, and in the case of religious symbolism, the experience itself presupposes a commitment. (Geddes MacGregor, 'The Nature of Religious Symbolism', *Introduction to Religious Philosophy*)

(c) A sign teaches: affects the 'head': a symbol is transforming, *affecting the* whole person.

A basic difference between a sign and a symbol is what it does in a person. Of a sign we ask the question, 'What does it mean?' and we learn something, gain some further, or deepening of, knowledge from it.

What a symbol is supposed to do in a person is the subject of the previous chapter 'The Experience of Responding.'

In religious circles there is frequently used a type of sign which is referred to as a symbol; but in reality is not, and that because of what it does for people. It is more of a 'visual illustration' or image. For example, an arrangement of six flowers around a candle to represent the six members of a community united in Christ; or a dead flower alongside a live one to indicate the Christian passing from death to life. Sitting with a bag over your head for a period of time and then having it removed has been used to simulate redemption. Catechists find this type of sign useful as a means of illustrating the points they make. It is also found in 'repository art', in first communion cards, plaques, and such like.

(d) A sign can be arbitrarily chosen: a symbol is born to life.

A sign is interchangeable at will; there is never any necessity for a sign to be what it is. It can be chosen, designed, altered and even abolished.

A symbol cannot be constructed; it is given birth and grows out of the individual or collective consciousness. It cannot be exchanged. It can disappear only when it loses its inner power, according to Paul Tillich. Symbols which lose their innate power become signs. A symbol can decay and die.

A symbol is socially rooted and socially supported. Hence it is not correct to say that a thing is first a symbol and then gains acceptance; the process of becoming a symbol and the acceptance of it as a symbol belong together. The act by which a symbol is created is a special act, even though it first springs forth in an individual. The individual can devise signs for his own private needs; he cannot make symbols. (Paul Tillich, 'The Religious Symbol,' *Myth and Symbol*).

Liturgical symbols are 'religious symbols'. They were created in the historical process of our Jewish-Christian faith. They express our Christian faith: the faith-experience of our People. When they evoke in us that same experience and only when they evoke that experience, they are liturgical symbols. They are there, not to bring us to any experience, but only to *one* experience: *the liturgical experience.*

(e) *A sign is* **apart** from *the reality it points to: a symbol is* **a part of the reality**.

This may seem to be leading us along a path of impractical theory. However, it is necessary to appreciate this difference between sign and symbol because of two wrong treatments of symbols which are quite widespread.

In the case of a sign, for example the road sign to Melbourne, the signpost is not by any means the *road* to Melbourne; nor does the road cause the signpost to be there. As a sign it is completely separate from what it signifies. It can be said to 'stand apart' from the reality. Similarly with smoke: although more connected with the fire than the signpost with the road, and is actually caused by the fire, yet the smoke is other than the fire and separate from it.

A symbol, however, is said to participate in, or is part of, the reality to which it points. The example is given of a flag: a country's flag participates in the power and dignity of the nation it represents. Hence the reverence with which a flag is always treated. On a more familiar level, think of the way in which you treat your letters, and the difference between what you do with bills, advertisements and all impersonal mail, and a letter from a close friend: how you handle it in a special way, slow to destroy it even when you have read its contents, and almost identifying it with the person of the sender!

The relation between a symbol and the reality is compared

to the tip of an iceberg in this quote from a paper by Denis Cox, 'Psychology and Symbolism' (*in Myth and Symbol*)

> We reach the idea of a symbol when we consider the act of looking at the gas to see if we have lit it, or at the coals to see if they are glowing. Like the smoke, the flame or the glow is a *sign* of the fire, but is itself a part of the fire in a way in which the smoke is not. Or we might detect the presence of the fire by passing a hand over the place where it might be to see if we could feel the heat. Like flame or glow, the heat is not merely caused by the fire but is involved in the idea of the fire as well, and most fires would be pointless and futile if they did not give out heat. These analogies show how a symbol may be at the same time a sign of something *and* a part or aspect of it. The flame or glow is a part or aspect of the fire, but it is not the whole of it. A symbol is like the top of an iceberg which shows above the water and shows that the rest of the iceberg is there though unseen.

It is this aspect of the liturgy to which the Constitution refers in paragraph 7: 'Christ is present in his Church, especially under the Eucharistic species. By his power he is present in the sacraments. . . He is present in his word. . . He is present when the Church prays and sings. . .' This, too, is what theologians endeavour to explain in theologies of 'presence.'

This could be a good time, before continuing with this treatment of the connection between symbols of liturgy and the liturgical experience, to delve a little more deeply into this aspect of a symbol as part of the reality to which it points.

A symbol: part of the reality

1. Choose any symbol that is important for you —
for example
— the BREAD as symbol of 'my body which is
given up for you;' or
— PEOPLE as a symbol of Jesus Christ;
-- any OTHER SYMBOL of your own choice.

2. Reflect on the implications of that symbol as
PART OF the reality.

What difference will it make to your RESPONSE
to that symbol?

The relation between a symbol and the reality

The relation that exists between a symbol and the reality
to which it points, as explained in (e) above, has very important consequences in regard to the liturgical experience, and
makes it necessary that a particular attitude is brought to
celebrations of liturgy. What follows here — although stated
negatively as it deals with how people can go wrong — says a
lot about the attitude that is part of 'symbol-treatment.'

There are two ways in which people can be deprived of a
liturgical experience through failing to respond to the symbol
as a symbol. The two ways arise from a misuse of symbols;
two misconceptions. Stated briefly, the first considers a
symbol as *identical* with the reality; the second, *ignores* the
reality. They are both currently in the Church, one more
widespread than the other. For this reason, we will look at
them both in a little more detail.

The first misuse: SYMBOL SEEN AS IDENTICAL WITH THE REALITY.

As has been already said, a symbol is part of the reality,
and part only: not the whole, not to be identified with the
reality. As long ago as the twelfth and thirteenth centuries
the seeds of the world-view known as humanism — which
focuses on man and his environment — undermined the 'part

of' aspect of symbolism. As a result the symbols which were in use became to be more and more mistaken for the reality which they signified: symbols were not seen so clearly to point beyond themselves.

The misuse has led to a type of 'white magic' mentality towards the sacraments, by equating the sacrament with its ceremony or rite — what is theologically expressed as the ' "confecting" of a sacrament by a validly ordained minister, with the proper intention, using the correct matter and form.' It led to strange practices in the celebration of the sacraments, for example, in the use of special wine and bread for the Eucharist: in attempts to baptise the foetus in the womb; in some use of sacramentals such as holy water; and in an attitude to the clergy which deified them; and many other instances.

Another consequence is contemporary fundamentalism, for this, too, equates the symbol with the reality. Instances of it are the interpretation of the dates and numbers in the apocalyptic books of the bible and the seven-day creation narrative in Genesis — an interpretation which obscures the truth to which these passages point. In general, this attitude is revealed when anyone asks concerning historical details in scripture, Did it really happen? It has been said of such people: 'They kill the symbols as symbols, and idolatrously enthrone them as realities in themselves.'

At the root of this mistaken attitude and misuse of symbols is the failure to 'SEE MORE'.

Jesus himself was faced with the same misunderstanding — the failure to receive him as he presented himself. Failing to see his miracles as symbols, they looked upon him as no more than a miracle worker: a miracle worker sent by God, but still just a miracle worker. It led him to say, 'Truly, truly, I say to you, you seek me, not because you saw signs, but because you ate your fill of the loaves.' (John 6:26)

The seriousness of this misuse lies in the result: because of it a symbol ceases to be the powerful influence it is intended to be: it no longer exists or functions as a symbol. 'Once a symbol is used for its own sake, and treated as a self-sufficient reality, it dies.'

The second misuse: THE REALITY IS IGNORED

Once symbols are neglected as symbols, as outlined above, it is a natural step for them to degenerate into signs. This attitude sees symbols as just another, an alternative way, of expressing ideas and facts: it is possible to 'translate' the symbols into ideas.

There is in this attitude a mentality which can desire to express the reality to which the symbol points without using symbols. This implies that the reality itself should be looked at immediately, and that it is capable of direct expression.

A practice which follows from this misuse of symbols is the use of 'themes' in the Eucharist. Those who follow the practice considered it helpful to the participants, especially to children, to have one selected theme as the basis of the planning and designing of the celebration. Hence, for a particular celebration a theme is selected; most likely a biblical theme such as given in Bible Dictionaries. This theme is then featured in the liturgy by means of selected readings and songs, maybe also by designing banners, and even composing prayers. Some of the themes we have heard selected are: vocation, faith, thanksgiving and — this gets the prize! — playfulness!!! The use of themes is a very good teaching strategy; but liturgy is not, as already mentioned, a teaching-learning situation. It is a praying situation. The experience in liturgy is a response in faith, trust and love; a prayer of repentance, petition, thanksgiving, praise — which is an experience. A theme in liturgy will not evoke experience of prayer any more than a meal in which the same food appears in every course would help a person's appetite. Imagine it — with pre-dinner drinks: thinly sliced raw carrots; soup: carrot soup; entree: curried carrots; main course: creamed carrots; dessert: carrot cake. To pursue the food analogy, liturgy is not like a bowl of minestrone soup, the many ingredients of which produce a consistent taste through the drinking of it. It is more like a plate of well selected and varied *hors d'oeuvres*, each with its own particular taste to stimulate the appetite.

A liturgy never has a single theme; a single reading may contain several themes. In the liturgy of the thirty-four Sundays of the year, the first reading is chosen from the Old

Testament 'in relation to the Gospel readings, in order to avoid too great a diversity of readings at each Mass and to show the unity of both testaments,' according to the Introduction to the Lectionary. The nearest to a theme are the liturgical seasons: Lent, Easter and Advent, which have very broad themes, containing, as they do, the whole spirit of the season.

During its time the Consilium which implemented the Constitution on the Liturgy received suggestions and requests for 'Theme Masses' for Sundays of the year. Archbishop A. Bugnini, then secretary of the Congregation for Divine Worship, wrote a very strong rejection of them in an article in *Notitiae* (November-December 1975). 'To "fabricate" the entire Mass or the greater part of it is a true distortion, the result of misunderstanding,' he wrote. 'Theme Masses do not respect the traditional course of the liturgical year – the wisdom of the ages – the history of salvation, which revolves around the mystery of Christ, unwoven during the course of the liturgical year.' Obviously it was felt that there was a need to make his views on the subject known to a wider public, and his article appeared in English in the *Newsletter* of the Bishops' Committee on Liturgy in the U.S.A., and in the National Bulletin on Liturgy (Canada) in 1976.

Another result of this tendency today is 'wordiness' in liturgy. To help the congregation to 'get something out of' the rite and text of the sacraments, explanations are offered; to prepare people to celebrate a sacrament, what they are offered is *ideas about* it. The preparation is directed towards registering facts, not enjoying an experience.

It was the attitude and practices treated of above that led to this reflection:

> In the Gospel of St John we read:
> The Word became flesh; he came to dwell
> among us. . . through him
> all things came to be;
> no single thing was created without him
> All that came to be was alive
> with his life, and that light was the life of men.
> The light shines in the dark,
> and the darkness has never quenched it.

. . .
Look steadily at the darkness. It won't be long
before you see the light.
Gaze silently at all things. It won't be long before
you see the WORD.
. . . The Word became flesh; he came to dwell
among us. . .
It is distressing to see the frantic efforts of those
who seek to change flesh
into words again,
WORDS, WORDS, WORDS. . .

> Anthony de Mello, S.J., *The Song of the Bird.*

Consequences for liturgy

The first consequence which follows concerns explanations
in liturgy. Liturgy is a symbol: the elements of the rite, the
text, the materials used, the movements and gestures, and
above all, the ministers are all symbols — not to be explained,
for that would be more of a hindrance than a help, but to be
experienced. *Rather than explanations which give every part
of the symbolic ceremony a 'meaning', what is needed is a
ceremony and presentation which is evocative: which results
in a response-experience for the congregation.* If liturgy
consisted of signs, explanations would be a very suitable
and valuable aid. Indeed, to include explanations serves to
give the wrong impression, and leads people to give liturgy
'sign-treatment'. As will be explained later in the appropriate
place in this book, the so-called 'directions or introductions'
recommended in the General Instruction to the Roman
Missal, n. 11, can be in other forms than explanations.

The inclusion of such 'thinky' activities as themes and
explanations inevitably leads to a neglect of the affective
element of the symbol, and a narrowing of interest to the
content element alone. The result is that the liturgy is deprived
of its festal and sacred character, and reduced to the level of
the 'everyday.' This can happen very easily, and indeed often
happens. When it does, those who plan liturgy have to take
steps to try to lift the celebration above the level of the
ordinary. Usually this is done by including singing and other
music. This can give a lift all right; it can also, and most often

H

does, end up as a spirited and enjoyable sing-a-long — but hardly a liturgical experience!

During World War II, there was a shortage of many imported commodities in Europe, among them coffee. In its place the people were sold a concoction made from dried dandelions — or something. We called it 'ersatz coffee' — very derogatorily. Ersatz means substitute; what we inferred was that it was no substitute at all for the real thing. In liturgy, an attitude that effectively ignores the reality and treats symbols as signs will produce nothing but ersatz liturgy: it will not, it cannot, evoke an experience.

Borrowing words from St Augustine, which he uses in a different context from ours, gives a way of expressing how necessary a 'symbol-response' is for a liturgical experience. He writes:

> The voice without the word
> strikes the ear
> but does not build the heart.

Because of the relation between a symbol and the reality it points to, in a liturgical experience — indeed any symbol-experience — the experience is the person's response, not to the symbol, but to what is symbolized, that is, to the REALITY SYMBOLIZED. For example, the joy experienced in celebrating the Eucharist is not a response to joyful music, but to the presence of Christ; the sense of oneness is not the result of the presence of people we know, nor greeting them or speaking to them, but to our shared life in the Holy Spirit symbolized by their presence.

It is possible, not only in liturgy but in all life, to give something the 'sign-treatment.' The example is given of a lock of hair. It is only a 'sign' to the lover if it merely indicates the fact of his love. But if the lock of hair awakens all the intimacy and involvement and mystery of his relationship with the one he loves when they are together, then it is a symbol. Hence, an object may be for one person something of no account, and for another a life-giving symbol. For the same person at different times, it may at one time be just a sign, and another a true symbol. It depends on the person's response; and that response depends on the person's attitude.

A certain attitude is necessary for responding to a symbol; that attitude is one of *active faith*. Oriented to the symbol it does not have the symbol itself in view but rather that which is symbolised in it. It is an attitude which will SEE MORE TO RESPOND.

Symbolism in our time

What we have called the misuse of symbols is widespread in our world today, and affecting more than liturgy. It is part of our world-view, and is reflected in many aspects of life, both religious and secular. The progressive infiltration of humanism has led to the killing of a symbolic sense. The contemporary situation is an insensitivity to all kinds of symbolic communication. People are conditioned to see empirical knowledge as the model for 'real' knowledge. Preoccupied with the outer world, they bring reason to bear on it to control and manipulate it.

If liturgy too is approached in this way, it must inevitably fail as an experience.

- A symbol is to be experienced; otherwise it is not a symbol.
- Liturgy is symbol; and therefore to be experienced.
- Liturgy is an experience; or it is not liturgy.

It is in liturgy more than anywhere else that the Christian is given the opportunity to live fully; to the full potential of human life; to his or her potential as the person she or he is.

With animals we humans share the capacity of reacting to the stimuli we call signs; it is not a specifically human endowment. Men and women have higher faculties: for example, the faculty of speech. This faculty is only one part of a 'symbolic system' in which we live and find ourselves in a new dimension of reality.

We, as human beings, live fully only by living symbolic lives: seeing more and responding more deeply. We live Christian lives only by seeing more with the eyes of our faith and responding. Living life to the full will not happen without coming to quiet in ourselves at regular times; coming to our centre, and focusing . . . waiting and listening . . . receiving and responding. That's liturgy! That's life!

We will conclude this section on Responding to a Symbol
— which concludes the whole treatment of Participation in
liturgy — by listening to a reflection on life, which also says
something significant about liturgy and life:

> You see, man is in need of a symbolic life —
> badly in need. We only live banal, ordinary, rational,
> or irrational things — which are naturally also with-
> in the scope of rationalism, otherwise you could
> not call them irrational. But we have no symbolic
> life. Where do we live symbolically? Nowhere,
> except where we participate in the ritual of life.
> But who, among the many, are really participating
> in the ritual of life? Very few. . .
>
> Have you got a corner somewhere in your
> house where you perform the rites, as you can see
> in India? Even the very simple houses there have at
> least a curtained corner where the members of the
> household can lead the symbolic life, where they
> can make their new vows or meditation. We don't
> have it; we have no such corner. We have our own
> rooms, of course — but there is the telephone which
> can ring us up at any time, and we always must be
> ready. We have no time, no place. . .
>
> Now we have no symbolic life, and we are all
> badly in need of the symbolic life. Only the sym-
> bolic life can express the need of the soul — the
> daily need of the soul, mind you! And because
> people have no such thing, they can never step out
> of this mill — this awful, grinding, banal life in
> which they are 'nothing but'. . .
>
> These things go pretty deep, and no wonder
> people get neurotic. Life is too rational; there is no
> symbolic existence in which I am fulfilling my role,
> my role as one of the actors in the divine drama of
> life.
>
> *(C.W. Jung, Collected Works,*
> *Vol. XVIII)*

When some, or all, of the symbols of liturgy die for us, and when they have degenerated into signs, we have to do something about reviving them as symbols. The following activity gives a suggestion how to go about this.

Reviving a Symbol

A symbol is like an embryo: it is brought to life in a womb, where, having been conceived, it is nurtured and develops. In the case of a symbol, the place inside me in which it is conceived and develops is in my heart, my centre.

* Select one response to a symbol in the Eucharist which you consider has become automatic for you, or not as vital as it could be (e.g. an action, a movement, a said or silent response).

* CENTER YOURSELF
* Take the symbol INSIDE you
* Place the symbol in a FRAME
* Enter into the Process of Responding:
  SEE MORE
  LISTEN
* RECEIVE the response.

You might like to record your response in writing, in some such form as: The prayer-response I received was —

Blessed be the God and Father of our Lord Jesus Christ. . .
who, before the foundation of the world,
chose us in Christ
so that we should be holy and blameless before him.
He destined us in love
to be his sons through Jesus Christ,
according to the purpose of his will,
TO THE PRAISE OF THE GLORY OF HIS GRACE,
with which he gifted us in the Beloved.

                                        (Eph 1:3-6)

Section Four

PRAYING THE EUCHARIST

**Father,
we thank you
for
counting us
worthy to stand
in your presence
and serve you. . .
through your Son, Jesus Christ
in the unity of the Holy Spirit.**

Eucharistic Prayer II

As we will be continually referring to the Rite of the Mass, you are advised to have a copy of it beside you while you are using this book. A Sunday or Daily Missal will suffice.

13

THE RITE OF THE MASS

On the opposite page is a summing-up of the experience of the Eucharist, using an extract from Eucharistic Prayer II.

How can the ceremony — the rite of the Eucharist — lead to that experience? That is the question which will be answered in this section on Praying the Eucharist. However, the question will be altered slightly to another form:

How are we, the congregation, to respond to the rite so that we may experience the Eucharist?

The answer will consist of applying what has been said about Response-Participation in the previous sections specifically to the rite of the Eucharist.

The rite of the celebration of the Eucharist in the Roman Catholic Church at present in use is the result of the revision of the rite of the Mass recommended by Vatican II in the

Constitution on the Liturgy, paragraph 50. The Text and Rite in current use is that of the Order of the Mass promulgated in 1969. The elements of this Text and Rite are given to us in two books: (1) The Roman Missal (*Missale Romanum*: also called the Sacramentary) published in 1970 in the translation of the International Commission on English in the Liturgy; and (2) The Lectionary (Order of Readings for use at Mass) promulgated in 1969, also in an official and authorised English translation. The structure of the Rite is described and explained in the General Instruction on the Roman Missal, available in the Missal/Sacramentary, and also as a separate book.

The new rite is different — very different — from that of the Roman Missal of St Pius V, promulgated in 1560. If this were not clear from the text of the rite, the General Instruction leaves no doubt. The key difference is expressed in paragraph 7, in the importance attached to the *people.*

> The Lord's Supper or Mass gathers together the
> people of God, with a priest presiding in the person
> of Christ, to celebrate the memorial of the Lord or
> eucharistic sacrifice.

light of the history of the people's participation in, and understanding of, the Mass.

History of Eucharistic devotion

From the beginning, the first Christian community 'devoted themselves to the apostles' teaching and fellowship, to the breaking of bread and the prayers.' (Acts 2:42). The 'breaking of bread' is the celebration of the Eucharist. Luke tells of 'being gathered together to break bread. . . on the first day of the week' at Troas (Acts 20:7). In early times the Lord's Supper was coupled with a meal. By the second century the meal was no longer part of the celebration, which now got a new name *EUCHARISTIA*.

> In the linguistic usage of the time it means to
> consider and conduct oneself as *eucharisticos*, that
> is, as one richly overwhelmed with gifts and graces.
> (Josef A Jungmann, S.J. *The Mass of the Roman Rite)*

Emphasis was thus on the people and their activity in the

celebration. They gathered as the 'called community' (*ekklesia*, church) 'on the day named for the sun.' There was no commandment governing it; they just assembled 'from the country as well as from the city.' It was part and parcel of their Christian living: 'Without the *Dominicum* we could not exist,' it was said. Proof of their devotion was that they continued to assemble to celebrate even in time of persecution.

Then, over a period, the focus changed from the people to the bread consecrated. At the time described above, there was no explicit emphasis on 'real presence' outside of Mass. It was certainly believed in. The Blessed Sacrament reserved in the tabernacle was given due reverence, but there was no 'devotion to the Blessed Sacrament' outside of Mass, as such. The sacrament was originally reserved for the sacrament of the dying, Viaticum, and for Communion of the sick. The reserved sacrament gradually assumed a new place for Christians. Reservation for the dying and sick led to 'the praiseworthy practice' of reservation for veneration and 'visits' to the Blessed Sacrament.

By the late Middle Ages, the emphasis was on the cult of the consecrated bread within the celebration of Mass and outside of the Mass, to the neglect of the context of the bread and the meaning of the celebration. The original meaning of the assembling of the community to celebrate the memorial of the dying and rising of Christ with thanks and praise was forgotten. The congregation's activities – assembling, praying, singing, praising, wishing peace, and partaking of the body and blood of Christ – all ceased. The people were ignored, and not seen as having any part in the celebration; they were regarded as just spectators. The ecclesial aspect of the Eucharist slipped out of memory.

The interest in the Mass came to be, in both theology and popular devotion, an interest in presence in the consecrated species. In popular piety there occurred a real impoverishment: devotion focused not so much on the presence of Jesus Christ active in his Paschal Mystery, but on a static view of the presence of 'God' – who was hardly God, the Father of our Lord Jesus Christ, but more of a 'deity,' a 'divine essence.' Phrases used at the time, like the 'terrible mystery', 'the dreadful table' are indicative of the God they found 'there' — and only there. For a further narrowing of focus regarded the consecrated bread as the *only* presence of God in the world; or, to use the terminology associated with this view, the only 'real presence.' This state implies the loss of interest in the Paschal Mystery of Christ's dying-rising, and in the Church as the Body of Christ; in the meaning of baptism, adoptive sonship in Christ, and many other aspects of Christian belief about people's relationship with God in Christ. *'Eucharist' had now acquired a new meaning: it was taken to refer, not to the thanks and praise in people's hearts and voices, but to the consecrated bread.* Hence the usage still in vogue of referring to the reserved Blessed Sacrament as 'Eucharist; and of using 'Eucharist' to mean, not the Mass, but the consecrated species on the altar, or received by the congregation, during the Mass.

Accompanying the focusing of interest in the consecrated bread was a focusing on the elevation at Mass. As well, Holy Communion acquired a new meaning, and with it, a change in attitude to, and the practice of, receiving Communion as part of the Mass. The place of thanksgiving and praise was taken by a type of reverence which was that of an unworthy person before an awesome deity, and Holy Communion became less and less frequent. New prescriptions were introduced, such as fasting from midnight (extended in popular piety in some countries to taking a bath the night before); and some which are typical of Old Testament prescriptions for ritual purity, such as husband and wife refraining from intercourse the night before receiving Communion.

It was taken for granted that a Mass would *not* include Communion for the congregation. Theology and popular devotion accepted this fact, and set about explaining the celebration of the Eucharist which omitted the principal act of participation commanded by Jesus Christ: 'Take, eat; this is my body. . . Drink of it, all of you. . .'! By the eighteenth and nineteenth centuries, Holy Communion was considered as a visit of the Saviour from the tabernacle. A child's first Communion was seen as a *first* encounter with Jesus Christ.

Here was a state of disintegration: Holy Communion was, in theory and practice, something that could stand on its own apart from the Mass. It was equally acceptable to receive

Communion outside of Mass, or at any stage of the Mass. The Mass was, of course, necessary for the supply of consecrated hosts. But there was a duality between altar and tabernacle. It was this duality which led Pope Pius XII to say at the time of the Assisi Congress: 'Is the tabernacle, where our Lord, come down among his people, dwells, superior to the altar and the sacrifice? It is more important to recognise the unity than the diversity.?'

The elevation was the high point of participation, and not any longer Holy Communion. Deprived of Communion, the congregation's only contact was *seeing* the consecrated bread. The elevation, introduced in 1200, catered for this seeing, and people came for the elevation and left after it. Out of this 'devotion' arose the popularity of exposition of the Blessed Sacrament in a monstrance, Benediction, processions with the Blessed Sacrament, and the feast of Corpus Christi.

Finally, devotion to the Eucharist, within Mass or outside of it, was utterly individualist – 'alone with the 'Alone.' The sense of community celebration was utterly absent!

The new Rite: Participation

We had remarked on the 'newness' of our present Rite, and this is the newness: the restoration of emphasis to the congregation participating.

Further, it is a change from 'I' to 'we'. That is, the whole congregation, with the presiding celebrant and other ministers, celebrate.

The high point of the celebration is , as Christ commanded, to eat his body and drink his blood. Hence, the unity is restored, and Holy Communion has its rightful place again.

The focal point of the Rite is the person of Jesus Christ, actively present – and no longer the 'how' or the 'where' of his static presence – not only in the bread and wine, but also in the congregation, the ministers and the word; and through, with and in whom the people are 'eucharistic' before the Father.

The most striking feature in the new Rite, and the one with greatest pastoral effectiveness, is the recognition of the place and role of the congregation. The designing and thrust of the Rite is directed towards fostering and improving their active participation. In his Apostolic Constitution promulgating the revised Roman Missal, Pope Paul VI expressed it as his hope that through it, 'in the great diversity of languages, one single prayer will rise as acceptable offering to our Father in heaven, through our High Priest Jesus Christ, in the Holy Spirit.'

The Rite is *for* participation, and participation will be our interest in this section. We do not intend to give a theology of the Eucharist, although a theology will be the basis for all that is said. Our intention is to keep looking at the liturgico-ritual structure with our particular question in mind. That is to say, we will not be writing about 'What do you have to do?' or 'Is it all right to do this, or that?' (which are concerned with the performance or ministering of the rite). *This section will rather deal with responding to the rite, looking at each element of the rite to discover such information as, 'What PRAYER is the rite aiming to evoke?' and 'How can we best be praying Christians through this rite?'*

By 'element' of the rite is meant all that is said, proclaimed or prayed; every moment and gesture of every person who is ministering; as well as every word, said or sung, by us the congregation, and every posture (sitting, standing, kneeling) and action (such as making the sign of the cross, eating and drinking the body and blood of Christ). These elements make up the Text and Rite: Area B. Each and every one of them is included in order to help participation. The explanation of the Rite of the Eucharist which follows in this book will always have this in mind. If we were addressing ministers, or those who plan celebrations, the emphasis would be different.

> We are addressing
> the praying people
> the congregation
> having in mind
> their EXPERIENCE in the Rite (see Chapter 11)
> in a RESPONSE
> which is a COMMUNAL PRAYER (Chapter 6)
> and
> the PRAYER OF THE CHURCH (Chapter 7).

Before going on with your reading, it could be well worth while to pause to reflect, and ask yourself some questions, as in this activity:

Eucharistic Devotion

Spend whatever time you consider is helpful for you, as you ask yourself:

1. What did the history of Eucharistic devotion 'say' to me?

2. Did I feel comfortable with it, or did I find it disturbing?

3. In what way did it help me to understand the difficulties some Catholics have with changes in the Mass and practices of Eucharistic devotion?

The Basic Structure: Four Stages

The celebration of the Eucharist according to the revised Rite is one continuous act of worship which moves in several stages. Official documents refer to them as 'parts' of the rite, but we prefer to call them 'stages' as indicating a movement, a development, and, as will be seen later, a dynamic progression.

The two main stages are the *Liturgy of the Word* and the *Liturgy of the Eucharist*. The Liturgy of the Word begins with the first reading and ends with the concluding prayer of the General Intercessions (Prayer of the Faithful). The Liturgy of the Eucharist begins at this point and ends with the Prayer after Communion. This stage leads on to the concluding rite, which is a *Dismissal Rite*. These stages are preceded by a preparatory stage, the *Introductory Rites*, which extend from the beginning to the Opening Prayer.

The *FOUR STAGES* in order are, therefore:
• The Introductory Rites,
• The Liturgy of the Word,
• The Liturgy of the Eucharist,
• The Dismissal Rite.

Each of the four stages has a distinctive character: that is, in each stage the congregation is called to make a response that is different from the other stages. Hence it is very helpful to know and understand the response which each stage aims at evoking, and in the course of the celebration to be consciously aware of the movement from one to another.

The ending of a stage has something of a climax built into it: a peak is reached in the form of a Collect-type prayer. The close of the first three stages is signalled by (1) the Opening Prayer; (2) the Concluding Prayer after the General Intercessions; and (3) the Prayer after Communion. The last stage, the Dismissal Rite, has no prayer, but is 'open-ended' – a significant difference which will be explained in Chapter 19. In each of these prayers the Presiding Celebrant presents himself to the congregation and prays in a distinctive style: that is, a very succinct, concise and terse prayer of Petition to God the Father (with rare exceptions), concluding with a formula which names Jesus Christ the Lord as the mediator through whom they pray. To the prayer the congregation responds 'Amen.'

There is no *logical* reason for the structure and form of the Rite of the Eucharist; no arguments can be given why it has to be, or should be, so. The answer to such questions as, 'Why do we have several readings in each Mass'? or 'Why has the Eucharistic Prayer to have the same form always?' or 'Why is the Our Father included every day?' is *'That is the way our People have prayed the Eucharist.'* There is no logical or 'reason why' explanation, any more than such an explanation could be given for other things in our lives. Take eating habits, for example. It could be asked, 'Why do Australians like to have a roast for Sunday dinner?' or 'Why do we always have coffee *after* dessert, rather than before it (as was done in France in centuries past)?' The answer is, it suits our people to eat in this way. It is not the only way, or the correct way; it is the most suitable way for us. Similarly, the form of the celebration of the Eucharist in this Rite is not the only possible way; it is a way that has grown among, and been tried and tested by, many generations of worshipping Christians.

The present revised Rite is an old, and very precious, form given to us by our People; a structure we value and appreciate. The New Testament accounts of the Institution of the Eucharist give us the essential features of the manner in which the Eucharist was celebrated in Apostolic times, in obedience to the mandate of Jesus, 'Do this in memory of me.' In the first Christian community, it was celebrated along with a meal. At first, the consecration of the bread took place before the meal, and, after the meal, the consecration of the chalice. Later, the two consecrations were joined and placed together either before or after the meal. What happened was: the person presiding took bread and the chalice, pronounced the thanksgiving prayer, the *eucharistia*, broke the bread, and distributed the body and blood of Christ to the community.

This basic structure of the Eucharist was to last. One great change, which occurred after a few decades, and which Jungmann considers to be 'the greatest perhaps in the whole history of the Mass,' *(The Early Liturgy)* was dropping of the meal. Hence, although the above structure remained, the emphasis was changed. Since the breaking of the bread was part of the meal once eaten in conjunction with the Eucharist, with the omission of the meal, emphasis moved from the breaking of bread and wine, which gave its name to the celebrations, namely, 'The Eucharist.' By the end of the first century the character of the celebration was no longer that of the fellowship of a meal in common, but of a prayer in common, and became in truth a Eucharistic celebration. Since the beginning of the second century, the commonly used name has been 'Eucharist.'

A little later, a scripture-reading service was added to the Eucharist: a Synagogue service, which was 'second nature to the Jewish Christians.'

The earliest concrete description of the combined form is given by St Justin (about 150 A.D.):

> And on the day called Sun-day an assembly is held in one place of all who live in town or country, and the records of the apostles or writings of the prophets are read for as long as time allows.
>
> Then, when the reader has finished, the president in a discourse admonishes and exhorts us to imitate these good things.
>
> Then we all stand up together and offer prayers; and as we said before, when we have finished praying, bread and wine are brought up, and the president likewise offers prayers and thanksgiving to the best of his ability, and the people assent, saying the Amen; and there is a distribution, and everyone participates in the element over which thanks have been given; and they are sent through the deacons to those who are not present.
>
> And the wealthy who so desire give what they wish, as each chooses; and what is collected is deposited with the president.
>
> He helps orphans and widows, and those who through sickness or any other cause are in need, and those in prison, and strangers sojourning among us; in a word he takes care of all those who are in need.'

(First Apology, chapter 67)

Evidence of a farewell blessing and dismissal goes back as far as the fourth century — and from that time gave the name 'Mass', missa. Jungmann says that 'there probably must always have been a formal dismissal at the end of the entire service.' (The Mass of the Roman Rite).

Nothing in the nature of an introductory rite appears until the fifth century. Until then the celebrant would enter the assembled community and the readings began without any preliminaries something like our present Good Friday liturgy. The introduction did not come into being all at the one time; many different stages can be distinguished in the structure as it evolved in different places in different centuries.

> *At the Last Supper, Jesus Christ said to those present, and to all his people in time to come: 'Do this. . .'*
>
> *In this Rite of the Eucharist — this ceremony of many elements — his People are saying to us: 'This is how we have been fulfilling the Lord's command. . .'*
>
> *The Rite is a liturgical expression of a whole People's — our People's — response to Jesus Christ: the response they make with him to the Father.*
>
> *It is given to us of today as a means of sharing in the response of Jesus Christ in his sacrifice that saved the world. There is only one way to approach it — prayerfully*
>
> *Lord,*
> *may the Spirit you promised*
> *lead us into all truth*
> *and reveal to us the full meaning*
> *of the sacrifice.*
>
> (Pentecost Sunday)

You may feel an urge to move on to discover what is going to be said about the Rite in the next chapter. It could be advisable to approach it with a deeper appreciation of what you need from it. The following activity will help:

The Rite and ME/US

Reflect sufficiently to find an answer to these questions:

1. What do you consider the Rite of the Eucharist can do for your EXPERIENCE of the Eucharist?

2. What would you see as your greatest NEEDS in regard to this experience?

14

THE INTRODUCTORY RITES

As its name indicates, this stage has the character of introduction and preparation: the congregation being prepared to participate. Since liturgy is 'people praying' the purpose of the Rite is to prepare the congregation for better praying.
That is to say, to give help to those present to be there, not as just physically present, nor as observing, nor learning; but as praying Christians.

Since we come to liturgy from the rest of our life, and bring to the Eucharist the person 'who I am,' and 'how I am,' we will be affected by, and under the influence of, what has been going on in us before — especially immediately before — the celebration. Each of us who comes to the liturgy comes to it, therefore, with personal needs, which if not catered for, will impair our prayer. The purpose of these Introductory Rites is to supply what we need: to do what is necessary for each of us and all together as community to begin to pray as well as we are capable of, as explained in Chapter 5.

To arrive at prayer there are two distinct needs to be met, though they may not be two distinct stages: the first is to come to *inner quiet*: the second, since quiet is not yet prayer, is to have one's *faith activated* in response. Without this latter, we will not be praying, and furthermore, the experience will not be a religious experience. There is a distinct and specific view, response and feeling belonging to faith. Take for example something that causes a lot of people concern, and which is regularly announced to us each Monday morning: the weekend road deaths. Different people respond to them in different ways. For those personally involved with it, relatives and friends of those who have lost their lives, it will be a time of loss, of grief and sorrow; and possibly anger, at the tragedy of it. For the police it will be a matter of discovering if anyone was at fault; they will be thinking in terms of traffic laws. Those responsible for safety in road construction will examine the place to try to discover if there are any shortcomings in the road surface, its camber, visibility and so on. Those, again, whose job is safety in car design and construction will want to see if there was any weakness in the car that was responsible. Their thoughts and expressions will be in engineering terminology. Insurance people will have a different reaction still to the accidents, and they will use a still different set of ideas and words. There is yet another view and response that a Christian can make; for example, he or she will believe that these people who were killed are not dead, but living — for the Christian never dies — and will be consoled by the fact of the happiness that is now the experience of these deceased people. This is to exercise one's faith in the event, to have one's experience altered by our faith, and to make use of the terminology of our Christian faith.

What this stage is intended to do for us, therefore, is:
— to bring about the change necessary in us so that we will be wholly present and centered;
— to take us into a communal prayer, by making us aware of the others present, responding to them in faith; and, in charity committed to help them in their participation, this

becoming our motivation for being present (Chapter 6);
—   to make us aware of the greater People to whom we
belong, accepting their prayer through accepting the faith
and this rite which they give us (Chapter 7).

The General Instruction puts it in these words: 'The purpose of these rites is to make the assembled people a unified
community and to prepare them properly to listen to God's
word and celebrate the eucharist.'

The Process

The process is the same process as dealt with in Chapter 5:
Beginning to Pray. In the Introductory Rites a succession of
stimuli is presented to the congregation, so that by responding
to them the required preparation takes place. Through their
response to what they see and hear in the various elements of
the preparation, the people come from 'outside to inside.'

In broad outline, the steps in the process are:
  becoming aware of myself, how I am and what I am
  experiencing;
  accepting how I am: that I am not as ready for prayer as
  I could be;
  realizing that I am now allowed the time to become
  ready;
  focusing on what is calling for my attention — whether
  that is a strong feeling inside me, or some urgent
  thought demanding attention;
  acknowledging these as 'hooks' keeping me from going
  deeper into my centre, parts of me holding me 'out
  there';
  gently putting them aside, or if they are insistent,
  asking their permission to allow me to be free to
  respond to the Rite;
  allowing myself to be led by what is going on: me with
  these people being led by the Rite, being taken into it to
  prayer.

'There is one archway after the other, one ante-room after
the other.' (J. Jungmann, *The Mass of the Roman Rite*).

The Elements of the Introductory Rite

  Assembling of the people

Entrance of the ministers; Entrance hymn
Greeting of the congregation by the presiding celebrant
Introduction
Silent reflection
Penitential Rite OR Holy Water Rite
'Glory to God in the highest'
Opening Prayer

These elements make up the Introductory Rites. They fulfill their function of preparation in the form of

— activities that quieten and give an experience of community;
— symbols to respond to;
— prayers to join in.

The more important elements are: Assembling; Greeting; and Opening Prayer.

Some remarks on these elements will help us from going astray in the course of the Introductory Rites. First, we should not expect to find, nor should we try to make, any connection between the different elements. They have been called 'a disparate series of devotional experiences,' (by Ralph Keifer). *We would consider them as a series of activities — centering activities, responding activities, and prayers — offered to the people to prepare them for their prayer-participation and liturgical experience.*

While it is a preparation for the Liturgy of the Word, it is not an introduction to the readings; nor should we expect any reference to the coming readings. It is neutral in that regard, and solely intended to bring us to quiet and activate our faith.

The series does not constitute a prayer-service: it is a preparation, and no more than a preparation. Without intending any disrespect, it has the characteristics of the customary knock-up before a game of tennis. In the knock-up the players have a definite and limited aim: to get warmed up, improve their co-ordination, and such like; they are not trying to win strokes, and are indifferent whether the ball goes out or not. They have a very different intent when the game actually starts. In the preparation we may well have to concentrate on other things than an actual prayer, as will be seen in what is to follow. However, we do so for the purpose of coming to prayer. Hence, the fact that we may be slow starters should not trouble us. We certainly are not expected to be in the full flow of prayer as the Rite begins.

It is, therefore, not to be expected that each of the elements will engage our attention to the same degree, nor that each one will have the same degree of effect on us. All of the elements are offered to us, but to be used as we find most helpful in order to come to be as prepared as possible when the next stage begins. What follows is intended to show how we can best benefit from all the possibilities offered.

Responding to the elements

We will see how the different component parts of the Introductory Rites can contribute to this process. As we consider each of the elements in some detail, it is to be kept in mind that this is not meant to be a comment on the Rite, but on *how we respond* to whatever is presented to us in the Rite, and in doing so, give it the specific character of preparation.

It is also essential for us to be aware that the process is in the form of a rite: we are engaged entirely in *ritual*. This applies to every element in the Introductory Rites. By accepting the rite, as mentioned before, we accept those — our People — who have given it to us.

The Assembling

The first element in the Rites is the coming together into the place where the celebration will be. First, however, we ourselves must come into the assembly, the group, and be part of it.

When people come together for liturgy, they do so as called by the Father into the prayer of Jesus Christ; to join together 'in him' in response with Christ. *The call of God is to assemble to pray.*

The first act of participation in the Eucharist, the first articulation of a response to God, is 'assembling.'

There is a difference between arriving in a church for the Eucharist and 'assembling.' Look at what happens very frequently in churches and chapels, especially on weekdays when there are very few there. The first person arrives and takes his or her place; the second will find a position well distanced from the first, possibly on the other side of the church; others, then, as they arrive, will take places that will maintain the maximum distance between them and those already there. They give the impression to anyone who looks at them in the seats that they want to have nothing to do with one another, that each wishes to be left quite alone. They certainly do not give the impression of an assembly, a body or anything bearing the character of people who are about to do something together. Remember what was said about communal prayer: the motivation is to help the others, and the help that our behaviour is to them. There is therefore a way to assemble, and that is by selecting our place so that we *look* like an assembly; we may not as yet *feel* like it, but that will come soon, and through the Introductory Rites. To deny one's interest in assembling as community would give very little hope for the other elements of succeeding.

This gathering can be a very powerful means of leading us to quiet and prayer: gathering in the sense of a deliberate choice to join the others in their prayer, and then externalize that attitude by as simple an action as selecting a position for myself that will contribute to the assembly, as such. We begin to have the experience that WE are present; WE are being prepared.

This important element can do yet more for us in preparing us for prayer. It will certainly do so if we apply to the people around us the Process of Responding, as explained in chapter 10: if we focus on them, put them in a frame, 'see more' in them, and listen to the response given in our hearts. This is about the best and most profitable way of spending the time after our arrival and before the Entrance.

It is a most valuable practice to focus on the people around us. To do so will certainly stop our meandering thoughts, give us a sense of being 'with' them and they with us, lead us to pray if we see them with faith, and give us a lead into communal prayer.

The call to respond will be repeated right through the celebration. This is the first; the next is. . .

The Entrance

The procession of the presiding celebrant with the ministers, especially when it starts at the rear of the church and comes through the assembled people, offers possibilities of a deepening response in faith.

The consciousness that there is movement, that something is happening, gives a sense that the action is starting and we are about to begin. It could be compared to a group waiting for a guided tour to begin; as soon as the guide comes in sight, the group acquires a new alertness, a readiness to listen and hear, a concentration that will ensure that they do not miss anything that is said.

WE have come here for something: WE have assembled for something; now WE are about to begin!

As the presiding celebrant arrives with the other ministers, what is presented to our sight is some persons. We may know them or not; we may have ideas about them; and strong feelings, too. To 'see more' in them is to come to see them as ministers: that is they are coming to do us a service, they are at our service. How did this come about? they are sent to us — chosen by God, given gifts and a charism, and a commission — one of the many means God is using to lead us to prayer-response.

This is an opportunity to get 'unhooked' from prejudices which would keep us from receiving these people as ministers, and as a consequence, from receiving the Holy Spirit through them.

The presiding celebrant and ministers are a symbol of the type of people we are as Christians: we are a servant-people — like Jesus himself. Our community life is made up of service: humbly serving others, and humbly accepting service from others. The WE now assembled, and about to go into the action of the Rite, have this great characteristic we were given by Jesus; it is a mark of our identity, as well as being a special gift — a gift that we are now going to put into use: they will minister to us, the assembled people; WE will minister to one another in communal prayer.

The accepted sign of responding to the Entrance and accepting the ministers is to stand. *WE, the assembled people,*

in standing up together give testimony to a oneness: strangers
we may be, but we believe that we have so much in common.
Traditionally in western rites the Entrance is accompanied by
song: the Entrance Hymn. Singing and other music in the
Eucharist will be dealt with in Chapter 24, but let us remark
here that singing has a special place at this point of the
Eucharist, especially in quietening and giving an experience
of WE.

In place of the Entrance Hymn there is available an antiphon to be recited by the assembly, or some of them, or one
of them or the presiding celebrant. It is by no manner of
means a substitute, and the general opinion of liturgists,
though not yet expressly stated in official documents, is that
it would be better to omit it. When the distance from the
sacristy to altar was considerably reduced in church, the hymn
was reduced to a shorter version. It developed into something
independent of the Entrance, and sung when the priest
arrived at the altar. When it was not sung it was recited by
the priest. What is offered now in the antiphon is one segment
of the original. It can be easily seen how far it has changed
from its original form, and how unsuitable it is to perform its
original function. Our reason for mentioning this is so that
not too much will be expected of it when it is used in recited
form.

On their arrival, the ministers call our attention to the altar,
and by the acts of veneration — genuflecting or bowing,
the ordained ministers kissing it, and sometimes the presiding
celebrant incensing it — present it to us as a symbol. It is a
symbol of Jesus Christ as well as of the whole Christian
community, the living stones from which the Lord Jesus
builds the Church's altar (*Dedication of a Church and an
Altar*). WE, assembled for this Eucharist, are part of that
People, part of Christ.

The Greeting

This segment, made up of the Sign of the Cross and the
Greeting, is an example, of which there are few in the revised
Rite, of 'doubling-up.' That is, there are two elements which
have the same purpose which they both fulfil in the *same
way*. One or other of them would have the same effect.

They are intended to do two things for us: (1) establish us

in communication with the presiding celebrant; and (2) give further depth to the experience of WE and who We are.

(1) For the first time, the presiding celebrant faces the assembled people; we look at him, see him, attend to him, and respond to him. A *relationship* between us is set up; we acknowledge him as the one who will preside over us in the assembly for this whole celebration of the Eucharist.

(2) Our faith is enlivened in the meaning of the assembly in the Sign of the Cross. The cross as a symbol of Christ's dying and rising is as old as the New Testament. The first way Christians made use of the symbol was by marking their foreheads with a small cross, as we still do at the gospel reading. The words used to accompany the action come from the baptismal command of Jesus in Matthew 28:19, 'In the name of the Father and of the Son and of the Holy Spirit,' and the signing has therefore got baptismal overtones. *It is an acknowledgement of Christ's Lordship over his People, a mark of his care, a badge of membership of his Body.*

The Greeting has several forms in the Missal. They all have in common a reference to the presence of Jesus Christ in the assembly: '. . . be *with* you.'

The General Instruction states: 'Through a greeting the priest expresses the presence of the Lord to the assembled community. *This greeting and the people's response manifest the mystery of the Church that is gathered together.'* (paragraph 28)

It is essential, if this exchange of words between the presiding celebrant and the assembly is to contribute to an experience of the Church assembled here, that they be accepted as *ritual*, that is a part of the Rite; hence, with *faith*. It is an act of 'seeing more' in faith; and something very different from what is sometimes practised. What we have in mind is the 'silence forbidden' situation in which the people introduce themselves, get-to-know-one another, and other activities that serve to start communication between them, and give the experience of community. It is a FAITH-COMMUNITY experience that we are concerned with here; that is to be experienced in this Rite. For the same reason, the 'Good Morning' greeting is not in place in these Rites.

Another characteristic of the Greeting is that we are responding to a prayer and not to a statement, such as 'The Lord is with you', that is sometimes given to the people. The presiding celebrant prays for the assembly, and the assembly in turn prays for him, the petition being that they may experience Christ's presence, grace, love, fellowship, and peace. As Ralph Keifer sums it up: 'To say either 'Good Morning' or to change the greeting formula into a flat statement is to treat the congregation as if they were bored or ignorant.' (To Give Thanks and Praise).

Introduction

After the Greeting, which is the most ancient element in the Introductory Rites, comes a very new element: there is no written evidence for such an element in the early Church.

'The priest or other suitable minister may very briefly introduce the Mass of the day.' (General Instruction, n. 29)

What we do not expect here is the introduction of a theme; nor a preview of the readings; nor any information or anything else for our 'heads'. Neither will we hear instructions or suggestions as to what we are to do, such as 'Let us place ourselves in God's presence" Rather will we expect to be led, facilitated by the presiding celebrant or a minister: by words of his choosing, or other means.

Called in Latin monitiones, and in English 'admonitions' in The Letter to the Presidents of the National Conferences of Bishops, 1973, their purpose is to 'enable the people to be drawn into a fuller understanding of the sacred action, or any of its parts, and to lead them to a true spirit of participation.' (n. 14) The function of the Introduction — and this is the help the assembly is to get from it — is to lead us deeper into the experience already initiated in the Introductory Rites. For this to happen, at this time we need

Silence

Periods of silence for reflection and prayer were suggested in the Constitution on the Liturgy, and Instructions belonging to the different rites emphasize its necessary place in their celebration. That this is so will not come as a surprise. The theory — and practice, we hope — will be very familiar to anyone who has persevered this far with us in this book.

Times of silence have a specially important place in the Introductory Rites, because of the character of beginning and preparing. It can be taken for granted that we are not yet in the full flush of prayer; that we may still be struggling to give attention and concentrate. *These periods of silence serve as an opportunity to make another start.* Like when you arrive at a bus stop when the bus is just pulling out; you have missed it. If it stops for you, though, you have an opportunity of getting on it. So too, the Introductory Rites stop at several places to give us the opportunity of 'getting on', of 'getting with' the experience.

It is not a time of withdrawal from the others — someone has called it a 'social silence' — but a time to deepen the experience of WE, and of the whole Christian People, whose gift to us this Rite and experience is.

The prayer in our hearts can connect us very naturally with

Penitential Rite

The new Rite gives three alternative forms. Rather than three versions of the same prayer, however, what we have in the Rite seems to be two different prayers — or at least with two different starting points.

The first form retains, in simplified form, the medieval 'I confess. . .' The second, and much shorter, form consists of two versicles and responses which lead into a single 'Lord, have mercy.' The stepping-off point for both of these forms is *our experience of our sinfulness before God and our need of his mercy.*

The third form is made up of the threefold 'Lord, have mercy' which is *troped.* A 'trope' is extra words added to a liturgical text, and here they serve to give deeper meaning and confidence to each invocation of 'Lord, have mercy' etc. They are statements ABOUT Christ and addressed TO Christ: 'Lord', 'Christ', 'Lord' all refer to our Lord, Jesus Christ. The starting point in this form is not us and our sinfulness, but Jesus Christ and his saving work. Hence, it is a misuse of it to give it the form, 'For our sins against. . . Lord, have mercy.'

'Lord, have mercy' (in English) can be two different

prayers: one is a translation of the Latin *miserere nostri, Domine* of the second form, and it is a prayer *pleading for* God's mercy. The gesture suitable to accompany it would be the striking of one's breast. Also translated as 'Lord, have mercy', *Kyrie, eleison* is a prayer *giving praise* to the risen Lord: we joyfully acclaim the presence of our merciful Saviour; and the gesture would be something like lifting one's arms in exultation. Hence the need of a different Introduction to the third form than to the other two.

It could be said that the three forms start with the experience of *our radical dependence on Christ*; the first two experience this dependence in regard to needs not yet supplied; the third form has as its basis the experience of dependence in regard to the riches we already have from him. It is helpful to know which starting point is chosen on any occasion so that we may be in tune with it and so drawn more easily into the prayer.

In place of this Penitential Rite the assembly can be offered

A Rite of Holy Water

This is very suitable for Sundays, especially Sundays in Easter time.

The ceremony consists of a blessing prayed over the water by the presiding celebrant, who then sprinkles the people, while they may sing a suitable hymn.

It reminds the assembly of their baptism: to renew their faith in their baptism: that is, in themselves as Christians assembled here.

The memory of what our baptism means can lead to an experience of being graced:

chosen by the Father;
given a new birth in Christ;
become his adopted children,
one of his People,
a member of the Body of Christ,
sharing the life of the Holy Spirit.

Stirring up our faith and love, and 'renewing the living spring of divine life within us', we can have deepened in us the experience of ourselves as WE, part of the great baptized community of Christians.

'Glory to God in the highest'

This next element is, and always has been, reserved for special occasions. It is used only on solemnities and feasts, and on Sundays except during Lent and Advent.

It is a very old Christian hymn; an Easter hymn for singing at dawn. Beginning with the words of the angels at the birth of Jesus, it continues in a hymn of praise of God the Father and his Son, Jesus Christ, using poetic figures and symbols to give exuberant expression to the people's worship of Father and Son.

It has, therefore, quite a festive character, and is meant to be sung by the assembly; at least alternating with a choir. When not sung, it is recited, and the effect is not at all the same. When sung, however, it can evoke in the assembly a stirring of heartfelt appreciation of the Father and Jesus Christ: who they are and who they have made us.

Opening Prayer

The presiding celebrant may not have said anything since the Greeting; he now comes before the assembly again for this final and climactic element in the Introductory Rites. There are four parts to this important element:
- -- An invitation;
- — a period of silent prayer;
- — the praying of the prayer by the presiding celebrant;
- — the 'Amen' of the assembly.

The form of invitation can mention the petition of the Opening Prayer; or it can be a simple, 'Let us pray.' Obviously, it does not mean 'Let us begin to pray,' at this stage of the Introductory Rites. It is rather to focus attention on this prayer that this summons is issued; being the conclusion of the preparation it is a critical time. Hence, what the presiding celebrant is inviting us to is to join in *this* prayer with him.

The assembly respond to the invitation first by praying in silence: for a period sufficiently long to allow them to pray in their hearts. It may well be that some are still trying to 'get on', and this silence can give them the opportunity to do so.

J

The prayer is a Collect: a prayer with a definite style. It is simple, concise and clear; a prayer of petition asking for petitions that are very broad and general. This very brevity requires special attention; otherwise it could be over before we realize that it has started!

We pray the petitions in our hearts, led by the presiding celebrant. His praying, and his gesture of extended hands, can be for us an extension of the invitation. *Drawn into the prayer, his prayer becomes the prayer WE now pray.*

This very prayerful element is not yet over; the climax is not yet. In the prayer we are praying we address God the Father. Now we name Jesus Christ, our risen Lord, as our Mediator, and the Holy Spirit. In a way, this is the part of the prayer most suited to revive our Christian faith. Because we hear it so often there is the possibility that it may not have much impact on us. Here again is the need for special attention.

The climax is 'Amen' prayed by the assembly. This short Hebrew acclamation is probably the most prayer-packed word in all liturgy and prayer. No suitable translation seems to have been found for it in liturgy. Hence it is a response that offers us marvellous scope for a prayer that concludes the Introductory Rites. We can put into it the flavours of: true, faithful, sure, enduring, reliable, constant, unvarying, sincere, trustworthy, certain, convinced. This is all in regard to our relationship with the Father in Christ.

St Augustine speaks of 'Amen' as our signature to a public petition: 'Your *Amen*, my brethren, is your signature, your approbation, your assent.' We are well prepared if we can make it what Clifford Howell, S.J. says of it: he calls it 'a word of downright emphasis, of enthusiastic faith, of categorical assent and dogmatic assertion.' There is a particular *sound* which goes with a prayer like this: 'spoken with firmness and assurance. . . from a congregation, a powerful unison, an acclamation, a stentorian pronouncement.'

* * *

This is the end of the time of preparation. We have been helped towards thoughts and feelings that are a faith-response.

Especially have we experienced our identity as *this* praying assembly; and we have a deeper sense of the presence of Christ among us.

We were going through a series of exercises — like flexing and loosening our 'praying-muscles' — but we did so as being prepared for something else to come. This was not the real prayer we assembled to pray. That is coming now.

Exercise of your skills will always help you to get greater help from the elements of the Introductory Rites — such as the following:

Exercising for the Introductory Rites

1. Select an object, a recording, or a radio programme, or something else suitable.

Sit with it for about ten minutes, letting it have all your attention and full concentration — as best you can at this time.

Afterwards, reflect on the experience: what you felt like in it; what were the results of your attention and concentration.

2. Making use of what you have now become familiar with, select *one* of the elements of the Introductory Rites, and frame it — for 'see more', listening and response.

You could make use of one of the actions, e.g. assembling; or one of the prayer formulas; or you could use an Opening Prayer; or 'Amen'.

Transition

The change to the Liturgy of the Word is signified by several changes:

> We turn our eyes to a *different place:* we now focus on the lectern;
>
> we give our attention to a *different person*: we respond to the reader as minister;
>
> we enter into a *different type of activity:* we respond to the Word of God in the readings, as explained in Chapter 9.
>
> we change our posture: *we sit down.*

We can take advantage of this movement to prepare us for the action in the Liturgy of the Word. There is a danger, and it is well to be aware of it, that our sitting down may result in our losing all we gained in the Introductory Rites. This can be, for the reason that we generally associate sitting down with relaxing and letting go: 'Let's take a rest now that that is over!' This, however, is a different sitting down: we are not now seated to rest, but *to listen;* not to give ourselves a rest, but to be in full activity.

We take with us all that happened in the Introductory Rites to present ourselves before God for him to speak to us his Word.

15

THE LITURGY OF THE WORD

The purpose and aim of the Liturgy of the Word, and the response we make, has been dealt with in Chapter 9, Responding to the Word of God in the Readings. In the new Rite its structure includes the following elements:

Elements of the Liturgy of the Word

INTRODUCTION to this stage

FIRST READING	PROCLAMATION
Introduction to the reading	
Proclamation of the reading	
Silent prayer	RESPONSE

PSALM
Introduction to the psalm

Responsorial psalm

SECOND READING	PROCLAMATION
Introduction to the reading	
Proclamation of the reading	
Silent prayer	RESPONSE
GOSPEL READING	PROCLAMATION
Alleluia/Acclamation	
Introduction to the reading	
Proclamation of the gospel	
HOMILY	PROCLAMATION
SILENT PRAYER	RESPONSE
CREED	RESPONSE
GENERAL INTERCESSIONS	RESPONSE

The dynamic

The dynamic operating in this stage through the above elements is evident in the right-hand column. The pro-clamation-response dynamic is the A-X type of response explained in chapter 9. Several features of the structure of this stage contribute to the assembly being activated in this dynamic. To help to enter into it there are:

(1) the *new place* of the minister;

(2) the *new person* who ministers

(3) a *new 'sound'* in the ministering.

(1) THE LECTERN is the new place. It is a place reserved to one type of activity only, and the more we associate it with this activity, the more it will help us. The activity is proclamation of the Word of God: the Good News of our salvation in Jesus Christ. It is GOD speaking to us; GOD inviting us; GOD offering to us — for our response. It is specifically God's initiative towards us. God taking the first step: initiating the process. The first movement is GOD'S.

The Lectern 'says' to us, is a reminder to us, that God does not ask us to do anything; he does it all.

(2) THE READER is the new minister. In her or him in the

words of the passage of scripture she or he proclaims, GOD makes himself heard by us. It is the word of GOD, with its special power to evoke a response in us. We are hearing God speak to us; he is here and now speaking his Word to us in the assembly.

The Reader is reading; God is NOW inviting, offering, giving.

(3) 'FOR YOU TO RESPOND TO' is the new 'sound' or atmosphere. The sound of proclamation is an *alerting, awakening sound*. It sounds like a summons: to listen and respond. "What?. . . what is on?. . . what am I going to say?' GOD expects a response from us: from each of us our 'X' response: my personal response from my heart.

Nothing is going to happen in us without our response: the response we make is more important than the proc- lamation of the reader, as we saw in connection with Responding to the Word of God. Our first response is a silent response: each of us, in the silent time provided, listens, and receives the response.

Then follows our communal response. Again, the differences contribute towards our being drawn into the dynamic under consideration. We will consider them in opposite order:

(3) OUR RESPONDING is the sound; the assembly praying their communal response. The prayer we pray is selected for us; it may, or may not be, the same as we silently prayed. Since it is a communal response, we accept the selected prayer, praying it in the manner of a 'structured prayer' (see Chapter 7). Whether we sing or recite the response, it is going to have a different sound and atmosphere about it. Not now a summoning sound, but the sound of people pleading for God's mercy, or humbly acknowledging their sinfulness, or exultingly thanking and praising God. Not a sound to stir to response, but the sound of what is in our very hearts; a sound that draws us together into this assembly's prayer.

The sound of proclamation is the sound of God DOING; the sound of our responding is the sound of our ALLOWING, YIELDING, ACCEPTING.

(2) THE PSALM-LEADER is the minister. It may be a

hymn we sing; it is usually a psalm, said or sung. The Lectionary provides a psalm for each first reading. We can be sure that it is a suitable response; it is certainly not the only suitable one. In the diocese of Auckland, for example, a psalm is selected from a book of psalms, and the whole assembly recites the psalm. The more common practice, following the Lectionary, is that someone prays the verse and the assembly repeat the response. In this way of praying the psalm it will have more meaning if it is not the Reader, but a different minister who prays the verses. It is a different ministry; a different kind of help.

To the Reader we make OUR RESPONSE (A-X); from the psalm-leader we ACCEPT THE PRAYER, the communal response of the assembly.

(1) THE PLACE IS THE ASSEMBLY. For this reason it is preferable that the psalm is not ministered at the Lectern, but from some other place. From the body of the assembly would be best, if practical. If the assembly is large, and if for the sake of being heard the minister needs to be in front, the place, and the microphone that is used, should be manifestly distinct from the Lectern.

Activated by the Word of God, moved by the Holy Spirit, and joined in the prayer of Jesus Christ, WE, THE ASSEMBLY here respond to the proclamation.

This dynamic is of importance not just in connection with this stage of the Eucharist, nor only in connection with liturgy. *It is symbolic, sacramental of all that goes on between God and us. God, in our regard, does nothing but give. We, in regard to God, do nothing but receive.* We take no initiative; all the initiative in our lives comes from God. We may think we are taking the initiative — we certainly do when we sin! — but we really do nothing but respond to God initiating, in some form or other. We live in dialogue with God: and he always has the first Word.

What we are engaged in, therefore, in the Liturgy of the Word is nothing different from what we are engaged in all the time. Or, to put it in the reverse way, we never do anything but what we do in the Liturgy of the Word.

Lectern — Assembly
Reader reading — WE praying a psalm
proclamation sound — prayer sound
is
GOD GIVING — WE RECEIVING
IS
LIFE

Introduction to the Liturgy of the Word

To draw this dynamic to the attention of the assembly, and to animate them into it, there can be an Introduction to this stage.

Introduction to the readings

A further help can be in the form of a sentence or two before each reading which serves to adjust our 'tuning' more finely. We can place the passage to be read in its context, hear the true message of the sacred writer and of our People.

Alleluia/Acclamation

This may, and would be better omitted if it is not sung. The Alleluia 'conveys the glory of the coming Christ as an introduction to the gospel' (A.G. Martimort). In Lent it is replaced by an acclamation of praise.

It can serve the purpose of stirring up our faith in Christ's presence among us. After the silent response following the second reading, if there is one — there is no other response to a second reading than the period of silence — we give expression to our feelings of appreciation of the awesome and wonderful event that is taking place: God is attending to us and gracing us.

Silence

As pointed out earlier, a time of silence after a reading cannot be dispensed with if we are going to make our response. It is not a 'nice' addition; it is a *must*. For us, it is not a rest period, but a vital activity. Indeed, there can hardly be much reason for listening to a reading, or having a reading at all, if we do not make use of the silence to receive the response.

The period of silence for the gospel-homily may be given to us either before or after the homily. Wherever it comes, it has the same purpose.

Homily

This is rated as a 'highly esteemed' part of the liturgy. It can do a lot for us; we should not, however, expect it to do too much. Far from being the main contribution of the presiding celebrant, or the high point of the whole celebration, the homily is but one component of the Liturgy of the Word: part of a movement that takes us on from the readings to the General Intercessions, and to the Liturgy of the Eucharist. We are not to expect it to be 'arresting' in tone, in a way that holds us there and does not move us on; nor are we to look for points that hold our interest. To find myself saying to the celebrant after Mass, 'You gave us plenty to *think* about, Father,' is to admit that the homily did not fulfil its purpose for me that day.

In this way, the homily is different from other 'talk times.' The one who delivers it is 'present-ing' the Good News to us; he brings the message closer to us, and us closer to the message in order to evoke a response in our hearts. That is where it is aimed at: our hearts — as all proclamation of the Good News is; that is where we receive it, and respond.

Creed

On Sundays and solemnities we have a Profession of Faith, the Creed, as a further opportunity for response to the Word.

To make a profession of our faith in the celebration of the Eucharist is very fitting. O. Cullmann writes: 'The need to confess one's faith according to a fixed text manifested itself in every gathering of the community. The believer wants to confess with the brethren before God what unites them before him' (*The Earliest Christian Confessions*). It was so in Israelite Temple worship, as in Psalms 105 (104), 106 (105) and many others. It was part of Synagogue worship, in pronouncing the *Shema*.

It was for those people — and is for us, too, — a heartfelt thanksgiving for the salvation which God has wrought, and in it, a renewal of commitment. *The experience is that of ⁊ part of this believing People.*

It is possible to be misled by the form of this commitment in the fourth century creed used in the Rite of Mass, which we call the Nicene Creed. It *looks*, perhaps, like a list of propositions, and our recital a giving of assent to these propositions: an adherence to the *truths* of our faith. There are creeds which ask this of anyone reciting them. A good example of this would be the Athanasian Creed, with its long list of propostions about the doctrine of the Trinity: 'We worship one God in the Trinity and the Trinity in unity; we distinguish among the persons, but we do not divide the substance. For the Father is a distinct person; the Son is a distinct person; and the Holy Spirit is a distinct person. Still, the Father and the Son and the Holy Spirit have one divinity, equal glory, and coeternal majesty. . .'

In our recital in the Eucharist, if we express our belief in, and adherence to, anything it is our People. We profess that we are WITH them in their/our FAITH. Similar in function and experience to singing one's national anthem, or school song, this is our Christian 'faith-anthem.' As well as a deepening of our faith-response in this assembly, there is the experience of a broadening of our WE-perspective, taking in a wider group than ourselves in this assembly. It takes us in our corporate prayer more towards the Prayer of the Church. Our profession is not just a tiny, thin wisp of prayer rising heavenward, but a mighty, broad column from all believers of all time. The very strangeness, and perhaps incomprehensibility, of the concepts and language brings us in contact with Christians of fifteen centuries ago. Phrases such as 'God from God, Light from Light, true God from true God', can give us a sense of appreciation of the people who coined those phrases in their effort to prevent our true faith from being contaminated at a time of struggle: a struggle which provided the faith in its authenticity for us. Our hearty recital of these phrases, and the whole Creed, is an opportunity to express our grateful solidarity with these people and all Christians, and ultimately to Jesus Christ, the 'author of our faith.'

General Intercessions

The Liturgy of the Word comes to its climax in this element. Unlike the Creed, which is reserved for Sundays and solemnities, the General Intercessions are an integral part of every

Eucharist. Called also the Prayer of the Faithful, it consists of:

— a brief *invitation* by the presiding celebrant which should flow from readings and homily, while evoking concern for people's needs and trust in God;

— prayers of *petition* prayed by the assembly;

— a *concluding* collect type prayer by the presiding celebrant.

There are several characteristics which this prayer must have, if it is to fulfil its climactic function.

• It is ONE ELEMENT in the Liturgy of the Word, the high point of this stage. It is not a session of petitionary prayer such as prayed in other, non-liturgical prayer gatherings; nor a period of spontaneous prayer inserted at this point of the Eucharist which can go on for as long as we have something more to pray for; nor an opportunity to give vent to whatever is on our minds or in our hearts. Making any element too predominant spoils its whole effect and purpose in a celebration of liturgy, and unfortunately because it has similarities with sessions of intercessory prayer, this element is sometimes prevented from fulfilling its part in the Liturgy of the Word.

• It is a prayer of THE FAITHFUL, that is of THE ASSEMBLY, as distinct from a presidential prayer, or a prayer led by a minister. The best form which will give us this experience would be a spontaneous praying of intercession from us in the assembly. This would be possible in a small group of six to eight, but is not practicable in a larger group, because if everyone wished to pray — and in any spontaneous situation no one should be deprived of an opportunity — this element would be out of proportion and the Liturgy of the Word unbalanced.

To deal with this difficulty, the usual form is a litany form: we pray our prayer of intercession as a response to a petition announced by a minister. Several forms of this are suggested in the Roman Missal (Appendix III, Sample Formulas for the General Intercessions). A deacon or other minister announces a petition, to which the assembly responds with a selected response, such as 'Lord, hear our prayer', 'Lord, have mercy,' or other short prayer of intercession. A lot of parishes rigidly keep to the one and only response every Sunday, but the response can be varied to aid our prayer. It is important to note that the minister does not pray: he or she only announces the intention, or the people for whom we in the assembly are going to pray. To be able to do this with attention and felt concern we need a *period of silence* after hearing the intention, to enable us to become really aware of for whom, or for what we are praying. The litany-form will then help towards a prayer of the assembly when we are provided with:

— the communal response we will use (which can be varied);
— some intentions to pray for;
— a period of silence in which we pray for them;
— an invitation to our communal response ('we pray to the Lord')
— our communal prayer.

• It is a prayer of INTERCESSION, and not a place for a prayer of thanksgiving, or anything else. We express our sense of responsibility towards the needy of the world, and our solidarity with them in filial dependence on our loving Father.

• It is a prayer of GENERAL or universal intercession, insofar as we pray for more than ourselves in this assembly. We allow our horizons to be extended to the whole world and Church. In this we give expression to our faith in Christ's universal influence on the world, and our trust in the unlimited nature of our faith and love.

• It is a PRAYER, therefore rising from concern and commitment to help; not a mentioning of known social evils and grievances. More important, as a prayer it is an expression of trust: an experience of hope. Hence there is in it a sense of relief, and uplifting of our spirits with a tinge of joy. This is the familiar prayer of the psalms: 'The Lord has heard my supplication; the Lord accepts my prayer.'

In this way 'the people exercise their priestly function by interceding for all mankind.' (General Instruction, n. 45)

This is the point to which we are brought in this stage; ready to move into the Liturgy of the Eucharist. The words to take with us are the last words of the concluding prayer: 'through CHRIST, OUR LORD.' The experience we take with us is of being taken into his prayer. . . in our People's prayer. . .in OUR prayer.

It is an experience of 'being graced': our constant state —

> For by grace you have been saved through faith;
> and this is not your own doing,
> it is the gift of God —
> not because of works lest any man should boast.
> For we are his workmanship,
> created in Christ Jesus. . .
>
> *(Eph. 2:8-10)*

The Experience of being Graced

1. What do you feel like when you receive a substantial gift — a gift with a lot of significance for you?

2. What sort of things do you think, and say aloud?

3. What does it feel like to be in a 'graced situation', such as the Liturgy of the Word?

16

THE LITURGY
OF THE EUCHARIST

The Response of Eucharist

Response to the Word

There are responses and responses: different degrees of
fullness of 'yes'. When you are asked by someone to do
something for them, you could give a very reluctant and
grudging 'yes', and then do it with very little enthusiasm: just
go through the motions, doing the very least possible. You
certainly responded with a 'yes'; but it could be remarked
that 'your heart was not really in it.' It was anything but a
full response. A full response, on the other hand, would be
something like you saying, 'Yes, I'd love to do that. Thank
you for asking me.' In this case you are pleased and delighted
with the opportunity offered; grateful for it. In your doing
whatever is asked of you, you have no reservations, no conditions. *All* of you will be in it.

Take note of what is characteristic of such a full response: the THANKFULNESS. We are fully responding only when we feel thankful in it. This is the Christian way of saying 'yes'. After a reading, ending with 'This is the Word of the Lord', our response is not 'I accept', or 'Yes, I will,' but 'THANKS be to God.' — 'I am quite thrilled. . .delighted. . . overwhelmed. . . at what you say to me!'

Let us take this full response a step further. Your thanks indicates a focus on yourself: you are grateful for what *you* now have; for what is happening to *you*. There is another way of indicating to a person how thankful you are to them: your response on receiving something from them could be a delighted 'You are so kind. You are marvellous!' In using such expressions the focus is on the person who gives, and no longer on you. What you receive makes you thankful — but not just with the gift; you are thankful for the PERSON. The gift evokes a response to the giver, his or her person.

This is a response of PRAISE. The fullest response will therefore have in it a feeling for the giver that stirs to praise of them. Again, this is our Christian way. After the gospel reading, with its 'This is the Good News of the Lord,' our response is 'PRAISE to you, Lord Jesus Christ.'

Our full response to the proclamation of the Word will be one of thanks and praise to God.

There is still another characteristic of the full Christian 'yes' to God. It is noticeable that children when given a gift do not so much thank the giver as run to another person: 'Mum, look what aunty has given me!' This is true, too of our Semitic people. They also expressed their thanks and praise to a third person. So, in their songs of thanksgiving, they are not content with addressing God; they want others to join with them, to share with them their feelings about their God, and have them join them in their praise of him. This we find in so many of the psalms:

Praise, O servants of the Lord, praise the name of the Lord (Ps 113)
Praise the Lord, all nations! Extol him, all peoples! (Ps 117)
Let everything that breathes praise the Lord! (Ps 150)

In this characteristic there is a PROCLAMATION-

INVITATION to join in the praise.

These three elements, thanks and praise, and proclamation-invitation constitute a specific Jewish prayer form: in Hebrew *berakah*. 'The *berakah* is a prayer whose essential characteristic is to be a response: the response which finally emerges as the pre-eminent response to the Word of God.' (Louis Bouyer, *Eucharist*). This is the prayer called, in Greek, EUCHARISTIA. In English, it is 'blessing', but since this has such strong, and almost exclusive, connotations of blessing people or objects, it is more satisfactory to opt for 'THANKS AND PRAISE' — a combination familiar to us from the Eucharistic Prayer of the Mass, and having the backing of sound scholarship. 'Although in the detailed study of the Last Supper we may have to allow for the distinction between 'thanksgiving' and 'blessing', they resolve essentially into one; and the universal tradition has been to characterize the chief prayer at the Church's chief act of worship as 'The Thanksgiving', whatever titles or contents it may have gathered to itself. (David Tripp, 'Shape and Liturgy', *Liturgy Reshaped*).

Form of *Berakah*

Putting it simply, there are three parts in this prayer. First there is the invitation, as mentioned above. Then there is the motive: 'praise God because. . . for . . .' The motive for praise comes in references to God's mighty deeds; creation, providence, redemption, etc; or to his attributes: his power, wisdom, fidelity, mercy, etc. — that is, what God has done, and what he is. There can be some intercession, but always in the praise context. Finally, there is a repeat of the invocation of praise of God.

The Eucharistic Prayers of the Rite of Mass are prayers in this form:

The invitation in the beginning: 'Let us give thanks. . .'; 'we do well always and everywhere to give you thanks. . .'
The motives follow, especially in the 'Preface'.
The final invocation is the doxology, 'Through him. . .' that end the Eucharistic Prayer.

Eucharistic Prayer IV gives a very good illustration of the motivation part, starting with its Preface which is praise of God in himself and source of all blessings on earth; in the next section, called 'Praise to the Father', the motive moves chronologically from Old Testament times ('formed man. . . offered a covenant. . . through the prophets taught him to hope. . .'), through the life, death and resurrection of Jesus Christ, and then the Holy Spirit (sent. . . as his first gift. . . to complete his work. . .). The motive, of course, continues into the Institution — to this assembly, now, as will be explained later.

Other prayers of this form are the prayers that the presiding celebrant may say over the bread and wine, in which the form of berakah is very obvious:

Blessed are you, Lord, God of all creation.
Through your goodness we have this bread to offer,
which earth has given and human hands have made.
It will become for us the bread of life.
BLESSED BE GOD FOR EVER.

'Grace before meals' is also of this form. It may have deteriorated into a blessing of the people and the food, but its true form is a berakah: the occasion of gathering to partake of food together gives a motive for praising God: 'Praise be Yahweh, our God, the king of the world, who makes bread come forth from the earth,' is a prayer, in the Mishnah, said over the bread at the beginning of a meal. It is good to see that it is regaining this form more and more today among us.

Spirituality

More than just a form, there is a spirituality which is part of this prayer. It was certainly Jewish spirituality, and we are of the opinion that it is also Christian spirituality. The Jews from whom we inherit it were a very down to earth type of people, with a great zest for living, and a capacity for enjoying life and all that is good on the earth. This is not to say that they are hedonistic: there is a very specific difference, and that is that the Jews enjoyed the good things of life — as God's gifts to them! The principle they lived on is given in the Talmud: 'He who eats or drinks or enjoys some pleasure of the senses, without offering a blessing, commits the theft of sacrilege, since to God belong the earth and all it brings forth, which, when consecrated by a blessing, it is man's privilege to enjoy.'

There is the realization and acknowledgement that all is God's; nothing is ours by right. God, however, in his love gives us his world — as his gift. What is not to be forgotten is that it is his gift, his favour, stirring a response not just to the world, but to God loving us. A short praise-thanksgiving prayer thus accompanied every action of the pious Jew from his awakening in the morning to the moment that sleep overtakes him in the evening. Quite obviously such people had the ability all the time to 'see more'!

If this spirituality and practice were part of our lives, then it would follow that *everything would be a sacrament*. Every event, person or situation would lead to an experience of God. There is nothing to be wondered at in this; God's purpose in creating was so that we would come to 'know' him in his creation. Things are good in themselves, for example water. It is right to use and enjoy water, and to appreciate its availability and marvellous qualities. However, we do not *fully* respond to water, or to anything until we 'see more' sufficiently to respond to *God*.

Full response

This is our aim and there is no doubting it. This is our avowed aspiration stated very clearly in every celebration of the Eucharist. In each 'Preface' we pray:

> Father, all powerful and ever-living God,
> we do well ALWAYS and EVERYWHERE to give
> you thanks.

Our thanks to God is not *for* a situation: there are many situations for which we are not thankful, nor should we be — they are waiting to be redeemed. We are concerned here with thanks IN a situation, and that is different. If I have an unpleasant cold I will surely not be thankful for the cold; but a cold does not rule out any thankfulness in me.

An outstanding illustration of this is to be found in Jesus Christ at the Last Supper. That night he knew very well what the next day was going to bring: the end of his mortal life, the end of his mission on earth; appearing as a failure, in a situation of defeat; the anguish and agony that would accompany his passion and death in the sight of his mother and friends. In no way was Jesus thankful *for* that situation. He feared it and found it as hateful and repulsive as anyone would. Yet, what way is he at the Last Supper with all this before him? Let the words of Eucharistic Prayer II tell us:

> Before he was given up to death,
> a death he freely accepted,
> he took bread
> AND GAVE YOU THANKS.

IN that situation, he was thankful! This, again, was through his 'seeing more' than just tragedy and suffering; he saw his Father in it, and fully accepted what the Father offered him in it.

We ourselves have the same experience at a Funeral Mass. Someone dies, and that is a loss and a sadness. Unless in rare circumstances, we are not thankful that a person has died. Still, where do we end up but at a Eucharist — thanking God and praising him. How do we happen to be thankful? Yes! Through 'seeing more' in the death: there is fulfilled for that person the hope of heaven: 'There we hope to share your glory when every tear will be wiped away. On that day we shall see you, our God, as you are.'

It is an indication that if I am not responding with thanks and praise of God, then I am not 'seeing more' enough.

It is this aspect of it that makes joy such an integral element in the Christian life. Joy for us is not like the icing on the cake or the shine on a car; it is of its essence. For our life is responding, and especially responding to God; and the full response is always a response with joy. We are not thinking of joy in the sense of gaiety, high spirits, or good cheer; but of the real Christian joy that can be experienced — and, we believe, can be only experienced — from the depths of a suffering situation. Such as Jesus was in in his passion, on the cross.

We have the assurance of St Paul that this is possible for us, in his assurance to the Colossians:

> You will be able
> to live the kind of life the Lord expects of you. . .
> You will have in you the strength,
> based on his own glorious power,
> never to give in,

but to bear anything joyfully,
thanking the Father
who has made it possible for you to join the
saints
and with them to inherit the light.

(Col. 1:10-11)

Rouse yourself, man, and recognize the dignity of your nature. Remember that you were made in God's image; though corrupted in Adam, the image has been restored in Christ.

Use creatures as they should be used: the earth, the sea, the sky, the air, the spring and the rivers. Give praise and glory to their Creator for all that you find beautiful and wonderful in them. See with your bodily eyes the light that shines on earth, but embrace with your whole soul and all your affections the true light which enlightens every man who comes into the world. . . If we are indeed the temple of God and if the Spirit of God lives in us, then what every believer has within himself is greater than what he admires in the skies.

A sermon by St Leo the great, pope, Office of Readings, Friday, fifth week in ordinary time.

Free choice

A response that is full will have, as well as the absence of restriction that is implied in thanks and praise, the quality of freedom. As explained in chapter 5, 'I' respond only when I am freed from 'hooks'; when it is 'I' who am responding, and not just a part of me reacting. *The only act that is fully 'me', is a free act: free from power exercised on me, whether it is inside me or outside of me.*

Freedom is exercised in making choices. The thanks and praise in my heart in the Eucharist can be there only when I am free, and freely choosing. An unwilling acceptance will not be accompanied with thanks and praise; far from it. On the other hand, feelings of thanks tell of my freedom of choice: when I am glad about something, I am free; when I am dominated by anger or fear, I am not free. ALL of me has to be a 'free me'; a 'free me' is me freely choosing to accept. A person praying a prayer of thanks and praise has to be 'free to worship him without fear,' as Zechariah prayed Luke 1: 74).

Jesus was acting with perfect freedom in the Last Supper, and as he was on the cross. He chose, and chose freely, to accept, all his passion and death. It is very relevant here to appreciate that people respond to what they 'see'. What Christ saw in his passion and death was 'more' than suffering and shame; otherwise he would not have chosen it. He saw the meaning of it, the reality of what God was offering to him, and giving to all people. His passion and death was the form, the 'packaging', in which he could 'see more', and it was to the 'more' that he responded fully, freely with thanks and praise.

Our responses are always IN concrete situations. Each situation is a 'package' — of which I have to see the 'more' than the wrapping in order to see what God wishes me to receive in it, and often in order to 'be free from fear' so that I can say a full 'yes' to it.

Eucharist

All this can explain for us the meaning, and the primacy, of the Eucharist. Jesus Christ gave to his apostles and to us a mandate at the Last Supper when he said, 'Do this. . .' Do what? He was telling us to do what he was doing. What was he doing — not what actions was he performing, nor what is the meaning of his actions — but what was *he* doing? In other words, what was going on in him at that time? It is obvious. He had been praying those psalms of praise called Hallel; the gospel accounts present him as 'blessing' God, in his prayer over the bread. This, then, is what was going on in him: his heart was full of thanks and praise of the Father. *This is what he was doing: praying a prayer of thanks and praise to his Father.*

The mandate to us is 'Do this. . .': YOU do this. . .There is more yet to the mandate. He told us that we were to express this prayer in a special way, that is by making use of bread and a cup of wine.

To celebrate the Eucharist,
to 'Do this. . .' is
to thank and praise the Father,
expressing it in eating and drinking
bread and wine
become his body and blood.

To 'Do this. . .' leaves nothing else to be done; it is
ALL any person can do.
To celebrate the Eucharist is to express a TOTAL
'yes'.
It is to accept ALL that God is giving to me;
with ALL that there is of me.
And when I do that,
there is nothing else to do.
That is all there is of living.
It exhausts the full potential of a human person.
When I have all that God is offering me,
I am living to the fullest;
I AM ALL I CAN BE!

That is how the Eucharist can be called 'the summit' of Christian living.

The Structure of the Liturgy of the Eucharist

Three phases

As well as having its meaning from what Jesus did at the Last Supper, this third stage of the Eucharist also takes its structure from his actions. The actions of Jesus, as told in the various New Testament narratives about the institution of the Eucharist, were:

he (1) took bread and wine,
(2) said the blessing,
(3) broke the bread, and
(4) gave the bread, and passed the wine, to his disciples.

'In that form and in that order these four actions constituted the absolutely invariable nucleus of every eucharistic rite known to us throughout antiquity from the Euphrates to Gaul,' writes Dom Gregory Dix, to whom we are indebted for the idea of the 'four-action' shape of the Eucharist (*The Shape of the Liturgy*, Dacre Press, 1945, p. 48). From the four actions we have the three phases of the Liturgy of the Eucharist:

The Preparation of the Gifts
The Eucharistic Prayer
The Communion Rite.

The Last Supper, although it is the source of the Liturgy of the Eucharist, is not its model. That is to say, in the rite of the Eucharist the presiding celebrant does not reproduce the words and actions of Jesus, as for example, would be done in a dramatic representation, such as the Passion Play in Oberammergau. The rite of the Liturgy of the Eucharist *expands the words and actions of Jesus* over the three phases, thus:

Actions of Jesus	Phase of Liturgy of the Eucharist
•Jesus took bread and wine	The Preparation of the Gifts: bread and wine are 'taken', and placed on the altar.
• said the blessing	The Eucharistic Prayer: the hymn of thanksgiving to God for the whole work of salvation; it includes the Account of the Institution — the actions and words of Jesus.
• broke the bread, and • gave the bread and wine to his disciples	The Communion Rite: the assembly receives the body and blood of Christ; before they do, there is the breaking of bread.

We will take each of these in turn in the following chapters.

The experience of the celebration of the Liturgy of the Eucharist will always include a change in response: that is towards a deepening of thanks and praise — as in the following activity.

Change in Response

Select one situation in your life in which you are conscious of a lack of thanks and praise in your responding.

To what in it *do* you respond? At what level?

Now, center yourself, and go through the process of 'framing' and responding in regard to this situation.

What is your response now? Has it changed?

17

THE PREPARATION
OF THE GIFTS

This next stage, the Liturgy of the Eucharist, changes the
focus of our attention from the Lectern to the altar. This
first phase serves as a help with the change. No more happens
at the Lectern; now the action starts around the altar: it is
being prepared for the Liturgy of the Eucharist. The presiding
celebrant will arrive there, and he will perform *the ritual of
placing the bread and chalice of wine on the altar*. This is the
main rite; there are other elements which surround it.

The elements

THE PREPARATION OF THE ALTAR is the beginning of
the activity around the altar which takes our attention
there. It is done by a minister, an altar server, not by the
presiding celebrant; he spreads the corporal on the altar
— at one time it was the altar cloth, but now it is

reduced in size — and places on the altar whatever else is needed, such as the missal/sacramentary.

THE PLACING OF BREAD AND WINE is the next major action — focusing our attention now on the PRESIDING CELEBRANT at the altar.

Several actions can precede it: The gifts can be carried up in procession from the assembly by representatives who make a PRESENTATION OF THE GIFTS, while all join in singing, thus establishing a *connection* between the assembly and the action at the altar which involves the bread and wine. This continues the spiritual value and meaning of the ancient custom when the people brought bread and wine for the liturgy from their homes.

This is also the time to have the COLLECTION taken up, and to bring it, as well as GIFTS FOR THE POOR, to be received and placed near the altar. Contributing to these gifts can be for us an expression of our concern for others and commitment to help when it is possible for us. However, it is not just utilitarian; it is a liturgical action, and as such must have as its purpose to help us to *pray better* at this Eucharist. It will be this help, provided we see it as still part of, and not an interruption in, the rite: it is part of the response we are making — an externalization of an act of faith and love. A little water is poured into the wine before the chalice is placed on the altar. Originally this was done because it was the custom to do so whenever wine was drunk, and not only in liturgy. Later the mixing was given a symbolic interpretation: the union of Christ with the faithful.

INCENSATION OF THE GIFTS AND ALTAR, and the WASHING of his hands, are two further symbolic actions of the presiding celebrant that can serve to prepare us for what is to take place at the altar.

PRAYER OVER THE GIFTS brings the Preparation of the Gifts to a close. It opens with the INVITATION, 'Pray, brethren'; originally this was an invitation to silent prayer, very like the 'Let us pray' before the Opening Prayer. After the silence was prayed the PRAYER

OVER THE GIFTS by the presiding celebrant. In the present Rite, in place of the silent prayer we now have the prayer 'May the Lord accept the sacrifice. . .'

The element with the greatest significance for the assembly, and the action for which we should depend for most significance, is the presiding celebrant receiving, first the plate with the bread, and later the chalice with the wine and water, holding them slightly above the altar — during which he may recite the two 'blessing' prayers — and then, as a ritual gesture, placing them on the altar.

The meaning

The meaning of this phase of the new Rite, the Preparation of the Gifts, is very different from the pre-1969 rite of Mass. In fact, there is hardly any part of the Mass which is more changed than this: changed, that is, in both form and meaning. To understand this new meaning, it is helpful to appreciate the difference, in form. Because many are still confused about the difference, we will take a little time here to outline the changes.

In the early celebrations of the Eucharist this phase was very simple, and even informal. Some bread and a cup of wine mixed with water were presented to the presiding celebrant — a bishop, in those days — who then began the Eucharistic Prayer. In time, he said a prayer over the bread and wine before beginning the Eucharistic Prayer. There was no procession; though there seems to have been a collection from the beginning.

The bread and wine were provided by the people — very naturally, as they were farming communities. A change was introduced when the people made a *ritual* presentation of the bread and wine: they formed a procession, and singing a psalm, brought the bread and wine to the presiding celebrant at the altar. The significance seen in this was linked with the dignity of the priesthood of the faithful; it was also connected with the Communion. Only what was necessary was used for the Eucharist; the surplus was given as alms to the poor.

Next, in addition to bread and wine, materials used in the celebration were brought: oil, wax and candles; as well as precious vessels for use at the altar. Later, contributions were made, in procession, not only for the Eucharist but also for the support of the clergy, such as immovable property by deed or voucher.

Money was introduced into the rite, and then superseded all other forms of gifts. Finally, all connection between the gifts and the celebration ceased when the 'stipend' was introduced, and the money was given to the priest in the sacristy before the Mass.

Once the procession with the gifts began to disappear, various prayers were added to fill out the action of the rite. They were intended for the priest only, and were said silently. These prayers had a quality about them that, in using sacrificial language they anticipated the consecration, and used the same references to the bread and wine as were later used of the body and blood of Christ. It came to be called the 'Offertory of the Mass', and even the Little Canon. Writing on the changes in the new Rite, Jungmann says:

> Those entrusted with the Mass reform imposed by Vatican II pondered whether the Offertory should not be restored to its original simplicity, i.e. shortened more or less to what was practically necessary, plus the Prayer over the Gifts as its conclusion. As they realized, since the essential event of the Mass must begin only now, attention should not be deflected from it by an overblown Offertory ritual; in other words, the sacrifice of the Mass as the Church's sacrifice is performed only in the consecration and should not be eclipsed by the occurrence of an independent, autonomous sacrifice of the Church. (The Mass).

In the present Rite, the name and meaning are both changed. Its name is now no longer Offertory (as we will see the 'offertory' occurs in the Eucharistic Prayer); it is Preparation of the Gifts. *Its purpose is PREPARATION.*

To appreciate what it is to do for us, we must see it as *only* a preparation: a preparation and no more. It did lose this 'preparation' character, and so it is necessary to ensure it is not made too much of, as Jungmann recommends. To borrow a phrase used by one of our politicians — in a different context, needless to say — the best policy to adopt in regard to the Preparation of the Gifts is 'to minimize it to the maximum!

On the other hand it *is* there for a purpose, and a very specific one. It is to the Liturgy of the Eucharist what the Introductory Rites are to the Eucharist. Why a second preparation along with the Introductory Rites? Is there anything *different* about the Eucharistic Prayer that needs another period of preparation?

There is this difference, that we are going to be taken to a further and deeper level of response — to the 'most' of thanks and praise. So we take some time *to re-center ourselves*. We can use the activity at the altar for this.

A further difference is that there is a change of place and person and of material to which we are called to respond. Now we re-focus: on the ALTAR, and on the PRESIDING CELEBRANT, and the BREAD AND WINE now brought to our attention.

We need to be involved with these right through the Liturgy of the Eucharist.

The ability to focus is needed in this preparatory phase of the Liturgy of the Eucharist. It could be developed by 'focusing activities', such as the following:

Exercise in Focusing

1. Begin by being CENTERED.
   In the place in which you are now, select a
   FOCAL POINT.
   Very deliberately FOCUS on it.
   Let it have ALL your attention. . .
   FRAME it.
   STAY with it for 5 to 10 minutes.

2. Now REFLECT on what happened:
   Ask yourself such questions as —
   — What was I like when I was really 'focused'?
   — What about the things I was hearing, seeing
   before being focused?
   — Was I FREE in it? Did I CHOOSE to focus
   on this focal point?
   — Could I have focused without this free
   choice?

3. What do I need to DO in order to focus?

HOW DO I NEED TO BE TO FOCUS ON THE
ALTAR, THE PRESIDING CELEBRANT, THE
BREAD AND WINE?

'Sacrifice' Language

The Prayer over the Gifts which concludes this phase, the Preparation of the Gifts, frequently makes use of the language of sacrifice, in phrases such as 'Accept our offering', or 'Receive our gifts.' We will now look at what we mean when we pray these prayers; and what we mean when we speak about 'offering sacrifice'.

We want to do no more here than present a clear understanding of one or two of the words and phrases used as part of this language. The concept 'sacrifice' which contributes so much in a theology of the Eucharist is so complex, so rich and so profound, that 'sacrifice language' must be expected to appear in the rite. We, however, have no intention of even attempting to uncover all that it expresses about the Eucharist. Our aim here is merely to clarify some phrases used in the rite of the Eucharist, because their misunderstanding will prevent a person's experience and prayer.

'To offer sacrifice'

Our concern here is strictly 'sacrifice' in the Jewish-Christian meaning of the word. Although it is a concept which is inextricably linked with other religions, and the word is also used in everyday speech, neither of these concern us now.

To start with the Old Testament, the source of our understanding. In it a 'sacrifice' is an umbrella word including a number of rites or ceremonies performed as Israelite worship. Sacrifices were of different types, of which there is a systematic treatment in the Book of Leviticus. In these ritual sacrifices animals, blood, wine, oil, flour were an element. Sometimes they were destroyed: burned, killed, poured out.

Whatever the form of sacrifice, they were all connected with the Covenant, and took all their meaning and significance from it; especially to renew it, when through infidelity, the people broke it. Looking further than the external form of the ritual to the meaning, the reality it contained, it is clear that the reality in the sacrifice was the making, renewing or strengthening of the Covenant relationship which God had established with his people, Israel.

The most important aspect of the Covenant, and therefore also of an Old Testament sacrifice, was GOD'S INITIATIVE: God's offer of this special relationship. Offered, of course, for the people's acceptance. This is the meaning of the ceremony: whatever was performed in it, the rite of sacrifice was an externalization of the people's acknowledgement of God's loving and merciful offer, and their acceptance of it. Their use of animals' blood, etc. was their statement of their condition before God: in utter dependence and yet richly favoured by him, they obediently received what he would give to them.

In short, their ceremony was their acceptance at this particular time. The phrase used to describe their acceptance

in the ceremony was 'to offer sacrifice'. The last meaning
it should have was anything like 'giving'. It is true that for
us today 'to offer' means to 'give', to let someone have what
we now have, enriching them insofar as they now are in
possession of something they had not got before the giving.
In no way is this meaning applicable to 'offering' in Jewish
sacrifice. It cannot mean to 'give something to God', to
transfer something to him, to make him richer; God having
something he had not got before. That their 'offering' was
misunderstood by Israel is clear from the denunciations of
many of the prophets. As in psalm 50 (49):

I do not reprove you for your sacrifices;
    your burnt offerings are continually before me.
I will accept no bull from your house,
    nor he-goat from your folds.
For every beast of the forest is mine,
    the cattle on a thousand hills.
I know all the birds of the air,
    and all that moves in the field is mine.
If I were hungry, I would not tell you;
    for the world and all that is in it is mine.
Do I eat the flesh of bulls,
    or drink the blood of goats?
Offer to God a sacrifice of thanksgiving. . .

They were wrong in limiting their view of sacrifice to the
external rite, the materials used and what they did, and
neglected to associate it with their inner selves. We can go
wrong in this way too, by limiting our attention to what we
do externally. We can also go wrong by limiting our attention
to what *we* do inwardly; we can neglect to see it as response
only, and forget that what we do is only a second activity,
and dependent on what God is doing.

We can go wrong in the way they were wrong, that is by
not seeing enough in sacrifice; limiting it to the ritual: what
we do, what things are used; and neglecting the most important aspect of sacrifice, God's initiative and presence. It
focuses on us and neglects to see ourselves as RESPONDING.

What is meant by 'offering a sacrifice' of animal or food
was more like what we see in a present we give to someone —
a real present though, with meaning and value beyond its

K

intrinsic value, and not like so many so-called presents today which are more in the nature of 'donations' or contributions! *That is to say, sacrifice language is a symbol, in which it is necessary to 'see more' in order to come to the reality: God's initiative and presence, and our responding in virtue of his prior action.*

The sacrifice of Christ

The Eucharist is spoken of in terms of sacrifice because Christ's dying-rising was referred to as a sacrifice, comparing it with the Passover sacrifice, the covenant-making sacrifice of Sinai, and the Day of Atonement.

The REALITY of Christ's sacrifice was the New Covenant: offered by the Father to the people of the world, now accepted on behalf of them in Christ's absolute obedience to the Father and total love of people.

The supreme EXTERNALIZATION of his obedience and love in response to the Father's loving favour were (a) his death on the cross and resurrection from the dead; and (b) the celebration of the Eucharist at the Last Supper. Because they are an externalization of God offering a New Covenant and Christ's acceptance of it, his death-resurrection and the Eucharist are both 'sacrifice'.

Let us again recall that 'sacrifice' is used here in the strict meaning of Jewish sacrifice. It is not used in the everyday sense of the word: a sacrifice because he 'gave something up', 'deprived himself of something.' Nor because he was killed as animals were killed in Old Testament sacrifice. Nor because he shed his blood: while the New Testament places saving value in Christ's 'blood', it is using it as a symbol — a very rich one — of the sacrifice of his death, in the sense in which we have been speaking. There is no value placed on, indeed no evidence of, Jesus shedding blood in the sense of 'bleeding', a devotional thought which came into circulation through misunderstanding. Christ can be said to offer himself in sacrifice in his death-resurrection and in the Eucharist because of his interior dispositions: his obedience and love — obedience and love given to him by the Father.

Our 'acceptable offering'

The Eucharist being 'the renewal of the Covenant between

the Lord and man' draws the assembly into the relationship of the New Covenant, and the rite presents that context of the relationship between the Father and us, his people, in Christ. The Father gives; he alone, and no one else, gives. We do nothing but receive. We have nothing whatever to give to God; all we can ever do is receive from him. For us, to offer sacrifice is to accept the New Covenant relationship from his gracious hands.

What about our offering being 'acceptable to God': does the prayer imply that God might not be well-disposed towards us, and we pray that he will change? Prayer is never to effect a change in God; but a change in us. *When we pray that our offering be acceptable, we are praying that OUR dispositions will be those of people accepting — and accepting with the fullness of thanks and praise.*

To round off what we have presented here we would like to offer this quote from Father David Power:

> The ritual gesture of offering can all be too easily misconceived. It is misconceived when it is made the *primary* gesture of sacrifice. The primary aspect is that God himself has given the means of expiation. This indeed is also the first thing that even the act of offering attempts to symbolize, since an act of offering is obliquely an act of receiving. As Irenaeus puts it, we take what God has given to us and offer back to him the first fruits. This is not done to placate him, but to thank him and thereafter to express the willingness to be the evidence of his love. The primary gesture of sacrifice, in that sense, is one of receiving in thanksgiving, and of proclaiming what has been received.

('How can we speak of the Eucharist as Sacrifice')

18

THE EUCHARISTIC PRAYER

The prayer and experience of this phase is that of being
- 'with the whole congregation
- joining Christ
- in acknowledging the works of God and in offering the sacrifice' (General Instruction, n. 54).

Elements

Introduction	
DIALOGUE	
PREFACE	Proclamation
'HOLY, HOLY'	Acclamation
PRAISE TO THE FATHER	Proclamation
INVOCATION OF THE HOLY SPIRIT	*Petition*
NARRATIVE OF INSTITUTION	Proclamation
MEMORIAL ACCLAMATION	Acclamation
MEMORIAL PRAYER/OFFERING	Proclamation
INVOCATION OF THE HOLY SPIRIT	*Petition*
INTERCESSIONS	*Petition*
DOXOLOGY	Proclamation
AMEN	Acclamation

The Eucharistic Prayer is ONE PRAYER, and not like the Introductory Rites or Preparation of the Gifts, which were more of a series of prayers. It is, as explained in connection with the Liturgy of the Eucharist (chapter 16), an extended *berakah*, that is, elements of thanks and praise, as well as some petition.

It opens with a summons to join in the coming prayer of thanks and praise; it continues by remembering and proclaiming God's wonderful works; and concludes with a doxology. In this way it enables us to do what Jesus commanded us to do 'in memory of me.'

It is one continuous prayer of thanksgiving and praise, having various elements fulfilling different functions. Note from the list of elements that some are in the nature of Proclamation-Response/Acclamation (hence the A-X dynamic, as in the Liturgy of the Word); others are prayers of Petition (and therefore A-A, as with the Opening Prayer).

There are nine Eucharistic Prayers in our Rite at present. Eucharistic Prayer I is a revised version of the old Roman Canon; Eucharistic Prayer II is brief and simple; Eucharistic Prayer III is a new composition; Eucharistic Prayer IV draws on eastern sources, and always has its own preface. There are two Eucharistic Prayers for reconciliation, which may be used when suitable. Finally, there are three Eucharistic Prayers for use in Masses with children. All Eucharistic Prayers have the same elements, as set out above.

They are proclaimed aloud for the response of the assembly, as is shown in the right-hand column above. It might seem that there is no need to point out that they are said aloud; after all we have been hearing them for ten years now. However, it is not so much a matter of how we hear them, as how we 'see', or understand, them. Before 1968, the Canon, as it was called, was always entirely *silent*. Liturgists cannot discover why; it certainly was *not* to give a sense of 'mystery'. The congregation accepted it, and saw value in being present, believing that in the silence something was happening — something sacred and awesome — and all remained equally still and silent. Their faith gave them an appreciation of the privilege of being in the same place with, and able to see, the priest in the act of offering the sacrifice of the Mass. It is

different in the new Rite: different not only in the proclaiming aloud; but different, too, in what the assembly does
— that is, in the manner in which they participate. To take
the two main differences: (1) the assembly prays aloud in
acclamations from time to time; (2) they are responding to
what they hear and see *all the time*.

We will consider each of the elements of the Eucharistic
Prayer, with a view to knowing how each can serve to contribute to this experience of Eucharist. Before entering into
this we need to become aware of the context, or the setting,
in which element occurs. In considering each element, there
are two very important aspects of the experience to be kept
in mind.

FIRST, Eucharist, thanks and praise, implies acceptance of
all that God offers to us in our lives; thanks and praise is the
'flavour', the 'colour' or the quality of fullness. It is a flavour,
though, that cannot exist on its own; as a colour cannot exist
on its own, either — we cannot speak of 'a red'; it has to be a
red something. Similarly, thanks and praise is a quality in our
response to God-and-me/us; thanks and praise must be rooted
in our lives. When there is acceptance with thanks and praise,
the response is full. *To speak of a response with thanks and
praise is really just a short way of expressing a thank-full and
praise-full acceptance of God's favours to us at this time.*

SECONDLY, the prayer of thanks and praise is not our
own doing, product of our own effort. It is 'the gift of God':
the effect of Christ's presence in us. The 'graced' experience
of the Liturgy of the Word is still alive in us: the first movement is God's; he does not ask us to do anything, for he does
it all; he is NOW inviting, offering, giving. *The experience of
the Liturgy of the Eucharist is that whatever happens in us,
in our minds and hearts, is Christ drawing, moving, changing
us.*

These aspects of the experience are to be kept alive in us
right through to the end of the Liturgy of the Eucharist.

Introduction

This is the place in which you will be given the Introduction
to this stage of the Rite. Since it occurs here, rather than at
the beginning, where it is in the two previous stages, it is to

be seen as an extension of the Preparation of the Gifts. It offers to the assembly the final preparation for the Eucharistic Prayer.

The Dialogue

The Eucharistic Prayer opens with a solemn dialogue. Whereas the invitation to join in a prayer with the presiding celebrant is usually a simple 'Let us pray', the importance of this prayer is shown by the increased formality of its introduction. It is addressed to us in the assembly; it insists that we join in this prayer of thanks and praise with the presiding celebrant, 'Let us give thanks.' Martimort suggests that 'This is probably what Jesus did at the Last Supper, and it would not be over-daring to believe that the origin of our formula goes back as far as that.' We give voice to our acceptance of the invitation, commit ourselves to be part of the thanksgiving in our response, 'It is right to give him thanks and praise.'

This invitation is preceded by another: 'Lift up your hearts.' These words express the mood in which the Christian should begin every prayer: 'see more' to the point of your hearts responding to God! Once again we raise our voices in consent to this proposal.

This quotation from Jungmann will give an idea of what this introductory dialogue can do for us:

> In ancient cultures acclamations of this kind played a grand role. It was considered the proper thing for the lawfully assembled people to endorse an important decision by means of an acclamation. And there are evidences that phrases like 'It is right' were used.

> An acclamation of this kind accorded well with the make-up of the Church and the nature of her worship. It is the ecclesiastical assembly that desires to praise God; but its organ, duly authorized from above, is the priest or bishop at its head. Only through him can and will she act, confirming this by her endorsement. But for his part, too, the priest does not wish to appear before God as an isolated petitioner, but rather only as speaker for the congregation. Thus, by means of a dialogue at the

great moment when the eucharistic prayer is about
to begin and the sacrifice is about to be performed,
the well-ordered community that is at work secures
an expressional outlet. At the same time there is
a manifestation of how self-evident and becoming
is the action which the Christian congregation has
undertaken.

(The Mass of the Roman Rite)

Preface

Taking up the response of the assembly, the presiding
celebrant enters into *the* prayer: 'in the name of the entire
people of God, the priest praises the Father and gives him
thanks for the work of salvation or for some special aspect
of it in keeping with the day, feast or season.' (General
Instruction n. 55a)

The name given to this beginning of the Eucharistic
Prayer, 'Preface' can be misleading, for the word denotes
for us something like introductory remarks prefixed to a
book — which could be omitted without spoiling the reading
of it; or preliminary sentences in a speech which have an
introductory character. In Latin it is *praefatio*, which would
be more accurately translated 'speaking out', 'proclamation'.
Indeed, *praefatio* may have been used for the whole of the
Eucharistic Prayer, 'recited aloud.' So, let us realize that we
are not now hearing a preface to anything; we are right into
the thanks and praise. It would be better if we called it the
Eucharistic Hymn.

There are eighty of them in the new Rite, all made up of
two fixed formulas at the beginning and the end; one linked
with the introductory dialogue (Father. . .we do well. . .');
the other with the 'Holy, holy' ('And so we join. . . and
sing. . .'). The body of the Preface is the *proclamation and
remembrance* of the special reason for praising God. It might
be helpful to know that tastes in the eastern church and our
western church differ here. In the East, they favour a type of
Eucharistic Prayer in which the Preface presents a rather long
and general view of the whole history of salvation, and is a
fixed part of the Eucharistic Prayer (as is the case in Eucharistic Prayer IV). In the West we tend to have fewer Eucharistic
Prayers, but a large variety of Prefaces which select a particular

aspect of salvation for the body of the Preface.

In our responding, we are not meant to note and list these reasons; they are motivations for our thanks and praise, and we are meant to *rejoice and thrill* at them. A situation similar to this one, and which will serve as an illustration here, is that of a little girl on her return home after being away on holidays. She runs to her mother, and she is full of the holiday, enthusiastically pouring out details of what she did, what the others were like, all that happened and all that she felt! The mother listens — and responds — but not to the facts and details: what she hears is the joy and delight in her daughter, and she is herself filled with joy and delight for her little girl.

The assembly hears, not a statement of facts by the presiding celebrant, but a lyrical and stirring proclamation of the reasons we have for praising God. The assembly hears this proclamation — which will continue right through the Eucharistic Prayer — and finds themselves taken by it: we are interested and moved, our hearts stirred with joy, delight, gladness, as people graced by God; marvelling at his goodness and power, we are lowly before him in reverence and respect; caught by wonder and awe and delight which leaves us inarticulate — what *can* we say?! Something like —

'Holy, holy'

We are given an opportunity to give voice to what we are feeling — to shout, or better to sing, our praise of God and his Son, Jesus Christ. It is our response to what has been proclaimed to us; it is done in this short, exclamatory form, called an 'acclamation.'

'Holy, holy, holy Lord' are the words Isaiah heard sung in his vision of God. We use them, as they were used in the vision, to express God's transcendence: his complete otherness from anything sinful or merely finite.

The second half of the acclamation, 'Blessed is he' was used by the people to greet Jesus at his solemn entrance into Jerusalem on Palm Sunday. To it they added their 'Hosanna', in the context an exclamation of joyful and trusting welcome.

Praise to the Father

We return to the proclamation of the reasons for praising

God. This element takes up the praise of the 'Holy, holy' – God's holiness, his greatness, and adds yet more reasons for us to respond to. Eucharistic Prayer IV does this in a very extended manner.

Our response is, of course, meant to be deepened and made more firm by the additional motives presented to us.

Invocation of the Holy Spirit

This element is a 'calling-upon' the Father to send the Holy Spirit to 'make holy' the gifts so that they may become the body and blood of Christ.

The wording here, and the gesture of the presiding celebrant, extending his hands over the bread and wine in the ancient gesture signifying the giving of the Holy Spirit, indicate to us that we are not now hearing a proclamation, but a prayer of petition. Our response, therefore, arises from the experience of our powerlessness to celebrate this Eucharist without the Holy Spirit, the giver of all our prayers.

In the petition that the coming of the Holy Spirit may change the bread and wine into the Body and Blood of Jesus Christ, we are asking, in effect, that we may be consciously aware of Christ present to us; that we may become present to him, and allow him draw us into his prayer of thanks and praise.

Narrative of Institution

The proclamation of God's saving deeds continues: the saving deeds proclaimed focus on *here and now*. Hearing the Words of Institution proclaimed by the presiding celebrant,
  – we 'remember' Jesus Christ in his Last Supper;
  – we 'see' him in his passion, death and resurrection – his action NOW;
  – we 'see' his infinitely gracious and loving Father 'in him' NOW,
and Christ accepting all from him, obediently and thankfully,
  receiving with heart full of praise;
  – we remember that it is FOR US: 'body given up for you,' 'blood shed for you,'
    and we 'see' ourselves drawn into Christ's *berakah*

response NOW.

— *we experience* ourselves allowing him to join us to himself in the prayer;

and *we look forward* to our fullest expression of it in the action of eating and drinking.

Memorial Acclamation

At the remembrance of Jesus Christ and all that the Father gives to us in him, present now in our midst, we cry out again, in another acclamation, voicing our feelings of thanks and praise towards Christ.

A good image for us at this time is Mary in her Song:

My soul proclaims the greatness of the Lord,
my spirit rejoices in God my Saviour. . .
the Almighty has done great things for me. (Luke 1:46-47,49)

or Zechariah overjoyed in his:

Blessed be the Lord, the God of Israel;
he has come to his people and set them free. (Luke 1:68)

or the people who witnessed the scene of the paralytic lowered through the roof: 'Amazement seized them all, and they glorified God, and were filled with awe, saying, "we have seen strange things today." ' (Luke 5:26)

Memorial Prayer

The result of the proclamation in this Eucharistic Prayer is our 'remembering'. We remember the saving work of God in our lives: in the lives of all people, and in our own lives, past and present; we remember his gifting us in the present in all the different circumstances of our lives, both the pleasant and welcome circumstances, and the painful and unwelcome.

The effect of our remembering is our acceptance and receiving of what God offers and gives us in these days of our life; accepting as one with Christ in his accepting, not necessarily *for* the circumstances, but IN them. For us, this, when stated in sacrificial language is 'being one with him in his offering sacrifice.' Accepting/offering in Christ's way is freely choosing with thanks and praise.

> Proclamation leads to remembering;
> remembering Christ leads to oneness in response with
> him;
> response in Christ is acceptance with him;
> acceptance with him is acceptance with thanks and
> praise.

> Proclamation – remembering – offering – thanks and
> praise, all go together.

The above is all included in the Memorial Prayer, a prayer
of remembering and offering. This is the 'offertory' of the
Mass; 'we offer you in thanksgiving', Eucharistic Prayer III
prays. The association of 'sacrifice' with 'thanksgiving' may
present some difficulty, and it makes it easier if we see a
sacrifice with more emphasis on GOD'S saving work in us
than on our action in response.

Memory of Christ, 'calling to mind', and all similar phrases
with which the prayer opens, are expressions of our faith and
trust in Christ's presence: his presence saving, healing, transforming us.

Words of 'offering' are our expressions of full and grateful
acceptance of whatever he wants us to have, wants us to be.
Thanks and praise are the colour, the flavour that reveals the
fullness, the 'Christ-ness' of our accepting prayer to the
Father.

> We thank you
> for counting us
> worthy to stand in your presence
> and serve you.

It is an important prayer: the high point of our *interior*
response. It is to be kept alive and fostered until the end of
the Liturgy of the Eucharist. This is what we will express in
the act of eating the body of Christ and drinking his blood.
This is what we pray for in –

Invocation of the Holy Spirit

We are going to spend some time in prayer of petition now,
in this and the following element. At this point, with thanks
and praise significantly affecting us, we are aware that we
have not yet had our full and final expression of it in Holy

Communion. The bread, his body, that Jesus gave us, is to be *eaten* by us; and the wine, his blood, is to be drunk by us. With a brief advertance to that coming action, we pause to pray that in it we will all be filled with the Holy Spirit.

Intercessions

Having asked God for the unifying presence of the Holy Spirit in those who communicate in Christ's body and blood, our prayers go on to pray for the living and the deceased (not in the same order in all Eucharistic Prayers), and for 'communion with the saints'. This last asks for a sharing in eternal life, 'to enter into our heavenly inheritance'; for unity among all God's people.

Final Doxology

The Eucharistic Prayer comes to a climax in a proclamation of thanks and praise in the form of a Trinitarian doxology, to which all respond Amen.

A striking gesture accompanies it: the presiding celebrant lifts up the plate with the bread and the chalice, and holds them aloft during the doxology.

Accompanying it, he proclaims, for our response that —
    through the Holy Spirit
    the People of God are one:
    one in Christ
      acting with Christ
        and through Christ
    they give perfect glory and honour
    to our almighty Father.

There is a gradation in the 'through', 'with', and 'in' Christ. 'Through' could give the impression that our oneness in Christ now is something after the image of our saying to him, 'Look, the next time you are with your Father, please tell him this for us. I'll leave you now.' And that obviously is not the oneness we have with Christ. 'With' could conjure up a different image: like Christ responding to us, saying, 'Come along with me to the Father; I will do the talking, and you just stand there and be with me.' Neither is that our oneness with him. *"IN" expresses what it is: as part of him — part of the total Christ, of whom we are part, in unity and communion, through the Holy Spirit. From US rises all glory and honour to the Father almighty.* Christ is not standing alone before the Father as a lone figure, as he was when during his earthly life he prayed alone. Now his redeemed are with him, taken up into the unity of his Body, 'in him', and are drawn into the current of his worship of the Father, his perfect thanks and praise.

To this we respond by asserting our commitment in the great expression of our faith —

Amen

The acclamation 'Amen' has already been mentioned in connection with the Introductory Rites (Chapter 14). This is a special one: it is called the Great Amen. The point has been made that it is not a punctuation mark: that is, it is not an indication that this is the *end* of a statement. It is a response, in the dynamic of the continuing dialogue between God and us. Because of this special time in the liturgy, when the assembly affirms and corroborates what has been said and done in the Eucharistic Prayer, it has unique importance. It can fail to convey this importance and significance, particularly if it does not *sound* like what it is.

As an attempt to remedy this weakness, in some places the whole assembly says the Doxology; but this is no remedy for a weak Amen. The Amen is a response, and if all recite the Doxology, it deprives the assembly of the experience, at this moment, of their Great Response. The remedy has to be applied to the Amen itself: to have it *sound* something special: something like *an assembly who are experiencing the presence of their Lord, and feel his life in themselves, and his love; and are aroused to feel strong and sure and so convinced about themselves — all of those present — and HIM!*

We 'do this' *in memory* when the remembering of God's saving us in Christ *affects us*, moves us to thanks and praise. Because the way in which we remember is so important in the Eucharistic Prayer, it is worth while to cultivate a remembering which affects us. The following activity might help:

Remembering

Have you ever seen a beetle lying on its back and struggling to get back again on its feet? Somehow or other it gets landed on its back. Its efforts to twist over seem frantic: it flaps its wings furiously — tremendous effort going into it. It flaps wildly for a while. Then another burst of effort — still to no avail. And that goes on. . .

There is no help available to it but its own energies, and they turn out to be no help at all.

Up to a certain point, WE are like that beetle. Our own energies are not any help at all in some things. But the difference between us and the beetle is that we can REMEMBER!

REFLECT, asking yourself:

— when did remembering change my attitude and feelings about someone or something?

— What did I remember? What was there about it that had such an effect on me?

— In my remembering now, how does it affect me? Anything like the original event? As much as the original event?

— Could it affect me as much? What would I have to do to allow it affect me as much now as then?

19

THE COMMUNION RITE

Character of the phase

'Eat. . .drink. . .', Jesus told us when giving us the form of
the celebration at the Last Supper. To eat and drink the
bread and wine, now become his body and blood, is the
symbol he bequeathed to his People as the visible sign of
their joining with him in his *berakah*. Now, having come to
the high point of our thanks and praise in response to the
Father's giving, we are ready to externalize what is in our
hearts in the rite of the Communion: it is the consummation
and fulfilment of the celebration of the Eucharist.

All that happens in this Communion Rite is oriented to the
Communion: the assembly prays the Lord's Prayer and they
exchange the sign of peace, the bread is broken, and, on
invitation, all come together in procession for the Communion.
The Communion Rite is, therefore, a preparatory rite —
another preparatory rite, like the Introductory Rites and the
Preparation of the Gifts. 'After the Eucharistic Prayer, the
community prepares by a number of prayers and rites for
communion in the sacrifice' (General Instruction n. 56)

It is important to participate in this phase as preparatory only. There is a different way we respond to, and behave in, activities that are merely preparatory to something else, and not the aim in itself. Take, for example, driving a car. If we are going for a drive for no other reason than to go for an interesting and enjoyable drive, we take all the time we want; we stop when we feel like it, linger and delay as long as we feel like it; getting anywhere is of no concern, and we leisurely savour all that we see and come across on the way. How very different it is when we are driving for the sole purpose of getting somewhere, and as soon as possible. Nothing is of interest except our arrival: we would not dream of stopping to look; any delay is an obstacle.

Coming to the Communion Rite with this attitude, and giving it this type of treatment, means that we have our eyes fixed on our Communion, and will move lightly through its elements. One thing must not happen, and that is that the Communion Rite would create a division between Christ's command to eat and drink (proclaimed in the Words of Institution), and our action of eating and drinking (in the Communion). The unity of the two elements must be preserved at all costs. In the earliest celebrations of the Eucharist, after the Amen there was just the one action of the breaking of the bread, and then ministers and assembly received the body and blood of the Lord. Gradually other elements were added; they constitute a rather long rite now — perhaps too long for a preparation — and anything that makes them longer, or presents them as an end in themselves must be avoided.

The overall thrust in the preparation is to retain our experience of that free choosing of all that God is giving to us in our life now, which we sum up as a response of thanks and praise; and, at the same time, to develop our experience of WE: to build up an awareness of our identity as the Christian People: the identity of this assembly. Not to make us 'more worthy', but to bring to life our experience of ourselves as a People 'in Christ'. We will have the opportunity of exercising, in our response to symbol and prayers, the principal aspects of US, the assembly.

We can experience ourselves as part of the total People:

extend our vision of US here.

The People are those baptized into Christ, sharing his life, his person. As used to be proclaimed in older liturgies at this point before the Communion: 'The Holy to the holy!' *(Sancta sanctis)*.

Four elements provide the experience, namely:
> The Lord's Prayer;
> Rite of Peace;
> Breaking of the Bread;
> Communion.

Lord's Prayer

This prayer has long been used as a preparation, and it is easy to see its suitability. The petition for 'our daily bread', as well as including all our daily needs, has close connection with the Eucharist, and is interpreted in a sacramental sense; further, we pray as a forgiven people, and as a people reconciled in mutual forgiveness. It is an important prayer in any Christian community: it is the first prayer that a catechumen recites as part of initiation into the Christian community; it is the one prayer that even in pre-ecumenical times all Christians would recite together — a Christian anthem; it is special because it was Jesus who gave it to us, not just as a suitable formula, but implying the right to use it and experience God as 'our Father'.

As an element contributing to our experience, it keeps alive what has already been stirred in us: the petition 'hallowed be thy name' echoes 'Holy, holy, holy Lord'; 'thy kingdom come', the two Invocations of the Holy Spirit; 'thy will be done' echoes the basic attitude of sacrifice — obedience.

The opening words, 'Our Father', say it all for us: ALL of our Christian experience. The Father is he who gives ALL; he is the source of ALL we have and are; he is OUR Father, the one Father of all in this assembly, and of every person, dead or living.

Out of reverence for the Lord's Prayer, it is customary to lead into it by an INVITATION. And also to round it off with an ancient doxology: the ACCLAMATION 'For the kingdom. . .'

By way of transition between the Lord's Prayer and the Acclamation there is a prayer which expands the final petition 'deliver us from evil', which is known as an EMBOLISM. It sums up deliverance from evil in 'peace', and adds two aspects of it, namely freedom from sin, and freedom from disorder. All of these expressions mean the same thing: peace. Peace, that is, in its full biblical significance. It is often heard in its Hebrew form, *shalom*, a word which means much more than absence of war, freedom from strife, or quiet and harmony. It is not acquiesence in the existing state of things, nor is it the avoidance of confrontation. *It is the quality of 'whole-ness': everything being as it should be, integrated. It is the experience of an integrated person, and of 'completeness' in relationships.* It is everything being saved and redeemed; reconciled, healed, free, which is to say, without sin. Peace is a global term including all that salvation in Christ is.

We should say something about the 'anxiety' in our English version of the Embolism: it causes a number of people a lot of confusion and annoyance. As we have been explaining, the prayer is for peace, and deliverance from what is not peace. Peace is a *quality of life*, not an emotional state; the 'anxiety' from which we ask to be protected is *not* the anxiety with which psychologists deal. It is not a word taken from psychology: it could not be, as the prayer, with that phrase, dates back to a time before there was interest in emotional disorders. What it means is 'not being together', or in the terminology we have adopted, not being centered, being 'hooked', kept 'outside' and acting from part of me.

In the petition we express the trust that we are graced with ALL aspects of Christ's salvation.

Rite of Peace

The assurance of possessing this peace of Christ because of the promise of Jesus is expressed in the PRAYER, 'Lord Jesus Christ, you said to your apostles' which begins this rite of peace. It is remarkable in being addressed to Jesus Christ — prayers in liturgy are usually addressed to the Father — and it alerts us to the closeness of the Communion.

There follows a WISHING OF PEACE by the presiding celebrant to the assembly, 'The peace of the Lord be with you always,' and the assembly's response, 'And also with you.' Then the people may greet one another.

How effective the people's greeting of one another will be in preparing them for the Communion by deepening their experience of being ONE in Christ, while keeping alive their response of thanks and praise, will depend on their attitude to this element. The form of the greeting is to be 'in accord with the customs of the people.' The greeting, however it is done, is to be natural and free, and certainly not causing embarrassment nor discomfort. There is one difficulty about it. It is not an everyday greeting, saying 'It's nice to see you,' nor 'Glad to be with you,' or anything like that. Least of all is it to develop into a minor 'orgy' of hand-pumping and back-slapping, like the players of a victorious team. This is wrong because it has the effect of stopping the movement of the preparation towards the Communion; as well, a greeting like this is not a faith-activity.

As a preparation for the Communion, it is *an expression and experience of faith*: a prayer said to one another, about one another: an expression of the experience of sharing Christ's life and prayer here and now; and wishing to one another the experience of Christ in our persons and our relationships. This thanks and praise we experience we have in common with one another and with Christ.

Breaking of Bread

Originally this was the only rite which occurred between the Eucharistic Prayer and the Communion. The celebration of the Eucharist once took its name from it, and was called 'the breaking of the bread' (Acts 2:43). It is *the* most important element in this Communion Rite.

In the pre-1969 rite this action had dwindled into insignificance, 'slipped in furtively' Martimort remarks, in that the celebrant broke only the host destined for his communion, as the other little hosts, called 'particles', were pre-broken. In the present Rite it can have a deep significance. The assembly need not expect this element to convey the experience it is intended to, unless it really is a symbol, and not as heretofore, 'slipped in furtively'. To be the symbol of Breaking of Bread there are several requirements in the new Rite, mentioned in the General Instruction: (1) 'The eucharistic bread, even though unleavened and traditional in form, should be made in such a way that the priest can break it and distribute the parts to at least some of the faithful.' (2) 'It is suitable to use one large paten for the consecration of the bread for the celebrant, ministers, and faithful.' The use of small hosts should be restricted to use only 'when the number of communicants is large or other pastoral needs require it.' (3) 'The gesture of the breaking of the bread. . . clearly shows the eucharist as a sign of unity and charity,' by giving it adequate time and expressive execution. (4) This takes for granted that 'the faithful should receive the body of the Lord in hosts consecrated at the same Mass.' (General Instruction nn. 283, 293,56)

After the breaking, there is an element, called the Commingling, which is the rite of dropping a small part of the bread into the chalice. It is so brief that it can hardly have any impact on the assembly.

It was customary to sing during the Breaking what was called a *confractorium*, that is a litany to accompany the action. This is the 'Lamb of God'. It is an invocation to Jesus Christ who is exercising his saving power in the assembly even now. It is, however, secondary to the action of the Breaking.

When performed as it should be, and clearly is a Fraction Rite, the breaking of the bread is the perfect sign of the relationship of the people with one another in Christ. St Paul wrote in 1 Corinthians:

Because there is one bread,
we who are many are one body,
for we all partake of the one bread. (10:16)

And the *Didache* gives this prayer over the broken bread:

As this broken bread was scattered over the mountains and when brought together became one, so let your Church be brought together from the ends of the earth into your kingdom.' (9:3)

We, who are receiving freedom from sin and peace from Christ, experience the oneness of his Body, being 'brought together' into it, in our thanks and praise.

Communion Invitation

'The priest then shows the eucharistic bread to the faithful. He invites them to participate in the meal and leads them in an act of humility.' (General Instruction, n. 56)

There is great joy in the PROCLAMATION-INVITATION:
> This is the Lamb of God
> who takes away the sins of the world.
> Happy are those who are called to his supper.

'Happy' is the 'blessed' of the beatitudes: the experience of those who are followers of Christ — all Christians, and not just 'we' who are here. Our thanks and praise is extended beyond ourselves, and bears on ALL.

The RESPONSE, 'Lord, I am not worthy. . .' is still expressing joy. It is not the exclamation of a wretched sinner, but of a *healed* sinner. Ralph Keifer offers a more suitable translation: 'Happy indeed are we, for though we are sinners, you call us to your table.'

The Communion

The assembly come to the Communion in PROCESSION, which, especially when they come singing, enhances the experience of being together in the action: hence 'communion' — people in a fellowship of faith and love.

Communion in the hand was the practice from the beginning. The change in Eucharistic devotion, dealt with in Chapter 13, was behind the change from hand to tongue. Each communicant has the right today to choose which way she or he will receive. Communion under both forms of bread and wine is a better symbol, and it is now being restored. The tendency seems to be that communion under both kinds is the normal practice; large numbers, however, create a difficulty.

The bread and wine are MINISTERED: Before handling the Lord's body to each communicant, a minister shows the bread to each person by raising it a little and saying, 'The body of Christ'. The communicant answers 'Amen' and receives the bread. A similar formula, 'The blood of Christ' precedes the ministering of the cup.

The AMEN response of each member of the assembly is

the acceptance — the full acceptance with thanks and praise — of WHO they are, and WHAT they are in Christ. The Amen is not a response just to the fact of the presence of Jesus Christ in the bread and wine. The minister does not say, 'This is the Body of Christ', or 'Receive the Body of Christ', referring only to the bread; but 'The Body of Christ' acknowledging who the person is by reason of baptism, and what the assembly is and does in this Eucharistic celebration. This point was made a few years ago in the U.S. Bishops' Liturgy Newsletter (September 1976), and in support of it they quoted St Augustine. Because this idea may sound strange to some, and even unacceptable, we feel that it would be helpful to quote the passage.

> Hear, in short what the Apostle, or better, what Christ says by the mouth of the Apostle concerning the sacrament of the Lord's table: 'We, being many, are one bread, one body.' That is all there is to it, as I have quickly summed it up. Yet do not count the words, but rather weigh their meaning; for if you count them they are few, but if you ponder them, their import is tremendous. One bread, the Apostle said. No matter how many breads were placed before him then, still they were only one bread. No matter how many breads are laid upon the altars of Christ throughout the world today, it is but one bread. What is meant by one bread? St Paul interpreted it briefly: 'We, being many, are one body.' This bread is the body of Christ, to which the Apostle refers when he addresses the Church: 'Now you are the body of Christ and his members.' That which you receive, that you yourselves are by the grace of the redemption, as you acknowledge when you respond Amen. What you witness here is the sacrament of unity.'

The use of the expression 'The Body of Christ. Amen', which dates back to the early Church, expresses what we are experiencing in the Communion:

-- that we, the assembly, are the Body of Christ;

— our assent, and full commitment of ourselves, to this People;

— Christ actively present among us, the worshipping assembly.

To the proclamation of the minister

'that which you receive,

that you yourselves are

by the grace of the redemption',

as we receive the bread in our hands and pronounce our Amen, we give voice to our acceptance of ourselves as we are in Christ. Amen is TOTAL ACCEPTANCE.

After Communion

At this point of the celebration, having experienced the high point of the Eucharist, there is really place for only one activity: SILENT PRAYER. The people need time to stop and reflect on what they have been doing, and its implications for them. The less time we spend with an experience the less impact it has on us. Hence it is natural and desirable to have a pause in activity in order to reflect and pray silently.

Before the new Rite, the time after Communion used to be called 'thanksgiving after Communion'. This could hardly be used today, since we have been engaged in thanksgiving at least since the Eucharistic Prayer began. It would appear to be more of a 'bridging' time. The people assembled for the Eucharist came from various places and situations, and will soon return there again. *This silence is an opportunity to realize, and experience, not 'I' returning, but 'I-who-have-celebrated-the Eucharist' returning.*

Sometimes another form of prayer can be used in place of silent prayer: a reflection or a hymn, for example. Whatever is chosen, its purpose remains the same: to integrate the Eucharistic response into our total lives.

The Communion Rite, and the whole Liturgy of the Eucharist, then comes to a close, with 'sober simplicity,' in a Prayer after Communion, a prayer of petition that asks, in some form or other, for the lasting effects of the celebration in our lives.

Summary

The prayer of thanks and praise of the assembly is, like everything else, the work of Jesus Christ.

The assembly comes to their Eucharistic response by focusing on, and responding to —
  (1) the presiding celebrant,
  (2) the bread and wine.

We come into the Liturgy of the Eucharist from the General Intercessions. The last words of the Concluding Prayer, '. . .through Christ our Lord. Amen' express our experience as we now commence this new stage: the experience is one of complete dependence on Christ, and the assurance of utter trust in him.

   (1) To us, then, through the PRESIDING CELEBRANT Christ causes us to remember gratefully and with praise God's saving deeds in the past — and in the present and future! He gives us in our hearts thanks and praise — *his* thanks and praise.

   While moved by this we also focus especially on what the presiding celebrant says and does with the bread and wine:
   (2) Through the BREAD AND WINE Christ gives us an experience, through progressively 'seeing more'
   -- of God's gifts to us (Preparation of the Gifts)
   — of the gift of Jesus Christ, now (Invocation of the Holy Spirit; Words of Institution),
   — of ourselves responding in him (Memorial Prayer),
   — of the fullness of thanks and praise 'in him' (Doxology),
   — of *all* of us sharing in it in him (Breaking of the Bread),
   — of being his 'body', People of the Covenant, of BEING CHRIST.

As so often in the celebration of the Eucharist we 'frame' something in order to respond, so we do in the Liturgy of the Eucharist. Indeed, that is *all* we do — or, that is what Christ does — for us HE frames (1) God performing saving deeds for us, and (2) the bread and wine; and HE responds in us.

'Eating and Drinking'

The action of eating and drinking, chosen by Jesus Christ and given to us as *the* action of the Eucharist, constitutes it as the 'summit of' all life's actions. It therefore warrants some further consideration of its meaning and significance. There is also another reason: that is a wrong understanding of its meaning that has arisen through the use of a model which is misleading. We are referring to the 'nourishment model'; it will be dealt with later.

The action of Communion — eating and drinking — is a symbolic action. It has the same meaning as the Amen we say on receiving the bread we will eat, and the cup from which we will drink. This is the meaning that Jesus gave it.

Bread from heaven; bread of life

The principal source of our understanding of 'eating and drinking' is chapter 6 of St John's gospel. In order to discover its meaning there we have to see how it is used in the full context. A re-reading of that chapter would be very helpful to see the full import of what we are saying here.

In John 6, Jesus is revealing himself for the people to believe in him: that is, to accept him in faith for what he is. In the opening of the chapter, Jesus reveals himself in two miracles, the miracle of the loaves, and the miracle of walking on the water. After each miracle, the gospel remarks on the response of the crowd.

The miracles are followed by Jesus revealing himself by means of a discourse, or homily, in the synagogue in Capernaum. He is not just a wonder-worker, he tells them: they should see more than that in the miracle of the loaves and fishes. In his elaboration of his homily we can learn the meaning of Eucharistic eating and drinking. The taking off point is 'bread', the bread for which the people had followed him to Capernaum. Jesus leads them to think of 'food which endures to eternal life'; and to a further idea: 'belief in him whom God has sent' — that is, belief in himself.

The Jews to whom he is speaking introduce the subject of the manna on which their ancestors lived during their sojourn in the desert. It was called 'bread from heaven', and it is associated with the concept of giving 'life to the world'; 'the bread of life.' The phraseology used is seen as making a reference to the great event of the giving of the Torah on Mount Sinai. Hence, 'bread from heaven' replaces the Torah in its life-giving power.

Jesus takes the association further: HE is that source of life, replacing manna, replacing the Torah: 'I am the bread of life. . .the bread which has come down from heaven.'

This claim is now driven home in John's gospel through the use of two more concepts — concepts familiar to John's readers — 'wisdom', and 'the one sent.'

Wisdom

That this chapter has also a number of allusions to Wisdom is obvious from the phrases used. The phrases associated with wisdom are: 'to come', 'to eat and drink' and 'to hunger and thirst'.

The words, 'he who comes to me' is a stereotyped phrase which John combines with a variety of words and ideas; for example 'No one can come to me unless. . .'; 'Everyone who has heard and learned from the Father comes to me.' There are examples of 'to come' also in the Synoptics: 'Let the children come to me' (Matthew 19:14); 'every one who comes to me. . .' (Luke 6:47).

'Coming' is also associated with 'eating and drinking', for example: 'he who comes to me shall not hunger, and he who believes in me, shall never thirst.'

Such phrases of invitation from Wisdom in wisdom literature are found in Proverbs:
'Come, eat of my bread
and drink of the wine I have mixed.' (9:5),
and in Sirach:
'Come to me, you who desire me,
and eat your fill of my produce. . .
Those who eat me will hunger yet more,
and those who drink me will thirst for more.' (24:19)

Hence the eating of the bread from heaven means the eating and drinking of wisdom. In different ways in John 6, those who eat and drink are promised eternal life, and will not die. The same promise is made in wisdom literature, for example in Proverbs:

'For he who finds me finds life
and obtains favour from the Lord.' (8:35)

In John the bread from heaven has been given the life-giving functions of the Torah and wisdom. This is Jesus' claim; this is how he presents himself for their acceptance. Jesus, not wisdom, is the living bread that finally satisfies: 'I am the bread of life'; 'I am the bread which came down from heaven.'

'The one sent'

The other concept which qualifies the significance of Jesus as bread from heaven is 'the one sent': 'For I have come down from heaven, not to do my own will, but the will of him who sent me'. Jesus presents himself as 'the one sent by the Father', — so that people can 'be drawn' to him, will believe in him. He is sent to be life-giving; those who accept him are given eternal life: 'Truly, truly I say to you, he who believes has eternal life.' 'Belief' includes confidence and trust in the Son. The claims made for his person, in the concepts used in John 6, are the basis of this trust. To accept Jesus is to place trust in him.

The claims are made in the images of Torah, wisdom, the one sent. Acceptance in faith is spoken of in the images of eating and drinking:

'the one sent' is to be accepted by 'belief in' him;
'Wisdom' is to be accepted by 'eating and drinking.'

It is the intention of Jesus that in the Eucharist the assembly perform the *action* of eating and drinking — the faith-expressing action of 'faith-eating' and 'faith-drinking.' This gets emphatic treatment in John: 'Truly, truly, I say to you, unless you eat the flesh of the Son of man and drink his blood you have no life in you.' This clearly refers to the action of partaking of the body and blood of Christ in the Eucharist.

Clearly, too, the action is not a hunger satisfying experience. The *quantity* of food and drink are not relevant. It is in the nature of drinking a toast — which is intended as a personal expression of an inner attitude, and not to satisfy one's drink-needs.

To eat and drink as Jesus told us requires that the person's faith and trust are active; in the same way as is required to say 'Amen.'

'Nourishment model'

It is a symbol which is open to misunderstanding in today's world. Food, in our time, has lost a meaning and significance: the personal meaning — or better, the 'interpersonal' meaning — is neglected. More than one factor has contributed to this change. We are very food conscious today: the right food and the wrong food; too much food for some, too little for others; food and nourishment, supplying energy, giving growth; the nutritional value of different foods in terms of protein, carbohydrate, vitamins, fibre and kilojoules; food as pleasure-giving, hunger-satisfying. Food has lost a lot of its association with meals; or rather, meals are losing their significance and are limited to 'eating food'. Fewer and fewer meals are being eaten today. There are young people who have *never* eaten a meal — though they have eaten plenty of food. Food, not meals, are our concern today.

A real meal is a gathering of people who experience fellowship together while they talk and eat and drink together: the food, is of secondary significance; a meal is a *personal experience*. People eating and/or drinking while viewing television, or rushing breakfast, or having a snack for lunch, or a business lunch — and in many more situations — are not having a meal; they are just eating food. Jesus' command to eat and drink was principally to have a meal together, in the sense of a faith-experience of one another: to share in the expressing of our shared thanks and praise.

The food/nutrition association can lead to a neglect of the importance of faith and trust in the heart in the action of the Communion. This, for the following reason. Some of the effects of food can now be obtained through pills. All that is necessary in order to benefit by the nutritional value of food is to digest the food, take the pill. It is automatic: get it into your stomach and the effects will follow. It is unfortunately too easy to approach the Communion in this same way; just swallow the bread and wine, and the effects will follow!

Then it becomes something that is no longer an expression of faith, nor an expression of anything at all.

The responses made in connection with the Communion are the most significant and important in the whole celebration. We agree that it is impossible for anyone to go through a whole Eucharist with uninterrupted attention, but if ever we should be attentive to what we are doing, and mean what we say and do, it should be in the Amen and the eating and drinking. Everything possible should be done for us in the celebration to ensure it; we should do everything we can for others, and ourselves, to ensure it. In this connection, there are few more uplifiting sounds than strong faith-filled Amens of the assembly echoing through the church, mingled with the singing, as each one receives the body and the blood of the Lord.

Your Communion is worthy of your attention and care. This activity is a simple and basic exercise that will certainly add to your Communion:

Responding 'Amen'. . .eating

•   Spend a while forming a picture of yourself in the act of having the body of Christ ministered to you. Hear the minister say, 'The body of Christ.' See yourself in your Amen, receiving the bread in your hand, then your eating the body of Christ.

•   Put yourself in a frame; reflect on what YOU 'hear' the minister proclaim, offer to you.

•   Then reflect on what YOU respond: what is on your lips? What is in your heart?

•   Is that what Jesus Christ wants?

20

THE DISMISSAL RITE

The fourth stage of the Eucharist is the Dismissal Rite. It consists of:
— Introduction to this stage, as in the other stages;
— parish announcements;
— 'the priest's greeting and blessing. . . the dismissal which sends each member of the congregation to do good works, praising and blessing the Lord.' (General Instruction n. 57)

The last word and action in the Eucharist is the dismissal of the assembly. There must always have been a formal dismissal in the celebration of the Eucharist, in some form such as 'Go, this is the dismissal.' The technical word used in Latin was *missa*, which can be translated 'dismissal' or 'sending'; it did not mean the end or the conclusion. It is quite extraordinary that this word came to be given to the whole celebration of the Eucharist, in Latin and in the modern languages of the West: the Mass. Extraordinary, because the designation for it was a word that indicated 'a separating', 'a going apart', whereas the whole concept associated with the celebration was an 'assembly', a 'gathering together'.

The simple form of dismissal was later placed in the setting in which we know it today:

The Greeting and response ('The Lord be with you. . .')
The Blessing given by the presiding celebrant, in simple or solemn form,
     leading to
The Dismissal, and
The Response, 'Thanks be to God.'
The going of the people.

A transition

It is misleading to call this stage a concluding rite. It is not an end. The thrust of the Prayer after Communion is the continuance, the non-ending: we are 'never separated from you,' The Eucharist 'has an effect on our lives,' 'brings us to new life', 'living the example of love'.

The 'Go' we hear is not saying 'Get out of here,' but 'Go to. . .' − 'to bring your salvation and joy to all the world,' 'to serve you in each other.' One petition ties together beautifully the thanks and praise of Eucharist with life: 'Help us to thank you by lives of faithful service.'

The Dismissal Rite is, like the Preparation of the Gifts, a transition, or as it has been called a 'crossing the threshold rite.' The late Dr Harold Leatherland makes a comparison with the Introductory Rites, and explains:

> The coming of the people into a congregation does not of itself immediately constitute them an assembly for the worship of God. They must be helped by appropriate words and ritual to become corporately prayerful and adoring, to be ready to listen to God's Word and respond to it in faith.
>
> Nor is it easy for the worshipping congregation, when the liturgy of the Word and Eucharist is over, immediately to see themselves in the role which is now theirs. In the assembly they have been in fellowship with one another and with the Lord. Now they are to be the Lord's witnesses, servants, indeed his Presence, in that part of the great

L

human enterprise where their responsibilities are. *Again they need an appropriate rite to bring home what the ending of the assembly means.*

The 'crossing the threshold' rites must prepare us to experience the two modalities of being the people of God — *fellowship and mission.*

A re-commissioning

We are not 'scattered' at the end of the Eucharist; we are 'sent'. The Dismissal Rite is the liturgical expression of something that belongs to the nature of Christian discipleship: a commissioning. When Jesus chose the original twelve, 'they were to be with him, and to be *sent out* to preach.'

We may regard the 'commissionings' in the gospels as models which give an understanding of the Dismissal Rite: the Twelve 'whom he summoned and gave authority. . . and sent out' (Matthew 10): the sending of the seventy-two 'into every town and place where he himself was about to come' (Luke 10): and the Great Commission at the end of Matthew's gospel, 'Go, therefore, make disciples of all the nations; baptize them. . . and teach them. . .'

In these commissionings those concerned received their mission from the Lord; in the Dismissal Rite those in the assembly receive anew their mission from the Lord. 'Go. . .' sends them FROM this Eucharistic assembly TO their mission in life; FROM one of the Christian's life-activities TO other life-activities of a Christian. *The Dismissal Rite establishes the link that makes a connection between the 'from-to', the connection between Eucharist and life.*

Eucharist and Life

We will consider the connection between our daily lives and our celebrations of the Eucharist by looking at them in the full context of our lives. We first look at our lives, at *ourselves, in a reflection on God's plan as it unfolded in the world, to see the place of mission in them.*

God the Father

God has a PLAN

a loving plan
for me, and all his creation.
His plan: unity
   harmonious order in the world
   wholeness in people
   oneness among them all
   a oneness which is very special:
   no greater oneness could be even imagined.

To implement it
he has to get inside people
in order to CHANGE us:
for when people have not wholeness in themselves
are not at-one with one another,
when there is division, conflict,
something coming between them
they come to integrity and harmony only when they *change*.

God, to fulfil his plan
has to get to people's hearts
in order to transform them.
His salvation, his kingdom will be
people in complete peace and harmony
with themselves, with others.
People perfectly at-one with one another.

God's plan is to change people,
but not by acting directly on them
— 'zapping' them from on high —
as he could do if he wished
but through 'instruments', using his own creation.
He wills to transform through INTERMEDIATE MEANS.
A special means:
this means will *show* the change
for which God is using it:
will be an example, an illustration
SHOWING what is happening to us.

   The visible, transparent means to bring oneness to people
was A PEOPLE already possessing this unity: 'his own
people', Israel.

   When he began to execute his plan on earth, God's first act

was to liberate an oppressed group of people living in Egypt: this was the Exodus.

These people he favoured by bringing them into a special relationship with himself: the Covenant on Sinai. He led them to the land of Canaan, and gave it to them as their own. He cared for them by sending them Judges, Kings and Prophets. All this was in the nature of a preparation, a formation, to make them more completely 'his own people,' 'a kingdom of priests, a holy nation.'

They were to be 'the light of the nations' — the visible means of changing the peoples of the world — 'so that my salvation may reach to the ends of the earth.' (Isaiah 49:6)

The elements in God's plan: • UNITY
                               • CHANGE
                               • VISIBLE MEANS

Jesus Christ

When the time had fully come,
to complete his PLAN
GOD sent his Son,
JESUS CHRIST.

He came to bring UNITY
proclaiming its presence in himself:
'the kingdom of God,' 'eternal life,' 'my peace.'

He came to CHANGE people:
his first preaching was a call to repentance,
'a change of heart.'

He taught that this transformation would take place
in anyone who believed in *him*:
that he, a man who was God, was the MEANS.
Jesus Christ, 'the image of the unseen God' (Col. 1:15)
REVEALED God, showed his saving plan.
No need, now, to try to know God by *imagining*.
We have only to look at Jesus to see what God is like
'To have seen me is to have seen the Father.' (John 14:9)

He showed the infinite power of God
exercising power over nature, whether bread or weather
he healed all manner of diseases

he brought the dead back to life
he forgave sins.

Everything he did, he did with love;
in all his dealings with people, he was moved by compassion.
In this he showed the other great characteristic of the Father:
In him 'the goodness and loving kindness of God our Saviour'
appeared.

That was his life, his life's work;
a life culminated and summed up in his death and resurrection
through which he achieved for us
that change which is salvation —
the special oneness which is God's plan.
'Making peace. . . in one body through the cross' (Eph. 2:15)
he won for the Father 'a holy people':
US.

The Holy Spirit in the Church

Jesus Christ accomplished God's plan;
it is now being completed in our time.
Through him, the Father
'from age to age gathers a people to himself'
into the oneness of the kingdom
by changing them
through visible means.

Now that Jesus Christ has ascended to the Father
and is no longer visible
a new means is being used for God's plan:
PEOPLE
whose life is the Holy Spirit.
The Holy Spirit is their LIFE:
the quality which makes the difference between
what is alive and what is dead;
the quality which is the source of all 'aliveness'
in what is living;
the dynamic in every vital movement
is nothing else, is no one else
than the HOLY SPIRIT.
A plant has life: its plant-life
a bird has life: its bird-life
we have life — which is not our human life

we have life: the Holy Spirit.
The Holy Spirit is *my* life;
the Holy Spirit is *your* life;
the Holy Spirit is *everyone's* life:
all SHARE this one life.
We really could not be more radically one;
it is as though we were all animated by the same soul.

This is the reality,
for every person;
those who profess their faith in it
are Christians.

'Christ has shared with us his Spirit, who, existing as one
and the same being in the head and in the members, vivifies,
unifies, and moves the whole body. This he does in such a
way that his work could be compared with the function
which the soul fulfils in the human body, whose principle of
life the soul is.' (*Constitution on the Church*, n. 7)

WE, this people,
are put in motion by the Holy Spirit.
The Holy Spirit in us gives us an impulse
which moves us
towards one another,
towards oneness
the oneness of Christian LOVE.

Even if Christ had never explicitly taught us
his commandment of love, we would 'know' it;
it is a 'law within us — written upon our hearts,'
the first fruit of the Holy Spirit.

We love, not because we are told to,   ———
but because *we cannot do otherwise if the
Spirit lives in us.*

As Jesus Christ is God made visible,
we, this People, are the 'visible means'
which God uses to complete his plan.
We are 'visibly' his means
in our love for one another and for all people:
'By this love you have for one another
everyone will know that you are my disciples.' (John 13:15)
Like Jesus

we are sent
and we come 'not to be served but to serve.' (Matt.20:28)

> Responding to God's call in their lives according
> to the requirements of social life and the demands
> of human partnership
> they commit themselves to the human community;
> putting their faith in action
> persevering through love
> serving one another in works of love.

> *(Constitution on the Church in the Modern World,
> n. 31)*

My loving acts
are *more* than a service:
the Holy Spirit in moving me towards people to serve them,
comes to life in them
through my serving them;
that is to say, I WITNESS to them.
Witness is communication, not of facts
but of a reality —
the reality of the Holy Spirit,
the life of Christ.

When I love someone, and act lovingly towards that person
he or she is changed, and becomes more loving
more at-one with others.

In this change, the UNITY which is God's plan comes
with me as a MEANS,
a VISIBLE-through-loving means.

We, the People who live by the Holy Spirit,
the body of Christ,
continue Christ's mission
complete his work on earth:
growing in all ways into Christ
every joint adding its own strength
each separate part working according to its function.
So the body grows
until it has built itself up in love
and GOD'S PLAN IS REALIZED.

God comes to us, not like a helicopter, coming
'vertically'; but like a plane coming in to land,
'horizontally' that is, *through* people: through us who
live by the Spirit.

I see myself as part of a missionary Church
an apostolic people.
If I am a Christian, I am on a mission
If I am not living an apostolic life,
I am not a Christian.
(There is no 'associate membership' of Christianity.)

My mission is to people —
to the ones to whom I am 'sent' in the Dismissal Rite —
beginning with those closest to me in my life:
the people I live with
work with
associate with;
the people God sends into my life.
As long as there is *one* person in my life
I have an apostolate.
I will never have to go searching for an apostolate, looking
for what is available, seeking out people to serve; God will
always provide them, and they will be easily at hand.

God the Father sends me
Christ lives in me
to spread ONENESS around me.
My only LIFE in the Spirit
is what contributes to peace and harmony
through being a loving, serving, witnessing person
towards those whom God puts into my life.

In this life our relationship with Jesus Christ is not to be
imagined as a 'face-to-face' one; one that consists in his
helping, consoling, strengthening me; nor of dialogue or of
reciprocal love. He made this clear to Peter, in the last scene
in St John's gospel, when Peter made his triple protestation
of love. On each of the occasions, Jesus responded to Peter,
his response speaking clearly of this relationship of love
between them:
'You love me! Then I send you on your apostolate. As if he
said: 'Those who love me are *with* me on my mission.' The
relationship is 'side-by-side' not face-to-face.

I do not live my relationship with Christ
if I only go *to* him;
I go WITH him!

These thoughts are summed-up for us in Eucharistic Prayer III:

Father, you are holy indeed, and all creation rightly gives you praise

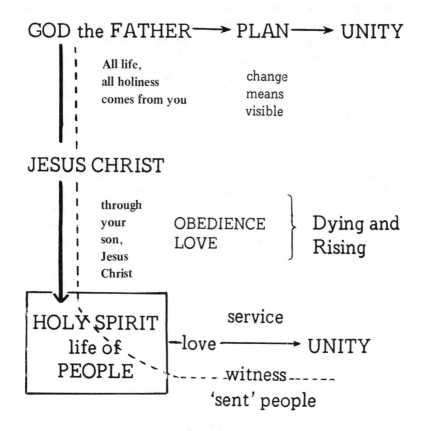

**by the working of
the Holy Spirit**

**from age to age
you gather a people
to yourself,**

**so that from east to west
a perfect offering may be made
to the glory of your name...**

We continue our reflection, now looking at ourselves as a missionary people, a 'sent-people' assembled at liturgy, or any prayer.

Life is building up the body of Christ:
it is in this that my life consists
I spend my life at it
I spend every day at it
just through my ordinary daily life.
All I have to do is to serve lovingly
and the Holy Spirit accomplishes growth and change in
people through my witness.

If this is accomplished through my daily life —
and if this is all there is to life —
what is the value of prayer,
what is the need to spend time at liturgy?

At one time, a spirituality was widespread which saw prayer as the *only* activity which gives life. My charitable activities were seen as causing spiritual energy to weaken. Hence, there was need to return to prayer at regular intervals to be 're-charged', as it were; to go out again to perform works of charity, and so to 'run down' again and require another 're-charging. through prayer or sacrament.

The value of prayer in my life
is not to restore the life which is lost through service.
Far from weakening my life, my service
gives growth and life to me:
growth in the Spirit, life in Christ.
I pray
because my life would not be complete without it.
I pray
because of the way God has made me,
because of the faculties and powers he has given to me
to make me the human person I am.
He has made me more than a person who serves
he has given me more than the power to 'do' lovingly.
He has made me so that
I can REFLECT;
he gave me the ability
to see MEANING in what I 'do'

through reflection.

He calls me to serve and witness
and
to find the meaning and value
of the circumstances and situations of my life
through looking at it in the light of,
through the 'grid'
of his plan.

God does not want me as an instrument
an automatic machine.
To live without reflection
is to half live only.

To live fully
I go out in service: my pre-reflective activity.
I follow it with my reflective activity:
I stop
take time
get in touch with myself
and 'see'
my activities and all about me
as *part of God's plan*;
and listen
and respond.
When I respond
I am praying.

I need both to serve *and* to pray.
To live a life of service without prayer
would be to drift into a faith-less humanism;
to live a life of prayer without service
would be impossible:
there would be nothing to find meaning in.

I move in a cycle
I serve — I pray — I serve — I pray — I serve — I pray
giving the amount of time to each
which gives me a full, human, vital, 'healthy'
life-in-Christ,
through the Holy Spirit
giving glory to the Father.

One manner of prayer, *the* prayer, is the Eucharist.

Eucharist and life: in both I am moved
by the inspiration and impulse of the Holy Spirit —
at one time to respond to the Father
by service
at another time to respond to the Father
by joining the assembly in this prayer.

Servant people

In the Dismissal Rite we accept our lives as people who serve, and we do so in the particular situations we find ourselves in at this time. We freely accept our mission from the Lord; and we thank and praise him for giving it to us, and for the confidence that we will fulfil it. This is something that we must do in the celebration of the Eucharist, and in all liturgical celebrations: there must be a Dismissal. In liturgy, the Prayer of our People, we make a full Christian response (see Chapter 7); we must, therefore, respond to this essential aspect of our Christian lives; our serving, apostolic life. We must make that response: seeing ourselves in our servant role, and appearing as such by acting as people on a mission, people 'sent to. . .'

The form of expression is by *(a) word and (b) action.* (a) We accept with the Christian form of 'yes', that is 'Thanks be to God.' The *berakah* in our hearts from the Liturgy of the Eucharist is still there. Very applicable are the words of Isaiah about Jerusalem:

Then you shall see and be radiant,
your heart shall thrill and rejoice. (60:5)

(b) The action is our 'going': our moving out of the church; leaving the assembly. We are not leaving as we do after a football match, or a show, has ended; because there is no point in staying there. We move out, not to leave that place, but to go to another; not to leave those people, but *to go to others —* *to whom we are sent.*

Because of the meaning in our obeying the command to 'Go', it spoils the significance if at this point a further hymn is sung — the so-called recessional hymn. It is really out of place: why it has come in, or how, nobody seems to know. In the U.S. Bishops' Committee on the Liturgy publication, *Music in Catholic Worship* (1972), it is stated: 'The recessional song has never been an official part of the rite. . .' If this were a concluding rite — which of course it is most definitely not — a song here would be most suitable in rounding the ceremony off. *There is no conclusion to any liturgy: it is always 'open-ended.'*

Some consider that the Eucharist ends too abruptly without a song. While the form of Dismissal Rite we have is perhaps a little on the curt side, the experience of being dismissed is meant to include in it a certain feeling of urgency. It could be compared to what I feel after offending someone I am fond of. I regret so much what I did, and my strongest urge is to see them again, explain and be reconciled. I cannot wait for this to happen; I will not be at ease until it does. That feeling of wanting to go to a particular person, or persons, and eager to get there, is part of the dismissal experience. We desire very strongly to be in action in service. To do this we are directed in the Dismissal; to do this the Holy Spirit is moving us.

Käsemann explains the urge to be 'going' when he writes:

> There is no grace which does not move to action.
> SERVICE is not merely the consequence, but the
> very FORM of grace.

What form will it take for me? I will discover that only when I 'go and open the door.'

> Go and open the door.
> Maybe outside there's
> a tree, or a wood,
> or a magic city.
>
> Go and open the door.
> Maybe a dog's rummaging
> Maybe you'll see a face,
> or an eye,
> or the picture of a picture.
>
> Go and open the door.
> If there's a fog
> it will clear.
> Go and open the door.
> Even if there's only

the darkness ticking,
even if there's only
the hollow wind,
even if nothing is there,
go and open the door.

At least
there'll be a draught.

This activity will help to clarify your understanding and deepen your experience of the Dismissal Rite: to see your response to the Eucharist as one of mission.

Eucharist and Life

1.   What do you consider you have to give as a consequence of celebrating the Eucharist?

Think of it in relation to
        Assembling
        the WORD you have heard
        the Body and Blood you have received, and
        the AMEN you have spoken
        the command 'GO' which is sending you.

2.   How do you see the connection between *praising God* for his gifts to you, and *sharing them* with others?

3.   How would you describe the experience of being 'sent' with thanks and praise?

Synopsis

THE DYNAMIC PROGRESSION OF THE EUCHARIST

We have been explaining the relationship between liturgy
and life: more specifically:
>   praying and living
>   *myself* at praying and living
>   myself in relationship with *others*
>   in living and praying.

The *experience* is of being on a journey — open-ended —
in both aspects of our life: living and praying. The Eucharist
is non-ending, it lives on and on in us; no end to it, open-
ended.

It is an experience through responding to symbols: therefore,
through 'SEEING MORE'.

It all begins with CONSCIOUSNESS — with 'seeing': to
see is to become consciously aware.

CONSCIOUSNESS EXPANDED: TO SEE MORE finds me
interested, involved, reflective, responsible.

TO SEE MOST is when I see that the above is my involvement with God: my relationship with him; my experience of
him.

TO BE MORE and BE MOST is to be a Christian; to be
CHRIST.
>   The Eucharist flows on;
>   we move on, as on a journey
>   in one continuous experience
>   through four stages
>   and many elements.
>   Each stage, as it ends,
>   moves itself to the next one.
>   We, once we are responding,
>   are moved to fullness in thanks and praise,
>   and to fullness in externalization in our lives.

THE DYNAMIC PROGRESSION
of the EUCHARIST

SEE...	MORE	BE...MORE	BE....MOST	BECOME MORE...MOST
ME as I am... OTHERS.... be conscious of...	I (in FAITH) ME IMe with others here and beyond	allow myself to be changed by the WORD as I LISTEN and RESPOND	A BERAKAH – EUCHARISTIC person = respond with PRAISE and THANKS with OTHERS	empowered – gifted – graced – equipped... to go to GIVE to GROW HIS KINGDOM will come.
INTRODUCTORY RITE	WORD – stage	EUCHARISTIC stage		DISMISSAL

Revitalizing

We need to revitalize signs — bring them back to the SYMBOLS they are meant to be — because many symbols have become signs.

The rite of the Eucharist is inexpressibly rich in symbols, as has been seen. Each symbol has the power in it to move us to a prayer-response. Each would do so, if we gave it the time: came to it centered, framed it to 'see more', and listened to receive the response. The continuous movement in the celebration, from one element to the next, gives little or no time for this. Hence it is very helpful, even necessary, to give attention to the symbols outside of the time of the Eucharist.

This is a practice that some people use in their time of prayer, and have found it very helpful, both for their celebration of the Eucharist and their personal prayer.

It entails an application, to any chosen symbol, of the method *'The Process of Responding'* (Chapter 10).

The Eucharist merits this attention and care, since —

Every liturgical celebration,
because it is an action
of Christ the priest and of his Body the Church,
is a sacred action surpassing all others.
No other action of the Church
can match its claim to efficacy,
nor equal the degree of it.

(*Constitution on the Liturgy. n. 7*)

*Begging them to keep silent and not prevent
his martyrdom, St Ignatius of Antioch wrote
in his Letter to the Romans:*

> *'If you keep silent about me,
> I become a word of God;
> but if you love me in the flesh,
> I become a meaningless cry.'*

> (Office of Readings, Tenth Sunday)

Section Five

MINISTERING

21

MINISTERS IN THE CELEBRATION OF THE EUCHARIST

Different ministers

Participating in the Eucharist is *one* activity in the Christian's life; ministering in the Eucharist is *one* ministry in the Christian's life.

We always had ministers in the Mass, especially the more solemn celebrations. The new Rite has not only introduced new ministries in the Eucharist, it has also clarified their role in the celebration and their significance in the Church. The General Instruction speaks of 'diversity of orders and functions' in the Eucharistic assembly, so that 'in the liturgy the Church may be seen in its variety of orders and ministries.' (n. 58) The different orders and functions in the Rite of Mass are:

Bishop: The bishop being the high priest of his flock, a celebration of the Eucharist with the bishop acting as presiding celebrant is the clearest revelation of the Church, the body of Christ.

Priest Celebrant: 'He presides over the assembly and leads its prayer.'

Deacon: When the deacon ministers he has his own special functions, such as proclaiming the gospel, and leading the General Intercessions; he may also preach sometimes.

Servers: They are also called acolytes or assistant ministers. Their distinctive ministry is to aid the other ministers, particularly the presiding celebrant, in a celebration of the Eucharist.

Reader: The reader is called by the Church to proclaim the scripture readings before the gospel reading.

Cantor: The cantor, or song-leader, sings the Responsorial Psalm, and may lead in other singing. If the Responsorial Psalm is not sung, but recited, this ministry will be performed by the —

Psalm Leader: This ministry consists in leading the assembly in the praying of the psalm, by reciting the verses.

Commentator: He or she will minister the 'Introductions' to the stages of the rite, the petitions of the General Intercessions, and sometimes give directives to the assembly.

Choir, or **singing-group**; **Instrumentalists**; **Music Director:** They give their service in the ministry of music in the celebration.

Special Ministers of Communion: They assist in the ministering of the bread and chalice in the Eucharist.

Collectors: Collecting the money offerings from the assembly is a liturgical action which takes place during the Preparation of the Gifts.

Ushers: Ushers meet the people at the door, lead them to their places, and in general offer a ministry of welcome and of bringing the assembly together.

Audio-visual operator: In contributing to the participation of the assembly, she or he can be considered to engage in a ministry.

Planner; organizer: The person designated to arrange the celebration, and see to the preparation of the ministers and the place in which the Eucharist will be celebrated.

It is being more and more recognized that these people should come from among members of the community, since ministries are functions of the community. Among others, Robert W. Hovda suggests that 'it seems a good general principle that the roles of leadership in the liturgical assembly should be related to leadership and active involvement in other aspects of the faith community's life' (*There are different ministries*). For example, it is fitting that the petitions or the Intercessions be read by someone engaged in helping the needy in the parish, that ushers be involved in social work, or leaders in catechetics, and so on. Fr Hovda also notes that liturgical ministers are servants within the servant-community of faith, and therefore, it is unfair to them and to the community to place children in the role of ministers: they are not yet community leaders.

Ministry in Eucharist reflects the servant nature of the Christian people and their servant-life. All those listed above as ministers have different functions, a different part to play, in the rite: different people perform different ministries.

Different ministries

God's plan for his kingdom as we outlined in Chapter 20, is to send people on different ministries to one another. St Paul expands this idea of diversity of ministries in the Church in First Corinthians, Chapter 12.

> Now concerning spiritual gifts, brethren, I do not want you to be uninformed. . .
> Now there are varieties of gifts, but the same Spirit; and there are varieties of service, but the same Lord; and there are varities of working, but it is the same God who inspires them all in everyone. To each is given the manifestation of the Spirit for the common good. . .
> All these are inspired by one and the same Spirit, who apportions to each one individually as he wills. For just as the body is one and has many members, and all the members of the body, though many, are one body, so it is with Christ. . .
> For the body does not consist of one member but of many. If the foot should say, "Because I am not a hand, I do not belong to the body," that would not make it any less a part of the body. . .

But as it is, God arranged the organs of the body, each one of them as he chose.

Now you are the body of Christ and individually members of it. And God has appointed in the church first apostles, second prophets, third teachers, then workers of miracles, then healers, helpers, administrators, speakers in various kinds of tongues. Are all apostles? Are all prophets? Are all teachers?. . .

God's plan:
ONE ultimate aim
MANY people
with DIFFERENT functions, different
SERVICES
endowed with a VARIETY OF GIFTS.

God will never call anyone to perform a particular service without giving them the necessary gifts. Everyone is called by God to some services or other; as parents, in our relationships with friends and other people, in the work force, etc. Hence people have different talents, different capabilities; and we do not all have the same capabilities

Christians believe that they are called, not just to services, but to bring Christ to people and people to Christ. This is called 'ministry', or 'apostolate' (both the same word, the former being the Latin, and the latter the Greek form, from the word 'sent'). The gift given to us to engage in an apostolate is called 'charism'. Charism is a gift to be used for others. We use our gifts for others; others use their gifts for us. We *must* use our gifts for others; and we must *allow others* to use their gifts for us. And so the body grows. . .

Purpose of ministries

As in life so in the celebration of the Eucharist there are different ministries performed by people with different gifts. When dealing with the Four Areas in chapter 2, Ministering was seen to be a specific area, Area C. It was said there that the minister is a person who comes between the text-rite and the assembly.

Different people with different tasks and different gifts to perform these tasks in the Eucharist is but one example of the call of Christians to serve the world. They have a symbolic function in the Eucharist. They are not there for convenience, to get things done smartly. Compare it with what you see at an airport when a plane lands. As soon as it stops an army of workers converge on it, and in a flurry of activity begin to clean the passenger area, put things on, take things off, stick pipes into it, and perform a multitude of different tasks – all in order to get the aircraft prepared as quickly and efficiently as possible for its next take-off. Speed and efficiency, the relevant factors in the servicing of aircraft, are not the reason for ministers in the Eucharist. Ministers have a 'theological' value: they speak to our faith, and about ourselves as Christians – ourselves in this celebration as in the rest of our lives.

The aim of each minister is to help us in our participation. They themselves and all their words and actions are for the service of aiding our prayer. Not because they present an impressive spectacle, nor because they look cute, nor to give as many as possible something to do in the ceremony – but to facilitate the assembly in their praying.

Prayer is, as we have always insisted, the work of the Holy Spirit. The minister is, therefore, the means used by the Holy Spirit. This brings us to the place of charisms in ministering; and to the difference between 'ministering' and performing a 'function.'

Let us explain the place of charisms by an example: that of the reader. We can, as we know from experience, take the bible or our breviary and by ourselves pray with its help. The text of bible and breviary have the power to awaken prayer in us. When, however, we have a minister as well as a text, then along with what bible and breviary can offer, we have a person: a person who is chosen by God, gifted for the task, and sent to us at this time specifically in order to move us to prayer. The Holy Spirit comes to us in many ways, and he certainly comes to us in the text of scripture. Much more powerful is it when he acts in us through a *person* whom he appoints and works in for our benefit. This is the reason why liturgical texts are always ministered: the Eucharist offers us 'the most' in help, and the most is a person to minister to us.

The reader whom we have used to illustrate this aspect of ministry, and every minister, contributes to our response by more than natural aids. Ministers do more than gain our attention, help us to know the content of a reading, or convince us by explanation or argument. Because they 'minister': they are not just 'functionaries'. A person can read beautifully and convincingly, or sing very movingly, or act most gracefully, and not act as a 'minister'. To act as a minister, as distinct from a functionary, the person must do something *more than perform*: not just do what a news reader does, or a musical performer. The difference arises not from what the person does, but from *what is going on inside the person* as she or he ministers.

> To encourage the active participation of the people and to ensure that the celebrations are carried out as they should be, it is not sufficient for the ministers to content themselves with the exact fulfilment of their role according to the liturgical laws. It is also necessary that they should so celebrate the liturgy that by this very fact they convey an awareness of the meaning of the Sacred Actions. (*Instruction on the Worship of the Eucharistic Mystery*, 1967, n. 20)

Ministering to the assembly

The minister will succeed in helping the assembly to pray — including overcoming their distractions, being attentive, and activated in faith — *only if the same is happening in him or her*. What ministering requires is —

That the minister be him or herself: Each minister is a particular person: unique; chosen by God as this particular person, including good qualities and bad qualities. This person who is chosen to minister, and not anyone else: with their own particular background and character; their own outlook and interests; and their own particular spirituality. All of these will influence how the person will act as minister; even how he or she will interpret a text. This is what God wants — the minister to be themselves, and not anyone else, or a copy of anyone else; above all not to act out of a 'role', or 'put on an act.'

That the minister is faith-activated: Another way of saying this is 'that the minister is praying', except that it might be misinterpreted as meaning that the minister is 'saying prayers'. What we mean is: that the minister be praying in the sense of making a faith-response.

If a person just performs, just vocalizes what is on the page of the lectionary, it would be just as useful to use a tape-recorder. The *person* is contributing nothing. When activated by faith in Christ's presence, the minister has a different feeling — about what she or he is doing, and about himself or herself:

- ministering, at the service of the assembly;
- called to it, by Christ and the Church;
- with the aim of an inner change in the people present to a deeper prayer;
- guided and activated by the Holy Spirit;
- not he or she alone, but Christ in him or her;
  etc.

Each minister, whatever the ministry, seeing more through the eyes of faith, will *be* different, *act differently* and *sound differently* from a functionary or performer.

That the minister loves and trusts the assembly: Only if we love and trust people is it possible to help them in their growth and inner activities. To come to them with anything of an attitude of 'I'll make the so-and-sos sit up!' or 'What's the point in bothering about them?' or any disapproval, judgement, or rejection would be a disaster as far as ministering is concerned.

With this goes a sensitivity to the assembly on this particular occasion, and a readiness to adapt to their needs. It requires the ability and caring that we can see and hear how they are, sense what is going on in them, and what can be done for them now as part of ministering to them.

That the minister is confident: This confidence is not, but definitely not, based on past performance, like 'No-worries! I've done this hundreds of times.' That, too, would be disastrous. The confidence will be in the God-given call and charism.

It goes without saying that a minister may have, with a feeling of confidence also a feeling of apprehension. That would be quite normal: we can have a mixture of opposite feelings.

That the minister use the skills of the specific ministry: 'As ministers our goal is to bring our whole lives — knowledge and talents, skills and hopes, creativity and love, enthusiasm and humour — to the service of the Christians gathered in worship. We take that small, sometimes overlooked out-pouring of the Spirit of Jesus in us, and we live it for others and for the Lord.' (William A. Bauman, *The Ministry of Music*).

The minister is required to perform well — but more important is the faith-response. 'Doing something well is not as important as allowing your soul to fill it. How you look or sound is not important; what is important is what you feel (as if God were feeling your prayer, not looking at your movements)' is advice that all ministers could follow. It will be demanding, and will require, for each minister, not only personal qualities, but also a formal preparation. Such a preparation would cater for (a) SPIRITUALITY, including an appreciation of the meaning of this ministry; and (b) TECHNICAL EXPERTISE in the skills of the specific ministry.

Then there will be fulfilled in the Eucharist what was foretold about the Church:

> We are to grow up in every way
> into him who is the head, into Christ,
> from whom the whole body,
> joined and knit together
> by every joint with which it is supplied,
> when each part is working properly,
> makes bodily growth and upbuilds itself in love.
> *(Eph. 4:14-16)*

If you act in any ministry, either regularly or from time to time, this activity will serve to deepen your awareness and your ministering:

Ministering to the Assembly

Ask yourself:

When I am called to act as a minister in the Eucharist —

What does that involve?

What personal resources are available to me?

The Assembly and the Ministers

Intrinsic to the experience of Eucharist, and all liturgy, is that of being ministered to. As well as the response of the members of the assembly to one another, and their response to objects (such as altar or crucifix), there is always *an encounter between each member of the assembly and another person, that is, a minister:* a response given by a member of the community to a person representing the Christian community, the Church; an interaction between the served and the servant.

In general we welcome anybody who serves us. We could give as instances a shop assistant, a doctor, a telephone operator. There are situations, however, when we do not welcome either the service or the servant. This is quite understandable, and it is well to realize what being served in liturgy implies for us and demands of us. Being served means renouncing independence and accepting someone else's help; it includes renouncing an 'I can do it myself' attitude, and allowing another person to take the initiative; it asks for a submission to a person we did not choose, may know nothing about; indeed, may not approve of. That is all part of the experience of Eucharist, because that is the manner of response in the rite: that is, the response of a person being served.

The rite is full of instances of this experience: it occurs in regard to *each and every* minister, the presiding celebrant and all the others who act as ministers in the celebration, even those we may not be able to see.

Responding to the minister

The experience is one of a relationship between me and *this* minister who is now in action. If he or she is going to minister to me, to help me as God intends, I must accept him or her as a minister — as a minister to me. What does it mean to accept a person *as a minister to me?* Let us start with this quotation:

> The spoken word in the liturgical service is not an eighth sacrament, yet it has sacramental value; and the minister, announcing the Gospel, explaining the liturgy, presenting to the people the mystery of the Word made flesh 'for us and for our salvation,' bringing them into the fellowship of heaven, giving them an insight into the present and future reality of the kingdom of God, acts in a capacity which is qualitatively different from that of an orator, a lecturer, a psychologist, a counsellor. He acts sacramentally, as channel of the Word.' (George A Tavard, 'The Function of the Minister in the Eucharistic Celebration').

I am in a special relationship with a person who ministers to me. My relationship is an *accepting* one. Remember that I accept only what I *see* in a person; hence, in order to accept this person as ministering to me, I 'see more' in the minister before me. I see in this minister a person who is unique, with his or her own character, ideas, interests, limitations, faults, spirituality and manner of ministering; who is selected by

God for me, to perform this service for me in this celebration. I see him or her as 'graced', specially endowed with gifts by God to perform this service to me, and sent to me.

I accept that minister not as clever, skilled or likeable but as the means through whom the Holy Spirit will affect me now. I yield myself to be ministered to, because Christ chose him or her for this occasion. It is not the person's good qualities that gain my assent, but my faith in Christ's presence and action in him or her. I accept, not because of my esteem for the minister's skills (a good reader, attractive speaker, impressive performer) but because I trust in the power of the Holy Spirit.

Responding to the person

The service which ministers give us is — themselves. In 'serving up' the text and rite for the assembly they are not like a shop assistant, by whom I can be served without even looking at his face. Ministers are not just reading for us to save us the trouble of reading ourselves, like a TV news reader — although they do that for us. Nor are they only helping us with the text, as a teacher would read with chosen emphases for the benefit of the pupils' understanding — and yet they do that, too. When the presiding celebrant lifts up the plate and the chalice, he is not just enabling us to have a better look at them — although he would want to do that. We respond, not just to the words they read, the ideas they present, the objects they use — but to THEM: the ministers speaking, the ministers making gestures and movements.

One way of illustrating this is by taking the example of a widespread practice among our people at the Eucharist. The practice we refer to is the using of hand-missals during a celebration. Originally introduced in order to give people the opportunity of understanding what the priest was saying, at a time when the Mass was all in Latin, small missals in various forms are still being published, even though the original reason — a language the people did not understand — no longer exists. They are available, and the congregation makes use of them. The result? The reduction of actual ministering, the eliminating of the effectiveness of ministers. The following story has become somewhat of a classic:

A visiting priest, one Sunday morning at the Eucharist he was celebrating, found the parishioners with the heads all buried in their missals. He found this disconcerting, and when he came to read the gospel, having started in the usual way, 'The Lord be with you. . . A reading. . .' and was confronted with the whole congregation assiduously reading their books and ignoring him, he said: 'I think that I read clearly, and that you will understand what I read without looking at your books. Could I ask you to put them aside, and for the benefit of us all, look at me and listen to me. I think you will see the advantage.' As soon as he stopped talking, the congregation responded with great spontaneity: 'Praise to you, Lord Jesus Christ!'

If we concentrate on the text alone, then it is to the text we respond — and not to the minister. If we respond to the text, there is no point in having a person minister to us, because the person is ignored. If we give our attention to *what* the person is saying, rather than to *the person* saying it, we are deprived of their ministerial help. We are rejecting the ministry. It is the ministers' own faith and trust and response that influence us and move us to prayer, not what they read or do. *The effect of ministers is from their charism, not from the content.*

To allow others to enter our lives in this way, to hand ourselves over to them especially in regard to our prayer, is demanding, and is something to be cultivated. The following reflection will open you up more to the experience:

Being Ministered To

Jesus, speaking about the last judgment, made this statement: 'Truly, I say to you, as you did it to one of the least of these my brethren, you did it to me.' If Jesus Christ in person were a minister in liturgy to you, how would you respond to him? What kind of attention would you give? How would you value his ministry?

A minister is 'one of the least of his brethren', so what would that ask of you in the Eucharist? What kind of response would it involve?

How would you describe the experience of being ministered to?

Section Six

EVALUATING-PLANNING A EUCHARIST

22

EVALUATING AND PLANNING
OF PARISH LITURGY

We began this book by focusing our interest on participation. The participation of the assembly, as we saw in Chapter 2, is affected, favourably or unfavourably, by Helps and Hindrances.

Ministry is directly concerned with what helps and what hinders participation. Its aim is to provide more Helps for this assembly, and to minimize Hindrances. Helps, that is, to improve their response to the rite.

Ministry has to concern itself with Helps/Hindrances not only during the Eucharist, but also at other times. This ministering outside of the time of celebration will be on two levels.

One will be a more or less permanent body (usually the parish liturgy committee) who will have responsibility for long-term changes and planning. These changes include whatever might be done in regard to structural changes or decoration of the place, new furnishings, training courses for ministers, and whatever is included in Area A (The Place) or Area C (Ministers).

The other level of responsibility is planning individual celebrations, one at a time. It is mainly contained in Area B (Text and Rite), and its principal activities are Evaluating and Planning.

Planning

Both levels have the same aim: to offer as much help as possible to the assembly in their response to the rite. Both also entail planning.

We are choosing to use 'planning' as a technical term, in order to make a distinction between planning and 'preparation'. We will reserve 'preparing' to refer to the personal preparation of ministers: that is, the time and activity immediately preceding the celebration.

When a person or a group sit down for the purpose of planning a Eucharist, they will be guided in their decisions by a definite aim. The answer to the question, 'Why do this rather than that?', must have some basis for it. If they see their planning as a ministry, the basis will have to be the participation of the assembly: this choice will result in giving greater help to the assembly in their prayer.

The next question relevant in their decisions is, 'How will we decide what gives greater help?' It is necessary to be explicit on the answer to this question. In quite a few groups we discovered that, without explicitly formulating it, they assumed as a principle, 'If you give people what they like they will participate better.' Hence their search was for 'what the people like', and their Eucharists were planned on the basis of 'the people's likes'. Obviously they did not see how wrong this was. It did not dawn on them that a Eucharist is planned to give people what they *need* in order to pray well. The point is that people are not helped by giving them what they like, but what they need. This must be appreciated by those who plan liturgies. Those who plan must also be very clear on the difference between 'a need' and a 'like' or 'want'.

The conflict between needs-wants exists not only in planning liturgy, but in all life. It will almost certainly influence the the effectiveness of a planner or planning group. It is worth while, therefore, to spend time in clarifying the difference for ourselves.

Needs and Likes

A.   A Story

The Master Nan-In had a visitor who came to enquire about Zen. But instead of listening, the visitor kept talking about his own ideas. After a while, Nan-In served tea. He poured tea into his visitor's cup until it was full, then kept on pouring. Finally the visitor could not stand it any longer. 'Don't you see it's full?' he said, 'you can't get any more in!'

'Just so,' replied Nan-In, stopping at last. 'And like this cup, you are filled with your own ideas. How can you expect me to give you Zen, unless you offer me an empty cup?'

Identify the conflict between the visitor's needs and wants in the above story.

What did he really *need*?

B.   Your own experience
List for yourself in two columns:

What do I NEED (is really necessary and helpful) FOR ME TO LIVE?	What do I FANCY (like, want)?

C. Reflection on your lists
Ask yourself such questions as:

— what made me put things in one column rather than the other?

— what made me put certain things in the second column?

Assuming that in the first column your list included something like: food, shelter, care, education, someone to love, being appreciated, faith, meaning etc.; and in the second things such as: plenty of money, nice clothes, theatre/concerts, travel, hi-fi equipment, playing sport, etc.

-- look at the second column as revealing *your own subjective tastes and preferences.* You chose these, because YOU like them, they appeal to YOU, the person YOU are.

D. The relevance for liturgy
Make two more lists:

What do I NEED (is necessary, helpful) FOR PRAYING THE EUCHARIST?	What do I FANCY (like, want) in the Eucharist?

E.   Reflection
Ask yourself:

— what difference is there between the influence of my needs and my likes in the Eucharist?

— what connection is there between *my* needs, and the communal needs of the assembly?

Needs and Likes

Needs can be elusive; at least, the discernment of them. During the time when religious congregations were first engaged in the work of renewal and up-dating, questionnaires abounded. The committees who were appointed to direct the work, wanting to proceed collegially, and to hear from every religious, asked for a response from each religious. Often, however, the religious failed to come up with any responses. When no replies came to such queries as: 'What do you want us to do? Let us know your NEEDS', or more simply, 'What do you NEED?', the committees experienced great frustration. 'Why don't they tell us what they need?'

The fact was that the religious did not themselves know what their needs were. Not surprisingly, for it is not to be expected that people can tell right away what their needs are, least of all in a particular area like religious life or liturgy.

People can feel that they have needs without being able to identify them. Unfortunately, many reach out for remedies, selecting them at random and applying them arbitrarily. The remedies may turn out to be quite harmful; at best they will be no more than band-aids.

This is what happened on the liturgy scene. As a result, the Church lost at least fifteen years when enthusiasm was high and plenty of attention and energy was directed to liturgy. What happened was somewhat like if a person went to the doctor with some ailment — say, a bad back or constant headache — and said to him: 'Doctor, I have a bad back. Will you prescribe a week's rest for me, please?' Or 'I have a constant headache, and I want you to give me a strong painkiller.' Of course he would refuse. He would first want to know more about the symptoms in order to diagnose the ailment, before he would decide on the treatment. The (1) treatment/remedy would depend on the (2) ailment, which would be revealed only by the (3) symptoms. In dealing with Eucharists which were crying out for improvement in the assembly's participation, what was done in those times was to decide on the treatment/remedy, but without discovering the ailment; that is, what the ailment *needed*. The opportunity for planning Eucharists was welcomed warmly. People were delighted with the possibility of selecting music for their celebrations, and of introducing variations of their own choice. And so, different things were 'done' with the rite; some good, some bad; some a help, some a hindrance. What changes were introduced depended solely on the planners, what they judged would be helpful. Certain things were pushed almost universally; such as singing and the greeting of peace. Singing is very desirable in the Eucharist, but that is not to say that for *every* assembly it is going to be a help. Some priests seemed to adopt it as an apostolate to have people shake hands at the greeting of peace, and were elated when they met with success. But — did it help the people to pray better? Was that their most urgent need right now? Or just a good thing to do?

'Like' is the real trap! If I were to live by what I like, I would soon die. It is no difficulty to give examples of this from life. Look at your list of 'likes' in the activity above.

Even though the 'likes' were very good for you, how would you be if your 'likes' were all you gave yourself? *You NEED more than your LIKES to live!*

'Like-behaviour' closes me. If I move only in the company of people who *agree* with me, who think *like* me — those who are the people I *like* — I would stop growing. 'Like is as big as my own skin', and as long as I stay with my likes, I stay my own little self. NEED TRANSCENDS SELF.

In the midst of arbitrary selection in planning liturgy there was a lot of talk about 'experimentation'. However, the kind of procedure we have been describing was not experimentation. It was merely doing a variety of different things. Experimentation includes, as well as doing things, an evaluation of what has been done.

Evaluation

How is it possible to evaluate my *prayer?* That is a question we are usually asked at this stage of our courses. The general impression people have is that their prayer is so intangible, so deep and personal, that it cannot be isolated so that it can be 'looked at.' To a large extent they are correct. However, even though we may not look at 'a prayer', we can certainly look at 'a person-praying'. Hence, answers to the following questions reveal a lot about a person's prayer on any particular occasion:

1. Was I sufficiently *centered?*
2. To what degree was I *present* to the celebration?
   a. To the others in the assembly?
   b. To the ministers?
3. Was I for the most part *responsive* or 'dull' in responding?
   a. Can I identify what hindered the response from coming?
   b. Anything I can do to facilitate it?

To remove scepticism and give them confidence, we usually give our participants an experience of evaluating their own prayer at this time. You could sample the following evaluation.

Evaluation of my Praying the Eucharist

To awaken consciousness about your praying at celebrations of the Eucharist, allow the answers to surface from within you.

1. How in general did I pray?

2. Did I have any striking difficulties in praying?

3. How was my conscious awareness of the others who were there?

4. How was my attention
   — to the ministers?

   — to the text (prayers, readings, Eucharistic Prayer)?

5. How responsive was I?
   — to the readings?

   — to the Liturgy of the Eucharist?

6. What took my attention away from the ministers or text?

7. Was I willing to allow my thoughts and attitudes to be led by the ministers?

8. Did I use the time given for reflection?

9. At what times did I 'see more'?

10. What would I single out as *my* most significant need in celebrating the Eucharist.

Changes in the Eucharist in a parish or religious community should only come in 'sandwich' form, and never an open plate. What we mean is that any and every change which is introduced into the rite of the Eucharist by the planners must (a) be the result of an evaluation, and (b) after a period of use, be subjected to a further evaluation, to discover if the change brought about the expected result.

'Careful planning and execution will help dispose the people to take their part in the Eucharist,' states the General Instruction, n. 313. In introducing this statement it further says:

> The pastoral effectiveness of a celebration depends in great measure on choosing readings, prayers and songs which correspond to the needs, spiritual preparation and attitude of the participants. This will be achieved by an intelligent use of the options described below.
>
> In planning the celebration, the priest should consider the spiritual good of the assembly rather than his own desires.

Genuine planning, as distinct from haphazard selection, rejects personal desires as a basis, and 'chooses what corresponds to the needs of the participants.' Those who plan the Eucharist must, therefore, have the knowledge necessary to choose what 'corresponds to the needs.' That knowledge will do nothing, however, unless they first know what the people's needs are. To discover their needs is the first task.

Needs do not always emerge clearly, or immediately. There is the problem of what are called 'presenting needs.' Quite often what is taken to be a need, is only an apparent need, clothing the real one. The task demands that whatever is necessary be done in order to discover the real one. For example, the need for a 'lively Eucharist' is frequently heard. The remedy? Liven it up with more lively music, and keep it moving along so that the people are occupied all the time! That sounds quite feasible. BUT could the *real* need be the ability to use the quiet times? That it often is, is betrayed by complaints like 'I wish he would not wait so long after the reading,' or '*Another* pause!' The question is, WHAT IS THE REAL NEED?

Discovering needs

Evaluating, whether life or liturgy, is a skill: a 'need-discovery skill.' *It is a skill of 'hearing'.* To 'hear' we need to be centered. We cannot hear the true needs in ourselves or in others unless we have brought our feelings into a subordinate position. Otherwise, what we hear will be our own frustrations, prejudices, and maybe, hurts. This has to be observed before, and during, a session devoted to an evaluation.

There is an opinion circulating that it is almost impossible to cater for the multitude of different needs that would be in any one assembly. This, however, is not the case. In fact, the different needs of people are very limited in number, and very ordinary. There is no point in looking for rare, exotic needs. This short list includes all the needs of the average assembly:

- they need to be attentive;
- the need to understand;
- they need to respond from the heart.

An evaluation of the celebration of the Eucharist in a

parish or religious community can be carried out by anyone who is sufficiently in touch with those who make up the assembly. Obviously, it would be better to have a group or committee do it. They will have to have some method in the way they proceed. Below we set out *one* possible way of going about it. We do not offer it as a hard and fast rule; it will serve to give some idea as to how an evaluating committee should proceed.

Evaluation for Planning

THE COMMITTEE

(1)   The members need to have sufficient knowledge and experience in order to arrive at responsible decisions.

(2)   They also need to be creative; they will very likely have to discover remedies that were never thought of before in the parish.

It has been our experience that in general people involved in planning liturgies have very limited and restricted suggestions to offer when they are asked to suggest changes. They can be helped in this by 'stretching' their imaginations. It is a very good idea for a committee to give some time at each meeting to their self-education and broadening of their vision. For example, a 'brain storming' session would loosen up their imagination. Like this —

> Recall and note the variations that are possible in Eucharist:
>> — in the period of time before the celebration begins;
>> — during the celebration:
>>> A. The Place
>>> B. The Text and Rite
>>> C. The Ministers
>> — independent of the celebration
>> (e.g. prayer groups, study groups, preparing the readings, etc.)

This is done without any discussion whatever, or any judgment. ALL LISTEN to the suggestions.

PRELIMINARY WORK

In the case of a parish, a committee must first take steps to find out about their participation at their celebrations of the Eucharist from a representative section of the assembly. They will require adequate information and facts to be able to answer the questions which reveal the sought for information — their needs. People cannot be asked directly, What do you need? — as mentioned above. The committee will have to design its questions and a method of enquiry that will be suitable to the people of the parish.

AT THE MEETING: REFLECTION to discover the Needs

(1) General

• Are there any very obvious things needing attention that make it difficult (or impossible) for the assembly to pray the Eucharist?

What NEEDS in the people does this (these) point to?

(2) Attention

• Is there anything which distracts, takes attention from responding, interferes with concentration, or prevents people hearing and seeing what is said and done by the ministers
  — before the celebration begins?
  — during the celebration
    outside the church?
    inside the church
    what people? (e.g. latecomers; servers)
    what activity? (e.g. the collection; the Communion)

Any remedy to suggest?

• What help could be offered to improve the people's concentration: to deepen their attention to the presiding celebrant and other ministers?

(3) Understanding

This enquiry is not about an understanding of theology, e.g. of redemption, of the Eucharist, but about a lack of appreciation of what is going on now, in this celebration.

- What could be done to help the assembly to appreciate what is expected of them in the various stages and elements of the Rite?

For example: what should they do while waiting for the ministers to arrive? what is the meaning of the Holy Communion?
or, in regard to the readings, Why this Old Testament reading? Why this reading for Advent?
or, the meaning of a feast, or ligurgical season.

(4) **Response from the heart in prayer**

- What could contribute to the assembly's:
  - inner quietness;
  - their listening;
  - their response from the heart?

- How effective are the ministers (presiding celebrant, readers, commentator, etc.) in getting a faith-response from the assembly?

The question is directed to the *ministers* here, rather than at the people. What has to be discovered is: do the ministers tend to teach and inform rather than *evoke, stir, arouse a response?* This applies especially to Introductions to the Stages, and the homily.

Summing up

WHAT IS THE NEED THE COMMITTEE SHOULD TURN ITS ATTENTION TO FIRST?

Decision

In view of that Need, in what Area (A, B, or C) would a change most likely give the desired improvement?

The NEEDS and SUGGESTIONS are heard, again without any response or comment.

Then, after discussion the committee decides:
THE CHANGE(S) WE WILL INTRODUCE INTO THE PARISH EUCHARIST WILL BE. . .

NOTE: The decision is never final and definitive, but subject to a further evaluation at some future time decided upon.

Hence, not being a 'life and death' decision, it should be arrived at with a certain ease and flexibility on the part of the committee.

23

PLANNING PROCEDURE

Necessity of planning

Planning was unknown in liturgy before the new Rite of the Mass; at least, planning as we see it today. Prior to 1969, a priest's preparation for Mass was personal and organizational (e.g. a roster for altar servers, training servers for a High Mass). Immediately before Mass, he had to attend to his own personal preparation; but apart from consulting the *Ordo* and marking the missal, there was nothing in the nature of 'planning'. In regard to the text he used, it was all fixed for him. The one exception was his sermon, if he gave one; this he would, of course, have had to prepare.

With the new rites of the Mass — and, indeed all the sacraments — it is impossible to omit planning. Even if he wants to, a presiding celebrant cannot avoid it: it has to be done, by himself or someone else. There are choices and selections which may be availed of, or not; but there are some which *must* be made. The General Instruction has a section on 'Choice of Mass Formula', and another on 'Choice of Individual Texts'. In the Lectionary, Chapter 1 has sections dealing with the choice of texts and the chants between the readings. While these possibilities may be ignored, the presiding celebrant, before he arrives at the altar, must have arrived at decisions about such elements as: the Greeting he will use, and which of the three Penitential Rites, which Opening Prayer, which Preface and Eucharistic Prayer he will use – to mention but some of them. There are about fifty different choices that *have to* be made in connection with every celebration of the Eucharist. That is not to say that they have to be made anew for every celebration; but at some time or other the decision has to be made. For example, without even thinking about the possibility of it, a priest may never sing the Eucharistic Prayer. In this, however, as in other instances, to keep on doing the same thing is to make a decision.

It is possible, of course, that the presiding celebrant may make his choices independent of any planning – 'on the run', that is, just as he comes to them. There is a priest who said that he never knew which Eucharistic Prayer he would use on a Sunday until he had finished his homily; and would then decide on the basis of the length of time he had spoken for. And he did not know how long that was going to be, either, until he had finished preaching! Another practice used in order to avoid making a choice is that of combining a definite Memorial Acclamation with each Eucharistic Prayer: thus, the first Acclamation is invariably used with Eucharistic Prayer 1, the second Acclamation with Eucharistic Prayer II, and so on. To practices such as these can be applied the warning of the Letter from the Congregation for Divine Worship in 1973:

> The many ways of increasing the pastoral effectiveness of a celebration are not always known, nor is sufficient attention paid to the spiritual good of the assembly in planning the celebration. (n. 3)

An exercise of faith and love

Considerations such as 'Do you have to. . .' or 'Must we. . .'

do not enter at all into planning. The only consideration is: What is best — best for this assembly on this occasion.

What is best for them is what they *need*: what they need here and now as a help in their participation. Planning takes into consideration the results of Evaluation, and includes the decisions following on it.

The motivation, therefore, in planning is concern for those who will be there.

Planning is a ministry: a ministry to people's prayer, and thus an exercise of faith and love. A well-planned liturgy is a work of art; a lot of skill as well as good taste and sensitivity goes into it. But it is more than that. Like every liturgical ministry, there are skills attached to doing it well; but it is above all a work of faith. Hence, the most suitable atmosphere in which to do the planning is a prayer-atmosphere. *It is a time for 'hearing' people and caring for them; and for listening to the Holy Spirit as we make our choices and decisions.*

Team planning

What is the most suitable size for a planning group? How representative should it be? Before answering those questions it is necessary to be clear about the function of those involved in planning, and especially about the difference between Evaluation and Planning.

Evaluation is a work of collecting information and making judgments. An evaluation needs to cover as wide a spectrum of the parish as possible. It has to have some type of structure that can reach out to, and hear from, the various classes and age-groups. The evaluating group has also to include in it those who are familiar with what remedies will suit the needs of the various classes and ages. Evaluation needs a variety of people, if it is to be done effectively.

Planning is very different. Planning, as we said, is an art; and works of art are very rarely the work of a group. The final plan of a Eucharist is the outcome of the Evaluation, but it also includes a lot of what is 'personal': it is *this person's/ group's* plan and design. It is the result of taste, and flair, and artistic ability.

About ten years ago, at an interview with Fr Gelineau, in

Paris, on the subject of team-planning, he said: 'Before you can have team-planning, you have to have a team. If you have not yet got a team, it is better to leave the planning to one person.' Anyone who has had much to do with planning-groups will appreciate this wisdom. A typical instance is retreats or seminars in which a group is appointed to look after the liturgy. So they meet to start their planning. Before they do anything in the nature of real planning, they discover that they need to come to some common consensus about more than one aspect of liturgy. What they are experiencing is that they are not yet a team, and until they are their planning will not be team-planning.

For the most part, the most practical number for planning a Eucharist is ONE. Maybe two can do it — but only if they have, over a period of working together, become blended into a planning-team. There are very few of them to be found. The larger group is needed for what we call the Survey and the Sketch (which will be explained below). But the art-work of Design of a Eucharist is usually best left to one.

Steps in Planning

There are four steps involved in planning:
1. **Survey**
2. **Sketch**
3. **Design**
4. **Organization**

STEP 1: SURVEY

Planning a celebration cannot proceed without certain information:

(a) **about the assembly**: who they are; how many; age group; whether they customarily celebrate the Eucharist together; their singing ability and taste; how at home are they with periods of silence; and whatever can provide a sufficient profile of the group for whom the Eucharist is being planned.

(b) **about the occasion**: A Sunday, a weekday, funeral, wedding, or other special occasion. What happened at previous celebrations? what is happening just before the Eucharist? and after? This information will help to place the Eucharist in a context: give a picture of what it will be like.

(c) **about the place:** a church, chapel or elsewhere; its size, appearance, atmosphere; placing of the altar relative to the assembly; availability of an organ, and/or other audio equipment; if it is not a church or chapel, seating arrangements; provision of materials, chalice etc., lectionary, etc. If it is feasible, the best thing to do is to go and see the place.

(d) **about their resources for ministering:** server, reader, singing leader, instrumentalist; someone to provide decor, etc.; possibility of seeing the ministers before the celebration.

Add to the above, any special features that might be requested or suitable: for example, a Water Rite in the Introductory Rites, a renewal of marriage or religious vows, or specific people as ministers. Or any restrictions imposed in the diocese, e.g. women not allowed as special ministers of the Eucharist.

A Survey is necessary for any special or first-time celebration. For weekly or daily celebrations, after it is done once, it it worth while repeating it at regular intervals; circumstances change with time, and undiscovered factors can come to light. The different Masses each Sunday should get separate treatment to allow for the different time of day, and the different type of assembly.

STEP 2: SKETCH

Before deciding on details, it is necessary to have a 'vision' of the type of celebration being planned. Very much like an architect, who will draw a sketch of a building before drawing a plan.

The vision or sketch of a Eucharist will consist of its characteristics. From imagining the celebration — the assembly , the occasion, the place and their resources — a picture can be formed, which will be of a celebration that is:

    — simple or solemn;

    — quiet or with music and sound;

— a lot of ceremony or little;
— a very reflective atmosphere, or short pauses only;
— etc. etc.

This sketch will give a unity and consistency to the Eucharist. Each element will be given its due and proper emphasis. This is necessary, for any liturgical rite is like a precision watch: it all fits together and works in order. If any element is given too much, or too little emphasis, the effect of the rite will be spoiled, and the assembly deprived of a true rite. This can happen, for instance when the Introductory Rite is extremely long; or when the Liturgy of the Word, due to a very long homily, goes on for thirty minutes, and is followed by a Liturgy of the Eucharist which lasts five.

> The above two steps in Planning would very suitably be the work of the Evaluation committee, dealt with in chapter 22. The work entailed in Design is ordinarily not suitable for a group.

STEP 3: DESIGN

A design includes *(1) selection*, and *(2) composition*. We will consider them together, as we take each stage of the Rite separately. Since the compositions may be attended to when the Design is complete, as a reminder we mark what has to be composed with an *.

Note that we are not including the selections and composition which is customarily left to the presiding celebrant, like the Greeting, homily, Eucharistic Prayer, introduction to the Our Father, etc.

Introductory Rite: What sort of an Introductory Rite does
    the Sketch call for? Will there be singing/music?
    What will be sung?
    I choose it.
    Which Penitential Rite? Who will lead it?
    *If it is Penitential Rite No. 3, I compose it.
    Which Opening Prayer will be used?

Liturgy of the Word: What are the readings of the day?
    I read them.
    Do any pastoral considerations indicate that others

should be chosen?
If so, I choose them.
*I write the Introductions to the readings and psalm.
Who will be the reader? Who will minister the Respon-
sorial Psalm?
Will we sing the Response? Or the whole psalm?
Will there be a sung Alleluia? Will the verse of the
Alleluia be sung or recited?
What else will we sing in the Liturgy of the Word?

*To compose the General Intercessions,
     I pray the readings,
     then compose the Petitions.
Who will minister them?
Will the presiding celebrant need a text of
Introduction and Concluding Prayer?
*If he does, I compose it.

Liturgy of the Eucharist: Will there be music/singing in this
stage? Where will it be?
I choose it.
What will happen during the Preparation of the Gifts?
Who will present the Gifts (if there is a procession)?
Will there be any special features (e.g. the assembly
standing around the altar, greeting of peace, a Fraction
Rite)?
I note the arrangements these features will require (e.g.
notifying the people, providing suitable bread).
Communion with chalice, or bread only?
Who will be Special Minister?

Dismissal Rite: Will we use a special blessing? A composed
dismissal?
*If so, I compose it.
Will the Parish Notices be read?
Will there be music?
If so, I select it.

Arising in the course of work on the Design will be
matters to be attended to. It is advisable to collect
these in a list for the work of the next step. Organization, so very different from the other steps, will

probably be done most effectively by some other(s).

STEP 4: ORGANIZATION

Many a well thought out and designed Eucharist has failed to come up to expectations through stopping work at the Design, and omitting this further step.

Included in its scope are:

Presiding celebrant and other Ministers: when they have been selected, they are to be notified in good time. If it would be helpful, they will also be prepared (by briefing and a practice session) for their role in the celebration. A previous practice can add to their confidence and their ministering.

The Place: the regular, routine arrangements (altar area prepared, lighting, microphones, sacristy); and anything special (holy water for a Water Rite, different arrangement of seating, special setting or decoration).

Materials: such as texts for ministers, hymn books, special booklet for the occasion, overhead transparencies.

Since so many choices are now possible it is necessary to make sure that. . . all know beforehand what they have to do. Nothing should be left for a hurried last-minute decision.

(General Instruction, n. 313)

In the following chapters, we will deal with one area of selection: Music in the Eucharist (Chapter 24); then some compositions (Chapter 25); and finally, with one special type of group: Masses with Children (Chapter 26).

You might like to try some planning now. You could practise your planning procedure on yourself. Admittedly, the only part of the celebration for which you can 'plan for yourself' is the time before the celebration begins. There is a lot of help, however, which you could get from attending to this time. This activity provides a suitable method of proceeding with it.

Planning for Myself

1. Planning needs a previous Evaluation. If you have not done so already, do a personal evaluation of your celebration of the Eucharist, such as suggested on page 353-4.

As in question 10, note down your most significant need:

2. Engage in a 'creative' session: discover as many possible ways as you can of catering for your need:

3. Center yourself for listening.
4. Entrusting yourself to the Holy Spirit, listen to his decision about what practice you will engage in in the time before the Eucharist.

24

PLANNING THE SINGING
IN THE EUCHARIST

Among the many signs and symbols used by the
Church to celebrate its faith, music is of pre-
eminent importance. As sacred song united to the
words it forms an integral part of solemn liturgy.
(*Music in Catholic Worship*, U.S. Bishops' Committee on the Liturgy, 1972).

At one time music *was* liturgy. Around the beginning of the
century, the efforts of the liturgical movement concentrated
its efforts on music, with special emphasis on Gregorian
chant. It was considered that good music in liturgy — performed by a group of experts — would mean good participation by the people.

There are recent instances of that identification of liturgy
with music. Up to fairly recently, musicians outnumbered the

others on liturgy commissions and at liturgical gatherings. Musicians were the principal, and in places, the only liturgists. It is still the same in many people's minds: a parish organist is, by the fact of musical ability, qualified in liturgy.

As a tradition, this way of thinking had very practical roots: for there was really nothing else that could be touched, adjusted or changed in any way in the rite. Hence all interest in liturgy, and all efforts to improve participation focused on its music. One result, and a very effective one, was the *Betsingmesse* ('Pray and sing Mass') begun in Germany in 1933, but based on a much older practice, the *Singmesse* which began in the eighteenth century.

We mention this trend so that we can appreciate fully the place of music in the new Rite of Mass. In it, following the Constitution on the Liturgy, music is but *one* of the means available for improving participation; certainly a very important one, but not to monopolize interest and effort as it did heretofore. In practical terms, there are other things to be done in planning a Eucharist *before* thinking about 'picking a few hymns'!

'Singing should be widely used at Mass depending on the type of people and the capability of each congregation' says the General Instruction in the section on 'Importance of Singing'. The new Rite certainly offers plenty of opportunities for singing. What will decide for us how we will use them? There are two questions in this. One, where will we sing: at what places in the Eucharist will we include singing? The other is, what will we sing in those places?

As in the case of all selections made in Planning, the choice of music is determined by the nature and purpose of the Rite. Lest this be neglected, it must be kept in mind by whoever is responsible for the Planning, that this is different from planning a concert or a sing-along. The basis of selection is not because 'it makes us feel good', or somebody or other 'loves that song', or because it was a favourite of the deceased at a Funeral Mass, or the last time we sang it it was very popular. The choice of music begins, not with any of our 'likes' or 'wants', but with the needs of the assembly: their prayer-needs. Like all Planning, the selection of music is *a ministry* which caters for these needs.

Ministerial function of music

The place of music in liturgy is based on what is called, in the Constitution on the Liturgy and other documents, its 'ministerial function.' The phrase indicates that it is 'at the service of': just as were all the items listed in the Four Areas (page 27). The ministerial function of a reader is to proclaim the Word of God, that of the plate and chalice is to evoke a response to the bread and wine, and so on. What is the ministerial function of music, or of particular hymns, in the Eucharist? Fr Lucien Deiss writes:

> This matter of the ministerial function is much like the simple yet important question a child asks when faced with an unfamiliar object: 'What is it for? What does it do?' Liturgically, why have an Entrance Hymn? A Responsorial Psalm? An Agnus Dei?
>
> The ministerial function constantly challenges each song and each rite concerning its reason for existing.' (Spirit and Song of the New Liturgy).

The two questions raised above, Where to sing? and What to sing? find their answer in the ministerial function of music and song in the Eucharist. Music performs two services:

- (1) a service to the rite, telling us *where* to sing; and
- (2) a service to the assembly, telling us *what* to choose.

A full and complete consideration of music in the Eucharist would include the parts sung by the presiding celebrant and other ministers, as well as the singing of the assembly, the choir/group and singing leader. It should also deal with the use of instrumental, non-vocal music. The purpose and scope of this book leads us to emphasize the assembly's singing, and to include a few remarks on instrumental music; but since our concern is with the assembly and their participation, it is not our intention to treat of the presiding celebrant's singing.

Music and the assembly

What service can music give to the assembly? What can it do for the people? What kind of help can it offer?

The help will be in their participation; they will be given

something that improves their response to the rite. In other words, it will cater for their *needs*. When discussing needs of the assembly at the Eucharist which are catered for in the Introductory Rites (Chapter 14), mention was made of these two: inner quiet in order to give attention to the rite; and the active faith necessary for prayer. Music assists both of these. Briefly, the contribution music makes to the assembly's response is an opportunity to experience and express their identity, and their motivation for assembling here. Music

— gives an opportunity to express in common their faith: a sharing which brings the faith of the assembly to life;

— gives a sense of unity: 'the unity of hearts is more profoundly achieved by the union of voices' (Instruction on Music in the Liturgy, 1967, n. 5)

— gives an entry into the eucharistic experience through the exercise of mind, heart and voice.

> Music, in addition to expressing texts, can also unveil a dimension of meaning and feeling, a communication of ideas and intuitions which words alone cannot yield. This dimension is integral to the human personality and to man's growth in faith. (*Music in Catholic Worship*, n. 24)

Music and the Rite

Writing on music in liturgy, St Pius X said that it 'enhances the beauty and splendour of the ceremonies'. The sound of music in the rite can be compared to extra lighting. When an element of the rite is accompanied by music, the effect is the same as training a spotlight on it. 'It should heighten the texts so that they speak more fully and effectively' (*Music in Catholic Worship*, n. 23). Since not all texts will be sung, but a choice has to be made of some of them, the texts to be 'heightened' should be the more important ones. This is also stated:

> The choice of sung parts, the balance between them and the style of musical setting used should reflect the relative importance of the parts of the Mass and the nature of each part. Thus elaborate settings of the entrance song, 'Lord have mercy' and 'Glory to God' may make the proclamation of the word seem unimportant; an overly elaborate

offertory song with a spoken 'Holy, holy, holy Lord' may make the Eucharistic Prayer seem less important. (n.31)

There is, therefore, a hierarchy of importance to be acknowledged in the choice of where we will sing. A good choice will highlight the more important elements by selecting them to be sung. 'Preference should be given to the more significant parts' (General Instruction n. 18).

Some elements in the rite are texts which are *meant to be sung* rather than to be recited. These texts fail to have anything like the impact they should when they are merely said. A good example is the Alleluia: there is just no comparison between a rousingly sung Alleluia and a recited one. For that reason, if it is not going to be sung, it is better to omit it altogether. (The same applies to the Entrance antiphon and and the Communion antiphon.)

The most important of these elements are ACCLAMATIONS.

Singing highlights the degree of importance attached to these responses of the assembly. If anything at all is sung in a Eucharist, it should be the Acclamations.

Next claiming the right to be sung are SONGS.

These are also of a nature to be sung, since they were composed for singing. They include the PSALMS and other HYMNS of the Rite.

In the next place are RESPONSES to the greeting of the presiding celebrant and ministers.

A final category which can be sung is PRAYERS.

By prayers are meant prayers of petition, as distinct from prayers of praise. In the Eucharist, not many of such 'prayers' belong to the assembly.

We will now consider each of these categories in detail.

Acclamations:

An Acclamation is a brief and forceful shout of joyful response. In style it corresponds in life to the spontaneous expression of a child's delight when given something very pleasing; or the 'Isn't that beautiful!' of a visitor to a picture gallery; or the words of approval, or disapproval, shouted at the players at a football match. The music of Acclamations is therefore strong and affirmative; and very different from the verses of a song. Hence an Acclamation should be sung just *once*; to repeat it spoils its effect, and makes it more like a song (a result which arises also from singing the Acclamation to the music of a song).

The Acclamations are —

Liturgy of the Word:	ALLELUIA VERSE/GOSPEL ACCLAMATION
Liturgy of the Eucharis	'HOLY HOLY' MEMORIAL ACCLAMATION AMEN EMBOLISM ACCLAMATION ('For the kingdom. . .')

Hymns/Psalms

Hymns can have two different functions in the Eucharist: (1) accompany a more important action, e.g. Processional hymns, 'Lamb of God'; (2) sung for the sake of embellishing a text which will be recited if it is not sung, e.g. 'Glory to God in the highest', Responsorial Psalm. These latter are marked with * below —

Introductory Rites:	Entrance hymn * 'Glory to God'
Liturgy of the Word:	* Responsorial Psalm
Liturgy of the Eucharist:	Hymn, Preparation of the Gifts 'Lamb of God' * Communion hymn

The Entrance hymn accompanies the processional entrance of the ministers. It also has the function of a kind of overture. After the manner of the music which introduces films and television shows, it acts as a prelude to create the right atmosphere. It puts the people in the proper frame of mind for the celebration; as well as introducing the particular flavour of a feast or liturgical season.

To have its proper effect it needs to be an alive and rousing, rather than quiet and reflective, type of music. It should always be a song which the people know well:

to have them struggle with a little known hymn is harmful.

The Responsorial Psalm may be sung in its entirety; or the response only, with the verses recited. The response chosen may be different from the one given in the Lectionary for the day. It is well worth while investigating the possibilities of singing the same response for a few weeks. This is suggested in the section in the Lectionary 'Common Texts for Sung Responsorial Psalms:Responses.'

The Procession with the Gifts is suitably accompanied with hymns of praise, to introduce the Liturgy of the Eucharist. Songs of 'offering' should *never* be used; what was suitable for the pre-1969 rite are no longer acceptable in the new Rite (see page 276).

Responses/Litanies

When the singing of Responses or Litanies is included in the Design, the Eucharist is acquiring a more than usual solemnity. The singing of them is very effective in giving a celebration the quality of being special.

Introductory Rites:	Greeting
	'Lord, have mercy'
Liturgy of the Word:	Gospel dialogue
	General Intercessions (Response)
Liturgy of the Eucharist:	Preface dialogue

Prayers

The same remarks apply to singing the Creed and the Lord's Prayer as were made in regard to Responses/Litanies.

Liturgy of the Word:	Creed
Liturgy of the Eucharist:	Lord's Prayer

The Lord's Prayer, with its preparatory function as one element in an already over-loaded preparatory rite, should not be made an obstacle in the flow from Eucharistic Prayer to the Communion (see page 297). This will be the result of singing it in a celebration of lesser solemnity. Furthermore, it seems more natural to pray prayers of petition in English by saying rather than singing them.

A balanced distribution

Planning the singing has to take into account *two* orders of importance:

A — The above order of the type of text
1. Acclamations
2. Psalms/hymns
3. Responses
4. Prayers

B — The order of importance in the four stages of the rite, which are:
1. Liturgy of the Eucharist
2. Liturgy of the Word
3. Introductory Rites

(On account of its form as a succession of responses, the Dismissal Rite does not give much scope for highlighting by singing. See Chapter 20.)

In a Eucharist in which there is a minimum of singing, the Acclamations in the Liturgy of the Eucharist would be chosen:

First, **Memorial Acclamation**
with 'Holy, holy'
and **Amen**

The choice might be narrowed to Memorial Acclamation and Amen by the limits of the assembly's singing ability.

If the singing were extended, it would be balanced by including singing in the Liturgy of the Word. First to be chosen would be:

'Alleluia' verse/Gospel acclamation

A yet further extension would bring in the Introductory Rites. Since there is no acclamation in this stage, what would be chosen would be:

Entrance hymn

Continuing, the next element to be included would come from the Communion Rite of the Liturgy of the Eucharist; and would be an acclamation, namely:

Embolism acclamation

As the Design calls for more and more singing, it is added according to this procedure: always retaining a balance, and respecting the relative order of importance in stage and nature of text.

Sufficient has been said here to let it be seen that an assembly can have plenty of singing in the Eucharist without drawing on hymns. Apart from the Entrance hymn, which is selected from the collection of hymns familiar to the assembly, much of the singing can be the singing of actual texts of the rite. Certainly, the planning of singing will never *begin* with selecting hymns. Much less will it be that favourite diet, 'the four-hymn sandwich'.

Well worthy of inclusion here is a 'rule' given by Lucien Deiss:

> Every time the quality of the music
> is not equal in value
> to the quality of the silence it is breaking,
> it is better not to sing at all.

A few samples of different degrees of solemnity in singing are given in an Appendix, (page 381-2).

Instrumental music

Singing is not the only form of music which can be of service to the rite and the assembly. The organ and other musical instruments, as well as accompanying singing, can also be played 'solo'. If sufficiently competent players are not available, recorded instrumental music can be used.

Instrumental music can have different functions in the Eucharist:

To create an atmosphere: it could be (a) to help the assembly to quieten down, for example, before the celebration begins;

(b) to assist their reflectiveness, in periods such as after a reading, or after the Communion;

(c) as background to some action, like the Entrance, the Preparation of the Gifts, or going at the Dismissal.

(d) to contribute to the spirit of the feast, or liturgical season; for example, the festivity of Easter time.

It is imperative that the music be carefully selected for the purpose it is expected to fulfil. In the above instances, (a) and (b) need 'neutral' music with a catchy tune, such as baroque music; a

N

well-known piece of music will draw attention to
itself and that would be a distraction rather than a
help. For these needs, single instruments such as
organ, flute, and other woodwind instruments will
be most effective.

For (c) and (d) familiar music with associations
serves its purpose well, e.g. Beethoven's 'Hymn to
Joy' or parts of Handel's 'The Messiah'.

For the sake of the words which are sung: as an aid to
reflection; or to instil the spirit of the liturgical season.

In this case, if the words are meant to be heard,
they must be sufficiently clear so that the assembly
can follow them without straining or distraction.

Again, there is no room for poor taste in selecting the
music; nor for mediocrity in performance. The music and the
instrumentalists must be of good quality. If recorded music is
used, the equipment — records, tapes, cassette deck, stylus —
must also be of good quality and in good condition; and the
speakers sufficient for the size of the place. People today,
without being aware of it perhaps, are accustomed to high
quality reproduction in sound, and they will be distracted
by anthing less.

Any musical instrument permitted in divine
worship should be used in such a way that it meets
the needs of the liturgical celebration, and is in the
interests both of the beauty of worship and the
edification of the faithful.

(*Music in the Liturgy*, n. 63)

Service to the assembly

The ministry of Planning is a service to the assembly. The
purpose of a good Design is their participation.

While selecting the music so that it is a ministry to the rite,
preserving balance and relative importance of elements, the
choosing is to be seen as *for* the people's benefit: their full,
conscious and active participation. The answer to the question
'What to sing?' is supplied by this consideration: the participation of *this* assembly, on *this occasion*. The choice of
music must, therefore, look to:

The quality of the music: Whatever style of music is used, it must be *good* music. In the long run, only music that is technically and aesthetically of good quality will be effective. The cheap and the trite may have a broad appeal, and be very popular. That makes it a 'like', but it does not make it effective.

The quality of the text: This applies only to newly composed songs which have a text other than scriptural or liturgical. While giving expression to emotions, the song must also give expression to Christian faith; and that in the fullness that is always found in liturgical prayers. The rite of the Eucharist is such that it brings the assembly to the 'most' in response. Hymns which do not come up to this standard may be used in other prayer-services, but not in liturgy.

What we look for in the song is its 'faith content': we expect that it will lead us to respond in faith and trust to God the Father, through Jesus Christ, by the Holy Spirit in us his People — hence including all the dimensions of our relationship with God as the Christian experiences it. To pray to Jesus, my friend, or anything on that level, will not be sufficient; much less to do no more than give expression to my loneliness or the lack of love in my life.

Suitable for this assembly: The music selected must be within the ability of the assembly: they should be familiar with it, able to sing it without any strain or distraction. It should be a style with which they feel quite comfortable.

The age of the assembly should be taken into account by choosing songs with suitable music and words. In particular, adults should never be given children's songs to sing. It might seem too obvious to be worthwhile saying it, but unfortunately it happens too often. It is nothing exceptional to hear adults singing music that is obviously of a style specially composed for little ones, with words that a five-year old will be comfortable with! That can do nothing to help the assembly make a Eucharistic response.

*   *   *

Those who perform the service of Planning celebrations of the Eucharist for a parish or community will find inspiration for their ministry in these words from Music in Catholic Worship:

> Flexibility reigns supreme. The musician with a sense of artistry and deep knowledge of the rhythm of the liturgical action will be able to combine the many options into an effective whole. For the composer and performer alike there is an unprecedented challenge. He must enhance the liturgy with new creations of variety and richness and with those compositions from the time-honoured treasury of liturgical music which can still serve today's celebrations. Like the wise householder in Matthew's Gospel, the church musician must be one 'who can produce from his store both the new and the old.'

Appendix

The following five sets present five different plans for singing in the Eucharist. They are graded according to solemnity.

A — Acclamations only
>   Before the Gospel reading:
>   'Alleluia' sung; verse *recited*.
>   Memorial Acclamation
>   'Amen'
>   Embolism Acclamation

B — Entrance Song + Acclamations
>   Entrance song
>   'Alleluia' (as in set A)
>   Memorial Acclamation
>   'Amen'
>   Embolism Acclamation

C —
>   Responsorial Psalm refrain,
>   with verses *recited*
>   'Alleluia' (as in A)
>   Memorial Acclamation
>   'Amen'
>   Embolism Acclamation
>
>   'Lamb of God'
>   *or* Communion Song
>   *or* Song after Communion *

D —
>   Entrance Song
>   Responsorial Psalm; refrain *and* verses
>   'Alleluia' and verse
>   Memorial Acclamation
>   'Amen'
>   Embolism Acclamation
>   'Lamb of God'
>   *or* Communion Song
>   *or* Song after Communion *
>   Recession: Instrumental music or recording

E —   Entrance Song
'Lord, have mercy' or 'Glory to God. . .' *
Responsorial Psalm: refrain and verses
'Alleluia' and verse
Response to General Intercessions

Preparation of the Gifts: song
'Holy, holy'
Memorial Acclamation
'Amen'
Lord's Prayer
Embolism Acclamation
'Lamb of God'
Communion Song

  or Song after Communion *
Recession: music while going out

* Where 'or' is stated, it will produce an imbalance to include more than one of these.

25

COMPOSITIONS IN THE EUCHARIST

This chapter will give some guidelines on how the person responsible for the Design of a Eucharist could go about work of composition. We will look at the compositions that are most likely to be part of his or her task, namely:

Introductions to the Four Stages
Penitential Rite, Third Form
Introductions to the readings and
responsorial psalm
General Intercessions:
Petitions;
Introduction;
Concluding Prayer

So as to have a definite base for examples, we will compose them for a particular day: that is *Holy Thursday, The Mass of the Lord's Supper.*

I – Introductions to the Four Stages

AIM: To help the assembly in their faith-response, by stimulating them to the particular activity expected of them in each of the four stages.

1. THE INTRODUCTORY RITES
(said after the Greeting)

Method: To release the people from whatever may be occupying their thoughts and interests now, so that they may be free to give their attention to what is presented to them by the ministers in the Rite; and to activate their faith so that they will be brought to respond in prayer.

It is best for the Planner to begin by asking a question: namely, What is most likely to be uppermost in the minds of these people? What is holding their attention and concern? The answer will give a starting-point to this Introduction.

It does not matter how far away it is from Eucharist, there is no other point from which to start. Even though it may be thoughts and feelings of rejection and unbelief, they cannot be ignored. If they are, they will remain right through the time of the Eucharist – only, for these people it will not be a Eucharist. They have to be led to acknowledge what is 'hooking' them; and to accept that that is how they are now. One way of proceeding from here, is to an acknowledgement of sinfulness, weakness, powerlessness.

The assembly's faith has to be touched in the Introduction: to be activated in some manner so that they become consciously aware of Jesus Christ. This has to be in the form of some aspect of their experience of their relationship with God in Christ: hence, belief in him, dependence on him; trust in him, or annoyance with him. This is only introductory: a beginning to pray.

People who come to celebrate the Eucharist on Holy Thursday will be people who are full of goodwill, and anxious to make as much as possible of it. They may have little idea of how to succeed. Maybe they have little hope of it in their hearts; and that is a problem to be faced by the

Planner. However, the goodwill and interest can be assumed; which gives an excellent starting point.

The following would be *one* possible Introduction which starts from these assumptions:

> This evening's Eucharist is one of those special ones in each year. We all want it to be special for us this evening. And special it will be! It is going to be *made* special for us.

> Holy Thursday night, and Jesus Christ is going to do for us what he did for the apostles at the Last Supper: make us feel the way they did — with all the reverence, and prayer and joy.

> As it is a special celebration let us do something different this evening: let us spend a moment in silent prayer and speak to Jesus in our hearts, and tell him what we would want this Eucharist to be, and how we trust him to do that for us.

Then, after what is for the assembly a suitable time of silence, proceed with the Introductory Rites.

2. LITURGY OF THE WORD
(said when the people are seated after the 'Amen' of the Opening Prayer)

Purpose: To draw the assembly into the proclamation-response dynamic of the Liturgy of the Word, as presented in Chapter 15.

To achieve it, a brief sentence, (or two, at most) can give them the orientation, such as:

> God will now speak to us in these readings. We listen to the message, and then we will make the response which the Holy Spirit will stir in our hearts.

Note: If the assembly would not understand the reference to the 'response the Holy Spirit will stir in our hearts', this phrase should be omitted.
OR

> God has something to say to us all now, and asks us, in the readings, to hear him speak to us.

3. LITURGY OF THE EUCHARIST
(said after the 'Amen' to the Prayer over the Gifts)

Purpose: To bring the assembly's conscious awareness the thanks and praise which is their response to the rite (see Chapter 16); to orient their prayer to it.

In what is said at this point, the attitude and feeling of thanksgiving could be further awakened in the people's hearts, by having them recall, or recalling for them, suitable motivations. For example:

> We say, 'It is right to give God thanks and praise.' What is there in my life that makes me feel that 'it is right' for me to do so?

OR

> God wants us to know how much he loves us. He is going to remind us of what he has done, and is doing, to show that love, so that we may appreciate him more.

4. DISMISSAL RITE
(said after any Parish Notices, or after the 'Amen' to the Prayer after Communion)

Purpose: To remind the assembly of the meaning of this transition (see Chapter 20); and to help them to experience themselves as 'sent' people.

To avoid introducing new thoughts or ideas here, as well as preserving a unity, the point of the homily could be referred to. In this Holy Thursday Eucharist, for example:

> One of God's greatest gifts to us is the ability to love other people. That would be one of our reasons for thanking him and praising him this evening. It is a gift to be used. Christ now sends us to put it to use.

Then follows the Dismissal.

II – Penitential Rite, Third Form

Style: Three well-balanced invocations, in the form of statements: expressions of faith in Jesus Christ as Saviour.
Each invocation is –
addressed TO Jesus Christ; and
is ABOUT his saving activity.

There are abundant sources available for anyone who wishes to compose these invocations. Especially to be noted are: scripture in general, the readings of the day, Prefaces, and Eucharistic Prayers. While we may not find there material for the three invocations, one or two can set us on our way, and we can compose the rest ourselves.

From Holy Thursday's liturgy we have:

Lord Jesus, you came from God to show your love for us,
Lord, have mercy.

In your life and death you left us an example to copy,
Christ, have mercy.

Through your resurrection you became our risen Lord
Lord, have mercy.

OR

Lord Jesus, you died for our sins,
Lord, have mercy.

Lord Jesus, you rose for our new life,
Christ, have mercy.

Lord Jesus, you reveal your love in this Supper
Lord, have mercy.

III — Introduction to the Readings and Psalm

AIM: To help the assembly to respond to the proclamation of the Word of God in the readings, by giving them some information about each reading.

Style: Two short sentences should be sufficient.

The Introduction should place the passage to be read in its full context: of scripture and liturgy. Therefore, it will include the meaning of the passage in the context of the teaching of the book; and further, the message of the Church during a liturgical season or on a particular feast.

To illustrate this from the readings of Holy Thursday:

Introduction to the First Reading

This reading gives an account of the institution of the Passover as a permanent feast in Israel. It is a 'memorial' of God's loving kindness and faithfulness to his covenant.

Introduction to the Second Reading

St Paul, concerned for its proper celebration, recalls the institution of the Eucharist at the Last Supper, and its meaning.

Introduction to the Gospel Reading

During a supper with his disciples, Jesus washes their feet, which is symbolic of his death and resurrection, and of the disciples' incorporation into his humble sacrificial death.

Introduction to the Responsorial Psalm

Our response to the memory of God's loving kindness is a grateful commitment to him:
the prayer of thanks and praise which is Eucharist.

IV — General Intercessions

The explanation of the function and context of this element as part of the Liturgy of the Word has been given in Chapter 15 (page 259). Here we will deal only with their composition: the Petitions, and the Introduction and Concluding Prayer.

It might be asked, why compose them when there are ready-made collections available? It is because Petitions need to be 'fresh'; like tea or coffee, they should be made fresh for each celebration, and then thrown out! They are composed with the same factors in view as in all Planning: this assembly on this occasion. If they are to be topical and striking, they need to be 'made to fit' each celebration, if for no other reason that needs and issues are very live things, and they fade from people's interest, and die in people's concern.

There will be at least four Petitions. Depending on the solemnity and duration of the celebration, it is hardly likely that there will be more than six or eight. In composing them, there are two stages:

1. Selecting the intentions to be prayed for;
2. Composing the Petitions in the chosen format.

The intentions

Each intention is concerned with people *in different situations of need*. To give the General Intercessions their proper universal character, the Prayer will include FOUR categories of intentions:

A. UNIVERSAL CHURCH

Included in this category are needs of the members of the Church as 'sacrament', that is, those aspects of their lives which are expressions of their Christian faith. For example:

Christian unity
Hierarchy (Pope, bishops, synod)
Missions
Apostolate of the laity
Religious
All Christians etc.

B. PUBLIC NEEDS

Corresponding to the diversity of human problems and the salvation of the whole world. Such as:

World (peace, justice, heads of state)
Nation (including the government and its leaders)
Social difficulties
Industrial unrest
Aspirations and ideals of the human race
etc.

C. PARTICULAR NEED

Those who are oppressed by any kind of need or are in any distress, physical, psychological or moral. Some of these would be:

Underprivileged
Poor
Sick
Unemployed
Lonely
Rejected
etc.

D. THE LOCAL CHRISTIAN ASSEMBLY

This community (parish or other) and its needs, including the needs of individual members in significant events, e.g. baptism, marriage, and those most commonly remembered at this time, the deceased.

The intentions need not be mentioned in any particular order.

Intentions are chosen because they are topical and relevant to this assembly: they will strike a sympathetic cord in the assembly and move them to pray. It is useless to include intentions that are too remote from the people present.

At least some of the needs to be prayed for will emerge from the readings and the homily. The following intentions would flow naturally from the readings of Holy Thursday.

1. Church unity
2. More love and concern in people
3. Those who suffer
4. Ourselves celebrating this Eucharist
5. Deceased

The format

The Petitions, when not spontaneous, will take some format or other. The form recommended in the document 'De Oratione Communi' of the Concilium for the Implementation of the Constitution on the Liturgy (1965) is the form given in the Appendix of the Missal and Sacramentary ('Sample Formulas for the General Intercessions'). Three different forms are suggested.

In each of these there is

(a) The statement of the intention, followed by
(b) An invitation to pray:
    'We pray to the Lord'
(c) The People's Prayer in communal response.

Example: For those who hold public office,
        we pray to the Lord,
        Lord, hear our prayer.

In order that the people may 'get with' the intention, and be in a position to feel concern and to pray, a time of silent prayer is a necessary element. Hence the full form will be:

(a) Intention
(b) silent prayer
    invitation to pray

(c) communal response of the assembly.

Composition of the format includes composing the (a) statement of the intention, and the selection of (c) the Prayer prayed by the assembly.

The simple form makes mention of categories of people only, thus:

      (a) 'FOR. . .'
      (b) Pause for silent prayer
          Invitation to pray
      (c) Selected communal response

(c) is a suitably short response of petition,

      e.g. Lord, hear us (the usual one)
           Lord, have mercy
           Show us your mercy and compassion
           Hear us, O Lord

(The Intercessions in Evening Prayer in the Breviary offer many different responses which could be used.
The Invocations of Morning Prayer are not suitable, and should not be used.)

A variation of this form would be to omit (b) and (c), and have a *silent response* to the petition.

The following is a simple form of Petitions for Holy Thursday, with the five intentions arising out of the readings as given above:

For an end of division between the Christian churches,
[silent prayer]
we pray to the Lord,
Lord, have mercy.

For the spread of the love of Christ in the world today,
[silent prayer]
we pray to the Lord,
Lord, have mercy.

For those whose life is one of suffering,
[silent prayer]
we pray to the Lord,
Lord, have mercy.

For all of us here together celebrating the Lord's Supper,
[silent prayer]
we pray to the Lord,
Lord, have mercy.

For all those close to us who have died,
[silent prayer]
we pray to the Lord,
Lord, have mercy.

The less solemn form mentions intentions along with the
different categories of people, thus:

    (a) 'THAT. . .MAY. . .'
    (b) [silent prayer]
        invitation to pray

    (c) response

The above Holy Thursday petitions in this form would be:

That all the Christian churches may grow into full unity,
[silent prayer]
we pray to the Lord,
Be mindful of your people, Lord.

That all the people of the world may show love for one
another,
[silent prayer]
we pray to the Lord,
Be mindful of your people, Lord.

That those who suffer may be given compassion and care,
[silent prayer]
we pray to the Lord,
Be mindful of your people, Lord.

That we who are assembled here may share in the prayer
of the Last Supper,
[silent prayer]
we pray to the Lord,
Be mindful of your people, Lord.

That all who have died may be with Christ in heaven,

[silent prayer]
we pray to the Lord,
Be mindful of your people, Lord.

The *solemn form* is more explicit in mentioning the categories
of people, thus:

    (a) 'FOR. . .THAT. . .'
    (b) [silent prayer]
        invitation to prayer
    (c) response.

In this form, the Holy Thursday petitions would be:

For all our Christian people: that they may all be one in
Christ,
[silent prayer]
we pray to the Lord
Lord, remember us your children.

For all nations and families: that they may love with the
love of Christ,
[silent prayer]
we pray to the Lord
Lord, remember us your children.

For all who suffer: that they may share in the patience of
Christ,
[silent prayer]
we pray to the Lord
Lord, remember us your children.

For all of us at this Eucharist: that we may be as Jesus was
at the Last Supper,
[silent prayer]
we pray to the Lord,
Lord, remember us your children.

For our friends and all who have died: that they may be
with Christ in heaven,
[silent prayer]
we pray to the Lord,
Lord, remember us your children.

Introduction

The Introduction is an invitation to the assembly, not unlike the introduction to the Lord's Prayer in the Communion Rite. The important point about it is that it is addressed to the people, and *not* to God. It is not a prayer; nor is it a petition. It is desirable that it flows from the readings and the homily. Its purpose is to evoke in the assembly a sincere concern for people in need, and of trust in God.

Concluding Prayer

The Concluding Prayer is an important prayer: it is the prayer of the presiding celebrant concluding, and bringing to a climax, the Liturgy of the Word.

In quality and tone, therefore, it is the same as the other presidential prayers which conclude a stage of the Eucharist: the Opening Prayer and the Prayer after Communion. These are 'collects' and should be taken as a model for its form.

In content, it is a prayer expressing confidence in God's love for his people, and asking that the petitions of the assembly be heard and answered. It should not contain a further petition. A very good source — since, unlike the other collects, it has to be composed — is the penitential psalms. These contain the authentic experience and expression of our needy people before God.

26

THE DIRECTORY FOR
MASSES WITH CHILDREN

The 'Directory for Masses with Children', a document from the Congregation for Divine Worship, November 1, 1973, is 'concerned with children who have not yet entered the period of pre-adolescence' (n. 6). According to Edward Matthews, a member of the commission responsible for the drawing up of the text of the Directory, 'for normal practical purposes this means that (it) is aimed at children in the 5-11 age group' *(Celebrating Mass with Children)*. It is a relatively short document (not much longer than some of the chapters of this book) yet a very excellent and very important one. Our reason for devoting a chapter to it is its value, not only for planning celebrations of the Eucharist for children of this age group, but also for all Planning. Although its concern is limited to this group, the principles underlying its suggestions bring to light the relative importance of the elements of the Rite, and how to give them their due emphasis.

We will first give a summary of the main points of the Directory, summarising them under the headings of the aim of the Directory, the difficulties foreseen in the Directory, and the means it suggests to overcome them. Then we will elaborate more fully on what it says about Planning, mainly from Chapter III. The numbers in parentheses indicate the paragraph numbers of the document.

Aim of the Directory

To help children quickly and joyfully to encounter Christ together in the eucharistic celebration and to stand in the presence of the Father with him. [55]

The principles of active and conscious participation are in a sense even more valid for Masses celebrated with children. Every effort should be made to increase this participation and to make it more intense. [22]

To lead children towards the celebration of Mass with adults, especially the Masses in which the Christian community comes together on Sundays. [21]

A liturgical and eucharistic formation directed toward a greater and greater response to the Gospel, in the daily life of the children. [15]

Difficulties to be faced

The children have not yet reached pre-adolescence. [6]

They have only recently made their first Holy Communion, if they have yet made it. [1]

Their parents may have neglected their religious education. [1]

Liturgy cannot exercise to the full its innate pedagogical force, because the words and signs have not been sufficiently adapted to the capacity of children. [2]

Means to overcome the difficulties

A – EXPERIENCES OUTSIDE THE CELEBRATION: First, an experience of the human values which are found in the eucharistic celebration. These values are: communal activity, exchange of greetings, listening, seeking and granting pardon, expressing gratitude, symbolic actions, a meal of friendship, and festive celebration.

A catechesis going beyond the human values, so that children may gradually open their minds to the perception of

Christian values and the celebration of the mystery of Christ. [9]

B – CATECHESIS: Directed to the child's active, conscious and authentic participation, and accomodated to the age and mentality of the children, it should be based on the text and principal rites, especially the Eucharistic Prayer and the acclamations. [12]

C – PLANNING OF CELEBRATIONS: by necessary adaptation, [20, 21] including additions [22].

In the choice of readings the criterion to be followed is the quality rather than the quantity of the texts from the scriptures. Everything depends upon the spiritual advantage which the reading can offer to children. [44]

> * Use of one of the three Eucharistic Prayers for Masses with Children, which, of course, are not mentioned in the Directory as they were not published until a year after the Directory.

Silence has its importance at the proper time as part of the celebration, lest too great a role be given to external action. [22; 37]

Singing and the use of musical instruments played by the children is to be encouraged. [30, 32]

It is to be kept in mind that external activities will be fruitless and even harmful if they do not serve the internal participation of the children. [22]

Discussion with the adults and the children. [29]

Children preparing the place and the altar. [22]   — N.B.

Also relevant in Planning: the time of day [26]: suitable interval between celebrations. [27]

(Suggestions for the Design are given in the next section, Arrangements, Adaptations).

D – STYLE OF CELEBRATION: The spirit of the celebration will depend upon the priest's personal preparation and his manner of acting and speaking with others. [23]

It is the responsibility of the priest who celebrates with children to make the celebrations festive, fraternal, meditative. [23] Much depends on his actions [33], and his use of the text, which should be spoken intelligibly and unhurriedly, with the necessary pauses [37].

The Eucharistic Prayer is of the greatest importance and the high point of the entire celebration. The children will be helped to be as attentive as possible by the dispositions of mind of the presiding celebrant, and by the calm and reverence with which everything is done. [52]

Arrangements, Adaptations (Chapter III)

PLACE
The primary place. . . is the church, in a suitable space; sometimes in another appropriate place. [25]

Visual aids are recommended. [35, 36]

MINISTERS
Diversity of ministries is to be encouraged. [24] As many children as possible to have special parts. [22, 34]

CHILDREN
Not too large a number. [28]

Should conduct themselves as a community; make use of gestures, postures and actions which could vary from what is indicated in the General Instruction, n. 21 [33], although the resulting rite should not differ too greatly from the Order of Mass celebrated with an adult congregation. [21]

AIM
To create the proper dispositions in the children, and to avoid any excess of rites in this stage. [40]

CONTENT
Some elements of the Introductory Rites may be omitted [40]. The OPENING PRAYER is always said — chosen, or adapted, from the Roman Missal. [50, 51]

Other possibilities:
Entrance procession of the children with the priest [34];

another appropriate sung text of 'Glory to God in the highest'. [31]

Liturgy of the Word [41-49]

AIM

To help the children to understand the readings, and make them their own; to give them a growing appreciaton of the value of God's word. [47]

CONTENT

There must always be a BIBLICAL READING [41]; a gospel is always read (the others may be omitted). [42]

The readings are chosen from the Lectionary or directly from the Bible; never paraphrased [45], though one or other verse may be omitted, provided that the sense is not mutilated. [43]
Translations suitable for children may be used. [45]

The RESPONSE may be selected verses of psalms; or a psalm may be sung; or the Alleluia with a simple verse sung between the readings. [46] or a reflective silence [46] aided by some kind of introduction. [22, 37]

The HOMILY should be given great prominence [48]; it may be given by one of the adults [24]. The children may just listen in silence, or sometimes the homily may become a dialogue with them. [48]

Other possibilities:

An introductory commentary [47, 23];
reading with parts distributed [47];
gospel procession with the participation of at least some of the children [34];

silent reflection after the homily, to which there
is an introduction [37];
Apostles Creed [49] or a different sung text of
the Nicene Creed. [31]

Liturgy of the Eucharist [50-54]

AIM

To make this stage appear as the high point of the
entire celebration; with an atmosphere of calm and
reverence; and the children attentive to the presence
of Christ. [52]

Special attention should be paid to the manner of
proclaiming the EUCHARISTIC PRAYER. [52]

CONTENT

Possibilities:

Eucharistic Prayer for Children I, II or III;
SUNG ACCLAMATIONS [30];
Procession with the gifts [34];
composed invitation ('Pray brethren. . .') [23];
adapted Prayer over the Gifts [50, 51];
explanatory comments before the Preface [23];
motives for giving thanks before the Preface [22];
singing of the 'Holy, holy'; use of another text
[30, 31];

The Rite of Communion will always have:

THE LORD'S PRAYER;
BREAKING OF BREAD;
INVITATION TO COMMUNION ('This is. . .') [53].

Other possibilities:

Composed introduction to the Lord's Prayer
[23];
greeting of peace: composed invitation [23];
sung 'Lamb of God'; different text [31];
composed Invitation to Holy Communion [23];
SINGING at the Communion Procession [54];
reflective silence, with introduction [22, 37];
adapted Prayer after Communion. [50, 51]

Everything should be done so that the children may go to the holy table calmly and with recollection, so that they may take part in the eucharistic mystery. [54]

Dismissal Rite [54]

AIM   To connect liturgy and life in the minds and lives of the children. [54]

Possibilities:
Introductory comments [23];
composed invitation before the blessing:
repetition and application [54];
solemn form of blessing [54]

. . . .*it is the very prayer*
which Christ himself together with his body,
addresses to the Father.
Hence all who perform this service. . .
are sharing in the greatest honour
accorded to Christ's spouse,
for by offering these praises to God
they are standing before God's throne
in the name of the Church their Mother.

(Constitution on the Liturgy)

The Liturgy Of The Hours: Our Prayer

Section Seven

PRAYING THE LITURGY
OF THE HOURS

The Liturgy Of The Hours: Our Prayer

The Liturgy of the Hours being our *prayer*, is influenced by the Four Areas. Our praying will be affected, therefore, by —
        A — Place
        B — Text and Rite
        C — Ministering
        D — Ourselves.

This section on Praying the Liturgy of the Hours will take these areas into account.

• To give emphasis to the PRAYER of the Hours, we will begin with what we use most for prayer in them: the psalms, with emphasis on Praying the Psalms. (Chapter 27)

• The Text and Rite will next be considered. We limit ourselves to Morning Prayer and Evening Prayer, as these are the most important and most used hours. Our concern will be to discover how the Text and Rite can be used to bring us to the best prayer in the morning and in the evening. (Chapter 28)

• Ministering of the Hours includes both Planning and Leading, and so the ministry of the Planner/Leader will be dealt with. (Chapter 29)

• Planning presupposes Evaluation. As the groups of those who gather regularly to pray Morning and Evening Prayer should be capable of a communal evaluation, the next chapter will be about Community Evaluation of Community Prayer. (Chapter 30)

• At certain times a community may feel called to undertake and enter into a period of serious renewal in their liturgical prayer-life. For such as these, in the final chapter we share our experience of Renewal Programmes in Communities. (Chapter 31)

27

PRAYING THE PSALMS

There is hardly a person who prays the Liturgy of the Hours who would not want to experience more 'prayer' from the psalms. The psalms are the largest element in all of the Hours, apart perhaps from the Office of Readings. The praying of the psalms in the different hours is what contributes most to its prayerfulness.

Everyone realizes that their praying of the psalms would improve if they spent time on them and gave the psalms some attention outside of the time of praying the Hours. Most think of that time spent in learning more about the psalms: some study of the psalms such as their history and background, or a separate study of each psalm in the psalter. There is no doubt that a study of the psalms *may* help one's praying them. However, it is not sure that it will. Information about the psalms may not be the most pressing need for a person.

There are courses in the psalms, for example in theological colleges, which are not intended to influence a person's prayer.

Our experience is that there is something that can be done with the psalms outside of the time of the Liturgy of the Hours which will help the praying of them: and it is not study. This chapter presents one form which this helpful activity could take. We would like to make it clear that it is not intended that a mere reading of this chapter is going to effect any change in anyone's prayer. The chapter does no more than present *what to do*: an activity to be engaged in with one psalm at a time which will yield results in prayer.

There will be two stages in the presentation: first, the expectations we can bring to a psalm; secondly, how to realize these expectations.

A — Psalm-Expectations

1. *The effect a psalm will have on me is 'me praying.'*

We are back at the concern of our Chapter 1: people praying. To pray is to experience; and the special experience it is was developed in Chapter 11. What we are going to say pre-supposes a familiarity with these previous chapters: it might be necessary to revise them.

2. *Psalms bring me to COMMUNAL prayer, and the PRAYER OF THE CHURCH.*

All the psalms are that type of prayer which was dealt with in Chapter 7, on the Prayer of the Church. They are the text of the prayer of a people: OUR People. They reveal and express that People's experience of their relationship with their God, with OUR God. It is a shared experience of God, refined over a long period; it is a response of their tried and tested faith in many different situations of their history.

Again we insist that it is necessary to appreciate the psalms as an example of what was presented earlier in this book. Most lack of appreciation of the psalms stems from an ignoring of this aspect: they are the Prayer of the Church.

3. *Psalms bring me into a 'WE' experience.*

Sometimes psalms pray an explicit 'we'; other times they

say 'I'. Whatever they say, their experience is 'we'. The mentality of the people among whom they were born was different to ours. Whereas we of the western world today have to come to an awareness of 'I' before we can experience 'we', and have to grow from the former to the latter, the Israelite started with an experience of 'we' and had to be educated into an experience of an individual, responsible 'I'.

4. *Psalms bring us into a COVENANT experience.*

The psalms are prayed by a people who experienced themselves as special: chosen by Yahweh as 'my people'. He is their God, who is characterized by his *hesed* (mercy, loving kindness); and by *emeth* (steadfastness, fidelity): a caring God who faithfully sustains the Covenant relationship.

> Great is his steadfast love towards us;
> and the faithfulness of the Lord endures forever.
>
> Psalm 117 (116)

Whether God is referred to in the third person as 'he', or in the second person as 'You', he is always the one who is in a special, intimate relationship with us.

5. *Psalms bring us to a deeper share in the Covenant EXPERIENCE of our People.*

The occasion of each of the psalms was different situations in the people's lives. Each psalm is a RESPONSE in a situation with its own circumstances. It is this response which we value.

We of today do not have the same experiences of that People: of being in exile, accused by enemies, attacked by the wicked. *Yet, while we do not share in those experiences of those situations, we do share in their experience of God which they express: that is, their hope, commitment, thanks, praise, recognition of God's Lordship, acknowledging him as Saviour, etc.*

> But I have trusted in your steadfast love;
> my heart shall rejoice in your salvation.
> I will sing to the Lord,
> because he has dealt bountifully with me.
>
> Psalm 13 (12)

6. *Psalms bring us to experience God in EVENTS.*

Psalms sometimes eulogize God as 'who is. . .'; but also as 'who *did*: an acknowledgement that it was God who acted in a past event, and that he still acts, and will continue to act, in the events of our lives.

> He it was who smote the first-born of Egypt,
>   both of man and beast;
> who in your midst, O Egypt,
>   sent signs and wonders. . .
>   *Psalm 135 (134)*

7. *Psalms bring us to pray from our suffering and sinful state.*

This occurs in the type of psalm called 'LAMENTATION' psalms. Israel experienced God in diverse situations, and these situations gave us psalms of different types. From the point of view of the 'starting situation', – and for the purposes of praying the psalms – they can be reduced to two categories, one of which, the lament, is the basic expression. For this treatment of the psalms we are indebted to Harvey H. Guthrie, in his study, *Israel's Sacred Songs.*

The characteristics of the lament are:

(a) They begin with the *plight of the suppliant*: mention is made, with a great display of emotion, of the present need, and possibly, who caused it.

Psalm 102 (101) begins with the complaint of a sick man, possibly suffering from fever.

> For my days pass away like smoke,
>   and my bones burn like a furnace.
> My heart is smitten like grass, and withered;
>   I forgot to eat my bread.
> Because of my loud groaning
>   my bones cleave to my flesh.

Different is the experience of the prayer of Psalm 88 (87). It is a person who feels that he has been removed from God's influence.

> For my soul; is full of troubles,
>   and my life draws near to Sheol.

I am reckoned among those who go down to the Pit;
  I am a man who has no strength,
like one forsaken among the dead,
  like the slain that lie in the grave,
like those whom you remember no more,
  for they are cut off from your hand.

(b) The psalmist then *remembers God* in his past mercies, and focuses on them. In psalm 7, having asked for refuge from 'my pursuers. . . lest like a lion they rend me', and prayed that 'the evil of the wicked may come to an end', the psalm takes on a different atmosphere with

My shield is with God,
  who saves the upright in heart.
God is a righteous judge
  and a God who has indignation every day.

Psalm 130, which begins with the plaintive, 'Out of the depths I cry to you, O Lord', changes to

But there is forgiveness with you. . .
I wait for the Lord, my soul waits,
  and in his word I hope.

(c) This leads to *a transition to confidence* the certainty of a hearing by God, and the granting of the petition. In the psalm last quoted, the climax of the prayer is

And he will redeem Israel
  from all his iniquities.

The person who prays Psalm 7 (quoted from above) ends the prayer with

I will give to the Lord the thanks due to his
righteousness,
  and I will sing praise to the name of the Lord,
the Most High.

The person who prays Psalm 6, who 'is languishing' and whose 'bones are troubled. . . my soul also is sorely troubled', can pray, after remembering God's 'steadfast love',

. . .the Lord has heard the sound of my weeping.
The Lord has heard my supplication;
  the Lord accepts my prayer.

How did such a transformation of experience come about

in the people who prayed these psalms? More to the point, how can such a transformation of experience come about in us? They were able to 'see more' than their suffering plight, and responded at a new level. We, by allowing the psalm to lead us, will be brought through the same process — the Process of Responding (Chapter 10).

9. *Psalms bring us to an experience of God's Lordship over all.*

The other category of psalms is the HYMN. The first category, starting with an experience of need, develops into an experience of God as Saviour. This second category is an experience of Yahweh, the Lord, as GOD in all the ways that counted.

Psalm 50 (49) acknowledges *God as Overlord:*

> The Mighty One, God the Lord,
> speaks and summons the earth
> from the rising of the sun to its setting.
> Out of Zion, the perfection of beauty,
> God shines forth.

And Psalm 81 (80):

> Sing aloud to God our strength;
> shout for joy to the God of Jacob!

In the same context there are songs which refer specifically to *God as king of the whole cosmos,* as in Psalm 29 (28):

> O give the Lord you sons of God,
> give the Lord glory and power;
> give the Lord the glory of his name.
> Adore the Lord in his holy court.

> The Lord's voice resounding on the waters,
> the Lord on the immensity of waters;
> the voice of the Lord, full of power,
> the voice of the Lord, full of splendour.

Psalm 104 (103) has a catalogue of different aspects of *God's control of the world:*

> You founded the earth on its base. . .
> You wrapped it with the ocean like a cloak. . .
> you made springs gush forth in the valleys. . .

> You made the moon to mark the months;
> the sun to know the time for its setting. . .

The Invitatory psalm, Psalm 95 (94) acclaims God as the chief of all gods:

> A mighty God is the Lord
> a great king above all gods.

Still in the same context, the supreme power of God is praised in *the person of the king*, to whom God has delegated his authority; and in the *place, Jerusalem*.

This is the background of Psalm 2:

> Why do the nations conspire,
> and the people plot in vain?
> The kings of the earth set themselves,
> and the rulers take counsel together,
> against the Lord and his anointed. . .
> He who sits in heaven laughs;
> the Lord has them in derision. . .
> 'I have set my king
> on Zion, my holy hill.'

Similar to it is the Sunday Evening Prayer psalm, Psalm 110 (109):

> The Lord says to my lord:
> 'Sit at my right hand,
> till I make your enemies
> your footstool.'

The importance of Jerusalem as the *place* of God's rule on earth appears in such psalms as Psalm 84 (83);

> How lovely is your dwelling place,
> O Lord of hosts!
> My soul longs, yea, faints
> for the courts of the Lord;
> my heart and flesh sing for joy to the living God.

The same motif occurs in Psalm 15 (14):

> O Lord, who shall sojourn in your tent?
> Who shall dwell on your holy hill?

These are the expectations with which we can come to the psalms: an enrichment of our experience of ourselves in our

O2

relationship with God; and of God himself almighty Lord of the universe and our loving Father. How can we come to share in this experience through the psalms? This brings us to the next section, on how to realize these expectations.

Psalm-Experience

To pray a psalm is to 'get inside the skin' of the person/ People who said those words, and to share in all that was going on inside them. In particular, to share in their feelings, their memories and hopes, their attitudes to God and people.

We have developed a way of doing this: a method which has been of help to people for quite a while. We now present this method in this chapter. It consists of asking several questions about the psalm, in order to arrive at the sharing of the experience with the person praying in the psalm. Hence, what follows will be nearly all in the form of an activity for you to engage in.

In order to become familiar with the 'technique', we will apply these questions to some very simple and familiar prayers, before applying them to a psalm. We find, however, that it is best to begin with a trial run, by asking these questions of some commonly used expressions.

This, then, will be the order in which we will proceed: first asking the questions of ordinary expressions; then of simple prayers; and finally of psalms.

The questions

ONE: The first question is directed to discover the SITUATION in which the expression is used. The situation is described by giving the circumstances: the facts about who? what happened? — the relevant details. It is completely objective and factual.

TWO: The second question is directed to discover the FEELINGS of the person who used the expression, including secondary feelings. Quite a mixture of feelings may be discovered.

THREE: The last question continues to look at the person who used the expression, but now to discover more than their feelings.

People's expressions contain a lot more than they explicitly say. In very ordinary expressions — provided that they are not just empty sounds — people 'say' something of their experience of their relationship to the person they address: something of commitment; something of their past; and something of their future hopes.

Three questions

1. WHAT IS THE SITUATION?
2. WHAT FEELINGS ARE EXPRESSED?
3. WHAT ELSE IS EXPRESSED?

Praying a Psalm: Preliminary

(You will need the text of the psalms for this activity: Bible or Liturgy of the Hours.

If at any stage you feel you need help with this activity, you could compare your replies with the lists on page 422.)

(a)   An ordinary expression

The first expression to which we will apply these questions is:

I am sorry to hear about your sister's accident

Write down your answers in regard to —
THE SITUATION in which that would be said:

FEELINGS EXPRESSED in the expression:

WHAT ELSE is expressed

(b)   Another ordinary expression
Take the expression:

> Isn't it a lovely day!

Again write down your answers —

1. One likely SITUATION:

2. FEELINGS expressed in that expression:

3. WHAT ELSE is expressed:

You cannot expect to see the relevance of these exercises just yet. You will, though, when we come to deal with a psalm. Let us now do the same with

(c)   A simple prayer
The prayer we select is:

> O my God, I am heartily sorry. . .

Now the questions

1. The SITUATION in which a person would pray this prayer:

(Give *facts* only; and be *complete*)

2. The FEELINGS of that person praying:

3. WHAT ELSE is expressed by that person in the prayer:

Before going on to the psalms, let us take just one more example. Please persevere; you will see the reason for these exercises soon!

(d)   Another simple prayer
This prayer is:

> Come, Holy Spirit, fill the hearts of
> your faithful.

Once more, the three questions

1. SITUATION from which the prayer arises

2. FEELINGS of those praying

3. WHAT ELSE do they express in these words:

Now we are ready to move on to the psalms. We begin with an example, and then we will leave you to work on your own on the others. The first psalm we will work on is —

Psalm 43 (42)

[*This psalm will be found in the Liturgy of the Hours, Week 2, Tuesday, Morning Prayer*]

Remember what was said: in order to pray a psalm it is necessary to 'get inside' the person who prayed it. To help us to do this we apply the three questions:

SITUATION: The person in the psalm is caught in a very live experience.

> He feels that he is 'oppressed.'
> The oppression is from a 'godless', evil source,
>   ('deceitful and cunning men').
> In it, he experiences God's rejection of him.
> Yet, he believes that God is his 'stronghold.'

FEELINGS:
- resentment (verse 1)
- sadness ('mourning')
- needy ('plead my cause')
- anxiety ('why have you. . ./do I. . .')
- trust (verse 3)
- hope (verse 4)
- *mixed feelings* (verse 5 'cast down', 'hope', 'will praise')

WHAT ELSE:
- He 'knows' that God is somewhere in it all
- He senses that the experience will pass
- He believes that God can give him what he needs
- He sees value in praying to God
- He is prepared to give time and attention to prayer

In order to PRAY that psalm
I must be in the SAME SITUATION,
with the SAME FEELINGS,
and the SAME 'ELSE':
the SAME EXPERIENCE.

You can come to that experience through this activity:

Praying a Psalm

1. Revive in your memory yourself in a
SITUATION in which:

— you experienced forces, influences
inside yourself, or outside of you
which were oppressing you,
taking away your freedom
— and you rejected them as bad
— you experienced no help from God
— yet you continued to believe in him and his
presence.
  Sometimes the objection is raised, 'Why revive
sad memories when you are feeling happy?'
The implication is that to feel sad is 'bad',
while to feel happy is 'good.' Our conviction
is that the only 'bad' feeling is *no* feeling:
feelings are not 'good' nor 'bad'. ('Good/
'bad' is not equivalent to 'pleasant/unplea-
sant'.) What is good is to be in touch with
what we are feeling, and to become aware of
the feelings that are deep in us.

2. Recall and re-live your FEELINGS. . . perhaps

mixed feelings, for example

— depression
— frustration
— disappointment
— anger
— fear
and
-- some trust
— a glimmer of hope

3. and the 'WHAT ELSE'

such as

— a deep- rooted faith in prayer
— a certainty that God could help
— a sense that it will pass sometime
— 'This is not really me'

now **PRAY the psalm yourself**

* * *

Psalm 119 (118) — I
[This section of the psalm is used on Week 1, Tuesday, Prayer During the Day]

A — Prepare to pray the psalm by making use of the three questions, proceeding as with Psalm 43 above:

SITUATION of the person in the psalm

FEELINGS of that person

WHAT ELSE is in that person

B — Revive the memory and experience of yourself sharing that person's situation and experience.

C — Pray the psalm.

D – Sum up the prayer of this part of the psalm in one phrase from the psalm itself.

*   *   *

Psalm 13 (12)
[*This psalm is used on Week 1, Tuesday, Prayer During the Day*]

As before, read the psalm to discover:

A – The psalmist's SITUATION, FEELINGS, and WHAT ELSE.

B – From the memory (if necessary) of a similar situation, share the psalmist's experience.

C – pray the psalm.

D – Sum up the prayer in a brief prayer of your own composition.

We are obviously implying that it is necessary to spend some time with a psalm before praying it in this way. The exercise could be profitably done with all of the psalms; the more the better. However, it would not be necessary to do all the 150 psalms. A representative selection of them will develop a 'taste' for them, and a familiarity with the prayer of our People in them.

Preparing the psalms in this way is a very good way of preparing to pray the Liturgy of the Hours.

To deepen in yourself the experience of what praying the Liturgy of the Hours can be, this activity gives a sample of what a psalm can offer.

Praying a Psalm: A Journey to the Centre

(You will need your breviary or bible for this activity)

1.
> Prayer is the response which comes from the still centre of our being. It is there that the Holy Spirit shapes us; it is there that the Holy Spirit says our prayer for us before God the Father.

Reflect on the meaning of 'still centre of our being', from your *awareness* of it and your experience of it.

2.
> Anthony Bloom suggests that we begin looking — not for the prayer that fires outward towards God, but the prayer that penetrates through the outer shell to the still point at the centre of our being.

If prayer is our response from the *centre* of our being, what activities may we need to engage in to penetrate the various shells of our being to come to the still point?

You might like to illustrate this diagrammatically, or symbolically:

3.

> Unless the words we say are those capable of penetrating to the centre then they are not prayers. They do not come from our whole being. Our words are not prayers until they arise from the centre of our being.

* Take a psalm; read it slowly, lovingly — not hurrying over the words. Let the ideas and the images seep into your being.

* Keep reading until one sentence, one phrase strikes you — that touches the centre of your being.
* Now focus on it.
* Say it over and over again.

* Now pray it as *your* prayer — using *your* 'heart-vocabulary'.

Lists for Comparison

(These lists are not intended to be a substitute for your completing the activities of this chapter.)

These are answers typical of those we have received back on our courses.

(a) *'Sorry to hear. . .'*

SITUATION: My sister had an accident.
                 A short time later I met a friend;
                 she had heard about the accident,
                 and she said. . .
                 (Note that there is nothing but facts; nothing of reaction or response)

FEELINGS: (that is, the friend's)

- sympathy;
- concern;
- sadness;
- anxiety;
- wanting to help;
- etc.

WHAT ELSE?

- hopes of her recovery;
- closeness to me;
- offer of help;
- would follow her progress with interest;
- a deepening of our relationship;
- etc.

These, and much more, are expressed in the friend's 'I am sorry. . .'

(b) *'Isn't it a lovely day!'*

The answers:

SITUATION: One day I was walking along the street.
                 The weather was beautiful.
                 I met a friend,
                 and she stopped and said. . .

            OR

I was at a get-together of some friends.
Everyone seemed to be enjoying themselves.
I was moving around, and mixing,
during which one person said to me. . .

FEELINGS EXPRESSED

- happy
- contented
- enjoyment
- secure
- looked-after
- grateful
- etc.

WHAT ELSE?

- 'I hope you feel happy, too'
- 'I'd like this to continue'
- 'Meeting you adds to my happiness'
- 'I like to talk to you'
- 'These are nice people here'
- 'I would like to be able to spend time together'
- 'I have an urge to share my happiness'
- etc.

(c) 'O my God. . .'

SITUATION: A person has sinned.
He or she becomes consciously aware of it.
He or she remembers God, forgiving sins,
and turns to him in repentance,
saying. . .
NOTE: An essential element in this situation
is the *conscious awareness* of one's state; an
actual remembrance and *explicit* thought of
God.

FEELINGS EXPRESSED

- regret
- sorrow
- guilt
- sadness
- disappointment
- unhappy

- lowly
- humble

- confident
- relief
- supported
- loved by God
- welcome
- etc.

> NOTE: There are two distinctive, even contrasting, types of feelings here, in the same person at the same time. The upper half is the response to sinful self; the lower half, the response to a merciful God.

WHAT ELSE?

- memories of the past: of self and God's care
- hope for the future
- serious commitment to Christian living
- purpose of amendment
- gratitude for forgiveness
- wonder at God's patience
- etc.

(d) *'Come, Holy Spirit. . .'*

SITUATION: A person/group experience a need.
They feel powerless to supply what they need.
They remember God,
and turn to him, praying. . .

Again note that necessary element in a prayer experience; awareness through focusing, or calling to memory.

FEELINGS EXPRESSED:

- powerlessness
- impatience
- dissatisfaction
- longing
- wanting
- needy

- trust

- hope
- assurance
- joy
- expectation
- a sense that we are provided for
- etc.

WHAT ELSE:

- glad we can do something
- conviction of the reliability of God
- willingness to submit to the Spirit
- awareness of our relationship with God
- a consistent stance of dependence
- etc.

28

PRAYING MORNING PRAYER
AND EVENING PRAYER

Morning Prayer and Evening Prayer both have the same structure. Yet they are a very different prayer. This chapter will consist of an examination of the Text and Rite with a view to discovering how it can be best used in order to —

(a) make the Liturgy of the Hours a real prayer,
(b) with the distinctive characteristics of Morning Prayer and Evening Prayer.

Prayer: morning and evening

The purpose of the Liturgy of the Hours is 'to sanctify the day and all human activity,' according to the General Instruction, n. 10. Time and activity are 'sanctified' when we are consciously aware of the saving presence of Christ in us, with us during those times and in those situations; when his presence is *realized* in our response. This gives to all the Hours an eschatological significance. On this Paul F. Bradshaw writes:

There are good grounds for concluding that the

primary purpose of the observance of fixed times of daily prayer in the early Christian community was none other than the liturgical expression of constant readiness for, and expectation of the *parousia*. . . For the observance of fixed times of prayer, far from being opposed to the expectation of an imminent *parousia*, was on the contrary the very expression of it: the realization that the new age was already begun was embodied in thanks and praise for what God has done, constant readiness for the Kingdom of God was embodied in regular petition for its final consummation, and participation in the apostolic mission of the world was embodied in intercession for the salvation of all mankind. *(Daily Prayer in the Early Church)*

The source of the difference between Morning Prayer and Evening Prayer is very simple: one we pray in the morning and the other in the evening. The difference between these prayers is the difference in *us* in the morning and evening: first, in how we are at those times; and secondly, the difference in our situation. In regard to 'how we are', I only have to look at myself at these times to realize the difference in myself in the first hour after getting up compared with myself at about six o'clock in the day. In one, I am only in the process of becoming fully awake and aware; in the other, I have a day's activity behind me, which has left its mark on me — possibly unnoticed by me, and possibly on one part of me more than another. *Hence, a person's needs are very different at those different times.* Most likely, lack of attention and awareness will be the morning need. Distraction, 'being hooked' and possibly weariness are more likely to produce evening needs.

The other difference — arising from the situation — *is the difference between myself beginning something and having completed it.* The difference between morning and evening is that in one I have the day, including all that it holds for me, ahead of me: with all my joyful or fearful anticipation; all my enthusiasm and zest for living, or, on the other hand, my lethargy and boredom. In the evening the day is just about ended, and it is behind me, with its pleasant and unpleasant situations, its agreeable and its uncomfortable moments. In one, I look forward; in the other, I look back.

Both situations make use of the same symbol: the symbol of LIGHT enters into both Hours. Morning Prayer recalls the resurrection of Jesus Christ, 'the true light, enlightening every man'. The General Instruction quotes St Cyprian who said: 'We should pray in the morning to celebrate the resurrection of the Lord with morning prayer.' Hence, Morning Prayer, recited as the light of a new day dawns, is a prayer of joyful anticipation.

Evening Prayer is celebrated when the day is drawing to a close, so that, as St Basil said, 'we may give thanks for what has been given us during the day, or for the things we have done well during it.' This prayer had its origin in an ancient ritual of lighting the evening lamp, called the *lucernarium*. For Christians it was a symbol of Christ, 'the light of the world.'

Ministering the Liturgy of the Hours

The prayer which is Morning Prayer and Evening Prayer will eventuate only if the Text is ministered to us. The Liturgy of the Hours is part of the Prayer of the Church, with all the qualities and requirements treated of in chapter 7. Enabling us to enter into the prayer of our People is the Text and Rite contained in the Breviary (or what is commonly referred to as 'Office Book.') This Text and Rite is ministered; we do not compose our liturgical Morning and Evening Prayer afresh each day.

The Text is given to us for our *prayer*; not to be 'said', or 'got in', or 'got through'! For this reason, it might be better if we abandoned the use of the word 'Office' in regard to this prayer. 'Office', from the Latin *officium* signifies a 'duty', an 'obligation.' As it was presented in the past, the 'obligation of the Office' was an important feature, an obligation which seminarians incurred as soon as they became subdeacons in those days. Although the notion of obligation is retained in the present Code of Canon Law, it is noteworthy that in the 'General Instruction on the Liturgy of the Hours', which is prefixed to the Breviary, (Congregation for Divine Worship, 1971), the expression used in connection with 'obligation' is, 'entrusted to sacred ministers in a special way.': it is more in the nature of a mandate to pray, rather than just the external fulfilment of a law, as heretofore.

If they choose to pray that prayer, they will choose the form in which it is given: the structure of Morning Prayer and Evening Prayer. The question before us is: What is its structure; And how can it be ministered — that is, planned and led by a minister — so as to accentuate its proper emphases? The first question will be dealt with in this chapter: What is available to the minister to work on? The second question will be answered in the next chapter.

Structure of Morning and Evening Prayer

> Introduction
> Introductory verse and Response
> INVITATORY and PSALM
> Hymn
> PSALMS (with Antiphons)
> Silence
> READING
> Silence
> Short Response
> GOSPEL SONG (with Antiphon)
> PRAYERS:
>> Invocations or Petitions
>> The Lord's Prayer
>> Concluding Prayer
> DISMISSAL/Blessing

The relative importance of the elements is indicated by the different emphasis given in the above list. We will take the elements singly, in order.

Introduction

The Introduction we are speaking about now is an Introduction composed by the Planner, similar to that recommended for the Eucharist.

The Liturgy of the Hours, like all other liturgical rites, begins with an introductory rite. Introducing Morning Prayer is: an INVITATION (called from its original Latin 'Invitatory') and a HYMN. The Invitation consists of an opening versicle and response, followed by Psalm 95 (94) with its antiphon. Evening Prayer is introduced by a versicle and response, the Glory be to the Father, and a HYMN.

Like all introductory rites, those of the Hours will be made more effective by including a composed Introduction, similar to that used in the Eucharist. This element, an absolute necessity in all liturgy, has been referred to and explained several times already. It is the content of 'Praying Liturgy I: Beginning to Pray' (Chapter 5). It was again dealt with in connection with the Eucharist, 'Introductory Rites' (Chapter 14). As in the latter, *the purpose of an Introduction to the Liturgy of the Hours is to supply what the community needs in order to pray as well as they are capable of praying.* The two distinct needs are: inner quiet and activation of faith.

What form this will take will be relative to the particular community on each particular occasion. It will be more suitable to take up its form when dealing with the work of the Planner/Leader in the next chapter. Here we will be content with insisting on the importance of this element, and the purpose of including it.

In the Liturgy of the Hours its purpose includes another function besides that of preparation to pray. It contributes to the *specific flavour of the prayer* — a morning prayer as different from an evening prayer.

The Introduction to prayer in the morning and in the evening will take our different needs into account, and be directed to supply what the community needs at those times in order to pray with full attention, awareness and presence.

Invitatory

'The whole Office is normally begun with an invitatory' (General Instruction, n. 34). Except in rare situations, this means that it will be the beginning of Morning Prayer. The Invitatory of Morning Prayer consists of:

Opening verse and response, 'O Lord open. . .'
Invitation psalm 95 (94) with its antiphon
('Glory be to the Father. . .' is *not* said)

This opening is very effective in establishing the character of a morning prayer. It dispels the notion that we should not pray morning prayer until we are wide awake. On the contrary. Here is a prayer — a 'Prayer for Sleepy People' — *specially designed to awaken us into Christian responding.* Very vigorously we are summoned to come before our Lord, our Creator and Lord of the Covenant; and before him to be joyful, and full of thanks. Further, we are called to commit ourselves to a day of 'listening to his voice.'

Psalm 100 (99) is a suitable alternative to Psalm 95, having the same thrust and character, and may be used in its place. The General Instruction also mentions Psalms 67 (66) and 24 (23) as alternatives. However, they do not carry the same content of 'morning-response' as the other two.

The Hymn

The singing of a hymn adds greatly to the praying of an Hour, and it should be included *if* it can be conveniently done. 'It makes an easy and pleasant opening to the prayer', says the General Instruction n. 42.

The hymns given in the different editions of the Liturgy of the Hours are selections on the part of their publishers; they are not, as psalms and scripture, part of the prayer of our People. The Constitution on the Liturgy recommended that the hymns be 'restored', and that 'other selections from the treasury of hymns be incorporated.' This is what has been done. Being just selections, they are easily interchangeable, always provided that they fit in with the character of each Hour.

Communities could also use their own collections of hymns: again, provided they are suitable to the Hour, and have the 'doctrinal and artistic value' expected in liturgy (see page 379).

It is hardly a substitute to have the words of a hymn recited, instead of sung, at this point of the Hour. While it may be a prayer, *saying* a hymn does not produce anything like the effect of singing. Worse still, the saying of some hymns produces nothing better than doggerel.

The Psalms

Our People have always regarded certain psalms as particularly appropriate for use in morning and evening prayer, and have continually used them. In our present Morning and Evening Prayer, the psalms have been selected to fit in with our morning and evening situations. The psalms of Morning Prayer are always:

1. a morning psalm
2. Old Testament canticle
3. a psalm of praise.

They are particularly suited to our needs at the beginning of the day. The morning psalm may explicitly refer to light or morning; or lead us to the thoughts and responses which are helpful to guide us into our day. Psalms of praise and thanksgiving, and those which acknowledge the glory of God in creation and history, are traditionally part of morning prayer.

In the early centuries only a few fixed psalms were used, notably Psalms 51 (50), giving a penitential character; 63 (62), with its warm, intimate longing for God: and the *alleluia* psalms 148-150. This was the style of the Cathedral Office, intended for the parish situation. Monasticism later introduced the Monastic Office, intended for the use of hermits and monks, which made use of all the psalms. Our Liturgy of the Hours is under this latter influence.

The psalms of Evening Prayer are two psalms or two sections of longer psalms, followed by a New Testament canticle. They are selected to suit the evening response and mood of a Christian looking back over the day, especially thanksgiving and trust.

The classic Evening Prayer psalm was, and is, 141 (140). Also used in the Cathedral Office were psalms 110 (109) — 147.

Antiphons

There are two types of antiphons. The more common are those used with the daily psalms. They usually are taken from, or based on, the psalm itself; often they use the words of the psalm.

The other type, which are generally longer, are found in feasts and the liturgical seasons. They are not taken from the psalm; often they are just connected with the feast or season.

While they are a help, antiphons are of far less importance than the psalms themselves. They do not have to be recited by the whole community: one person could recite them, while the community listens. This is particularly applicable to communities who use a one-volume breviary, in which it can be very difficult to find the correct antiphon in a given group of three or four antiphons. This happens a lot during the liturgical seasons. The search for the text of an antiphon in the breviary by members of the community should never be allowed to distract from the praying of the psalm.

It would seem to be worth while calling attention to the use of antiphons recommended in the General Instruction: 'An antiphon may, *if so desired*, be repeated after the psalm.' (n. 123. Italics ours)

Ways of using the psalms

There are a variety of ways of using the psalms suggested in the General Instruction nn. 121-123, and they may all be made use of by communities, as they contribute to the prayerfulness of the Hour.

(1) The oldest way was having the psalm sung by one person while the rest listened and responded with a refrain. This is the most common way of praying the psalm in response to the first reading in the Liturgy of the Word in the Eucharist. It is called praying a psalm *responsorially*.

(2) Another way is for *all* to recite or sing the whole psalm together.

(3) Praying alternate verses (or strophes in our present breviaries) by two choirs or two parts of the community is called praying *antiphonally*.

(4) The verses (strophes) may be alternated between one person, the leader, and the rest. This way can be used to advantage to introduce a more meditative pace into praying the psalms.

(5) Finally, one person alone can recite or sing the psalm, while all listen and pray silently.

Psalms are meant to be sung, and singing them is something to be desired. Some psalms lend themselves more readily to singing than others; this applies especially to the hymns of praise. (General Instruction n. 278)

'Glory be to the Father. . .'

It is customary to conclude each psalm with this short doxology. It is meant as a help to the 'christianization' of the psalms. It is to be regretted, as Fr Crichton points out *(Christian Celebration: The Prayer of the Church)*, that we do not have the form 'Glory be to the Father, *through* the Son, and *in* the Holy Spirit', which was still current in the time of St Basil, and which gave way to 'the old relic of the anti-Arian campaign of the fourth century' — our present form of doxology.

Silent Prayer

What was said in Chapter 10 on the 'Process of Responding' points to the suitability and, indeed, necessity of time for reflective prayer in the course of the Liturgy of the Hours.

It is not intended that any of the Hours be prayed through without some breaks for silent prayer. Quoting the *Constitution on the Liturgy*, the General Instruction states that 'opportunity for silence should be given in the recitation of the Liturgy of the Hours' (n. 201). It suggests that these periods can be after the psalm; and after the reading; either before or after the Short Response. They need not, of course, be limited to these times.

In this connection, mention could be made of 'Psalm-Prayers' or 'Psalm-Collects' as they are called. In the early centuries, the custom had arisen of having a pause after the recitation of a psalm. This pause gave time for reflection and private prayer; it slowed down the pace of the Hour and prevented a mechanical recitation of the psalms. At the end of the period of silence the person leading the Hour prayed a collect-type prayer of his own composition. These psalm-prayers were collected from different traditions. Many are now available in different collections. A selection of them is included in the supplement to the Latin edition of the Liturgy of the Hours, and is included in the U.S. edition of the Liturgy of the Hours published by the Catholic Book Company, New York. They could be used in communal or private praying of the Hours. However, as everyone will not find each of them helpful on every occasion, *people could be recommended, and given time, to pray their own psalm-prayer after each psalm*.

Scripture Reading

The readings for Morning and Evening Prayer are usually short in comparison with those of the Eucharist. As will be seen when speaking of the work of the Planner in the next chapter, they do not have to be short (see Choice of Text, pp. 445-6).

Somewhat the same as with antiphons, some of them are chosen to express and interpret the significance of the feast or season being celebrated. Others have been included to 'emphasize certain passages and help to highlight short sayings which receive less attention in the continuous reading of the scriptures.' (General Instruction n. 45)

They help to bring out the morning or evening character of the Hour; as well as the special character of Sundays and Fridays.

A short Introduction to the reading, similar to those recommended in the Liturgy of the Word, will be helpful (see Chapter 25).

The reading is always meant to evoke a response in prayer. To aid this, a *Short Responsory* follows each reading. Originally selected to be sung to a very rich musical melody, they do not have anything of the expected impact when recited. In many instances they are a summarizing of the thought of the reading rather than a response to the reading (as envisaged in Chapter 9). As stated in the General Instruction, n. 49, they may be omitted if so desired.

Whether the Short Responsory is used or not, a period of SILENT PRAYER must be included (see Chapter 9).

Gospel Song

Perhaps more than any other element the Gospel songs contribute to the special character of prayer in the morning and evening.

Morning Prayer has the Song of Zechariah, the *Benedictus*. We pray it as a People who 'live on a promise', and the hope it inspires in us. This emphasis is brought out better in the ICET (International Consultation on English Texts) Text, sometimes given as an alternative on the last pages of the breviary.

> As he promised 'through his holy prophets', and before them, promised 'to our fathers', and before them again, 'to our father Abraham', God will 'visit us' in Jesus Christ in this coming day. We will live today — we are promised — as people who are saved; people who are free to respond to God. In this day to come, as sure as the sun rises to usher in the dawn, soon the Son will shine on our 'dark' and 'dead' parts, and guide us to the wholeness which is 'peace.'

We enter the day, as it were, floating on God's promise!

Evening Prayer has the Song of Mary, the *Magnificat*. We pray it *remembering*: remembering the day that is past with appreciation of God's part in it. There is also an alternative ICET text for this song.

> God has bestowed his 'favours' on us; he 'has done great things' for us in the day past. We collect all the blessings we have received from God during the day — blessings unearned and by us all-unworthy — and we bless him as great and merciful.

As we end the day, we remember that God has remembered us!

There is a distinct spirituality in the way the Prayer of our People in the Liturgy of the Hours leads us to begin and end our days. While the aspect of penitence is not absent from either Hour, Morning Prayer is full of hope in the blessings and the good to come in the day. Evening Prayer is full of thanks for the good we are able to do through God's faithfulness to his promise; like one great *berakah* which takes up into one prayer the many occasions for it during the day. This is in keeping with the spirituality mentioned in connection with *berakah*, in Chapter 16.

For this reason it will seriously impoverish, even distort, the Hour if the songs are omitted. Unfortunately, the practice does exist in some communities of solving the difficulty of people being bored with their daily recitation by leaving them out. We can be fairly sure that the very fact that our People experienced the suitability of praying these, and other prayers, every day — and so included them each day in the Liturgy of the Hours — that they are of the utmost importance to our prayer life. If people are bored and the Songs have no impact, then something can be done to 'un-bore' them! As will be seen, it will then be the task of the Planner-Leader to serve them up attractively. The Gospel Songs are as an essential part of Morning and Evening Prayer as psalm and scripture reading.

Antiphons

These Songs have their antiphons, too, and like the psalms, they are of the same two types: the ones given for each day of the week, closely connected with the text of the Song; and others, given for Sundays and the liturgical seasons, drawn from elsewhere.

The remarks made about the use of antiphons with the psalms also applies to their use with the Gospel Songs (see above).

Prayers

The Prayers which follow are again very different in Morning Prayer from those of Evening Prayer.

Morning Prayer, being a looking-forward prayer, leads us to pray about *ourselves and the coming day*. 'Since traditionally prayer is offered in the morning to commend the whole day to God, INVOCATIONS are given at Lauds to consecrate the day to him.' (General Instruction n. 181) They may include, as well as petitions, prayers of trust, commitment, thanksgiving etc.

Evening Prayer, while looking back, includes INTERCESSIONS 'for the whole Church, indeed for the salvation

of the whole world' after the manner of the General Intercession in the Eucharist (see Chapter 15).

These Prayers are part of a very long and unbroken
tradition in the Liturgy of the Hours. However, the particular
ones which are given in the breviary are not traditional, but
recent compositions for the revised (1971) edition of the
Liturgy of the Hours.

Format

The form of these prayers given in the editions of the
Liturgy of the Hours is somewhat elaborate. After an introductory invitation there are a succession of two-part invocations, to which there is a response. These compositions,
too, are often very elaborate, too packed with details and
very 'wordy.' The responses sometimes are more a separate
petition, and do not follow on smoothly from the invocations.

To use them with effect, many of them will need some
alterations. First, they could be pruned to the minimum of
detail and words, remembering their function as an element
in the Hour. The style of some is more suitable than others
to evoke prayer: for example such as 'Father, through the
victory of the cross you have lifted up Jesus from the earth;
— may he draw all men to himself.' In this style, the first half
sets up the motivation of trust for the petition in the second
part. Secondly, more suitable responses could be substituted:
short, simple and a natural response to the invocations used.
In using them in the Hour, there would have to be a slight
pause for silent prayer in between the two parts.

In view of what was said in regard to the General Intercessions in the Eucharist, that they should be produced fresh
for each community for each occasion, *a simpler form could
be used to advantage, especially in small gatherings.* Perhaps
the most suitable form would be the mentioning of a petition
by the Leader, with a period of silent prayer, followed if
desired, by a short response. When a community knows what
is expected in these prayers, spontaneous invocations would
be suitable for a small group.

The Short Intercessions given in an appendix in breviaries
for use at Evening Prayer could be taken as a model for

composed invocations.

What is to be remembered is that the best form to use for a particular group on any occasion is the format that results in the best prayer.

The Lord's Prayer

The Lord's Prayer 'has the place of honour at the end of the Prayers', according to the General Instruction, n. 194. Because of this, and its ranking in the prayers of our People, it is very fittingly preceded by an introduction. A list of suitable ones is included in the breviary (in an appendix, or in the Ordinary).

Concluding Prayer

This section of Prayers is completed with a collect type Concluding Prayer. These Concluding Prayers are another element which highlight the particular character of the Hour, as well as the liturgical season.

The Concluding Prayer is prayed by the Leader. Neither its function in summing up the Hour, nor its special collect form makes it suitable for recitation by the whole community.

Dismissal

The essential place of a Dismissal in the Eucharist was discussed in Chapter 20. What was presented there applies also to the Liturgy of the Hours: the final element is a Dismissal in some form or other. The breviary gives the same form as used in the Eucharist.

A difficulty arises in that it is only an ordained representative of Christ and the Church, namely a bishop, priest or deacon, who can, in the name of Christ and the Church, 'send' an assembly. So often the Liturgy of the Hours is celebrated by an assembly which does not include any such person. This situation is catered for by an alternative form, 'when no priest or deacon is present.' The form consists of a blessing, and omits any element of dismissal. This results in the absence of an opportunity for the community to express their acceptance of their missionary nature and role. This we see to be, as has been said at length elsewhere, a serious omission: dismissal is as integral to a liturgical experience as being apostolic is to the Christian life. Is there any solution?

The purpose of the 'Go' is to re-awaken our awareness of this apostolic aspect for ourselves; and to evoke a new acceptance, fully and thankfully, from us of our missions in life. The acceptance is expressed by our response of 'Thanks be to God,' and our going out. Granted that not every Leader of an Hour is one who is entitled to pronounce a 'Go' to the community, surely she or he would say something else, which, while not a full re-commissioning, *would suitably evoke the same dismissal-response*. Perhaps this will become more urgently experienced as a need according as our missionary self-awareness develops.

*   *   *

Rites in celebration

The General Instruction mentions a 'principle of progressive solemnity' in the celebration of the Liturgy of the Hours. Contributing to added solemnity are:

POSTURES; MOVEMENTS of the community. These include making the sign of the cross; standing at certain times. Details are given in General Instruction, nn. 263-266.

SINGING: everything except the readings can appropriately be sung. 'The principle of progressive solemnity is one which admits several intermediate stages between the singing of the Office in its entirety and the recitation of all its parts' (n. 273). In selecting the music of an Hour the nature of each element should be taken into account. Hymns are obviously meant to be sung. Psalms are greatly enhanced by singing, and 'this form is to be preferred' especially for hymns and psalms of thanksgiving (nn. 278, 279).

MINISTERS in the Hours include a Leader who presides (priest, deacon or non-ordained minister); reader, cantor (nn. 253-260).

INCENSE may be used during the Gospel Songs (n. 261).

VESTMENTS of the ministers are also given as a factor in signifying the degree of solemnity of a celebration.

Celebration of Saints

There are different degrees of importance of celebrations: they are called *solemnities, feasts and memorials*. The breviary will indicate the type of each day, and the General Instruction gives details about the arrangement of the Liturgy of the Hours on those days in Chapter Four, 'Various Celebrations in the Course of the Year,' nn. 204-240.

Most saints' days are celebrated as a memorial. However the breviary caters for any saint's day to be celebrated as solemnity or feast. It provides the text in the two sections Proper of the Saints, and Common Offices (Commons). It should be noted that it is only when, because of the particular place or community, a saint's day is elevated to solemnity or feast, that all that is provided in these sections is used, especially the special antiphons and psalms. Normally a memorial of a saint follows the current day, apart from Invitatory and Gospel Song antiphons, Reading and Concluding Prayer, as outlined in the General Instruction n. 235. Of relevance to this arrangement is what is said in the next chapter on Choice.

29

THE PLANNER-LEADER
IN THE LITURGY OF THE HOURS

If we are called to pray the Liturgy of the Hours as a community, then we are called to do what it takes to pray these hours. 'What it takes' is: planning; someone to lead; and regular evaluation on the part of the community. In this chapter we will take up the first two of these needs. In case there might be any misunderstanding, we are not catering just for special occasions; *we are talking about what will go on all the time, every day.*

A ministry

The Leader has already been specified as a necessary minister in the communal celebration of the Liturgy of the Hours (page 440). A Planner is equally necessary. The structure of an Hour permits of choices, and someone has to make them; if there is an Introduction, someone will have to compose it; if there is singing, it may need selection and organizing. Who will take care of these tasks? The Planner will: this is part of his or her ministry.

The Hours are presented in the breviary in such a way that they need someone to minister them to the community. The

Text and Rite of the Liturgy of the Hours is not the prayer; it is a *means* which we use to come to the Morning and Evening Prayer of our People, and we make use of it for our prayer — like any prayer-book. The Text is to be seen as at our service; we are not slaves to it. Applying to it what Jesus said about man and the Sabbath, 'Man was not made for the sabbath, but the sabbath was made for man,' it can be said: 'Man or woman was not made for the breviary, but the BREVIARY WAS MADE FOR THEM.' *For as community celebration it cannot fulfil its function without being ministered.*

Planning and Leading are two distinct ministries. We are here envisaging them as being done by the same person, since that is the most practical arrangement at present for the daily celebration of the Liturgy of the Hours in communities.

Planning and leading is a service to the community: a response to their needs; in particular their prayer-needs.

To the Planner-Leader a community gives their mandate. All that the Planner-Leader does is in response to that mandate, to its extent and within its confines. It is all *for* the community; all begins *from* the community.

Community Evaluation will be dealt with in the next chapter. Here it is well to note that the Planner-Leader's concern is with the *community* and their (corporate) needs; not with individual's needs — or wants. One of the difficulties in this ministry is to ensure that the prayer of the community is not retarded, or robbed of its vitality because of one or two individuals. This difficulty is not just a difficulty in community prayer; it is a difficulty in *community life*. It means, however, that a Planner-Leader has to deal with it, with all the wisdom, strength and discernment that it takes.

The Planner-Leader and the community

The ministry of each Planner-Leader has as its basis the relationship she or he has with the community. The actual planning and leading is but an expression, an externalizing, of that relationship. Love, trust and commitment are what are operative primarily; method and procedure, technique and skill, important though they be, are a second to these human qualities, attitudes and feelings. Let us then look at ourselves in this ministry.

As a Planner-Leader I am conscious of being *called* to plan and lead for the community: called by God *through* the community. 'I' am called; as I am, with my degree of faith, of maturity, of competence; with my particular spirituality; and my particular way of doing it.

- I accept this call, this service to my community.

- My starting point for what I do is not me, but *them*: their needs. (I have 'heard' these needs in our Community Evaluation.)

- I do not do the things *I* would like to do, follow my own tastes and likes, but I do what helps them.

- I am committed to this service; I must be faithful to it!

- It is not an opportunity to display my talents, my ideas; it is not intended for my sense of self-fulfilment; or to meet any of *my* needs.

- I will do nothing that would in any way put them off their prayer.

- I trust my community, and in the power of the Holy Spirit to enable them to pray.

- I believe in them: in their commitment, and particularly their commitment to prayer.

- I believe that they accept me, as I am: my Planning and my Leading.

- In my planning and leading I will willingly change whatever is not helpful, as soon as I become aware of what will help them.

- I do not expect to be without apprehension, some doubt. In fact, I welcome it, for if there is no room for doubt, there is no room for faith!

Planning an Hour

The time and activity of planning is one of loving and prayerful service. I sit down, and set myself down, therefore, to do something for others. It is an occasion — and an opportunity — for centering myself once again; and then to become present to my community.

The AIM of the Planning cannot be brought to consciousness too often. The question: *What am I hoping to do for the community? What is my overall purpose?*

TO LEAD THEM TO PRAY!

I look at them, and how they will be when I will lead them in the Hour. They may have been praying for a while before the Hour: maybe only just arriving in the chapel.

What would I hope to bring alive in them?

> e.g. their *call* to this prayer;
> *trust* in their ability to pray well;
> confidence that *I* can help them;
> their attitude to one another;
> concern for the others' prayer
> etc.

What have they — or will they have then — that I can start from?

What *is* alive in them: distraction; anxiety; pre-occupation; a worry; disappointment or delight; or what?

What can I do, present to them, or say to them that will make them attentive to me? And then, how to awaken their faith?

These will guide me in the composition of an INTRODUCTION. (see pp. 429-430).

From here on, Planning will be done from the text of the breviary. The text of the day is the obvious starting point, and it will normally be followed. Only if it is obviously unsuitable and 'unprayable' would an element be exchanged for another. The General Instruction gives as sufficient reason for change 'a good spiritual or pastoral reason' (n. 252)

A section of the General Instruction caters for such an exchange. It is entitled 'The Choice of Text' (nn. 246-252).

P

It begins

> Provided that the general arrangement of each
> Hour is maintained and that the rules which
> follow are observed, texts other than those found
> in the Office of the day may be chosen on par-
> ticular occasions. (n. 246)

As would be expected, in order to preserve their particular
characteristics, changes are not made

> on Sundays, solemnities, feast of Our Lord; and in
> general, during the liturgical seasons (for details,
> see General Instruction, n. 247).

On Sundays, however, psalms of the current week may be
replaced with the Sunday psalms of another week.

Apart from these exceptions, 'for a good spiritual or
pastoral reason, instead of the psalms assigned to a particular
day other psalms may be said which are found in the same
Hour of a different day' (n. 252). Note the qualification
about 'psalms from the *same Hour*'.

Under the same conditions, readings, collects and prayers
for the weekdays of a particular season may be changed for
others of the *same season*. (n. 251)

A Planner will have to take into account the 'praying
tolerance' of the community. There is just so much a community can pray before their capacity is exhausted. This
applies especially to the number of psalms. There are indications that three psalms may be too many in the morning
and evening. Another factor is the length of time which
communities have been accustomed to allocate to Morning
and Evening Prayer. The addition of an Introduction, the
inclusion of times of silence, and possibly also a slowing of
pace in their recitation, forces the alternative: do not change
anything in the Hour, or reduce the number of psalms. Our
work has led us to be engaged in a renewal of the Liturgy of
the Hours with about forty religious communities in Australia
and overseas, and they each shared the same experience.
They all came to the conclusion that, in a period of renewal,
*when a community is endeavouring to improve its praying
of the Hours, it is a distinct advantage to the prayer to pray
only one psalm in Morning and Evening Prayer.* It can be

looked on as a temporary measure in a period of adjusting to something new. It is to be hoped that the community will be in a position to schedule a longer period of time for these Hours; and that the members of the community will grow sufficiently in their prayer to include the three psalms. In the meantime, quality is more important than quantity.

Writing on this same difficulty, and how the revised Liturgy of the Hours reduced the number of psalms (from five to three in Morning and Evening Prayer), Fr A.M. Roguet, O.P., says:

> The purpose of the liturgical reform in cutting down the number of Hours, in reducing the number of psalms and readings, has not been to minimize the importance of prayer. To assert the contrary would be to identify the number of words with the spiritual quality of the prayer. By reducing their number and their length, the value of the Hours has been re-asserted. They can recover their original meaning by being able to be said at the right time of day without demanding a tremendous effort of willpower to do so.' ('Commentary on the Renewed Liturgy of the Hours,' in *The Liturgy of the Hours*).

Hence, if a Planner, with the community's agreement, selects one of the psalms, she or he is acting on the same principle as the compilers of the revised Liturgy of the Hours. To pray one psalm is to return to the original practice in the Cathedral Office in the West. There is evidence from St Augustine that in North Africa in his day (fifth century) there was only a single psalm and not a group of psalms.

Planning will include *selections* and *compositions* which take into account and cater for the treatment of each element of the Hour.

FEATURING: The Planner will consider whether the Hour would benefit by highlighting any one element. This is what we have come to call 'featuring': that is, giving special treatment to an element in the case, for example, that members of the community are 'bored' with it. This element is then 'served up' with particular attention.

INTRODUCTION: This has been dealt with above. Anyone who is regularly called upon to act as Planner-Leader would be well advised to make a collection of ideas for centering/Introductions.

INVITATORY (Morning Prayer): It is helpful if it flows from the Introduction. Then the decisions as to: Which psalm will we use? Will it be sung or recited?

HYMN: Will we have one? If so, which one?

PSALM: In keeping with the aim, and guided by her or his sensitivity to the community, the psalm is chosen from the three of the Hour. Again: Will it be sung or recited? What way will we pray it: antiphonally, responsorially, or how? Would an Introduction to the Psalm be helpful? How would I best help them to pray it? Here the method given in Chapter 27 would produce a suitable short Introduction to the Psalm.

READING: I compose an Introduction to the Reading, if it would be helpful.

RESPONSE to the Reading: SILENCE only; or will the Short Response be used? If the latter, will the Silence be before or after it?

GOSPEL SONG: To be sung or recited? Would an Introduction be helpful to it? How will I help to bring out its morning/evening character?

NOTE: Not every element should have an Introduction at every Hour. Too many Introductions would be irksome rather than helpful.

PRAYERS: What form will these take: as in the breviary, or an altered form, or composed by me? A vocalized or silent response? What response will we use?

LORD'S PRAYER: Sung or recited? As it will always have one, I select or compose a suitable Introduction.

CONCLUDING PRAYER: I get familiar with the petitions. It is often worthwhile to practice my praying of it aloud.

DISMISSAL/BLESSING: Will I use the usual form, or compose one?

As well as the above Design, the Planner might consider the use of:

A SETTING: a candle, picture etc, to contribute to the atmosphere.

MUSIC: Before, after, and/or within the Hour, such as after the psalm or reading.

OTHER treatment of the Place, Text and Rite; Leading and using other ministers; and whatever the Planner's creativity would consider as helping in her or his aim.

When the work of Planning is completed, it is wise to check it for BALANCE: how does it all fit together, especially in regard to the silent pauses, Introductions, and use of music?

The Leader needs a copy of the result of the Planning to consult during the Leading. It should therefore be very clear and such that every element stands out and can be found without difficulty. To give the paper some solidity and to prevent any distracting rustle, we strongly recommend that it be placed in a plastic envelope for its use during Leading.

Lastly, if there is anything about the Planning that the community would need to know, then write a list of the items which you will tell them in a BRIEFING.

How long?

The above outline of procedure in Planning might raise the question, How long would it take to plan an Hour? With practice and familiarity, it can be expected that the time will get shorter. Although it may not take all of it, in the beginning about twenty to thirty minutes would need to be available for it.

Leading the Community in an Hour

The Planning is completed. Now comes the time for Leading the community in this Hour. The first requirement for Leading is —

Preparation

When I come before the community to begin the praying of the Hour, I myself need to be *praying*: that is, centered and my faith activated.

The main factor in my Leading is ME: what I diffuse; what I communicate through body-language. A scattered, distracted Me can give no help to others to become centered; a Me without conscious awareness of Jesus Christ will never awaken that faith in the community. *I* am the first means — God-chosen and Spirit-endowed — to help them with their praying. Consider also this realistic thought: I, too, can turn out to be a hindrance, even an obstacle, to them.

Before the Hour begins, I need to lead myself to prayer: act as my own prayer-leader for a while.

Part of the preparation needs to bear on my relationship with the community I am about to lead, as already mentioned above.

- I come to them anew in the light of faith, and our relationship in Christ.
- I see this special relationship of my Leading, and what that means for them and for me.
- I respond in faith and trust to the God who is calling me to lead; and to the Christ who lives in them and shares his prayer with them.

Then, just being myself — myself as I really am at this moment — I am prepared to come to the community.

More time! Yes, time is needed for Preparation as well as Planning. How long? That is relative to how I am when I begin my Preparation. To give a figure, no matter how suitable my condition before it, at least ten to fifteen minutes would need to be left free for it. It could quite well require much more. Experience will indicate to each how long.

Leading

The LEADING-POSITION from which it is most effective to lead a community depends on the place, its size, and the size of the group. The normal and natural position is *in front* and *standing* at some lectern-like support for breviary and the copy of the Planning. NEVER at the Lectern, though!

A BRIEFING to inform of anything different in the format of the Hour, if it is needed, should come before anything else in Leading.

The LANGUAGE used needs to be chosen with sensitivity for the community. A suggestion may be welcomed more than a command: 'Let us think about. . .', rather than 'Think about. . .' Some communities, through their past experiences, for example in renewal programmes, are threatened by a terminology associated with painful moments in their lives: for example, 'reflect', 'sharing', even 'feelings'. If this is so, other words should be chosen in their place.

ADAPTING to the circumstances and the occasion is part of the ministry of Leading. A group of sisters who are at home all day, and have spent a lot of it praying, will need different treatment to a group of teachers or social workers who just 'fall into' the chapel at the time of the Hour. Monday morning is different from Sunday, and so is the community.

ADJUSTMENTS on the spot may be necessary. They will be indicated by what the Leader 'hears': what is seen on their faces, their bodies and the 'sound' of the community at the time. It may not be possible for the Leader to make a change, but at least, the response of the people should be noted and taken seriously. If something unexpected happens to shorten considerably the time available for an Hour, the response to the situation by the Leader must be an adjustment, and not a rushed effort to complete what has been planned.

RE-CENTERING will almost always be called for. As soon as a Leader realizes that he or she is caught by something other than the community's praying, a brief re-centering should be unobtrusively engaged in.

Hearing comments

A Leader needs some feedback from the members of the community. It can be given in evaluation sessions; but also informally, and may have to be asked for. People seem reluctant to say more than a general, though uninforming, 'Thanks very much. That was great!' It is hard to come by; but some feedback is very necessary.

Roster of Planner-Leaders

Rostering may be on a volunteering or appointment basis: whichever the community prefers.

Two very important conditions must be catered for:

(1) Sufficient notice for those involved as Planner-Leaders to complete the task beforehand. They should be consulted as to how long a notice they would like.

(2) Sufficient space between the times of their ministry. It is not possible, given the usual conditions of community life at present, for anyone to lead for a whole week. That is, if the Planning and Leading is conducted in the way we are advocating. One day at a time is enough; or maybe one Hour a day. With the usual apostolic involvements today, the best method is to put up a list for volunteers for Morning Prayer and Evening Prayer to discover when the members of the community would find themselves most free to take on the ministry.

We consider in the next chapter what a Planner needs in order to minister: Community Evaluation.

Those who act as Planner-Leader will find that their ministering will gain in depth and confidence through reflections such as the following activity:

The Planner-Leader

Ask yourself these questions:

1. What is my aim in planning and leading?

2. What means are available to me to achieve this aim?

3. What preparations are necessary for me to achieve my aim?

4. What is my commitment to this ministry?

How would I state my commitment?

30

COMMUNITY EVALUATION
OF COMMUNITY PRAYER

Purpose

The importance of Community Evaluation cannot be appreciated, nor can the running of them be explained, without first being clear about what they are. So before we consider *why* we have Community Evaluations, and *how* they are conducted, we will begin with *what* they are.

Community Evaluations are community meetings
held in order to discover
the *community's needs* in the praying of the Liturgy
of the Hours,
with a view to meeting these needs
by introducing a *change* (or changes)
in the Areas of Place, or Text and Rite, or in the
Ministering.

A lot has already been written about the matter earlier in this book, in Chapter 22, on Evaluating and Planning. We will presuppose a familiarity with the contents of that chapter. Of special relevance to the matter of Community Evaluation are:

— the nature of 'needs', and the difference between needs and likes or wants;

— the necessity of discovering needs before making changes;

— the kind of questions that can be asked in order to discover needs (see pages 50 and 350);

— the more common types of needs in liturgical praying: attention, inner quietness; understanding; listening; prayer-response from the heart.

Necessity

Any community which regularly assembles to pray communal prayer must also meet *to speak about* their praying together. To maintain their prayer together they need to express to one another their ideas, expectations, hopes, as well as their complaints, disappointments and struggles; and to listen to one another, and 'hear' what each wants to express about their community prayer. Such meetings are a must, even apart from evaluation.

The necessity of evaluation gives a further reason for meeting. Even if all the members of the community were expert in their understanding of prayer-needs, they would still be required to meet together and talk in order to discover the needs, not of individuals, but of the *community* as such.

For the most part that expertise cannot be presumed — would that even *one* person in each community had it! Hence there is no point in asking the direct question, What are your needs in communal prayer? Answers to it would be very misleading. Instead, questions have to be thought up and put to the meeting — questions such that the answers will reveal the needs underlying them. Further, a community will most probably need some facilitation to answer the questions from a reflective and serious, rather than critical and angry, level.

Lastly, and most importantly, communal praying needs *corporate commitment.* That is to say, the community has to express and hear expressed — either through just engaging in a Community Evaluation, or explicitly articulating it — one another's belief in their communal prayer and their serious commitment to the prayer and its growth.

The first Evaluation

There has to be a first time that a community gathers for an Evaluation of the Liturgy of the Hours. Before this first time, they will not really know what it is all about, or what will go on at it. An announcement of a forthcoming Community Evaluation may arouse fears, and therefore opposition, possibly in the form of cynicism. Hence, a special approach has to be taken to the first evaluation that is conducted.

It is better that it be un-announced: introduced in a community meeting or gathering in an informal way. The word 'evaluation' itself should be avoided: it can call up too easily a sort of 'examination of conscience', as well as sounding too scientific for the kind of atmosphere that is desirable. Whoever is leading the meeting could do something like this:

- Introduce the topic as filling in time that is to spare, or as a matter of personal interest. For example: 'As we have a few moments, is there anything you would care to say about our praying the Office together?'

- This is a general question which allows to surface *anything* that is there — and needs to come out anyway. Suggest that we listen to whatever anyone who chooses to speak has to say without any discussion.

- Be firm in applying this rule: hear everyone, but no response at this point.

- Their contributions should be written down in brief form, for all to see. Say something like; 'Would you mind if I write some of these things down; we might like to spend a little time on them afterwards.'

- Anything that is said is received; no comments; no dialogue.

The group is then invited to look at the summary. This is the time to invite comments: 'Anyone like to comment on these?' If nothing comes, make a start: 'A lot of these seem to be the same; I wonder what that says to us?' Or, 'There are some quite negative things there.'

- If the summary is fairly negative, leave it for the time being: 'Let's leave these for a while and make another summary. We can come back to it later.'

- Invite positive comments: 'Would you like to think for a moment on how the praying of the Office has helped me; or aspects of it that appeal to me?' This pushes individuals to look at *themselves*. The negative will be 'outside'; this bring them, 'inside.'

- Collect and collate these. Again invite comments.

- Finish up by calling attention to an item which seems to suggest itself as a *start* for helping to pray better: a change until the next meeting.

- Ask their consent. Also ask their agreement to meet again for an evaluation of the results of this change, in three or four weeks, or earlier depending on the community.

(To give an idea of what a community might reply, a list of typical responses is given at the end of this chapter.)

Regular Community Evaluation

Once a start has been made, regular Community Evaluation meetings can be announced and run along somewhat similar lines as the first. That is to say, the meeting will —

1. provide an opportunity — though they may choose not to use it — to off-load feelings, grievances, proposals, etc. about the community's praying of the Liturgy of the Hours;

2. always come to the 'inside': How am *I* praying the Hours?

3. then proceed to look at: What can help *us* to pray better?

4. preserve the 'on trial' character of any change by making a decision about the next Community Evaluation.

A meeting of the community is envisaged. This does not mean that it is a 'command performance,' in that every single member of the community has to be there whether they want to or not. All should certainly be not only invited, but encouraged to come. In this way, if they choose not to attend, they will know that they had been offered the opportunity to express to the community what they felt or thought about the Liturgy of the Hours.

The Evaluation meeting need not necessarily be led by the superior. Anyone capable and suitable may take the role of facilitator.

Devotional prayers

This would seem to be the most appropriate place to take up the subject of devotional prayers. When dealing with Communal Prayer, the difference between it and devotional prayer was explained, and the need people have of devotional prayer (page 91). Expressions of preference for devotional prayer, or confusion about the two types of prayer, are frequently made in the course of an Evaluation. After all, this meeting is likely to be the only time people speak about their prayer in community, so it is not to be surprised at. As the occasion arises, they should be affirmed in their devotional practices, and encouraged to give their devotions the time they require.

A problem of another kind is 'congregational prayers.' Most religious congregations have specified non-liturgical prayers which are to be said in common every day. The problem can be reduced to one of time and opportunity: When can we pray them, since it is impossible to be together in the chapel at times other than the celebration of the Eucharist and Morning and Evening Prayer? The inevitable solution has to be that the congregational prayers are said at the same time! While this is not the best arrangement, as devotional prayer should not be mixed with liturgical prayer, it seems to be the only one. So let us look for the best way of doing this.

The best time to include the congregational prayers is before the Hour begins. They can be before the Leader's Introduction, or after it, or become part of it.

A distinction between them and the liturgical Hour can be made by having the Leader lead them from a different place: for example, not from the front but from the community. When the congregational prayers are concluded, the Leader can take up the leading of the Hour by moving to the front.

After the Evaluation

The ones who will take away most from a Community Evaluation are those who plan and lead. Each Planner-Leader will have heard the community speak about the Hours which they will minister to them. They are now better acquainted with the community's feelings about the prayer, and their ideas. They can come nearer to making a true judgment about how the members of the community are when they begin to lead them; and what they will cater for in their planning.

The expression of community commitment to the Liturgy of the Hours will be a help to each Planner-Leader, and a source of confidence in the ministry.

Most important, perhaps, is that they will go away from an Evaluation with a *more specific mandate* from the community. The community has spoken to them, as clearly as they can, about what the Planner-Leader can do for them to help their prayer.

The Sorts of Things a Community Might Say

FIRST REQUEST

> I wish they would use the hymns from the book —
> not all the bits and pieces of other books.
> I would like to ask a question: Is the Office obligatory?
> I heard the other day that a Community invited lay-people to pray with them.
> We ought to be on time: always punctual.
> I prefer my private prayer any time.
> I can't stand it when they use records or tapes.
> Everyone should be there.
> I like the weekends to be free.
> Who does the leader think she is, telling me what to think!

SECOND REQUEST

> I have always liked the Office.
> Since I did that course in. . ., the Office really means something to me.
> I find it easier to pray when I pray *with* someone.

It is just about the only time when most of us are
together, and I like that.
I need the commitment of everyone.
I would not be there every day if it were not for
the community: sometimes I need to be 'carried.'
When Sister. . . leads, prayer comes alive.
As I am now, I would not pray at all were it not
for the group.

31

RENEWAL PROGRAMMES
IN COMMUNITIES

It is our hope that this book will provide a renewal in their liturgical prayer for everyone who uses it as we intend it to be used.

This final chapter is about a renewal for a whole community: a renewal, in particular, of their praying of the Liturgy of the Hours.

Our scope in this renewal is limited to this one part of their liturgical praying — and does not include the Eucharist — because a renewal of the Liturgy of the Hours can be undertaken by a community themselves; whereas a renewal of the celebration of the Eucharist would need to include in the programme the full involvement of the priest or priests who regularly celebrate the Eucharist for them.

What is it?

What we have in mind is a community activity: the community all together for a period of time, in which they are led through a programme, very much after the manner of so many other community courses or workshops.

461

In the programme the community will be helped:
to experience a deeper prayer in the Liturgy of the
Hours;
to learn more about this form of prayer;
to become more skilled and competent in what this
prayer demands;
and to evaluate their community prayer.

The content, it will be seen coincides with the content of this book.

How long?

It will need a substantial amount of time: around fifteen hours. It is desirable that it be in as large blocks of time, and as close together, as possible. Communities doing these programmes have chosen many different ways of dividing that time. Usually individual and community commitments prevent much choice in the matter of times. The following are samples: five consecutive days; two weekends, with a few weeks interval in between; a weekend followed up by a week of 'twilight' sessions (from 5.00 to 9.00 p.m.). It takes at least that amount of time to effect any permanent results in community praying.

When?

Equally important for a community as available time is their *willingness*. There is an opportune time, a *kairos*, which is when a community is 'ripe' for such a renewal. They experience the need of it, are prepared to commit themselves to it, and make what sacrifices it will entail for them. The desire needs to arise from the community: not from a judgement of a superior that they need it, or it would do them good; nor from the enthusiasm of a few which is not shared by the majority.

The time also needs to be when the community is not under pressure: when they can have, and experience that they have, 'space' to integrate the programme and adjust to change.

The timing is critically important. If for any reason a renewal programme fails, it cannot be attempted again with any hope of success for quite a length of time.

How prepare?

Some preparatory work can help to get a community interested and motivated. The best way to go about this is to avail of structures that already exist, and avoid introducing any extra activities for it.

For example, on special community days — such as feast days, community reflection days, community evenings, or chapter preparation time — the atmosphere of the occasion could be availed of to give an experience of a different way of praying: to lead a prayer in a slower, more reflective way — even if it is only meal-time prayers, or a prayer before a meeting. This will open up some possibilities of change in those present.

Community meetings could include in the agenda Community Evaluation, and what we have called in this book Framing Activities. These could be done by suggesting a discussion on a phrase from the Constitutions, such as what we mean by the phrase, 'deepen our prayer life'; or 'frame' a phrase from the liturgy, e.g. 'counting us worthy to stand in your presence', or 'Say but the word and I shall be healed.' That sort of activity — with no discussion, no comments at all.

At the beginning of the year, when emphasis is on apostolate, and the value of our work stemming from our spiritual life, the question could be raised: How can we foster that life of the Spirit in us? And so, to community prayer!

> How important is it to us?
> 'The most important thing in our lives.'
> Is it? Then, let's look at the consequences; for myself:
> for us, as a community.

Then there is also the beginning of the year topic, our commitment to community prayer:

> 'What price am I prepared to pay?'

The aim and procedure of the type of activity proposed should be stated clearly, and adhered to: 'We will just share what each one thinks: NO discussion; NO dialogue.'

How to deal with the 'difficult'?

If individuals try to spoil these preparatory efforts, or

express their unwillingness to take part in them, they should seriously have the situation pointed out to them, with such as: 'You may not need these activities for yourself, but would you give *us* the right to spend some time on our prayer in an effort to improve it, please?'

Difficulties can arise in connection with the very thought of a prayer-renewal programme. Individuals may reject the idea: maybe along with a lot of other things they reject; or maybe because they are old and set in their ways of praying, and change would be well nigh impossible for them.

Although a renewal is a community-wide, or even province-wide, project, all must be left *free*: they make the choice. The choice may be to absent themselves. They are to be allowed to make that decision. If community decisions about prayer are arrived at without them, or against their wish, they should again be approached: 'All of *us* want it; would you allow us to have it?' Individuals must *not* be allowed to prevent the rest of the community taking steps to improve their praying.

Some may just need a little coaxing and encouragement — a little sign of kindness and care.

Who will conduct it?

A renewal of prayer programme will have best and most lasting results when it is conducted by a small group from the community itself. This has been proved over the years. When the time arrives for a renewal programme, this is the first possibility to be investigated. There are many advantages: the group's knowledge and experience of the community; the group's enthusiasm stimulates the motivation of the community; the group provides an on-going presence, and a continuing resource group.

The first step is the selection of the group. Certain qualities and conditions are necessary in the members of it. Usually the following are put forward:
They need to be religious who:
— are themselves convinced of the value of praying the Liturgy of the Hours;
— are interested in a project involving work within the community (or communities), and are willing to take it on;

— have sufficient time to devote to it: both the training period, and work after that with the community;

    — have the support of the superiors, both major and local;

    — are acceptable to the sisters, in general;

    — are not working through any 'problems', either psychological or faith, and who because of them are selected for this preparation course in the hope that it will help them with their personal problems. Experience shows that such religious hold back the group's formation, and are not at all helpful to a community in this work.

One way to make a start is to get together a wider group of likely religious, and put this to them: Without coming to any conclusions as to what it might entail, would you be prepared to commit yourself to make a contribution in a project or programme for the Renewal of the Praying of the Office in your communities? Believing that even though you may not consider yourself competent for it, if God calls you to it, he will give you what you need, would you volunteer to become part of a training group?

The formation of this group for the programme would be very satisfactorily assured by working through this book together. If there is someone with more experience to lead them, either from their congregation or outside of it, all the better.

The group would decide themselves when they are ready to begin the programme; and what form they choose for it.

If it is a province-wide project — and it seems a pity not to avail of a trained group in the province for more than one community — some combining of communities might be considered. It usually is more effective, however, to give each community the opportunity of being together with just themselves. They have *their* own special difficulties and problems; they are the ones who will be putting it into practice together.

Role of superiors;

In a word *indispensable!* The superior's expressed approval is necessary for a programme even to be accepted at all by some religious. But it is the superior's commitment that plays an essential part in the success of a programme. There is first, the element of support to the group, and leadership of the community. Equally essential, and even more critical, is the superior's organization — a role no one else can take on; if the superior fails in this, the program cannot continue. It will die. Too often has this been the end result of the programmes of very hopeful groups and very willing communities.

If the superior of any community cannot or will not play her or his necessary part, then it would be better to postpone any renewal project.

Effects?

More than might be expected: certainly more than just community prayer. Many communities in Australia tell of the result of their working together on their prayer, and the good effects it had on their life. Many attempts have been made to build community spirit; all sorts of means have been tried, by a wide variety of facilitators and lecturers, both local and from overseas. Perhaps this is one means that has not yet been sufficiently tried.

You can only find out by trying!

A final activity: one to help anyone who, through using this book, hears a call to help others with their praying:

'Helping People to Pray Requires that I am a PRAY-ER'

1. Do you agree with this statement?

2. What implications has this statement for you?

3. What means are at your disposal to be a PRAY-ER?

'LEAVE TAKING'

We began this book by introducing ourselves. We would like to end it by taking leave of you. To say good-bye, and to thank you for staying with us through this book.

We heartily hope that it has helped you! It has certainly helped us. Writing it has required a new look at some of our presentations, now being put in written rather than spoken form; we gained some new ideas and insights; and became confirmed in the value of our approach, and more eager to share it with others.

An undertaking of this size is a first for us, and aspects of it demanded a lot of hard work. However, from beginning to end we experienced a growing joy and hope. Your use of the book makes the work worthwhile, and is that hope fulfilled for us!

For a long time we have adopted the practice of bringing our courses to an end by one of us singing the Blessing of Aaron ('Hebrew Blessing') and the other sending with a Dismissal. (You will know from reading the book which of us does which.) The Dismissal was composed by our dear friend, Dr Harold Leatherland, with whom we worked closely until his death in 1977.

We take our leave of you by saying:

The Lord bless you and keep you:
the Lord make his face shine upon you
and be gracious unto you:
the Lord lift up his countenance upon you
and give you peace.
Amen.

Go in the power of the Spirit;
in all things, at all times,
remember that Christ is with you;
make your life your worship
to the praise and glory of God.
Go in peace to love and serve the Lord.

GLOSSARY

A-A/A-X: An outline of the two different types of responses in PARTICIPATION: one, joining in the prayer which I hear somebody (a minister) pray [A-A], for example, the Opening Prayer; the other, allowing what I hear [A], for example a reading, to evoke my personal response [X]

BEGINNING TO PRAY: This refers not just to a time — the first minutes in praying — but more so to a specific pre-prayer activity which is always required before celebrating liturgy. The quality of participation, that is full, conscious and active, requires that a person is 'WHOLLY PRESENT', which in turn implies that he or she has become free from whatever would prevent them moving 'OUTSIDE' TO 'INSIDE', and is 'CENTERED'. A further need in the activity of beginning to pray is the activation of the person's faith.

BRIEFING: Giving a congregation whatever information they need about the coming celebration, so that they will not be distracted by anything unexpected. They need to know, for example, what they will be singing; and anything that is different from what is usually done. A Briefing is given prior to, but separate from, the celebration, by a minister. It should be well prepared, preferably written, so that it can be delivered accurately, clearly and concisely.

CENTERING: A process of moving closer to my real self, my CENTRE, where I can be truly present, quiet, listening and make free choices. This requires a movement from 'OUTSIDE' TO 'INSIDE': becoming free through a recognition and acceptance of what HOOKS me.

COMMUNAL PRAYER: It is first, the prayer of a group of people praying a STRUCTURED PRAYER. In addition, accompanying their prayer is a special attitude towards the people in the group: loving concern, which is the outcome, not of previous acquaintance, but of how they see one another in faith.
This gives them the motivation for joining in the prayer; and, as well, moves them to pray internally, and express it externally, in a manner that will help the others in their prayer.

DESIGN/SHAPE OF A CELEBRATION: The Text and Rite which result from the use of (1) SELECTIONS from given options, and (2) COMPOSITIONS for which there is provision in the Rite.

ELEMENTS OF THE RITE: The components which give a rite its particular structure, DESIGN/SHAPE; every single item which is part of the ceremony: the prayers, readings, movements, gestures, and all that is said and done.

EVALUATION: a process that aims at discovering the prayer needs of a congregation (or person), by means of 'hearing' a representative number of them, for the purpose of deciding what changes in Place, Text and Rite, and Ministering would be most helpful to the people's participation.

EXPERIENCE: How we are affected as a result of what is 'outside' us (people, events, what we hear and see), and 'inside' us (feelings, memories, motivations etc.). An experience has both cognitive and affective aspects. Participation in liturgy is always an experience with these characteristics and aspects.

FEATURING: Giving special attention to one element of the Eucharist, Liturgy of the Hours, or other celebrations, by using different means to highlight it in PLANNING and LEADING. For example: an Introduction; music; reflection (perhaps guided).

FORMATION IN LIFE AND LITURGY: Because participating in liturgy (that is, praying) is a response of the *whole person*, it is not imporved by information and understanding only; it needs attention to a person's growth which is usually called a 'formation'.
The connection between liturgy and the rest of a person's life is such that growth in praying liturgy cannot occur without personal growth and development. Hence, help given in liturgy – a formation in liturgy – will at the same time be a formation in life. Similarly, any help given towards growth in life becomes a help in liturgy.

FOUR AREAS: The four groups of factors which significantly influence people's praying, through being a help or a hindrance to them in their participation in celebrations of liturgy; areas in which there are possibilities of making changes in order to improve participation. They are: A – the PLACE, B – TEXT AND RITE, C – MINISTERS, D – CONGREGATION.

FRAMING: A technique useful in focusing on, and 'staying with', something, when we wish to 'SEE MORE' in it. It consists of (physically or mentally) putting a frame around the subject/ object. The frame serves the purpose of keeping us inside it, or making us aware when we move outside it.

'HOOKED': This is how we are when part of us is taking control over us and directing us, preventing us from choosing, or in any way acting, freely. For example: states of body, like sleepiness or tiredness; strong emotions like those that go with hurt, worry, insecurity or rejection; and what we have on our minds in the nature of preoccupations, memories, plans, expectations. ("I'm too tired/too upset/I've too much on my mind to pray right now.") Until we are freed from these, moving from 'OUTSIDE' TO 'INSIDE', and becoming CENTERED, we are not in a position to participate fully, consciously and actively in liturgy.

LEADER OF THE LITURGY OF THE HOURS: The person who performs the ministry of facilitating the group's prayer, first by PLANNING (making selections, composing, organizing), and then by helping them in BEGINNING TO PRAY by a CENTERING/ Introduction, and in the course of the Prayer, leading in a manner that will help the community to pray.

LITURGICAL SYMBOLS: Symbols being a type of sign which contain and evoke an EXPERIENCE, liturgical symbols are those words and objects which grew among OUR PEOPLE, the Church, as their expression of their experience of their relationship with God in Christ. We enter into this experience through their symbols.
A liturgical rite is a symbol of this nature, and is composed of many such symbols: including the prayers and readings, as well as the persons, movements and objects.

OUR PEOPLE: The Church; our Christian People; all those, living and deceased, who experience God as revealed by his Son, Jesus Christ; and, indeed, all who experience the God of Exodus and Covenant. They are the People with whom we share — and 'handed on' to us — a living experience of God, their faith and their prayer: THE PRAYER OF OUR PEOPLE.

'OUTSIDE-INSIDE': All the activities and experiences that have been ours previous to our time of prayer remain part of us, and can be discovered by noting the effect they had on us: that is, on the three levels of body, feelings and mind. Further, they can hold us 'out there'; HOOK us, and prevent us coming 'inside' to our CENTRE. (We are more than our bodies, feelings, mind.) This keeps us from praying, because it is only when we are at our CENTRE that we can receive the prayer which the Holy Spirit is offering us.

PARTICIPATION: The internal activity of mind and heart of the assembly in faith-response to the Place, Text and Rite, and Ministers, externalized by them in sound and movement. Hence, it is their PRAYER in the celebration.

PHASES OF THE LITURGY OF THE EUCHARIST: These are: Preparation of the Gifts; Eucharistic Prayer; and Communion Rite. This structure has its origin in the actions of Jesus at the Last Supper, 'He took bread, said the blessing, broke the bread and gave it to his disciples. . .'

PLANNING A CELEBRATION OF LITURGY: The work done by a person or group which ensures that a particular celebration of the Eucharist, Liturgy of the Hours, or other celebrations of liturgy, will best meet the prayer needs of the congregation and be the most suited to the occasion.
It is based on an EVALUATION, and consists of four steps: SURVEY; SKETCH; DESIGN/SHAPE; ORGANIZATION.

PRAYER OF THE CHURCH: The prayer of OUR PEOPLE, the text of which is given to us in the liturgical books: that is, Missal/ Sacramentary, Lectionary, Liturgy of the Hours and the other Rites of the sacraments. it is a STRUCTURED PRAYER and requires a special attitude towards OUR PEOPLE, the Church; and towards the Text and Rite being celebrated, which leads to our accepting it as drawing us into sharing with them *their* faith-experience of God and their prayer to him.

'Liturgy' is just another name for the Prayer of the Church.

PREPARING FOR A CELEBRATION OF LITURGY: In common with PLANNING, preparing is something that has to be done before a celebration of liturgy. In contrast to it, preparing refers to the personal preparation of the ministers: what they do in the time immediately preceding the celebration in CENTERING and becoming FAITH-ACTIVATED. It is the activity of BEGINNING TO PRAY.

PRESENT; WHOLLY PRESENT: In liturgy, as in life, there are varying degrees in the quality of our 'presence' to what we are doing. When we act purely mechanically, there is a complete absence of 'presence'. At the other end of the scale there is a state, with recognizable characteristics, in which we are 'wholly present': *all* of us is focused on, and responding to, this one person/thing. While God is always present to us, we are not always present to God, and it is this latter which is our concern here.

PROCESS OF RESPONDING: An activity that takes me from an initial reaction, through 'SEEING MORE', to an inner experience in my CENTRE, where I receive the response as given to me. In liturgy it is the prayer given to me in my heart by the Holy Spirit.

The process is completed when I return to life, now as a RE-SPONDING PERSON.

RESPONDING: A movement awakened in my heart when I am affected by something or someone. As distinct from 'reacting', which comes from a *part* of me that is affected, responding is always from my CENTRE. I respond to the depth of my 'SEEING MORE'.

SEE MORE: A new vision, arrived at through reflection, which sees beyond the surface appearance of anything to the point of seeing 'with the heart'. The result is an experience of change in myself, in what I see, and in my RESPONDING to it.

SKILLS: Since people's participation is greatly affected by 'how they are' in a celebration, they need skills — the ability and facility to deal with obstacles to prayer, to come to quiet inside, to 'be present' and respond. All the necessary skills are included in the one skill of responding to a symbol.

STAGES OF THE EUCHARIST: The Rite of the Eucharist moves and develops in these Stages: Introductory Rites; Liturgy of the

Word; Liturgy of the Eucharist; Dismissal Rite.

STRUCTURED PRAYER: In contrast to a 'spontaneous prayer' which has its beginning *inside* a person, a structured prayer makes use of a previously composed formula. Hence, it begins *outside* us, and becomes our prayer when we allow our thoughts, attitudes and feelings to correspond to those it expresses.

INDEX